The Land and Conveyancing Law Reform Act 2009: Annotations and Commentary

To the team!

from John

February 2010

The Land and Conveyancing Law Reform Act 2009: Annotations and Commentary

by

PROFESSOR J.C.W. WYLIE

LL.M. (Harvard), LL.D. (Belfast)

Emeritus Professor of Law, Cardiff University
Consultant, A&L Goodbody, Solicitors
Dublin, Belfast, London, Brussels, Boston, New York

Bloomsbury Professional

Published by
Bloomsbury Professional
Maxwelton House
41–43 Boltro Road
Haywards Heath
West Sussex
RH16 1BJ

Bloomsbury Professional
The Fitzwilliam Business Centre
26 Upper Pembroke Street
Dublin 2

ISBN 978 1 84766 100 5
© J.C.W. Wylie 2009

British Library Cataloguing-in-Publication Data
A catalogue record for this book is available from the British Library

Typeset by Marlex Editorial Services Ltd., Dublin, Ireland
Printed and bound in Great Britain by
Athenaeum, Gateshead, Tyne and Wear

Preface

Forty years ago, when I began the research which led to the writing of *Irish Land Law* (which was first published in 1975), I never thought that the day would come when I would write this book! I am sure that neither the Law Society, which commissioned, nor the Arthur Cox Foundation which sponsored, that book thought so either. I cannot help wondering what the late Mr. Justice John Kenny would have thought. As then Chairman of the Foundation and Consultant Editor for both *Irish Land Law* and *Irish Conveyancing Law*, he played a huge role in shaping those books. Having spent so many years in the 1970s discussing with him the mysteries and absurdities of Irish land law, I really do think that he would have approved of the 2009 Act, at least most of it!

This book has been produced with some speed because of, at the time of writing, the Act's imminent commencement (1 December 2009, except for s 132). The Bill was drafted originally within the Law Reform Commission as long ago as 2004, as part of a joint project with the Department of Justice, Equality and Law Reform, and introduced by the Government in 2006 (initially in the Seanad). It then had a lengthy passage, interrupted by a General Election, during which numerous additions and changes were made at different stages, even at the Final Report Stage last summer. All this made it impossible to complete definitive annotations until very late in the day. Nevertheless my publisher was understandably anxious to provide practitioners with a guide as near as possible to the commencement date and I have done my best to comply. I regard this as the first shot! Like other authors in this area I am now faced with producing new editions of books which will have to undergo a radical change of content. It is difficult to underestimate the wide-ranging nature of the changes to our basic land law and the law which underpins the conveyancing process made by the 2009 Act. These are explained in the detailed annotations to each of the Act's provisions which follow.

Many will be aware that in my role as a consultant to the Law Reform Commission and Department of Justice, Equality and Law Reform I played a major role in the drafting of the original Bill. It is important, however, to acknowledge that many others in both the Commission and Department had considerable input. Furthermore, as I explain in the Introduction, many of the provisions stem from numerous Reports and Consultation Papers published over the past 20 years or so by the Commission, to which many practitioners contributed. There are too many to list here but they are all referred to in those publications. I must, however, also pay tribute to four people. Michael McDowell SC, as former Minister for Justice, Equality and Law Reform was the prime mover in getting the reform project underway and drove it from the start with extraordinary enthusiasm and encouragement. It was he who secured Government adoption of the Bill and initiated its parliamentary process. Dermot Ahern TD, current Minister for Justice, Equality and Law Reform saw the Bill through its various stages in the Dáil with consummate skill and exhibited a knowledge of land law which I doubt he ever expected to have to show. Two officials in the Department, Seamus Carroll and Tracy O'Keeffe, were active members of the joint project group and nursed the Bill through its various stages with truly splendid dedication. If any good comes from this Act we all owe them a considerable debt.

The rest of what I want to say is to be found in the Introduction, save this. The drafter of an Act is wont to claim that he or she knows exactly what is intended, and having spent an inordinate time putting it into the words of a section, cannot understand why others, particularly lawyers, cannot see what is startlingly obvious! This is, of course, absurd and anyone who thinks that human language and phraseology is so precise that it can always be couched in terms totally free of ambiguity and doubt is naïve indeed! In writing the annotations which follow I have endeavoured to keep this in mind, in the hope that readers will obtain some benefit from them. I emphasise above all else that they are written entirely in my personal capacity and must not be treated as representing the views of anyone else, still less the views of the Department of Justice, Equality and Law Reform, the Law Reform Commission or any other body.

Finally, I must express my appreciation of the support provided under considerable pressure by my new publishers, especially by Sandra Mulvey in the Dublin office. Marian Sullivan, who has applied her keyboard skills to previous books of mine, surpassed herself this time in deciphering the most wretched of manuscripts!

Professor J C W Wylie

1 December 2009

Contents

Table of Legislation

Primary Legislation: Post-1922

1922 Constitution

1937 Constitution

United Kingdom

Conventions

Statutory Instruments

Table of Cases

C

I

L

M

P

Q

R

T

Y

Introduction

[1]

The Land and Conveyancing Law Reform Act 2009 introduces the most momentous changes to land law and the law which underpins the conveyancing system of Ireland since the legislation of the late nineteenth century – in particular the Conveyancing Acts 1881–1911 and the Settled Land Acts 1882–1890. For the most part it replaces those Acts, although not entirely because provisions in the former relating to landlord and tenant law will survive until further recommendations made by the Law Reform Commission are implemented (see Notes to Schedule 2 of the 2009 Act).

[2]

In some respects the enactment of the 2009 Act may be compared with the "Birkenhead" legislation enacted for England and Wales in 1925, but it is important to note that such a comparison would be somewhat misleading. To some extent the 1925 legislation was broader in scope, comprising six major Acts. Two (the Land Charges Act and the Land Registration Act) dealt with registration matters, which are only touched on marginally by the 2009 Act. Ireland does not have a land charges registration system (which was introduced for the first time in England and Wales in 1925) and, instead, has long had a universal registration of deeds system applicable to unregistered land (see Lyall, *Land Law in Ireland* (2nd edn, Round Hall, 2000), ch 5; Wylie, *Irish Land Law* (3rd edn, Tottel Publishing, 1997), ch 22). A registration of title system has operated since the nineteenth century (Lyall, *Land Law in Ireland* (2nd edn, Round Hall, 2000), ch 24; Wylie, *Irish Land Law* (3rd edn, Tottel Publishing, 1997), ch 21). Both systems are governed now by modern legislation: see Registration of Title Act 1964 and Registration of Deeds and Title Act 2006. The 2009 Act makes only minor changes to those Acts (see Notes to Part 13 and Schedule 1).

[3]

The 1925 legislation also included a Trustee Act and Administration of Estates Act. The former was a comprehensive Act replacing the more limited Trustee Act 1893. The 1893 Act remains in force in Ireland, but the Law Reform Commission has proposed its replacement: see *Trust Law: General Proposals* (LRC 92–2008). The 2009 Act does contain substantial provisions relating to trusts, but they are not intended to replace the 1893 Act or other aspects of the general law of trusts which, at the time of its drafting, were the subject of a separate study by the Commission. Part 4 deals with trusts of land and during the Bill's passage through the Oireachtas, the Government added Part 5, which deals with variation of trusts (see further the Notes to these Parts). The subject of administration of estates (curiously the 1925 legislation did not deal with the other major branch of the law of succession, the law of wills) was dealt with in Ireland as part of an overhaul of the entire law of succession by the Succession Act 1965.

[4]

The result is that the 2009 Act largely covers only the ground covered by the Law of Property and Settled Land Acts 1925. However, in doing so it also deals with matters which were the subject of later legislation enacted in England and Wales, such as the Law of Property (Miscellaneous Provisions) Act 1989 and Trusts of Land and Appointment of Trustees Act 1996. In many respects the 2009 Act has taken a different approach. This is also illustrated by Part 3, Chapter 3 (Party Structures), which contains a scheme somewhat different to that contained in the (E & W) Access to Neighbouring Land Act 1992 and Party Walls etc Act 1996.

[5]

It is also important to note that the 2009 Act departs quite radically in some instances from the current law in England and Wales. The most obvious example of this is the abolition of the rule against perpetuities by Part 3. The rule was retained and amended by the (E & W) Perpetuities and Accumulations Act 1964 and further amendments will be introduced by enactment of the Perpetuities and Accumulations Bill 2008 currently before the Westminster Parliament (see further the Notes to Part 3). The provisions in Part 7 relating to co-ownership are also in marked contrast to the English legislation (see the Notes to Part 7).

[6]

In other respects the 2009 Act reforms the law in ways which have long been mooted for England and Wales but have never been put into effect. Thus Part 8, Chapter 1 (Easements and *Profits à Prendre*) overhauls the law of prescription and clarifies the law relating to acquisition by implication. Chapter 4 of that Part deals with the enforceability of freehold covenants and removes the limitations of the rule in *Tulk v Moxhay* (1848) 2 Ph 774. Substantial changes have been made to the law of mortgages by Part 10.

At this point it may be useful to say something about the background to the 2009 Act, its underlying principles and primary objectives.

Background

[7]

The impetus for reform of land law and the conveyancing system began in the late 1980s when the Law Reform Commission responded to a request made on 6 March 1987 by the then Attorney General to formulate proposals relating to conveyancing law and practice "in areas where this could lead to savings for house purchasers". The Commission set up a Working Group convened by one of the Commissioners (John F Buckley, solicitor and later Circuit Court Judge) and comprising members of the judiciary, practising barristers and solicitors and an academic lawyer (the late Professor JC Brady of UCD). With changing membership over the years between then until the turn of the century, the Working Group produced for publication by the Commission a series of reports on discrete aspects of land law and conveyancing practice. These are referred to throughout the Notes to the various provisions of the 2009 Act which follow.

[8]

Sadly most of the recommendations in these reports were never implemented. The one notable exception was the *Report on Land Law and Conveyancing Law: (2) Enduring Powers of Attorney* (LRC 31–1989), which was implemented by the Powers of Attorney Act 1996. Recommendations contained in the *Report on Land Law and Conveyancing Law: (3) The Passing of Risk from Vendor to Purchaser* (LRC 39–1991) and *Report on Land Law and Conveyancing Law: (4) Service of Completion Notices* (LRC 40–1991) were acted upon by the Law Society through changes made to the *General Conditions of Sale* (see Wylie and Woods, *Irish Conveyancing Law* (3rd edn, Tottel Publishing, 2005), paras 12.36–43 and 13.20–24). Most of the rest of the recommendations have now been implemented by the 2009 Act.

[9]

The Law Reform Commission had always made it clear that it did not have the resources to carry out a comprehensive review of the law (see LRC 30–1989, para 1). That did not get under way until the Department of Justice, Equality and Law Reform and the Commission established in late 2003 a Joint Project for reform and modernisation of the land law and conveyancing law. In fact this was seen at the time as part of a larger programme of reform, other elements of which included reform of landlord and tenant law (see the Commission's publications on this: *Consultation Paper on Business Tenancies* (LRC CP 21–2003); *Consultation Paper on General Law of Landlord and Tenant* (LRC CP28–2003); *Report on the Law of Landlord and Tenant* (LRC 85–2007), and development of an eConveyancing system (see on this *Report on eConveyancing: Modelling of the Irish Conveyancing System* (LRC 79–2006)).

[10]

The Joint Project involved three phases. The first concerned the screening of all pre-1922 statutes relating to land law and conveyancing. This was seen as part of the Government's overhaul of the statute book and removal of reliance on old statutes pre-dating the foundation of the State. Another major step in this process was enactment of the Statute Law Revision (Pre-1922) Act 2005 and the Statute Law Act 2007. Those Acts did not, however, affect statutes relating to land law and conveyancing (see Schedule 1 to the 2007 Act). Instead these are dealt with by the 2009 Act. Thus the first phase of the Joint Project involved identifying all such pre-1922 statutes and then assessing how far they still had relevance to twenty-first century law and practice. This aspect of the process is returned to later under the heading of "Primary Objectives". It was also contemplated that the first phase would involve the sort of general review of the law (not just statute law) and practice which the Law Reform Commission had hitherto not had the resources to carry out. The author was appointed by the Department in February 2004 to carry out this first phase of the Joint Project and chaired the Commission's new Working Group established to oversee the Project.

[11]

The second phase of the Joint Project involved publication by the Commission of the *Consultation Paper on Reform and Modernisation of Land Law and Conveyancing Law* (LRC CP 34–2004) and a subsequent period of consultation. The *Consultation Paper* contained detailed recommendations for reform (and replacement of old statutes) covering the broad range of land law and conveyancing law. As explained above, it did not cover areas of the law which had been the subject of recent reform and legislation (such as succession law and land registration) or which were intended to be covered as separate projects (such as landlord and tenant law and the general law of trusts). It is, perhaps, to be regretted that few responses were received at this stage, although those that were were generally supportive of the recommendations. That remained the case when further responses were received or published later, mostly after the Bill had been introduced to the Oireachtas. These indicated that some provisions were controversial and resulted in some amendments during the Bill's passage (as indicated by the Notes to the Act's provisions which follow). The second phase culminated with a Conference, involving also speakers from England, held at UCD on 25 November 2004.

[12]

The third phase of the Joint Project involved the drafting of a Bill to implement the Commission's recommendations which had been accepted by the Government in late 2004. The Government instructed the Law Reform

Commission to undertake responsibility for the drafting and this was done by a small team led by the author. This resulted in publication in July 2005 of the *Report on Reform and Modernisation of Land Law and Conveyancing Law* (LRC 74–2005) to which was appended a Land and Conveyancing Bill (with notes to each section). That Bill formed the core of the Land and Conveyancing Law Reform Bill 2006 (No 31 of 2006) introduced in the Seanad by the then Minister for Justice, Equality and Law Reform (Michael McDowell TD, SC) on 9 June 2006. It is important to note, however, that numerous additions, amendments and deletions were made to the Bill by the Government during its lengthy passage through the Oireachtas (one of the main causes of delay was the calling of the General Election in 2007). These changes are outlined below and further details are provided in the Notes to the Act's provisions which follow.

Underlying principles

[13]

It may be useful at this stage to reiterate the underlying principles which drove the Joint Project established by the Department and Commission and discussed above. These were set out in the 2004 Consultation Paper (LRC CP34–2004, p 3) as follows:

"(a) updating the law, so as to make it accord with changes in society;

(b) promoting simplification of the law and its language, so as to render it more easily understood and accessible;

(c) promoting simplification of the conveyancing process, in particular the procedures involved, including the taking of security over land;

(d) facilitating extension of the registration of title system, with a view to promoting a system of title by registration; and

(e) keeping in mind the overall aims of the eConveyancing Project and facilitating introduction of an econveyancing system as soon as possible."

These points were reiterated in the lengthy Explanatory and Financial Memorandum which accompanied the Bill and by the Minister of State (Deputy Fahey) in introducing the Second Stage in the Seanad on 20 June 2006. Bearing these underlying principles in mind the primary objectives of the Act may be stated as follows.

Primary objectives

(a) Repeal of old statutes

[14]

In furtherance of the underlying principle of updating the law and the Government's policy of statute law revision, the Act replaces numerous pre-

1922 statutes which hitherto governed land law and the conveyancing system. The screening process which formed part of the first phase of the Joint Project discussed earlier ultimately led the Law Reform Commission to one of three conclusions with respect to particular pre-1922 statutes or provisions within statutes. Sometimes only part of an old statute would relate to land law or conveyancing and that would be the only part relevant to the Project. Another point also made earlier should be reiterated, that not all areas of land law were covered by the Project, such as landlord and tenant law. This explains why not all the provisions in the Conveyancing Acts 1881–1911 are repealed (see the Notes to Schedule 2 of the Act).

[15]

(1) **Repealed without replacement**: in such instances the conclusion was reached that the statute, or a provision within a statute, should be repealed without replacement in the new Act. This might be because the statute in question was obsolete or served no practical purpose in the twenty-first century. Examples would be statutes relating to the old feudal system, such as the Statute of Uses (Ireland) 1634. In other cases the statute would be rendered redundant by reforms introduced by the Act, such as those relating to the fee tail estate (De Donis Conditionalibus 1285 and the Fines and Recoveries (Ireland) Act 1834: see the Notes to s 13 of the Act).

[16]

(2) **Replaced with substantial amendment**: in such instances the conclusion was reached that, while the statute or provision within a statute, continued to serve a useful purpose in the twenty-first century, it was not doing so in the most appropriate way or otherwise needed substantial amendment or recasting to cure defects or to make it conform with other changes being made by the 2009 Act. Thus the provisions of the Settled Land Acts 1882–1890 are replaced by a new system governing "trusts of land" introduced by Part 4 of the Act (see the Notes to this Part which follow). The same applies to some of the provisions in the Conveyancing Acts 1881–1911 (see, for example, ss 80 and 81 and Schedule 3 which replace the covenants for title provisions in s 7 of the Conveyancing Act 1881 and Notes to those provisions in the 2009 Act which follow).

[17]

(3) **Replaced without substantial amendment**: in such instances the view was taken that the particular statute, or provision within a statute, continued to serve a useful purpose and could be carried forward into the Act without substantial amendment. The most that might be done would be to recast the statute or provision in clearer language or to make it accord

more with the rest of the Act. This applies to many of the other provisions in the Conveyancing Acts 1882–1911.

The result of this process is that the Act repeals over 150 pre-1922 statutes (see Schedule 2 and Notes which follow).

(b) Consolidation, not codification

[18]

While the 2009 Act aims to contain in one statute much of the statute law relating to land law and the conveyancing system, so that to that extent it involves an element of consolidation, that element is, in fact, strictly limited. As has been explained above, this element relates only to pre-1922 statutes and mention has been made earlier that several post-1922 statutes relating to land law and conveyancing continue in force, such as the Registration of Title Act 1964, Succession Act 1965 and Registration of Deeds and Title Act 2006. Furthermore, as has also been explained above, in so far as pre-1922 statutes, or provisions within them, have been incorporated into the Act, often this has been done with changes to their wording or even with changes of substance. Such changes mean that the process has not simply been one of consolidation.

[19]

It follows from what has been said above that the Act is even less an exercise in codification of the law in the sense in which that concept is usually understood. There is no question of it attempting to enshrine in legislation all the law relating to land law and conveyancing. This is so even within the confines of those aspects of the law which the Act covers. The Law Reform Commission recognised that much of our law has been developed through the practice of conveyancers and by the courts. In particular it has been much influenced by exercise of equitable jurisdiction, through which the courts developed the concept of "uses" and then the law of trusts (see Lyall, *Land Law in Ireland* (2nd edn, Round Hall, 2000), ch 4; Wylie, *Irish Land Law* (3rd edn, Tottel Publishing, 1997), ch 3). In more modern times the courts have increasingly recognised the creation of equitable (or beneficial) interests by developing the concepts of resulting and constructive trusts and proprietary estoppel (see Delany, *Equity and the Law of Trusts in Ireland* (3rd edn, Round Hall, 2003), chs 7, 8 and 17). The Act does not seek to curtail or inhibit the exercise of such jurisdiction or the development of such concepts (see ss 11(7) and 51(2) and the Notes to them).

(c) Simplification

[20]

The objective of simplification has two aspects: substance and language. Many of the provisions of the Act are designed to simplify the law. In some instances this involves removing outmoded concepts (such as the concept of feudal tenure: see s 9 and its Notes), abolishing types of grants (such as the fee tail, fee farm grants and leases for lives: see ss 12–14) or conveyances (such as mortgages by conveyance or assignment: see s 89) which have outlived their usefulness or getting rid of rules which complicate the law and do more harm than good (such as the rule against perpetuities: see ss 16 and 17). In other instances the previous law is replaced with much more simple and straightforward provisions (such as that relating to settlements and trusts of land (see Part 4) and acquisition of easements and profits by prescription (see Part 8, Chapter 1). As was mentioned previously, the Act contains several provisions which exceed what has been done in England and Wales either in 1925 or subsequently and some of which are probably unique in the common law world.

[21]

Simplification of language is a very tricky area. As would be expected of legislation emanating from the Law Reform Commission every effort was made to abide by the principles set out in its *Report on Statutory Drafting and Interpretation: Plain Language and the Law* (LRC 61–2000). However, it was recognised that there were limits to what could be achieved in an area of the law such as the Act covers. Land and conveyancing law is a highly technical subject which involves abstract concepts of considerable antiquity. Although, as indicated above, simplification was a primary objective, the Commission concluded that it would be counterproductive to try to substitute an entirely new terminology for well-established and generally well-understood concepts which were being retained. Thus the Act refers to concepts like estates in land (such as the fee simple) and interests like easements and *profits à prendre*. Use of such terms necessarily imports the generally understood characteristics of such concepts without the need to provide detailed definitions in the Act. Had the Act not used such terms it would have been necessary to invent new terms and to provide an explanation of their meaning and scope. The result would have been a more complex and much longer piece of legislation.

[22]

The Commission did recognise that the final draft of the Bill which formed the core of the Act was something of a compromise in terms of its language. The continued use of technical language would mean that many, if not most, of the provisions would not be understood easily by the lay person. In the end it concluded, for the reasons given above, that the Act was primarily "lawyers' law" and that the main objective in this regard should be to use language which was at least clear to lawyers, particularly conveyancers relying on its provisions in carrying out land transactions on behalf of clients. The Commission was also mindful that many provisions in the Act were being carried forward from previous legislation, such as the Conveyancing Acts 1881–1911. The view was taken that it would be unwise to change the language of such provisions, especially where it had been the subject of judicial interpretation, unless this was necessary in order to correct some defect which had emerged or to resolve some ambiguity or doubt as to meaning. Where, on the other hand, the provision being carried forward derived from some ancient statute, couched in the archaic language of a bygone age, the view was taken that it would have been absurd to retain such language and recasting in modern language was done (an example is s 51 of the Act which replaces s 2 of the Statute of Frauds (Ireland) 1695).

Additions, amendments and omissions

[23]

As indicated earlier, it is important to note that the Bill originally drafted under the auspices of the Law Reform Commission and attached to its 2005 Report (LRC 74–2005) was altered in several respects by the Government when introduced to the Oireachtas and during its passage. Those alterations fell into three main categories: additions, amendments and omissions.

(a) Additions

[24]

A number of substantial provisions were added to the original Bill. As originally drafted it did not contain provisions relating to variation of trusts. In fact, the Commission had recommended that the abolition of the rule against perpetuities should not be implemented until such variation provisions were also enacted (see the Notes to s 16), but it was originally contemplated that such provisions would be introduced by other legislation. In the event it was decided to include them in the Bill and Part 5 was added at the Dáil Select Committee Stage.

[25]

The original Bill had a limited provision relating to registration of a *lis pendens* (then s 113), but again it was decided at Committee Stage to consolidate the provisions relating to the *lis pendens* register (in the Central Office of the High Court) contained in the Judgments (Ireland) Act 1844, Judgment Mortgage (Ireland) Act 1850, Lis Pendens Act 1867 and Judgments Registry (Ireland) Act 1871. Those are to be found now in Part 12 of the Act.

[26]

At the final Report Stage in the Dáil the Minister for Justice, Equality and Law Reform introduced a very controversial provision purporting to prohibit "upwards-only" rent reviews in business leases. This is to be found in s 132. It is, no doubt, a sign of the controversy that this provision was not brought in to force, unlike the rest of the Act, on 1 December 2009 (see the Notes to ss 2 and 132).

(b) Amendments

[27]

As is only to be expected with a statute as complex as the 2009 Act various amendments were made to the Commission's original Bill, many during its lengthy passage through the Oireachtas. Many of these were largely technical adjustments to particular wording and are referred to in the Notes to the sections in question. A few are of more substance, such as adjustments to ensure the constitutionality of particular provisions (see, eg, the Notes to s 13) or clarify the operation of certain provisions (see, eg, the Notes to ss 48 and 49). Rather more controversially the provisions in Part 10 (Mortgages) of the Act underwent substantial changes during the Bill's passage. This is discussed in the Notes to that Part. Finally some adjustments were made as a consequence of representations made to the Government (see, eg, the Notes to s 133).

(c) Omissions

[28]

The Commission's original Bill contained a Part (Part 11) dealing with limitation of actions (adverse possession). Initially this was intended to implement technical adjustments recommended by the Commission in its *Report on Title to Adverse Possession of Land* (LRC 67–2002). However, at the time the Bill was being drafted the controversial case in England, *JA Pye (Oxford) Ltd v Graham*, had just completed its journey through the domestic courts (see [2000] Ch 676 (HC), [2001] Ch 804 (CA), [2003] 1 AC 419 (HL)). During this journey doubts had been expressed about the compatibility of the doctrine of adverse possession with the European Convention on Human Rights and Freedoms (as also raised in the English High Court in *Beaulane Properties Ltd v Palmer* [2006] Ch 79). The Commission decided to include in Part 11 provisions designed to counter such fears, but they proved to be very controversial (see Buckley, 'Adverse Possession at the Crossroads' (2006) 11 (3) CPLJ 59; 'Calling Time on Adverse Possession' (2006) Bar Rev 32). The Law Society made representations objecting to those provisions in Part 11 and in the end, in view of the ongoing *Pye* case, the Government decided to omit Part 11 in its entirety from the Bill introduced to the Oireachtas. The Commission had noted that the *Pye* case was being appealed to the European Court of Human Rights (LRC 74–2005, para 2.04). Although that Court initially ruled that the doctrine was incompatible (*J A Pye (Oxford) Ltd v UK* (2006) 43 EHRR 43), on appeal (in which both the British and Irish Governments made submissions) the Grand Chamber by a majority ruled that the doctrine was compatible (2007) 46

EHRR 1083). In essence it took the view that it involves a control of the use of land rather than a deprivation of possession (see Buckley, '*Pye (Oxford) Ltd v United Kingdom*: Human Rights Violations in the Eye of the Beholder' (2007) 12(4) CPLJ 109).

[29]

Although the ultimate decision in the *Pye* case may have resolved human rights issues (this has been accepted by the English courts: see *Ofulue v Bossert* [2009] Ch 1), there remain the technical issues which had been dealt with by the Law Reform Commission's original Report (LRC 67–2002) and which Part 11 of the original Bill would also have covered. The Commission is returning to these issues and other aspects of the doctrine as part of its ongoing programme.

Land and Conveyancing Law Reform Act 2009

Number 27 of 2009

ARRANGEMENT OF SECTIONS

PART 1
PRELIMINARY AND GENERAL

PART 2
OWNERSHIP OF LAND

PART 3
FUTURE INTERESTS

PART 4
TRUSTS OF LAND

PART 5
VARIATION OF TRUSTS

PART 6
POWERS

PART 7
CO-OWNERSHIP

PART 8
APPURTENANT RIGHTS

CHAPTER 1

Easements and profits à prendre

CHAPTER 2

Rentcharges

CHAPTER 3

Party structures

ACTS REFERRED TO

Accumulations Act 1892	55 & 56 Vic. c. 58
Administration of Justice Act 1707	6 Anne c. 10
Bankruptcy Act 1988	1988, No. 27
Bodies Corporate (Joint Tenancy) Act 1899	62 & 63 Vic. c. 20
Boundaries Act 1721	8 Geo. 1 c. 5
Building Societies Act 1989	1989, No. 17
Capital Acquisitions Tax Consolidation Act 2003	2003, No. 1
Central Bank and Financial Services Authority of Ireland Act 2004	2004, No. 21
Charities Act 1961	1961, No. 17
Charities Act 1973	1973, No. 13
Charities Act 2009	2009, No. 6
Chief Rents Redemption (Ireland) Act 1864	27 & 28 Vic. c. 38
Circuit Court (Registration of Judgments) Act 1937	1937, No. 3
Clandestine Mortgages Act 1697	9 Will. 3 c. 11
Commons Act 1789	29 Geo. 3 c. 30
Commons Act 1791	31 Geo. 3 c. 38
Companies Act 1963	1963, No. 33
Consumer Credit Act 1995	1995, No. 24
Contingent Remainders Act 1877	40 & 41 Vic. c. 33
Conveyancing Act 1634	10 Chas. 1 sess. 2 c. 3
Conveyancing Act 1881	44 & 45 Vic. c. 41
Conveyancing Act 1882	45 & 46 Vic. c. 39
Conveyancing Act 1911	1 & 2 Geo. 5 c. 37
Conveyancing Acts 1881 to 1911	
Copyhold Act 1843	6 & 7 Vic. c. 23
Copyhold Act 1844	7 & 8 Vic. c. 55
Copyhold Act 1852	15 & 16 Vic. c. 51
Copyhold Act 1858	21 & 22 Vic. c. 94
Copyhold Act 1887	50 & 51 Vic. c. 73
County Hospitals (Amendment) Act 1767	7 Geo. 3 c. 8
County Hospitals Act 1765	5 Geo. 3 c. 20
County Hospitals Act 1777	17 & 18 Geo. 3 c. 15
Courts Act 1981	1981, No. 11
Courts and Court Officers Act 1995	1995, No. 31
Courts (Supplemental Provisions) Act 1961	1961, No. 39
Criminal Justice (Theft and Fraud Offences) Act 2001	2001, No. 50
Crown Land Act 1819	59 Geo. 3 c. 94
Crown Land Revenues Act 1854	17 & 18 Vic. c. 68
Crown Lands Act 1823	4 Geo. 4 c. 18
Crown Lands Act 1825	6 Geo. 4 c. 17
Crown Lands Act 1841	5 Vic. c. 1

Crown Lands Act 1845	8 & 9 Vic. c. 99
Crown Lands Act 1848	11 & 12 Vic. c. 102
Crown Lands Act 1851	14 & 15 Vic. c. 42
Crown Lands Act 1852	15 & 16 Vic. c. 62
Crown Lands Act 1853	16 & 17 Vic. c. 56
Crown Lands Act 1866	29 & 30 Vic. c. 62
Crown Lands Act 1873	36 & 37 Vic. c. 36
Crown Lands Act 1885	48 & 49 Vic. c. 79
Crown Lands Act 1894	57 & 58 Vic. c. 43
Crown Lands Act 1906	6 Edw. 7 c. 28
Crown Lands Act 1913	3 & 4 Geo. 5 c. 8
Crown Lands (Ireland) Act 1822	3 Geo. 4 c. 63
Crown Private Estate Act 1800	39 & 40 Geo. 3 c. 88
Crown Private Estates Act 1862	25 & 26 Vic. c. 37
Crown Private Estates Act 1873	36 & 37 Vic. c. 61
Drainage (Ireland) Act 1842	5 & 6 Vic. c. 89
Drainage (Ireland) Act 1845	8 & 9 Vic. c. 69
Drainage (Ireland) Act 1846	9 & 10 Vic. c. 4
Drainage (Ireland) Act 1847	11 & 12 Vic. c. 79
Drainage (Ireland) Act 1856	19 & 20 Vic. c. 62
Drainage and Improvement of Land (Ireland) Act 1866	29 & 30 Vic. c. 40
Drainage and Improvement of Land (Ireland) Act 1892	55 & 56 Vic. c. 65
Drainage and Improvement of Lands (Ireland) Act 1853	16 & 17 Vic. c. 130
Drainage and Improvement of Lands (Ireland) Act 1855	18 & 19 Vic. c. 110
Drainage and Improvement of Lands (Ireland) Act 1864	27 & 28 Vic. c. 72
Drainage and Improvement of Lands (Ireland) Act 1878	41 & 42 Vic. c. 59
Drainage and Improvement of Lands Act (Ireland) 1863	26 & 27 Vic. c. 88
Drainage and Improvement of Lands Amendment Act (Ireland) 1865	28 & 29 Vic. c. 52
Drainage and Improvement of Lands Amendment Act (Ireland) 1869	32 & 33 Vic. c. 72
Drainage and Improvement of Lands Amendment Act (Ireland) 1872	35 & 36 Vic. c. 31
Drainage and Improvement of Lands Amendment Act (Ireland) 1874	37 & 38 Vic. c. 32
Drainage and Improvement of Lands Supplemental Act Ireland 1864	27 & 28 Vic. c. 107

Drainage and Improvement of Lands Supplemental Act (No. 2 Ireland) 1865	28 & 29 Vic. c. 53
Drainage and Improvement of Lands Supplemental Act (Ireland) 1866	29 & 30 Vic. c. 61
Drainage and Improvement of Lands Supplemental Act (Ireland) 1867	30 & 31 Vic. c. 43
Drainage and Improvement of Lands Supplemental Act (Ireland) (No. 2) 1867	30 & 31 Vic. c. 139
Drainage and Improvement of Lands Supplemental Act (Ireland) (No. 3) 1867	31 & 32 Vic. c. 3
Drainage Maintenance Act 1866	29 & 30 Vic. c. 49
Ecclesiastical Lands Act 1634	10 & 11 Chas. 1 c. 3
Ecclesiastical Lands Act 1795	35 Geo. 3 c. 23
Electronic Commerce Act 2000	2000, No. 27
Family Home Protection Act 1976	1976, No. 27
Family Law Act 1995	1995, No. 26
Family Law (Divorce) Act 1996	1996, No. 33
Fee-Farm Rents (Ireland) Act 1851	14 & 15 Vic. c. 20
Fines and Recoveries (Ireland) Act 1834	4 & 5 Will. 4 c. 92
Fines and Recoveries Act 1833	3 & 4 Will. 4 c. 74
Forfeiture Act 1639	15 Chas. 1 c. 3
Harbours Act 1946	1946, No. 9
Hospitals Act 1761	1 Geo. 3 c. 8
Housing Act 1966	1966, No. 21
Housing (Gaeltacht) Act 1929	1929, No. 41
Housing (Miscellaneous Provisions) Act 2002	2002, No. 9
Housing (Miscellaneous Provisions) Act 1992	1992, No. 18
Housing (Private Rented Dwellings) Act 1982	1982, No. 6
Illusory Appointments Act 1830	11 Geo. 4 & 1 Will. 4 c.46
Improvement of Land Act 1864	27 & 28 Vic. c. 114
Improvement of Land Act 1899	62 & 63 Vic. c. 46
Inheritance Act 1833	3 & 4 Will. 4 c. 106
Interpretation Act 2005	2005, No. 23
Judgments (Ireland) Act 1844	7 & 8 Vic. c. 90
Judgment Mortgage (Ireland) Act 1850	13 & 14 Vic. c. 29
Judgment Mortgage (Ireland) Act 1858	21 & 22 Vic. c. 105
Judgments Registry (Ireland) Act 1871	34 & 35 Vic. c. 72
Land Debentures (Ireland) Act 1865	28 & 29 Vic. c. 101
Land Drainage Act 1845	8 & 9 Vic. c. 56
Land Drainage Act (Ireland) 1863	26 & 27 Vic. c. 26
Landed Estates Court (Ireland) Act 1858	21 & 22 Vic. c. 72
Landed Estates Court (Ireland) Act 1861	24 & 25 Vic. c. 123
Landed Estates Court Act 1866	29 & 30 Vic. c. 99

Landed Property (Ireland) Improvement Act 1860	23 & 24 Vic. c. 153
Landed Property Improvement (Ireland) Act 1847	10 & 11 Vic. c. 32
Landed Property Improvement (Ireland) Act 1849	12 & 13 Vic. c. 59
Landed Property Improvement (Ireland) Act 1852	15 & 16 Vic. c. 34
Landed Property Improvement (Ireland) Act 1862	25 & 26 Vic. c. 29
Landed Property Improvement (Ireland) Act 1866	29 & 30 Vic. c. 26
Landlord and Tenant (Amendment) Act 1980	1980, No. 10
Landlord and Tenant (Ground Rents) Act 1967	1967, No. 3
Law of Property Amendment Act 1859	22 & 23 Vic. c. 35
Law of Property Amendment Act 1860	23 & 24 Vic. c. 38
Leases Act 1849	12 & 13 Vic. c. 26
Leases by Schools Act 1781	21 & 22 Geo. 3 c. 27
Leases by Schools Act 1785	25 Geo. 3 c. 55
Leases for Corn Mills Act 1785	25 Geo. 3 c. 62
Leases for Cotton Manufacture Act 1800	40 Geo. 3 c. 90
Leases for Lives Act 1777	17 & 18 Geo. 3 c. 49
Leases for Mills (Ireland) Act 1851	14 & 15 Vic. c. 7
Leases for Schools (Ireland) Act 1881	44 & 45 Vic. c. 65
Leasing Powers for Religious Purposes in Ireland Act 1855	18 & 19 Vic. c. 39
Leasing Powers Amendment Act for Religious Purposes in Ireland 1875	38 & 39 Vic. c. 11
Life Estates Act 1695	7 Will. 3 c. 8
Limited Owners Reservoirs and Water Supply Further Facilities Act 1877	40 & 41 Vic. c. 31
Lis Pendens Act 1867	30 & 31 Vic. c. 47
Maintenance and Embracery Act 1634	10 Chas. 1 sess. 3 c. 15
Married Women's Status Act 1957	1957, No. 5
Minerals Development Act 1940	1940, No. 31
Mines (Ireland) Act 1806	46 Geo. 3 c. 71
Mining Leases Act 1723	10 Geo. 1 c. 5
Mining Leases Act 1741	15 Geo. 2 c. 10
Mining Leases Act 1749	23 Geo. 2 c. 9
Mining Leases (Ireland) Act 1848	11 & 12 Vic. c. 13
Mortgage Debenture Act 1865	28 & 29 Vic. c. 78
Mortgagees Legal Costs Act 1895	58 & 59 Vic. c. 25
Partition Act 1868	31 & 32 Vic. c. 40
Partition Act 1876	39 & 40 Vic. c. 17
Pensions Act 1990	1990, No. 25
Perpetual Funds (Registration) Act 1933	1933, No. 22
Planning and Development Act 2000	2000, No. 30
Plus Lands Act 1703	2 Anne c. 8
Powers of Appointment Act 1874	37 & 38 Vic. c. 37

Powers of Attorney Act 1996	1996, No. 12
Prescription Act 1832	2 & 3 Will. 4 c. 71
Prescription (Ireland) Act 1858	21 & 22 Vic. c. 42
Public Money Drainage Act 1850	13 & 14 Vic. c. 31
Real Property Act 1845	8 & 9 Vic. c. 106
Registration of Deeds and Title Act 2006	2006, No. 12
Registration of Title Act 1964	1964, No. 16
Renewable Leasehold Conversion Act 1849	12 & 13 Vic. c. 105
Renewable Leaseholds Conversion (Ireland) Act 1868	31 & 32 Vic. c. 62
Renewal of Leases (Ireland) Act 1838	1 & 2 Vic. c. 62
Sales of Reversions Act 1867	31 & 32 Vic. c. 4
Satisfied Terms Act 1845	8 & 9 Vic. c. 112
School Sites (Ireland) Act 1810	50 Geo. 3 c. 33
Settled Estates Act 1877	40 & 41 Vic. c. 18
Settled Land Act 1882	45 & 46 Vic. c. 38
Settled Land Act 1884	47 & 48 Vic. c. 18
Settled Land Act 1889	52 & 53 Vic. c. 36
Settled Land Act 1890	53 & 54 Vic. c. 69
Settled Land Acts (Amendment) Act 1887	50 & 51 Vic. c. 30
Settled Land (Ireland) Act 1847	10 & 11 Vic. c. 46
Settled Land Acts 1882 to 1890	
Sites for Schoolrooms Act 1836	6 & 7 Will. 4 c. 70
Stamp Duties Consolidation Act 1999	1999, No. 31
State Property Act 1954	1954, No. 25
Statute De Donis Conditionalibus 1285	13 Edw. 1 Stat. Westm. sec.c. 1
Statute of Frauds 1695	7 Will. 3 c. 12
Statute of Limitations 1957	1957, No. 6
Statute of Uses 1634	10 Chas. 1 sess. 2 c. 1
Statute Quia Emptores 1290	18 Edw. 1 Stat. d'ni R. de t'ris, & c.
Succession Act 1965	1965, No. 27
Taxes Consolidation Act 1997	1997, No. 39
Tenantry Act 1779	19 & 20 Geo. 3 c. 30
Tenures Abolition Act 1662	14 & 15 Chas. 2 sess. 4 c. 19
Timber Act 1735	9 Geo. 2 c. 7
Timber Act 1765	5 Geo. 3 c. 17
Timber Act 1767	7 Geo. 3 c. 20
Timber Act 1775	15 & 16 Geo. 3 c. 26
Timber Act 1777	17 & 18 Geo. 3 c. 35
Timber Act 1783	23 & 24 Geo. 3 c. 39
Timber (Ireland) Act 1888	51 & 52 Vic. c. 37
Tithe Arrears (Ireland) Act 1839	2 & 3 Vic. c. 3
Tithe Rentcharge (Ireland) Act 1838	1 & 2 Vic. c. 109

Tithe Rentcharge (Ireland) Act 1848	11 & 12 Vic. c. 80
Tithes Act 1835	5 & 6 Will. 4 c. 74
Tithing of Turnips Act 1835	5 & 6 Will. 4 c. 75
Trustee Act 1893	56 & 57 Vic. c. 53
Trustee Savings Bank Act 1989	1989, No. 21
Vendor and Purchaser Act 1874	37 & 38 Vic. c. 78
Voluntary Conveyances Act 1893	56 & 57 Vic. c. 21

MARGINAL ABBREVIATIONS

AJA 1707	Administration of Justice Act 1707	6 Anne c. 10
BC(JT) A	Bodies Corporate (Joint Tenancy) Act 1899	62 & 63 Vic. c. 20
CA 1634	Conveyancing Act 1634	10 Chas. 1 sess. 2 c. 3
CA 1881	Conveyancing Act 1881	44 & 45 Vic. c. 41
CA 1882	Conveyancing Act 1882	45 & 46 Vic. c. 39
CA 1911	Conveyancing Act 1911	1 & 2 Geo. 5 c. 37
IAA 1830	Illusory Appointments Act 1830	11 Geo. 4 & 1 Will. 4 c. 46
JA 1844	Judgments (Ireland) Act 1844	7 & 8 Vic. c. 90
JMA 1850	Judgment Mortgage (Ireland) Act 1850	13 & 14 Vic. c. 29
JMA 1858	Judgment Mortgage (Ireland) Act 1858	21 & 22 Vic. c. 105
JRA 1871	Judgments Registry (Ireland) Act 1871	34 & 35 Vic. c. 72
LEA 1695	Life Estates Act 1695	7 Will. 3 c. 8
LPA 1867	Lis Pendens Act 1867	30 & 31 Vic. c. 47
LPAA 1859	Law of Property Amendment Act 1859	22 & 23 Vic. c. 35
LPAA 1860	Law of Property Amendment Act 1860	23 & 24 Vic. c. 38
PA 1868	Partition Act 1868	31 & 32 Vic. c. 40
PA 1876	Partition Act 1876	39 & 40 Vic. c. 17
PA 1832	Prescription Act 1832	2 & 3 Will. 4 c. 71
PA 1858	Prescription (Ireland) Act 1858	21 & 22 Vic. c. 42
PAA 1874	Powers of Appointment Act 1874	37 & 38 Vic. c. 37
RPA 1845	Real Property Act 1845	8 & 9 Vic. c. 106
SF 1695	Statute of Frauds 1695	7 Will. 3 c. 12
QE 1290	Statute Quia Emptores 1290	18 Edw. 1 Stat. d'ni R. de t'ris, & c.
SLA 1882	Settled Land Act 1882	45 & 46 Vic. c. 38
SU 1634	Statute of Uses 1634	10 Chas. 1 sess. 2 c. 1
VCA 1893	Voluntary Conveyances Act 1893	56 & 57 Vic. c. 21
VPA 1874	Vendor and Purchaser Act 1874	37 & 38 Vic. c. 78

Number 27 of 2009

Land and Conveyancing Law Reform Act 2009

[30]

AN ACT TO PROVIDE FOR THE REFORM AND MODERNISATION OF LAND LAW AND CONVEYANCING,[1] TO REPEAL ENACTMENTS THAT ARE OBSOLETE, UNNECESSARY OR OF NO BENEFIT IN MODERN CIRCUMSTANCES,[2] TO PROVIDE FOR THE VARIATION OF TRUSTS,[3] TO MODERNISE THE LAW RELATING TO *LIS PENDENS*,[4] TO AMEND THE REGISTRATION OF DEEDS AND TITLE ACTS 1964 AND 2006[5] AND CERTAIN OTHER ENACTMENTS AND FOR RELATED MATTERS.[6]

[21st July, 2009]

Notes

1　This phrase reflects the title of the Law Reform Commission's Consultation Paper (LRC CP 34–2004) and subsequent Report (LRC 74–2005) which contained the draft Bill upon which the Bill ultimately introduced by the Government was based (see Introduction above).

2　The reference to statutes reflects a primary objective of the Act, namely the replacement of over 150 pre-1922 statutes relating to land law and conveyancing (see Schedule 2 and the Notes to it).

3　This refers to Part 5 of the Act which was added during the Act's passage through the Oireachtas (see Introduction above and the Notes to that Part below).

4　This refers to Part 12 which was also added during the Act's passage (see Introduction above and the Notes to that Part below).

5　This refers to Part 13 which contains some substantial amendments (see Notes to that Part below). Note, however, that there are other consequential amendments to the 1964 and 2006 Acts in Schedule 1 (see the Notes to it).

6　Schedule 1 contains consequential amendments to other Acts.

BE IT ENACTED BY THE OIREACHTAS AS FOLLOWS:

PART 1
PRELIMINARY AND GENERAL

[31]

1.—This Act may be cited as the Land[2] and Conveyancing[3] Law Reform Act 2009.　　　**Short title.**[1]

Notes

1   Although the Act is concerned for the most part with land law and conveyancing law, it should be noted that some of its provisions have a wider scope. For example, the rule against perpetuities which is abolished by s 16 applied to future interests in all kinds of property (see the Notes to that section). Although Part 4 (Trusts of Land) is necessarily confined to land, Part 5, which was added to the Bill during its passage through the Oireachtas, applies to trusts of any kind of property. This Part is linked with the abolition of the rule against perpetuities (see the Notes to Part 5). Other provisions which have a wider scope are those in Part 6 (Powers), Part 7 (Co-ownership) and Part 10 (Mortgages) (see the Notes to those Parts).

2   Parts of the Act which deal particularly with land law are Parts 2, 4, 8 and 11–14 (see the Notes to them).

3   The Part of the Act which deals particularly with conveyancing law is Part 9 (Contracts and Conveyances) (see the Notes to it).

---

[32]

Commence-
ment.[1]

2.—This Act shall come into operation on such day or days[2] as the Minister[3] may appoint by order or orders either generally or with reference to any particular purpose or provision and different days may be so appointed for different purposes and different provisions.

Notes

1   This is what is now the standard provision enabling the Act to be brought into force wholly or partially by a statutory instrument or instruments made by the Minister.

2   The Land and Conveyancing Law Reform Act 2009 (Commencement) Order 2009 (SI 356/2009) specified 1 December 2009 as the appointed day for the whole Act other than s 132 (see the Notes to that section).

3   The Minister for Justice, Equality and Law Reform: see s 3.

---

[33]

Interpreta-
tion gener-
ally.[1]

3.—In this Act,[2] unless the context otherwise[3] requires—

"Act of 1957" means the Statute of Limitations 1957;[4]

"Act of 1963" means the Companies Act 1963;[5]

"Act of 1964" means the Registration of Title Act 1964;[6]

"Act of 1965" means the Succession Act 1965;[7]

"Act of 1976" means the Family Home Protection Act 1976;[8]

"Act of 1988" means the Bankruptcy Act 1988;[9]

"Act of 1989" means the Building Societies Act 1989;[10]

"Act of 1995" means the Family Law Act 1995;[11]

"Act of 1996" means the Family Law (Divorce) Act 1996;[12]

"Act of 2000" means the Planning and Development Act 2000;[13]

"Act of 2005" means the Interpretation Act 2005;[14]

"Act of 2006" means the Registration of Deeds and Title Act 2006;[15]

"assent" has the meaning given to it by section 53 of the Act of 1965;[16]

"consent" includes agreement, licence and permission;[17]

"conveyance"[18] includes an appointment, assent, assignment, charge, disclaimer, lease, mortgage, release, surrender, transfer, vesting certificate, vesting declaration, vesting order and every other assurance by way of instrument[19] except a will;[20] and "convey" shall be read accordingly;

"the court"[21] means—

(*a*) the High Court,[22] or

(*b*) the Circuit Court[23] when exercising the jurisdiction conferred on it by the Third Schedule to the Courts (Supplemental Provisions) Act 1961;

"covenant" includes an agreement, a condition, reservation and stipulation;[24]

"deed" has the meaning given to it by *section 64(2)*;[25]

"development" has the meaning given to it by section 3 of the Act of 2000;[26]

"development plan" has the meaning given to it by section 3(1) of the Act of 2000;[27]

"disposition" includes a conveyance and a devise, bequest or appointment of property by will and "dispose" shall be read accordingly;[28]

"exempted development" has the meaning given to it by section 4 of the Act of 2000;[29]

"fee farm grant"[30] means any—

(*a*)   grant of a fee simple, or

(*b*)   lease for ever or in perpetuity,[31]

reserving or charging a perpetual rent, whether or not the relationship of landlord and tenant[32] is created between the grantor and grantee, and includes a sub-fee farm grant;

"freehold covenant" has the meaning given to it by *section 48*;[33]

"freehold estate" has the meaning given to it by *section 11(2)*;[34]

"housing loan" has the meaning given to it by section 2(1) of the Consumer Credit Act 1995, as substituted by section 33 of, and Part 12 of Schedule 3 to, the Central Bank and Financial Services Authority of Ireland Act 2004 and "housing loan mortgage" means a mortgage to secure a housing loan;[35]

"incumbrance" includes an annuity, charge, lien, mortgage, portion and trust for securing an annual or capital sum; and "incumbrancer" shall be read accordingly and includes every person entitled to the benefit of an incumbrance or to require its payment or discharge;[36]

"instrument"[37] includes a deed, will, or other document in writing, and information in electronic or other non-legible form[38] which is capable of being converted into such a document, but not a statutory provision;[39]

"judgment mortgage" means a mortgage registered by a creditor under *section 116*;[40]

"land"[41] includes—

(*a*)   any estate or interest[42] in or over land, whether corporeal or incorporeal,[43]

(*b*)   mines, minerals and other substances in the substratum below the surface,[44] whether or not owned in horizontal, vertical or other layers[45] apart from the surface of the land,[46]

(*c*)   land covered by water,[47]

(*d*)   buildings or structures of any kind[48] on land and any part of them,[49] whether the division is made horizontally, vertically or in any other way,[50]

(e) the airspace[51] above the surface of land or above any building or structure on land[52] which is capable of being or was previously occupied[53] by a building or structure and any part of such airspace,[54] whether the division is made horizontally, vertically or in any other way,[55]

(f) any part of land;[56]

"Land Registry" has the meaning given to it by section 7 of the Act of 1964;[57]

"landlord" means the person, including a sublandlord, entitled to the legal estate immediately superior to a tenancy;[58]

"lease" as a noun means an instrument creating a tenancy; and as a verb means the granting of a tenancy by an instrument;[59]

"legal estate" has the meaning given to it by *section 11(1)*;[60]

"legal interest" has the meaning given to it by *section 11(4)*;[61]

"lessee" means the person, including a sublessee, in whom a tenancy created by a lease is vested;[62]

"lessor" means the person, including a sublessor, entitled to the legal estate immediately superior to a tenancy created by a lease;[63]

"Minister" means the Minister for Justice, Equality and Law Reform;[64]

"mortgage" includes any charge or lien on any property for securing money or money's worth;[65]

"mortgagee" includes any person having the benefit of a charge or lien and any person deriving title to the mortgage under the original mortgagee;[66]

"mortgagor" includes any person deriving title to the mortgaged property under the original mortgagor or entitled to redeem the mortgage;[67]

"notice" includes constructive notice;[68]

"personal representative" means the executor or executrix or the administrator or administratrix for the time being of a deceased person;[69]

"planning permission" means permission required under Part III of the Act of 2000;[70]

"possession" includes the receipt of, or the right to receive, rent and profits, if any;[71]

"prescribed" means prescribed by regulations made under *section 5*;[72]

"property" means any real or personal property or any part or combination of such property;[73]

"Property Registration Authority" has the meaning given to it by section 9 of the Act of 2006;[74]

"purchaser"[75] means an assignee, chargeant, grantee, lessee, mortgagee or other person who acquires land for valuable consideration; and "purchase" shall be read accordingly;[76]

"registered land" has the meaning given to it by section 3(1) of the Act of 1964;[77]

"Registry of Deeds" has the meaning given to it by section 33 of the Act of 2006;[78]

"rent"[79] includes a rent payable under a tenancy or a rentcharge, or other payment in money or money's worth or any other consideration, reserved or issuing out of or charged on land, but does not include interest;[80]

"rentcharge"[81] means any annual or periodic sum charged on or issuing out of land, except—

(*a*) a rent payable under a tenancy,[82] and

(*b*) interest;[83]

"right of entry" means a right to take possession of land or of its income and to retain that possession or income until some obligation is performed;[84]

"right of re-entry" means a right to forfeit the legal owner's estate in the land;[85]

"strict settlement" has the meaning given to it by *section 18(1)(a)*;[86]

"subtenancy" includes a sub-subtenancy; and a "subtenant" shall be read accordingly;[87]

"tenancy"[88] means the estate or interest which arises from the relationship of landlord and tenant however it is created but does not include a tenancy at will[89] or at sufferance;[90]

"tenant" means the person, including a subtenant, in whom a tenancy is vested;[91]

"trust corporation" has the meaning given to it by section 30(4) of the Act of 1965;[92]

"trust of land" has the meaning given to it by *section 18(1)*;[93]

"unregistered land" has the meaning given to it by section 3(1) of the Act of 1964;[94]

"valuable consideration" does not include marriage or a nominal consideration in money;[95]

"will" includes codicil.[96]

Notes

1 This section contains a wide range of definitions, but it is important to remember that others which may apply are contained in the Interpretation Act 2005. Of particular relevance in this context is Part 4 and the Schedule in that Act. Thus s 18 of the 2005 Act contains important provisions such as the singular including the plural (and *vice versa*), "person" including a body corporate, the masculine gender including the feminine gender (and *vice versa*) and various provisions relating to distance and time. The Schedule includes important provisions such as "month" meaning a calendar month (cf *Vone Securities v Cooke* [1979] IR 59) and the meaning of "writing". The definitions in s 3 and in the Interpretation Act 2005 (and rules of construction in that Act) are given very important added significance by s 75, which applies them to private instruments relating to land executed after 1 December 2009 (see the Notes to that section).

2 But note again the significance of s 75.

3 This is a standard qualification. Note that a similar qualification is contained in s 75. For an example of a "contrary" context in relation to the definition of "conveyance" see s 79(*a*) (and the Notes to it).

4 The 1957 Statute is referred to in several places in the Act: see ss 48, 49(6)(*a*)(ii), 99(2) and 119 (see the Notes to those sections).

5 In fact this reference became redundant in the enacted version of the Act. The original Bill contained provisions to implement recommendations made by the Law Reform Commission to amend the law relating to judgment mortgages as they operate in respect of companies (in particular under s 291 of the Companies Act 1963) and on the bankruptcy of an individual (in particular under s 50 of the Bankruptcy Act 1988) (see *Consultation Paper on Judgment Mortgages* (LRC CP 30–2004), paras 2.58–2.67). The Commission also recommended that judgment mortgages should be treated like other charges required to be notified to the registrar under s 99 of the 1963 Act (see LRC CP 30–2004), paras 2.69–2.73. The provisions in question were contained in ss 115 and 116(4) of the original Bill (as initiated) but during its passage the view was taken that it was not appropriate in such a Bill to amend company or bankruptcy law. Section 115 was deleted at the Seanad Committee Stage and s 116(4) at the Dáil Select Committee Stage. A consequential amendment to the references in s 3 was overlooked.

6   There are several references in the Act to the 1964 Act: see other parts of s 3 itself (see the definitions of "Land Registry", "registered land" and "unregistered land") and ss 21(3)(*b*)(iii), 96(1)(*b*) and 104(4). Apart from that Part 13 contains a number of textual amendments to provisions in the 1964 Act and there are further amendments set out in Schedule 1 (see the Notes to those parts of the Act).

7   References to the 1965 Act will be found in other parts of s 3 (see the definitions of "assent" and "trust corporation") and ss 9(3)(*a*)(ii) and 80(4) (see the Notes to those sections).

8   References to the 1976 Act will be found in ss 21(6), 31(5), 101(7) and 117(4)(*a*) (see the Notes to those sections).

9   This reference also became redundant as a consequence of the amendments made to the Bill at the Committee stages which were mentioned in Note 5 above.

10 The 1989 Act is referred to in s 103(5) (see the Notes to that section).

11 The 1995 Act is referred to in ss 22(5), 31(5) and 117(4)(*a*) (see the Notes to those sections).

12 The 1996 Act is referred to in ss 31(5) and 117(4)(*a*) (see the Notes to those sections).

13 The 2000 Act is referred to elsewhere in s 3 itself (see the definitions of "development", "development plan", "exempted development" and "planning permission") and s 50(2)(*c*) (see the Notes to s 50).

14 The 2005 Act is referred to in ss 5(3)(*b*), 8(2) and 75 (see the Notes to those sections).

15 The 2006 Act is referred to elsewhere in s 3 itself (see the definitions of "Property Registration Authority" and "Registry of Deeds" and Notes 74 and 78 below).

16 An "assent" is referred to in the definition of "conveyance" (see Note 18 below) and is also referred to in s 63(1)(*a*) (see Notes to that section). The concept of a "conveyance" is a key feature of Part 9 and Schedule 3 (see the Notes to those parts of the Act).

17 This definition of "consent" makes it clear that it does not matter how the giving of a required consent to something is couched. It may, therefore, be worded as an "agreement" or "licence" or "permission" instead of as "consent" or, since this is an "including" definition, referred to by some other appropriate term, eg an "assent" or "acceptance" or "acquiescence". There are references to "consent" in ss 26(2)(*b*)(i), 30(1) and (2), 31(2)(*e*), 33, 97(1), 100(2), 112(1), (2) and (3)(*c*), 114(5)(*a*) and (*b*) and 122(*a*) (see the Notes to those sections).

18 This is a wide definition of a fundamental concept which, as mentioned above, is a key feature of parts of the Act (see Note 16). It is also used in other provisions: see ss 21(1), 30(1), 89(2)(*a*) and (*b*), 90(1) and (2), 104(1), (2) and (3) and 105(1) (see the Notes to those sections). Cf s 79 and the Notes to it.

19 Note the definition of "instrument" which includes a very wide range of private documents (see Notes 38–39 below).

20 Note that, unlike an "instrument", a "conveyance" does *not* include a "will". The essential point here is that many of the provisions of the Act, in particular those in Part 9 and those relating to the position of purchasers, such as ss 21, 104 and 105,

cannot apply to wills and those who succeed to land on the death of the owner. Those matters are governed by the Succession Act 1965.

21 The effect of this provision is that, apart from the exceptions mentioned below, the Circuit Court has jurisdiction to deal with any matter arising under the Act, subject to the current prescribed limits on its jurisdiction set out in successive amendments to the Third Schedule to the Courts (Supplemental Provisions) Act 1961. In relation to proceedings in respect of land these are mostly based on the rateable valuation. Note the additions to the Third Schedule relating to proceedings under the 2009 Act contained in Schedule 1 to the Act (see the Notes to that Schedule). There are two exceptions to this general rule:

(1) jurisdiction is conferred on the District Court by ss 6(3) (offences), 43 (party structures) and 98 (abandoned mortgaged property) (see the Notes to those sections);

(2) exclusive jurisdiction is conferred on the Circuit Court in respect of possession applications under s 97(2), and applications for authorisation to exercise the power of sale under s 100(3) in relation to property the subject of a housing loan mortgage, by s 101(5) (see the Notes to those sections).

22 This is defined by the Schedule (Part 1) to the Interpretation Act 2005.

23 This is also defined by the 2005 Act.

24 A "covenant" is another fundamental concept which features in several of the Act's provisions, most of which derive from provisions in the Conveyancing Acts 1881–1911 which the Act replaces (see further s 8 and its Notes below): see ss 11(4)(*b*), 12(3), 48–50, 59(2), 78, 80–83 and Schedule 3 (and the Notes to those provisions). Note also s 82(4) (see the Notes to it).

25 Section 64 introduces substantial changes to the law governing when a document constitutes a "deed" as opposed to some other instrument (see the Notes to that section). The need to distinguish between different instruments remains because the Act establishes (what, in practice, has long been the case) the general rule that a conveyance of a *legal* estate or interest in land must be by deed: see s 62 and note the exceptions in s 63 (see the Notes to those sections).

26 This key feature of planning law is referred to in ss 44(1)(*b*) and 48 (see the Notes to those sections).

27 This concept is referred to in s 50(2)(*c*) (see the Notes to that section).

28 As the definition makes clear, "disposition" is a wider term than "conveyance" because it includes also dispositions of property by will. Use of this concept is to be found in ss 11(1), (4), (8) and (9), 12(6), 23, 40(2), 51(1), 55(1), 58(2)(*b*), 60(1) and 74(1) and (2) (see the Notes to those sections).

29 This concept is referred to in s 44(1)(*b*) (see the Notes to that section).

30 This definition is important for the purposes of s 12 (see the Notes to it).

31 Most fee farm grants involve the grant expressly of a "fee simple", but older precedents took the form of a lease "forever" or "in perpetuity" (see Stubbs and Baxter (eds), *Irish Forms and Precedents* (Butterworths, 1910), pp 117–126) The Renewable Leasehold Conversion Act 1849 automatically converted post-1849 leases "in perpetuity" into conveyances "for ever" at a fee farm rent (see ss 37 and 38; Wylie, *Irish Land Law* (3rd edn, Tottel Publishing, 1997), paras 4.081–4.086).

Lessees holding under leases for lives renewable for ever were given the right under the 1849 Act to convert the lease into a fee farm grant and the Landlord and Tenant (Amendment) Act 1980 automatically converted any lease whose holder had not exercised this right into a fee simple probably held under the equivalent of a fee farm grant (see s 74 and Wylie, *Landlord and Tenant Law* (2nd edn, Tottel Publishing, 1998), para 4.45). The object of this definition is to catch all forms of fee farm grant – note also the word "any".

32 Most fee farm grants create the relationship of landlord and tenant in the modern "non-feudal" sense, either because they are "conversion" grants (ie converted from leases) or are made under Deasy's Act 1860, s 3 of which removed the need for retention by the grantor of a lease of a reversion (see Wylie, *Irish Land Law* (3rd edn, Tottel Publishing, 1997), paras 4.079–4.103). However, some older grants created feudal tenure (ie freehold subinfeudation which had been prohibited by the statute Quia Emptores 1290: see Wylie, *Irish Land Law* (3rd edn, Tottel Publishing, 1997), ch 2; Lyall, *Land Law in Ireland* (2nd edn, Round Hall, 2000), ch 3) because 17th century Crown grants of confiscated Irish land gave the grantees special dispensation to make sub-grants *"non obstante Quia Emptores"*. Exercise of such powers was subsequently confirmed by a series of statutes enacted by the Irish Parliament during the 17th century (see Wylie, *Irish Land Law* (3rd edn, Tottel Publishing, 1997), para 4.059). It is very doubtful whether many of such Crown grants containing dispensation powers have survived the operation of the Land Purchase Acts (see Wylie, *Irish Land Law* (3rd edn, Tottel Publishing, 1997), para 4.060) but any that do come within this definition.

33 Section 49 concerns the enforceability of freehold covenants entered into after 1 December 2009, but note that s 50, which concerns discharge and modification by court order, applies also to freehold covenants created before that date (see Notes to those sections).

34 The concept of a "freehold estate" is used in the Act to indicate what estate will, from 1 December 2009, have legal title attached to it. Any other estate will not involve legal title, unless it is a "leasehold estate". This reflects other changes made by the Act, such as abolition of the fee tail estate (s 13) and conversion of life estates into equitable interests only (s 18(4)). It also reflects the replacement of the Settled Land Acts 1882–1890 with the "Trusts of Land" provisions of Part 4, under which the freehold estate (in essence the fee simple) and, therefore, the legal title will always be vested in trustees and not the holder of some more limited estate (see the Notes to s 11 and Part 4).

35 This definition was added at a late stage in the Bill's passage through the Oireachtas (at the Dáil Select Committee stage) to deal with various changes which were made to the provisions relating to Mortgages in Part 10. In essence the issue had arisen as to how far the provisions of that Part were mandatory and could not be varied by the express terms of mortgages. The end result is that from 1 December a distinction has to be drawn between a "housing loan" mortgage coming within the 1995 Act (as amended by the 2004 Act) and other mortgages (see the Notes to Part 10).

36 This definition is based on the one in s 2 of the Conveyancing Act 1881 (which is repealed by the Act: see Schedule 2). Note that it is a wide "including" definition (see *Robinson v Barton-Eccles Local Board* (1883) 8 App Cas 798 at 801; *Rodger v*

Harrison [1893] 1 QB 161 at 167; *Rye v Rye* [1962] AC 496 at 507). The concept of an "incumbrance" is relevant to several parts of the Act: see ss 11(4)(*c*), 60(1)(*a*) and (2)(*a*), 93(2), 94(3)(*d*), 107(1)(*a*), 114(5), 117(2)(*a*), (3) and (4) and Schedule 3, Part 2 (see the Notes to those sections and Schedule 3).

37 This definition is a wide one covering all forms of written documents (note that it is an "including" one). The definition of "writing" in the Interpretation Act 2005 (which applies to the 2009 Act and has the additional significance for private documents under s 75 which was referred to in Note 1 above) includes "printing, typewriting, lithography, photography, and other modes of representing or reproducing words in visible form and any information kept in non-legible form, whether stored electronically or otherwise, which is capable by any means of being reproduced in legible form." The concept of an "instrument" is relevant to several provisions in the Act: see ss 10(3), 12(2) and (4), 13(2), 18(1)(*a*), 19(1)(*a*)(ii), (*b*)(i)–(iii) and (*c*), 20(1)(*b*), 26(1) and (2), 28(2), 29(2), 32(2), 49(6)(*b*), 58(1), (2), (3), (7) and (10) (note here the additional meaning given by para (*a*)), 59(1), 60(1)(*a*) and (2)(*a*), 64(2), 65, 72, 75, 85, 86(1) and (2) and 89(2) (see the Notes to these sections). Note that s 127 amends s 3 of the Registration of Title Act 1964 by inserting this definition.

38 This confirms the application of the meaning to modern methods of storing information electronically also referred to in relation to the meaning of "writing" under the Interpretation Act 2005 (see Note 37 above).

39 The Act is concerned primarily with private documents relating to land transactions and not statutory material. On the rare occasion where a substantive provision also relates to a statutory provision this is indicated expressly: see, eg, ss 58(3) and 59(1) (and the Notes to them).

40 The provisions of Part 11 replace those in the Judgment Mortgage (Ireland) Acts 1850 and 1858 (see the Notes to that Part).

41 This is a much wider "including" definition than that in s 2 of the Conveyancing Act 1881 or, indeed, in Part 1 of the Schedule to the Interpretation Act 2005. It incorporates some of the features of the definition in the English Law of Property Act 1925 (s 205(1)(ix)), which is much wider than the definition in the 2005 Act (or its predecessor, the Interpretation Act 1937). The narrowness of that definition was referred to by the Supreme Court in *Metropolitan Properties Ltd v O'Brien* [1995] 1 IR 467 in the context of separate horizontal layers of land, such as flats, and so-called "flying freeholds" (see O'Flaherty J at pp 481–482 and *Bank of Ireland v Gleeson* (6 April 2000), SC; cf the views of Peart J in *A O'Gorman & Co Ltd v JES Holdings Ltd* [2005] IEHC 168; see also Lyall, *Land Law in Ireland* (2nd edn, Round Hall, 2000), pp 38–40; Wylie, *Landlord and Tenant Law* (2nd edn, Tottel Publishing, 1998), para 30.05; Wylie and Woods, *Irish Conveyancing Law* (3rd edn, Tottel Publishing, 2005), paras 8.08 and 19.13). See further on this particular aspect of the definition Notes 44 and 51 below. Note that s 127 substitutes this definition for the definition in s 3 of the Registration of Title Act 1967.

42 The Act reinforces the long-established distinction between a major interest in land comprising an "estate" (whether freehold or leasehold) and other "interests" which fall short of an estate, such as mortgages, charges, easements and profits (see ss 10 and 11 and the Notes to them). The essence of the distinction is that an estate confers

greater attributes of "ownership" and benefits of enjoyment in respect of the land in question, such as the right of occupation. An interest falling short of an estate usually confers much less in the way of benefits, although in such instances (such as the case of a mortgage) it may enable the holder to acquire such benefits (eg on default by the owner-mortgagor). The distinguishing feature of the right to occupy or enjoy physical possession is also relevant to the distinction between "corporeal" and "incorporeal" hereditaments: see Note 43 below.

43 This recognises a traditional distinction in land law. An "incorporeal" hereditament (the latter word was the traditional word for "land" and stemmed from the former distinction between land and other property under the feudal law of "inheritance" which was abolished by the Administration of Estates Act 1959 and Succession Act 1965) is a right over land which does not confer the right to occupy or possess it (the "corpus"). It is a right exercisable in respect of someone else's land, such as a easement or *profit à prendre* (see Lyall, *Land Law in Ireland* (2nd edn, Round Hall, 2000), ch 22; Wylie, *Irish Land Law* (3rd edn, Tottel Publishing, 1997), ch 6).

44 This recognises the traditional maxim that the owner of the surface of land owns also both the airspace above it and the substratum below it – *cuius est solum, eius est usque ad coelum et ad inferos*. However, it is important to emphasise that the maxim should not be taken literally – the surface owner cannot claim ownership right up to the sky nor down to the centre of the earth. Although there is no direct Irish case law on the point, there is much guidance from that of other common law jurisdictions that the surface owner can only lay claim to that much of the airspace and substratum which is physically or commercially exploitable (see, eg, *Bernstein of Leigh v Skyviews and General Ltd* [1978] QB 479; *Bocardo SA v Star Energy UK Onshore Ltd* [2009] EWCA Civ 579; Tolson, "'Land' without Earth: Freehold Flats in English Law' (1950) 14 Conv 350; Gray, 'Property in Thin Air" (1991) 50 Camb LJ 252).

45 This recognises that the layers of the substratum may not be divided either horizontally or vertically but may be separated at different angles. This would be particularly the case with many minerals which are owned separately from the owner of the surface. Most are now vested in the State under Article 43 of the Constitution and their exploitation is governed by the statutory regime contained in the Minerals Development Act 1979.

46 This recognises the point made in the previous Note, that ownership of the substratum, or layers of it or materials comprised in it, may be separate from ownership of the surface of the land (see the discussion involving oil in the recent English case *Bocardo SA v Star Energy UK Onshore Ltd* [2009] EWCA Civ 579).

47 This recognises that land may comprise the bed of a river or lake and ownership usually rests with the owners of the banks (riparian owners) (see *Toome Eel Fishery (NI) Ltd v Cardwell* [1966] NI 1; *Tennent v Clancy* [1987] IR 15; *Gannon v Walsh* [1998] 3 IR 245). Such land may not be covered permanently, such as the foreshore which lies between the high and low tidal marks. The foreshore is vested in the State under Art 10 of the Constitution and its exploitation is governed by the regime in the Foreshore Act 1933.

48 Buildings have long been regarded as part of land and other structures, which may not be regarded strictly as buildings, may nevertheless be regarded as part of land if they are sufficiently attached to the surface or to a building as to constitute a "fixture" (see Lyall, *Land Law in Ireland* (2nd edn, Round Hall, 2000), pp 623–625; Wylie, *Landlord and Tenant Law* (2nd edn, Tottel Publishing, 1998), ch 9).

49 This recognises that parts of a building may be owned separately, such as a flat or apartment (see Note 51 below).

50 This recognises that the divisions or layering of land or buildings on land may not only be horizontal or vertical but also be created at an angle, eg, where the base of a stairway or elevator forms the division between difference parts of a building.

51 This recognises that different layers or parts of the airspace may be owned separately and be the subject of conveyances to different persons. Notwithstanding doubts which seem to have underpinned statements made by O'Flaterty J in the *Metropolitan Properties* case referred to above (Note 41) the fact is that the common law recognised such separate ownership over 100 years ago (see *Humphries v Brogden* (1850) 12 QB 739 at 755–757, *per* Lord Campbell CJ; *Bonomi v Backhouse* (1858) El Bl & El 622 at 654–655, *per* Willes J; *Dalton v Angus* (1881) 6 App Cas 740; cf *Stadium Capital Holdings (No 2) Ltd v St Marylebone Property Company plc* [2009] All ER (D) 166 (Oct)). On this basis separate ownership of flats and apartments came to be recognised and the only problem was facilitating such ownership from the "technical conveyancing" point of view (see Wylie and Woods, *Irish Conveyancing Law* (3rd edn, Tottel Publishing, 2005), paras 19.12–19.22). That problem stemmed largely from the failure of the common law to develop an effective scheme for enforceability of freehold covenants, so that "multi-unit" developments have hitherto been leasehold ones (on this and other problems which arise in relation to such developments see the Law Reform Commission's *Consultation Paper on Multi-unit Developments* (LRC CP 42–2006) and note the recently initiated Multi-unit Developments Bill 2009 (No 32 of 2009)). The conveyancing problem relating to enforceability of freehold covenants is resolved by the provisions in Chapter 4 of Part 8 of the Act (see the Notes to those provisions).

52 This recognises that it is possible to convey a layer or block of the airspace separately from the surface of the land, provided it is capable of being exploited by putting a building or structure in it. Where no such building or structure is in existence at the date of the conveyance care must be taken to identify clearly the location and precise dimensions of the airspace in question (by reference to the surface of the land). Otherwise there is a danger that a court might declare the conveyance void for uncertainty (see Wylie and Woods, *Irish Conveyancing Law* (3rd edn, Tottel Publishing, 2005), ch 17 and paras 18.58–18.70).

53 This recognises that where a building is destroyed the owner still owns the airspace previously occupied by that building.

54 This reiterates the point made above (see Note 51) that different parts of the airspace may be owned separately, usually occupied by different parts of a building, such as flats or apartments.

55 Just as the division of a building may be at an angle out of the horizontal or vertical so may be the division of the airspace (see Note 50 above).

56 This saves having to refer to parts of land in the various references to land throughout the Act.

57 Notwithstanding the establishment of the Property Registration Authority by the Registration of Deeds and Title Act 2006 (see Part 2 of that Act) the Land Registry continues to function for the purposes of registration of titles. The Authority's function is primarily to manage and control both the Land Registry and the Registry of Deeds and to promote and extend registration of ownership of land (see s 10 of the 2006 Act). References to registration in the Land Registry are to be found in ss 21(3)(*b*)(iii) and (4), 30(3), 35(4), 39(1), 50(4), 68(3), 116(2) and Part 13 (see the Notes to those sections and that Part).

58 This definition is linked with the definition of a "tenancy" (see below), which in turn is linked with the provisions of s 11. That section draws the distinction between legal estates and interests on the one hand and equitable interests on the other hand. This is important for determining who holds legal title to land and what interests are "overreached" on a conveyance of legal title to a purchaser under s 21 (see the Notes to ss 11 and 21).

59 This definition does two things. One is that it confines use of the word "lease" to situations where a tenancy is created expressly by some instrument (see Notes 37–39 above) and not simply orally or by implication. The other is that it recognises that commonly the word is used in two senses: as a noun when it is referring to the instrument creating a tenancy ("the lease") and as a verb when it is referring to the process of granting a tenancy by means of an instrument ("leasing" the premises): for examples see ss 66(2)(*a*), 81, 99(1)(*b*), 112–114 and 132 (and the Notes to them).

60 Section 11 draws a distinction between legal "estates" and legal "interests" (see the Notes to it).

61 See again the Notes to s 11.

62 This is also linked with the definition of a "tenancy" and the provisions of s 11 (see Note 58 above).

63 This is also linked with the definition of a "tenancy" and the provisions of s 11 (see Note 58 above).

64 The Minister has power to make regulations under s 5 (see the Notes to that section).

65 This is similar to the definition in s 2 of the Conveyancing Act 1881 which is repealed by Schedule 2 (see the Notes to it). The definition in s 3(1) of the Registration of Title Act 1964 cross-referred to that in the Conveyancing Acts but by virtue of s 8(2)(*b*) and (*c*) that should be read as referring to the definition in this Act (see Notes to s 8). Note that it is an "including" definition and that, unlike most of the Act, it covers mortgages or charges of property other than land. This is an important feature of the provisions of Part 10 (see the Notes to that Part). The definition in the original Bill included a reference to a "judgment mortgage" but the view was later taken that this was not appropriate. Judgment mortgages are confined to land and are the subject of separate provisions in Part 11 (see the Notes to that Part). The reference to a "judgment mortgage" was dropped at the Seanad Committee Stage.

66 This is also similar to the definition in s 2 of the Conveyancing Act 1881 (see Note 65 above).

67 This is also similar to the definition in s 2 of the Conveyancing Act 1881 (see Note 65 above).

68 This relates to the doctrine of notice, which may govern priorities as between competing interests or claims to land. It has nothing to do with notices which may have to be served on people (as to which see s 4 and its Notes). The doctrine of notice has a limited role in Irish conveyancing because of the operation of the Registry of Deeds, which governs priorities between deeds and other documents relating to unregistered land, and because it is generally irrelevant to registered land (see Lyall, *Land Law in Ireland* (2nd edn, Round Hall, 2000), chs 4, 5 and 24; Wylie, *Irish Land Law* (3rd edn, Tottel Publishing, 1997), paras 3.069–3.090). This definition is linked with s 86 which deals with the doctrine of notice, replicating the provisions of s 3 of the Conveyancing Act 1882 (repealed by Schedule 2) (see the Notes to s 86). References to "notice" in this sense are to be found in ss 21(1), 57(4), 74(4)(*a*), 77(2), 86(1) and (3) and 95(2) (see the Notes to those sections).

69 This is similar to the definition in s 3(1) of the Registration of Title Act 1964. There are references to a "personal representative" in ss 19(1)(b)(iv), 63(a), 80(2) and (4) and Schedule 3 Part 2 paragraph 5 (see the Notes to those sections and Schedule 3).

70 This concept is referred to in ss 44(1)(*b*) and 50(2)(*d*) (see the Notes to those sections).

71 This replicates the definition in s 3(1) of the Registration of Title Act 1964. It has particular relevance to s 11(2) and confirms that the owner of a fee simple who has granted a tenancy (and receives the rent under it) is nevertheless owner of a fee simple "in possession" and, therefore, of a legal (as opposed to an equitable) freehold estate (see the Notes to s 11). See *Clarence House Ltd v National Westminster Bank plc* [2009] EWHC 77 (Ch).

72 Matters in respect of which things are required to be, or may be, prescribed are referred to in ss 63(*g*), 88, 100(1), 103(2), 121(3) and 122. Apart from such specific references, whenever the Act refers to registration in the Land Registry (see Note 57 above) or Registry of Deeds (see Note 78 below) appropriate rules and forms may have to be made under s 126 of the Registration of Title Act 1964 or s 48 of the Registration of Deeds and Title Act 2006 (these are referred to in the Notes to the relevant sections in the Act).

73 As was pointed out earlier (see Note 1 to s 1), although the Act is concerned primarily with land law and conveyancing transactions, some Parts apply also to other property (as is explained in the Notes to those Parts).

74 This is the body established by the 2006 Act to manage and control the Land Registry and Registry of Deeds (see Note 57 above). The Act generally refers only to those Registries rather than the Authority, though there are references to the Authority in the amendments to sections of the Registration of Title Act 1964 contained in Schedule 1 to the Act (see the Notes to that Schedule).

75 This definition is similar to the one in s 2 of the Conveyancing Act 1881 and is particularly relevant to the operation of the doctrine of notice and the issue of priorities between competing interests in land (see Note 68 above). For this reason a "purchaser" is not confined to someone who "purchases" the land outright but extends to anyone who acquires for valuable consideration (see Note 95 below) any interest in the land, such as a lease or mortgage. This use of "purchaser" is

particularly relevant to ss 21(1), Part 9, Chapter 2 and ss 74(1), 77(2), 86, 87, 88, 102(*d*)(iii), 104(2)(*a*) and (*c*), 105, 106(2) and 125 (see the Notes to those sections).

76 In relation to the primary significance of "purchaser" in relation to the matter referred to in Note 75 above, the definition of "land" is important, in particular the references in that definition to "any estate or interest" (see Note 42 above) and to "any part of land" (see Note 56 above).

77 References to registered land (apart from references to registration in the Land Registry: see Note 57 above) will be found in ss 21(3)(*b*)(iii), 61(3), 111(4)(b) and 129 (see the Notes to those sections).

78 Notwithstanding the establishment of the Property Registration Authority by the Registration of Deeds and Title Act 2006, the Registry of Deeds continues to function for the purposes of registration of deeds and other documents relating to land transactions (see Part 3 of the 2006 Act and Note 57 above). References to registration in the Registry of Deeds are to be found in ss 21(4), 30(3), 35(4), 39(1), 50(4), 68(3), 116(2) and 118 (see the Notes to those sections).

79 This is a much wider definition than that in the Conveyancing Act 1881, but, like it, is not confined to the traditional concept of rent payable under a tenancy or a rentcharge (see *Brown v Peto* [1900] 2 QB 653 at 664). This wider meaning is relevant to the definition of "possession" (see Note 71 above) and ss 31(4)(*b*)(iv) and 109(1)(*a*) (see the Notes to those sections).

80 Interest involves payments of a different order from rent and other sums issuing out or charged on land; it is usually a payment on top of some other sums issuing out of or charged on the land (like a mortgage).

81 Such charges, which do not create the relationship of landlord and tenant (see Lyall, *Land Law in Ireland* (2nd edn, Round Hall, 2000), pp 757–764; Wylie, *Irish Land Law* (3rd edn, Tottel Publishing, 1997), paras 6.131–6.145), are comparatively rare nowadays, hence the provisions at ss 41 and 42 (see the Notes to those). They are also referred to in s 11(4)(*h*) (see the Notes to that section).

82 Such a rent by tradition creates a rent "service" rather than a rent "charge" (see Lyall, *Land Law in Ireland* (2nd edn, Round Hall, 2000), p 757; Wylie, *Irish Land Law* (3rd edn, Tottel Publishing, 1997), paras 6.131–6.132).

83 See Note 80 above.

84 The Act recognises a distinction which is often confused or overlooked, that between a "right of entry" strictly so-called, which confers the limited powers specified in this definition, and a "right of re-entry", which confers much wider powers, in particular the power to forfeit the interest in land to which it is attached (such as a landlord's right to forfeit a lease for breach of covenant) (see Wylie, *Irish Land Law* (3rd edn, Tottel Publishing, 1997), paras 6.142 and 8.023; see also s 44 of the Conveyanicng Act 1881 and the Notes to s 42 below). Reference to such a right is to be found in ss 11(2)(*b*) and (4)(i) (see the Notes to that section).

85 See Note 84 above.

86 This was a key feature of traditional family settlements of land to which the Settled Land Acts 1882–90 applied. The provisions of those Acts are replaced by the provisions of Part 4 (see the Notes to it).

87 This is a standard provision to save having to refer to such further subgrants. Subtenancies are referred to in ss 57(1), (2) and (5) (see the Notes to that section).

88 This definition is linked with the provisions of s 11, in particular sub-s (3) (see Note 58 above and the Notes to that section).

89 Although a tenancy at will was once regarded as arising when a landowner informally allowed someone to occupy the land rent-free, it is more likely nowadays that such an arrangement would be regarded as creating, instead, a licence (see Wylie, *Landlord and Tenant Law* (2nd edn, Tottel Publishing, 1998), paras 4.21–4.33). If rent is paid, the arrangement is more likely to be regarded as a periodic tenancy. If no rent is payable, such an arrangement cannot create the relationship of landlord and tenant within the meaning of Deasy's Act (Landlord and Tenant Law Amendment Act, Ireland 1860): see s 1 of that Act). The Law Reform Commission recommended that such a "tenancy" should no longer be regarded as creating that relationship (see *Consultation Paper on the General Law of Landlord and Tenant* (LRC CP 28–2003), para 1.24; a similar definition to the above was contained in s 3 of the draft Landlord and Tenant Bill appended to the Commission's subsequent *Report on the Law of Landlord and Tenant* (LRC 85-2007).

90 The Law Reform Commission took the view that there was even more reason for not regarding a tenancy "at sufferance" as creating the relationship of landlord and tenant (LRC CP 28–2003, para 1.25). The only reason such a "tenant" is not regarded as an out-and-out trespasser is that the initial occupation was lawful under a tenancy which has since expired. (see Wylie, *Landlord and Tenant Law* (2nd edn, Tottel Publishing, 1998), paras 4.34–4.39). A "tenancy" is referred to in the definitions of "fee farm grant" (see Note 32 above) and "rentcharge" (see Note 81 above) and ss 11(3) and (4)(*d*), 36, 57, 59(2) and (3), and 63(*d*) (see Notes to those sections).

91 This definition is also connected with the provisions of s 11 (see Note 58 above and the Notes to that section).

92 This concept is related to the provisions of s 21, especially sub-s (2)(*a*) (see the Notes to that section).

93 This is the key concept in Part 4 the provisions of which replace the Settled Land Acts 1882–1890 (see the Notes to that Part).

94 References to unregistered land (apart from reference to registration in the Registry of Deeds: see Note 78 above) will be found in ss 21(3)(*b*)(iii) and 67(1) and (2) (see the Notes to those sections).

95 This definition is tied to the meaning of "purchaser" (see Note 75 above) and is particularly relevant to the overreaching provisions of s 21 and the operation of the doctrine of notice under s 86 (see the Notes to those sections). The concept of "valuable consideration" was also used in the definition of "purchaser" in s 2(viii) of the Conveyancing Act 1881, but not defined. The definition here clarifies what amounts to such consideration. Under the common law it probably did not include "nominal" or "good" consideration (such as "natural love and affection"): see *Re Browne's Estate* (1862) 13 Ir Ch R 283; *Re Rorke's Estate* (1865) 15 Ir Ch R 316; *Bryce v Fleming* [1930] IR 376. It probably did include marriage (see *Stackpole v Stackpole* (1843) 6 Ir Eq R 18; *Dennehy v Delaney* (1876) IR 10 Eq 377; *Greenwood v Lutman* [1915] 1 IR 266), but that is now ruled out. Apart from the concept being

imported in references to "purchaser" it is also referred to in ss 74(4)(*a*), 80(2), and 81(2) and Schedule 3 (see the Notes to those sections and that Schedule).

96 This is a standard provision. A similar definition was in s 2 of the Conveyancing Act 1881.

---

[34]

Service of notices.[1]
[CA 1881 s. 67][2]

4.—(1) A notice authorised or required to be given or served by or under this Act shall, subject to *subsection (2)*, be addressed to the person concerned by name and may be given to or served on the person in one of the following ways:[3]

(*a*) by delivering it to the person; or

(*b*) by leaving it at the address[4] at which the person[5] ordinarily resides or, in a case in which an address for service has been furnished, at that address; or

(*c*) by sending it by post in a prepaid letter to the address at which the person[6] ordinarily resides or, in a case in which an address for service has been furnished, to that address; or

(*d*) where the notice relates to a building with which the person is associated, and it appears that no person is in actual occupation of the building, by affixing it in a conspicuous position on the outside of the building or the property containing the building; or

(*e*) if the person concerned has agreed to service of notices by means of an electronic communication (within the meaning given to it by section 2 of the Electronic Commerce Act 2000) to that person (being an addressee within the meaning given to it by that section) and provided that there is a facility to confirm receipt of electronic mail and that such receipt has been confirmed, then by that means; or

(*f*) by sending it by means of a facsimile machine to a device or facility for the reception of facsimiles located at the address at which the person ordinarily resides or carries on business or, if an address for the service of notices has been furnished by the person, that address, provided that the sender's facsimile machine generates a message confirming successful transmission of the total number of pages of the notice; or

(*g*) by any other means that may be prescribed.[7]

(2)[8] Where the notice concerned is to be served on or given to a person who is the owner, landlord, tenant or occupier of a building and the name of the person cannot be ascertained by reasonable inquiry it may be addressed to the person at that building by using the words "the owner", "the landlord", "the tenant" or "the occupier" or other like description, as the case may require.

(3)[9] For the purposes of this section, a company shall be deemed to be ordinarily resident at its registered office, and every other body corporate and every unincorporated body shall be deemed to be ordinarily resident at its principal office or place of business.

(4)[10] Where a notice required or authorised to be served or given by or under this Act is served or given on behalf of a person, the notice shall be deemed to be served or given by that person.

(5) A person shall not, at any time during the period of 3 months after the notice is affixed under *subsection (1)(d)*, remove, damage or deface the notice without lawful authority.

(6) A person who knowingly contravenes *subsection (5)* is guilty of an offence.[11]

Definitions

See s 3 for definitions of "landlord"; "prescribed; "tenant".

Notes

1   Although this section relates primarily to service of notices under the Act's provisions, note that it applies also as a "default" provision where notices are to be served in accordance with a private document, but it does not make provision for how such a notice is to be served: see s 85 (and the Notes to it). This section does not apply, however, to service of notices relating to proceedings in court which are governed by Rules of Court.

2   This section replaces the provisions in s 67 of the Conveyancing Act 1881.

3   This extends the provisions in the 1881 Act to cover modern technology such as email or fax. Using one of these ways constitutes valid service even though the intended recipient does not actually receive the notice: *Re 88 Berkeley Road, London, NW9* [1971] 1 All ER 254.

4   It has been held to be sufficient service to hand the notice to a person who can reasonably be expected to pass it on to the intended recipient: see *Cronin v Rogers* (1884) Cab & E 348; *Cannon Brewery Co Ltd v Signal Press Ltd* (1928) 139 LT 384.

5   As regards corporate or unincorporated bodies see sub-s (3) and Note 9 below.

6   See again sub-s (3) and Note 9 below.

7   This enables regulations to be made adding new methods to take account of new technology.

8   This enables a notice to be served where the intended recipient's actual name is not known but his or her status is, such as being the occupier or tenant of the building in question.

9   This relates to the provisions in sub-s (1)(*b*) and (*c*).

10 This facilitates service by an agent such as a solicitor acting on behalf of a client.

11 Section 6 provides the penalties for offences under the Act.

---

[35]

Regulations.[1]   **5.**—(1) The Minister may make regulations—

  (*a*) for any purpose[2] in relation to which regulations are provided for by any of the provisions of this Act,

  (*b*) for prescribing any matter or thing referred to in this Act as prescribed or to be prescribed,[3]

  (*c*) generally for the purpose of giving effect to this Act.[4]

(2)[5] A regulation under *subsection (1)* shall be laid before each House of the Oireachtas as soon as may be after it is made and, if a resolution annulling the regulation is passed by either such House within the next 21 days on which that House has sat after the regulation is laid before it, the regulation is annulled accordingly, but without prejudice to the validity of anything previously done under it.

(3)[6](*a*) If in any respect any difficulty[7] arises during the period of 5 years[8] from the commencement of any provision[9] of this Act (including a provision that amends another Act), either in bringing into operation or in giving full effect to the provision or the Act as amended, the Minister may by regulations do anything which appears to be necessary or expedient for removing that difficulty.

  (*b*) In *paragraph (a)* a reference to another Act is a reference to an Act falling within either paragraph (a) or (b) of the definition of "Act" in section 2(1) of the Act of 2005.

(4) Regulations under *subsection (3)* may, in so far only as it may appear necessary for the removal of such difficulty, modify a provision referred to in that subsection provided such modification is in conformity with the purposes, principles and spirit of this Act.[10]

(5) Where the Minister proposes to make regulations under *subsection (3)*—

(*a*) he or she shall, before doing so, consult[11] with such other (if any) Minister of the Government as the Minister considers appropriate having regard to the functions of that other Minister of the Government in relation to the proposed regulations, and

(*b*) he or she shall cause a draft of the regulations to be laid before each House of the Oireachtas and the regulations shall not be made until a resolution approving of the draft has been passed by each such House.[12]

(6) A regulation under this section may contain such consequential, supplementary and ancillary provisions as the Minister considers necessary or expedient.

Notes

1 The original draft of the Law Reform Commission's Bill (appended to its Report LRC 74–2005) contained the usual provision for regulations, but the Bill introduced by the Government to the Seanad had this extended version inserted in it. The extensions are contained in sub-ss (3)–(5). For a precedent see s 36 of the Nursing Homes Support Scheme Act 2009.

2 Purposes for which the Act permits regulations to be made are specified in s 88 (see the Notes to it). Apart from that regulations may be made in relation to matters under the Act involving registration in the Land Registry or Registry of Deeds (see Notes 57, 72 and 78 to s 3 above).

3 Apart from rules and forms relating to registration matters (see Note 2 above) the Act refers to prescribed matters in ss 63(*g*), 88, 100(1), 103(2), 121(3) and 122 (see the Notes to those sections).

4 This enables the Minister to make regulations on matters which are not specifically referred to in the Act as matters in relation to which regulations may be made or matters to be prescribed.

5 This is the standard provision relating to such regulations.

6 This is the "non-standard" provision added to the Bill when it was introduced (see Note 1 above).

7 It remains to be seen how a "difficulty" will be interpreted. It is anticipated that this power to remove difficulties by regulation will be exercised only in respect of non-controversial, technical matters, otherwise the exercise of this power could be seen as trespassing on the legislative powers of the Oireachtas. This does, of course, put at issue the extent of the delegation of powers which the Oireachtas is to be taken as making in this regard. Note the parameters set by sub-s (4) (see Note 10 below). Note also that this power is limited in time (see Note 8 below).

8 This 5-year period is an important limitation on the special power conferred by sub-s (3).

9 The power might be used to remove redundant provisions (see Notes 5 and 9 to s 3 above), but it might be questioned whether redundant provisions cause a "difficulty" within sub-s (3).

10 Note that any modification must conform with the "purposes, principles and spirit" of the Act. This seems to rule out any regulation designed to change the substance of any provision unless, possibly, it could be shown that a particular provision is an obvious mistake and, therefore, inconsistent with the rest of the Act and its clear purposes, principles and spirit: see Note 7 to s 27.

11 The need for such consultation stems from the power in sub-s (3) to modify other Acts which are amended by this Act and which do not come within the jurisdiction of the Minister for Justice, Equality and Law Reform. Several of such Acts are listed in Schedule 1, such as the Housing (Gaeltacht) Act 1929, Minerals Development Act 1940, Harbours Act 1946, Charities Acts 1961 and 1973 and Companies Act 1963 (see the Notes to that Schedule).

12 Note that unlike regulations made under sub-s (1) (as to which see sub-s (2)), regulations under sub-s (3) laid before the Oireachtas have to be positively approved by resolutions passed by each House.

---

[36]

Offences.[1]

6.—(1) A person convicted of an offence under this Act is liable on summary conviction to a fine not exceeding €3,000 or imprisonment for a term not exceeding 6 months or both.

(2) Proceedings for an offence under this Act may be instituted at any time within one year after the date of the offence.

(3) Where a person is convicted of an offence under this Act the District Court shall, unless it is satisfied that there are special and substantial reasons for not so doing, order the person to pay the costs and expenses, measured by the Court, incurred in relation to the investigation, detection and prosecution of the offence.

Notes

1 This is a standard provision for offences. Offences are created by ss 4(6), 60 and 103(3) (see the Notes to those sections).

---

[37]

Expenses.[1]

7.—The expenses incurred by the Minister in the administration of this Act shall, to such extent as may be sanctioned by the Minister for Finance, be paid out of moneys provided by the Oireachtas.

Notes

1 This is also a standard provision.

[38]

8.—(1) Each provision specified in column (2) of *Schedule 1* **Amendments** opposite the mention in *column (1)* of that Schedule of an **and repeals.**[1] enactment is amended in the manner specified in *column (3)*.[2]

(2)[3] Subject to *subsection (1)*, and without prejudice to section 26(2)(*f*) of the Act of 2005[4]—

   (*a*) any reference in an enactment to—

      (i) the Settled Land Acts 1882 to 1890,

      (ii) an Act included in that collective citation, or

      (iii) any provision of such an Act,

      shall be construed as a reference to this Act or to the equivalent or substituted provision of this Act, as may be appropriate,

   (*b*) any reference in an enactment to—

      (i) the Conveyancing Acts 1881 to 1911, or

      (ii) an Act (other than an Act repealed by this Act) included in that collective citation,

      shall be construed as including a reference to this Act, and

   (*c*) any reference in an enactment to—

      (i) an Act that is included in the collective citation "the Conveyancing Acts 1881 to 1911" and that is repealed by this Act, or

      (ii) any particular provision of such an Act,

      shall be construed as a reference to this Act or to the equivalent or substituted provision of this Act.

(3) Each enactment specified in *column (2)* of *Schedule 2* is repealed to the extent specified in *column (3)* of that Schedule.[5]

Notes

1 This section contains the standard provisions for amendments and repeals. These are set out respectively in Schedules 1 and 2. As was pointed out in the Introduction (see pp 5–7) a primary objective of the Act is the repeal of numerous pre-1922 statutes and provisions within statutes (not wholly repealed because some provisions

unrelated to land law and conveyancing remain) (see further the Notes to those Schedules). However, this section also includes "default" provisions dealing with the Settled Land Acts 1882–1890 and Conveyancing Acts 1881–1911 (see Notes 3–4 below).

2   This is the standard provision governing amendments. Note, however, that Part 13 contains other amendments to the Registration of Title Act 1964 (see the Notes to that Part). Note also the amendments to other Acts contained in the body of the Act: see ss 99(2), 119 and 126 (see the Notes to those sections).

3   This subsection is an amended and amplified version of a provision included in the original draft of the Bill. It is a "default" provision to catch any existing statutes which refer to the Settled Land Acts 1882–1890 or Conveyancing Acts 1881–1911, or particular provisions within those Acts. Those Acts are replaced for the most part by the 2009 Act and so sub-s (3) provides, in essence, that such references should be construed, instead, as a reference to the 2009 Act. In the case of a reference to a particular provision in those replaced Acts, the reference is to be construed as a reference to its equivalent or substituted provision in the 2009 Act. This saved having to identify each such replaced statute or provision and including a specific amendment in Schedule 1: see, eg, Note 21 to s 80. Note, however, that that Schedule does contain some specific amendments to mostly post-1922 statutes. The reason for the differing treatment of the two sets of pre-1922 statutes in sub-s (2) is that the 2009 Act repeals the 1882–1890 Acts entirely, whereas parts of the 1881–1911 Acts remain in force (see the Notes to Schedule 2). The view was taken that s 26(2) of the Interpretation Act 2005 (see Note 4 below), which is expressed to apply to enactments "repealed and re-enacted, with or without modification", could be applied to the 1882–1890 Acts. On the other hand, more specific references should be made to the 1881–1911 Acts, so that references to those Acts or to unrepealed Acts included in such references should be read as including (but not necessarily confined to) references to the 2009 Act.

4   It is arguable that the provisions of sub-s (2) were not strictly necessary because of the general provision dealing with replacing statutes contained in s 26(2)(f) of the Interpretation Act 2005, but that general provision will operate in respect of other statutes replaced by the 2009 Act and this saving was included to make this clear.

5   This is the standard provision for repealing statutes.

[39]

PART 2[1]
OWNERSHIP OF LAND[2]

Notes

1   Part 2 of the Act contains fundamental provisions relating to key concepts of land law as it developed from the feudal system imposed on Ireland by the English Norman Kings many centuries ago. In particular, it deals with the concepts of tenure

and estates (see Lyall, *Land Law in Ireland* (2nd edn, Round Hall, 2000), ch 3; Wylie, *Irish Land Law* (3rd edn, Tottel Publishing, 1997), chs 2 and 4). Part 2 reflects the Law Reform Commission's underlying principles of updating the law and simplification of the law and its language and the conveyancing process (see Consultation Paper, LRC CP 24–2004, p 3 and Introduction above).

2   In dealing with the twin concepts which were embedded in the feudal system of land ownership, tenure (the notion that all land is held ultimately from the Crown) and estates (the notion that land so held is held for a limited period of time only, for an "estate"), Part 2 dramatically changes the theoretical basis of land ownership. It is important to note, however, that in implementing the Law Reform Commission's recommendations Part 2 does not adopt completely the concept of absolute ownership which is common in civil law jurisdictions. The Commission recommended adoption of what was done in many of the American states after the Revolution and Declaration of Independence in 1776. They too had had the feudal system of land ownership imposed on them as former British colonies and took the view that the concept of tenure in particular had no place in their new constitutional status. Several State legislatures enacted statutes declaring that feudal tenure no longer existed and all land would in future be "allodial", ie owned by their citizens as "absolute" owners and not held from the State (see Alexander, "Time and Property in the American Republic Legal Culture" (1991) 66 NYU L Rev 273; Vance, "The Quest for Tenure in the United States" (1923–24) 33 Yale LJ 248). However, the American States retained the other fundamental concept embedded in the feudal system, the concept that what is owned is not the land itself (the physical entity) but rather an "estate" (of limited duration – the duration varying according to the estate in question). The Law Reform Commission took the view that this was appropriate for Ireland also, given that much land remains unregistered land, the title to which derives from deeds and other documents referring to the estates granted to the grantees in question (see LRC CP 34–2004, ch 2). The Commission took the view that, on balance, it was more appropriate to retain the well-established and understood concept of estates, which remains the position also in the USA despite what was done by many States immediately after Independence. It was also pointed out that Article 10 of the Constitution refers to "estates and interests" in land. It is, however, important to note that the Commission did state that the issue of the abolition also of the concept of "estates" (and moving to a system in which what is owned is the land itself) should be reconsidered in the future, suggesting that the more appropriate time to do this would be when the title to most, if not all, land in the State becomes registered (LRC CP 34–2004, para 2.11). Given the drive by the Property Registration Authority set up under the Registration of Deeds and Title Act 2006 to achieve this, that time may come sooner than the Commission contemplated.

[40]

Ownership[1] and abolition of feudal tenure.[2]

9.—(1) From the commencement of this Part,[3] ownership of land[4] comprises the estates and interests[5] specified in this Part.[6]

(2) In so far as it survives,[7] feudal tenure is abolished.[8]

(3) *Subsection (2)* does not affect[9]—

    (*a*) the position of the State[10] under—

        (i) the State Property Act 1954,[11]

        (ii) section 73 of the Act of 1965,[12]

    (*b*) the concept of an estate under section 10,[13]

    (*c*) any fee farm grant made in derogation of the Statute Quia Emptores 1290,[14]

    (*d*) any surviving customary right[15] or franchise.[16]

[SQE 1290]

(4) A fee simple remains freely alienable.[17]

Definitions

See s 3 for definitions of: "fee farm grant"; "land".

Notes

1 Section 9 states how ownership of land operates from 1 December 2009. In essence, as indicated by the Notes above the notion of feudal tenure is abolished (see Note 2 below), but, while a landowner no longer holds the land from the State (as "successor" to the Crown), what is owned remains an "estate" in the land with the usual attributes of that concept (see s 10 and the Notes to it).

2 It is vitally important to note the qualification "feudal". What is being abolished is the notion of tenure imported to Ireland in the 12th and 13th centuries. That concept was confined to what came to be known as freehold (and when it applied to Ireland copyhold) land (see Lyall, *Land Law in Ireland* (2nd edn, Round Hall, 2000), ch 3; Wylie, *Irish Land Law* (3rd edn, Tottel Publishing, 1997), ch 2). The other form of "tenure" which eventually developed, leasehold tenure, was never part of the feudal system. That was a much later development which only took root in the 17th century, when it ceased to be regarded as a purely contractual arrangement binding the original parties only (see Wylie, *Landlord and Tenant Law* (2nd edn, Tottel Publishing, 1998), paras 1.02–1.04). Of course, things changed dramatically in Ireland with the enactment of Deasy's Act (the Landlord and Tenant Law Amendment Act, Ireland 1860), s 3 of which abolished "tenure" as the basis for landlord and tenant law. Instead, it provided that in future the relationship of landlord and tenant would be based on "contract", but with considerable "proprietary" characteristics (eg, a lease or tenancy binds successors in title and not just the original parties: see ss 12 and 13 of Deasy's Act and see Wylie, *Landlord and Tenant Law* (2nd edn, Tottel Publishing, 1998), chs 2 and 21–22). Deasy's Act was, of course, a statute passed by the Westminster Parliament specifically for Ireland and the irony is that the English courts in recent decades have increasingly

been treating the relationship of landlord and tenant as more akin to a contractual relationship (see Bright, *Landlord and Tenant Law in Context* (Hart Publishing, 2007), ch 2). The Westminster Parliament has never enacted an equivalent of s 3 for England and Wales. Part 2 does not affect the law of landlord and tenant in this regard (see also s 11(3) and the Notes to that section). All it does in relation to landlord and tenant law is deal with some outmoded types of leases and grants involving the relationship of landlord and tenant (see ss 12 and 14 and the Notes to them).

3   The change in the theoretical basis of ownership operated only from 1 December 2009 (see Note 2 to s 2 above).

4   Note that, unlike in the USA (see Note 2 to Part 2 above), there is no reference to land being "allodial". The view was taken that this term would not be familiar to Irish lawyers and might cause some confusion (see also Note 5 below). Note also that Part 2 is concerned with ownership of "land", which includes only the estates and interests in land which such ownership encompasses. It is not concerned with rights or interests which do not amount to interests in land or which have become divorced from the land. Thus the controversial subject of "titles" and "honours" is not referred to because, although these were once considered to be incorporeal hereditaments, they became divorced from ownership of land and so the better view is that they then ceased to be properly regarded as incorporeal hereditaments (see the Editor's (Charles Sweet) notes in *Challis's Law of Real Property* (3rd edn, 1911), pp 468–472 – "merely personal privileges" and "not rights of property"). This is a point often overlooked when the sale of titles such as "baron", "baronet" or "lord of the manor" takes place. The conferring of titles or honours is prohibited by the Constitution and no Irish citizen may accept one from a foreign power without prior approval of the Government (Article 40.2 of the Constitution, replacing Article 5 of the 1922 Constitution) (see Lyall, *Land Law in Ireland* (2nd edn, Round Hall, 2000), pp 767–768). Part 2 of the Act does not affect any pre-1922 personal titles or honours as it is concerned only with ownership of land.

5   This emphasises the point made above (see again Note 2 to Part 2). Part 2 retains the concept of "estates". It also recognises what has long been the position in our land law system, that what can be owned in respect of land may be also an "interest" which falls short of an estate. This is often an interest held by someone else, such as mortgage or charge over the land, or by some neighbouring landowner, such as an easement or *profit à prendre*. This distinction is reflected in s 11 (see the Notes to it).

6   See especially ss 10 and 11 (and the Notes to them).

7   The point here is that very few vestiges of the feudal concept of tenure survived to modern times, as a result of later legislation like the Tenures Abolition Act (Ireland) 1662 and modern reforms such as those instituted by the Succession Act 1965 (see Lyall, *Land Law in Ireland* (2nd edn, Round Hall, 2000), ch 3; Wylie, *Irish Land Law* (3rd edn, Tottel Publishing, 1997), ch 2). Note that "copyhold" tenure, which was a central feature of the feudal "manorial" system, operated in Ireland centuries ago but died out in the 19th century, probably as a result of the Land Purchase Acts (see LRC CP 34–2004, paras 1.08 and 2.08). What did survive, however, was the theoretical concept of feudal tenure which was difficult to reconcile with the position of the State and its citizens under the Constitution (see Lyall, *Land Law in Ireland*

(2nd edn, Round Hall, 2000), p 87). In particular, notions which were inherent in the feudal concept of tenure, such as the "tenant" (in this context meaning the holder of the land) paying homage to the superior owner (and ultimately to the Crown) and owing loyalty, seemed totally inconsistent with the position of Irish citizens as individuals having fundamental rights protected by the Constitution which they can assert even against the State. The removal of such notions drove the State legislatures in the USA in declaring land "allodial" (see the remarks of Woodward J in the Supreme Court of Pennsylvania decision in *Wallace v Harmstead* 44 Pa 492 (1863), quoted in LRC CP 34–2004, para 2.04; see also *Van Rensselaar v Hays* 19 NY 68 (1859); *Stuart v Easton* 170 US 383 (1893); *Waltz v Security Trust & Savings Bank* 197 Cal 263 (1925); and see Note 2 to Part 2 above).

8   As a result of this provision various old statutes relating to the feudal system of tenure could be repealed by Schedule 2. These include the Statute Quia Emptores 1290, Forfeiture Act (Ireland) 1639 and Tenures Abolition Act (Ireland) 1662. It was pointed out above (Note 7) that at one time copyhold tenure did exist in Ireland, which explains why 19th century statutes enacted at Westminster providing for commutation of manorial rights and enfranchisement of copyhold tenants applied initially. However, the consolidating Copyhold Act 1894 did not, presumably because the copyhold system had been destroyed by the Land Purchase Acts. Schedule 2 lists for repeal the earlier Acts which did apply to Ireland.

9   The purpose of sub-s (3) is to reiterate the limited, and largely conceptual or theoretical, change resulting from abolition of feudal tenure (see Notes 2 and 7 above). As the provisions of the subsection make clear, the practical effect of the abolition is probably zero (see Notes 11 and 12 below).

10 The point here is that the position of the State so far as ownership of land is concerned is nowadays governed by the Constitution and statute law, not by notions derived from feudal tenure and, in particular, the position of Crown under that system. The Supreme Court has emphasised that the State is not to be regarded in this context as the "successor" to the Crown and the so-called Crown prerogatives associated with concepts like tenure are inconsistent with the character of the State as enshrined in the 1922 and 1937 Constitutions (see *Byrne v Ireland* [1972] IR 24; *Webb v Ireland* [1988] IR 353; *Howard v Commissioners of Public Works* [1994] 1 IR 101; see also the discussion in Kelly, "Hidden Treasure and the Constitution" (1998) 10 DULJ 5; Morgan, "Constitutional Interpretation" (1998) 10 DULJ 24; Lenihan, "Royal Prerogatives and the Constitution" (1989) 24 Ir Jur (NS) 1; Costello, "The Expulsion of the Royal Prerogatives from Irish Law: Qualifying and Remedying the Loss of the Royal Prerogatives" (1997) 32 Ir Jur (NS) 145).

11 The management and control of land, and the exercise of all powers, functions, rights and "prerogatives", vested in the people by Articles 10 and 49 of the Constitution are carried out on behalf of the people by the State in accordance with the State Property Act 1954. In particular the vesting of land in the Crown under feudal tenurial concepts like escheat in certain circumstances (but not on death of an owner: see Note 12 below) is dealt with by Part III of the 1954 Act. Thus s 28 deals with land vesting on dissolution of a corporate body (see Courtney, *The Law of Private Companies* (2nd edn, Tottel Publishing, 2002), paras 12.145–12.148). This

illustrates how the notion of tenure had ceased to have practical effect in modern times.

12 The tenurial notion whereby land "escheated" to the Crown when a landowner died without leaving an effective will or intestate successor was abolished by s 11(3) of the Succession Act 1965. Instead, on death of a person intestate with no other person entitled to take the estate (in accordance with Part VI of the 1965 Act), the State takes the estate under s 73 as "ultimate intestate successors" (see Brady, *Succession Law in Ireland* (2nd edn, Tottel Publishing, 1995), paras 8.44–8.53).

13 This confirms the point made earlier that, although the concept of feudal tenure is abolished, the concept of an estate survives and continues to denote the nature and extent of land ownership (see Note 2 to Part 2, Note 5 above and the Notes to s 11 below).

14 Although s 12 prohibits the creation of fee farm grants from 1 December 2009, existing fee farm grants created prior to that date survive. Most of these will have created the modern relationship of landlord and tenant but some earlier ones will have created feudal tenure through exercise of powers conferred by old Crown grants to do so "*non obstante Quia Emptores*" (see Note 32 to s 3 and Lyall, *Land Law in Ireland* (2nd edn, Round Hall, 2000), p 87; Wylie, *Irish Land Law* (3rd edn, Tottel Publishing, 1997), paras 4.059–4.077). It is unlikely that many of these will have survived the operation of the Land Purchase Acts or various redemption statutes (see Wylie, *Irish Land Law* (3rd edn, Tottel Publishing, 1997), paras 4.074–4.076). A saving was, however, necessary to cover the possibility.

15 It is arguable that this provision was not necessary because customary rights as such did not derive from the feudal concept of tenure (this saving was not in the Law Reform Commission's original Bill, but it was added to the Bill as initiated in the Seanad). Customary rights are rights held by a section of the community (not the public at large as is the case with "public rights"), such as the inhabitants of a particular village or parishioners of a church. They are recognised at common law on production of evidence that they are ancient, certain, reasonable and continuous (see Lyall, *Land Law in Ireland* (2nd edn, Round Hall, 2000), pp 729 and 856; Wylie, *Irish Land Law* (3rd edn, Tottel Publishing, 1997), paras 6.043–6.045). In theory "ancient" means dating back to or before the beginning of "legal memory" (fixed as 1189 by the Statute of Westminster I 1275 c 39), but in practice the courts will often presume such long enjoyment if 20 to 40 years' recent enjoyment is shown with no counter evidence of a post-1189 grant. However, in Ireland many so-called customary rights, or rights claimed by local communities or a section within a local community, derive from grants of land made by the Crown in the 17th and 18th centuries as part of the confiscation and resettlement programmes (see Wylie, *Irish Land Law* (3rd edn, Tottel Publishing, 1997), paras 1.27–1.34 and 6.045). Those grants often involved the creation of feudal tenure (see Note 14 above). "Customary rights" are listed in s 72(1)(g) of the Registration of Title Act 1964 as amongst the burdens affecting registered land without registration. For these reasons this saving was included to make it clear that the abolition of such tenure does not affect such rights.

16 This saving was also included in the Bill as initiated in the Seanad for the same reason. Franchises (such as the right to hold a fair or market or to run a ferry) were

exclusive rights or privileges granted by the Crown (see Lyall, *Land Law in Ireland* (2nd edn, Round Hall, 2000), pp 764–765; Wylie, *Irish Land Law* (3rd edn, Tottel Publishing, 1997), para 6.020). A recent case in the High Court involved the right to hold a market in Listowel granted by letters patent by James I in 1612 and James II in 1688 (see *Listowel Livestock Mart Ltd v William Bird & Sons Ltd* [2007] IEHC 360). Franchises are also listed as burdens within s 72(1)(g) of the Registration of Title Act 1964 (see Note 15 above).

17 This saving preserves a fundamental principle of the feudal system of tenure, namely, the rule against inalienability applicable to freehold land which was enshrined in the Statute Quia Emptores 1290. The original Bill as initiated referred to that rule, but at the Report Stage in the Seanad Senator Tuffy and others tabled an amendment designed to restate the rule in more positive terms, especially in view of the fact that the 1290 Statute is repealed by the Act (see Schedule 2). The Minister for Justice, Equality and Law Reform proposed what is now sub-s (4) at the Dáil Report Stage. It is important to reiterate that this rule is confined to freehold land (for its application in recent times see *Re Dunne's Estate* [1998] IR 155). It does not apply to leasehold land (see Lyall, *Land Law in Ireland* (2nd edn, Round Hall, 2000), p 341; Wylie, *Irish Land Law* (3rd edn, Tottel Publishing, 1997), para 5.034). It should also be noted that the rule against inalienability applies also to personal property, where it is often referred to as the rule against perpetual trusts or against trusts of undue duration (see Note 10 to s 16).

[41]

Estates and
interests in
land.[1]

10.—(1) The concept of an estate[2] in land is retained[3] and, subject to this Act,[4] continues with the interests specified in this Part[5] to denote the nature and extent of land ownership.[6]

(2) Such an estate retains its pre-existing characteristics,[7] but without any tenurial incidents.[8]

(3) All references in any enactment[9] or any instrument[10] (whether made or executed before or after the commencement of this Part[11]) to tenure or estates or interests in land, or to the holder of any such estate or interest, shall be read accordingly.[12]

Definitions

See s 3 for defintions of: "instruments"; "land".

Notes

1 This section is linked with both s 9 and s 11 (see the Notes to those sections). Section 10 establishes that Part 2 abolishes the concept of feudal tenure but not the other concept embedded in the feudal system, the concept of "estates" (see Note 2 to Part 2 and Note 5 to s 9).

2   Note the distinction between an "estate" and other "interests" enshrined in s 11 (see the Notes to that section).

3   The existing concept is retained (see Note 1 above) for the moment (see Note 2 to Part 2 above).

4   This qualification is made because of the provisions in ss 12–14 which alter the law relating to certain estates. Note also as a result of s 11(2), a life estate ceases to be a legal estate and becomes an equitable interest subject to the Trusts of Land provisions of Part 4 (see the Notes to that Part and note s 18(4) and see the Notes to that section).

5   This refers, in particular, to the interests less than an "estate" listed in s 11(4). Those are legal interests, but the Act recognises that they may also exist as equitable interests only (see s 11(6) and the Notes to that section).

6   This confirms that the principle that the estates and interests hitherto recognised as being what a landowner "owns" in relation to land (rather than the physical entity ("the land") itself) continues under the Act (see again Note 2 to Part 2 above). What rights are enjoyed in respect of the land and for how long continues to be determined by whatever estate or interest is held by the person in question.

7   This confirms the point made in Notes 1, 3 and 6 above. Note that the word "such" imports the qualification "subject to this Act" in sub-s (1) (see Note 4 above).

8   This qualification stems from the abolition of feudal tenure by s 9(2) (see Note 2 to that section).

9   This includes both statutes and statutory instruments (and any portion of them): see ss 2 and 4 of the Interpretation Act 2005.

10 Note that the provisions of sub-s (3) apply to both the enactments and private documents.

11 Note that this provision has retrospective effect.

12 Subsection (3) reiterates the provisions of sub-ss (1) and (2) that the law relating to estates and interests in land continues (except where changed by the Act: see Note 4 above). Any reference to tenure, on the other hand, must be read on the basis that it has ceased to have any significance as a result of ss 9 and 10(2).

---

[42]

11.—(1) The only legal estates in land[2] which may be created[3] or disposed[4] of are the freehold and leasehold estates specified by this section.[5]

Restrictions on legal estates and interests.[1]

(2) For the purposes of subsection (1),[6] a "freehold estate" means a fee simple[7] in possession[8] and includes—

(*a*)   a determinable fee,[9]

(*b*)   a fee simple subject to a right of entry[10] or of re-entry,[11]

(*c*)   a fee simple subject only to[12]—

   (i)   a power of revocation,[13]

(ii) an annuity or other payment of capital or income for the advancement, maintenance or other benefit of any person,[14] or

(iii) a right of residence which is not an exclusive right over the whole land.[15]

(3) For the purposes of *subsection (1)*, a "leasehold estate"[16] means, subject to *sections 12* and *14*,[17] the estate which arises when a tenancy[18] is created for any period of time[19] or any recurring period[20] and irrespective of whether or not the estate[21]—

(*a*) takes effect in immediate possession or in future,[22] or

(*b*) is subject to another legal estate or interest,[23] or

(*c*) is for a term which is uncertain[24] or liable to termination by notice,[25] re-entry[26] or operation of law[27] or by virtue of a provision for cessor on redemption[28] or for any other reason.[29]

(4) The only legal interests in land[30] which may be created[31] or disposed of[32] are—

(*a*) an easement,[33]

(*b*) a freehold covenant,[34]

(*c*) an incumbrance,[35]

(*d*) a rent payable under a tenancy,[36]

(*e*) a possibility of reverter,[37]

(*f*) a *profit à prendre*,[38] including a mining right,[39]

(*g*) a public[40] or customary[41] right,

(*h*) a rentcharge,[42]

(*i*) a right of entry or of re-entry attached to a legal estate,[43]

(*j*) a wayleave or other right to lay cables, pipes, wires or other conduits,[44]

(*k*) any other legal interest created by any statutory provision.[45]

(5) A legal estate or legal interest under this section has, subject to this Act,[46] the same attributes[47] as the corresponding legal estates and interests existing at the commencement of this Part and may exist concurrently with, or subject to, any other legal estate or interest in the same land.[48]

(6) Subject to this Act,[49] estates and interests other than those referred to in *subsections (1)* to *(4)* take effect as equitable interests only,[50] but this does not prevent the creation of the

estates and interests referred to in those subsections as equitable interests.[51]

(7) Nothing in this Act affects judicial recognition of equitable interests.[52]

(8) Subject to this Act,[53] a power of attorney, power of appointment or other power to dispose of a legal estate or interest in land operates with the same force and effect as such powers had before the commencement of this Part.[54]

(9) All estates and interests in land, whether legal or equitable, may be disposed of.[55]

Definitions

See s 3 for definitions of: "disposed"; "freehold covenant"; "incumbrance"; "land"; "possession"; "rent"; "rentcharge"; "right of entry"; "right of re-entry"; "tenancy".

Notes

1   This section supplements ss 9 and 10 by setting out in more detail the estates and interests in land which since 1 December 2009 comprise ownership of land (shorn of its feudal tenurial incidents: see the Notes to ss 9 and 10). It also draws a distinction between "legal" estates and interests, on the one hand, and "equitable" interests. This is linked with the doctrine of notice (see s 86 and the Notes to it) and the concept of overreaching (see s 21 and the Notes to it). These concepts are fundamental to the issue of priorities as between competing claims to the same land. Under traditional law such priorities depend to a large extent on whether the claim is based on a legal estate or interest or an equitable one only (in Ireland this has to be qualified because of the operation of the Registry of Deeds and the Land Registry systems: see Lyall, *Land Law in Ireland* (2nd edn, Round Hall, 2000), chs 5 and 24; Wylie, *Irish Land Law* (3rd edn, Tottel Publishing, 1997), chs 3, 21 and 22). So far as unregistered land is concerned, generally legal estates and interests "bind the world", whereas equitable interests are more vulnerable as they may not be enforceable against a *bona fide* purchaser of a legal estate or interest without notice or, in the case of registered land, against a transferee for valuable consideration if no prior steps were taken to protect priority (eg by lodging a caution or entering an inhibition: see Fitzgerald, *Land Registry Practice* (2nd edn, Round Hall Press, 1995), pp 161–169).

2   Subsection (1) designates the only "legal" estates in land which can operate since 1 December 2009. This is not as significant as it might appear. As sub-ss (2) and (3) make clear what this means, in practice, is that so far as freehold land is concerned the legal title will be vested in the owner of the fee simple in possession. Where the fee simple is the subject of a settlement or trust whereby some prior estate (such as a life estate) exists (rendering the fee simple an estate in reversion or remainder), a trust of land will exist under Part 4. Under the provisions of that Part the legal title (fee simple in possession) will be vested in trustees (see the Notes to that Part). This extends the provisions of the Settled Land Acts 1882–1890, under which a tenant for

life had power to deal with the fee simple even though holding a life estate only. Thus even under those Acts the life estate had little significance for the purposes of dealing with the land and the Act carries this principle through to its logical conclusion. The other freehold estate established under the feudal system, the fee tail, is abolished essentially by s 13 (see the Notes to that section). So far as leasehold estates are concerned, sub-s (3) confirms that these continue to operate largely untouched by the Act. The two qualifications to this general principle are the removal of tenancies at will and at sufferance from the concept of a tenancy (and therefore a leasehold estate: see Notes 89 and 90 to s 3) and the modifications to certain grants and leases involving tenancies made by ss 12 and 14 (see the Notes to those sections).

3   Subsection (1) is concerned both with the initial creation of a legal estate and its subsequent disposal.

4   Note that "dispose" includes both an *inter vivos* conveyance or transfer and leaving by will (see the definition in s 3 and Note 28 to that section).

5   That is sub-ss (2) and (3) (see the Notes to those subsections).

6   That is in order for the freehold estate to be a legal as opposed to an equitable one (see Note 2 above). Note the exception for continuing fee farm grants in s 12(5) (see Note 15 to that section).

7   As explained above (see Notes 1 and 2), only the fee simple of the three freehold estates recognised by the common law continues as a legal estate. The other two, a fee tail and life estate, necessarily involved a fee simple reversion or remainder and so created a settlement within the Settled Land Acts 1882–1890 (see Note 2 above). Apart from that, the fee tail is abolished by s 13 and a life estate continues as an equitable interest only (see sub-s (6) and s 18(4) and the Notes to these provisions).

8   Again a fee simple in reversion or remainder would have created a settlement within the Settled Land Acts 1882–1890 and since 1 December 2009 a trust of land within Part 4 (see s 18 and the Notes to that section). Under that Part the fee simple in possession is vested in trustees (as to which see s 19 and the Notes to that section). Note that where the owner of a fee simple has granted a tenancy, he or she (the landlord) still has a fee simple "in possession" and, therefore, retains legal title to the land. This is because s 3 defines "possession" as including "receipt or, the right to receive, rent and profits." There is also no question of a tenancy creating a trust of land within Part 4.

9   This used to be a fairly common category of "modified" fee simple, created when land was conveyed to someone "until" some event occurred or "as long as" some situation lasted or for some similar uncertain period (see Lyall, *Land Law in Ireland* (2nd edn, Round Hall, 2000), pp 177–182; Wylie, *Irish Land Law* (3rd edn, Tottel Publishing, 1997), paras 4.046–4.047). Such a modified fee is subject to a "possibility of reverter" retained by the grantor. It has been a matter of controversy whether this was sufficient to create a "succession of interests" so as to bring such a modified fee within the Settled Land Acts 1882–1890 (see Wylie, *Irish Land Law* (3rd edn, Tottel Publishing, 1997), paras 8.022–8.023). The practical consequence of that would have been that the holder of the fee simple could only deal with the land by invoking the powers of a "tenant for life" under those Acts. That involved the complications of ensuring that capital money (eg the proceeds of a sale) were paid

not to the fee simple vendor, but to "trustees of the settlement". Given that in such cases the fee simple is subject only to a mere "possibility" of reverter (which may never occur), the Law Reform Commission took the view that it was unnecessary to impose on the owner of a determinable fee such complications (including the provisions relating to trusts of land in Part 4 which replace the 1882–1890 Acts) (see LRC CP 34–2004, para 2.15). The Act implements this recommendation. The result is that the holder of a determinable fee is free to dispose of it by himself or herself, as legal title is held. How marketable such a fee simple is depends on the view the market would take of the potential impact of the possibility of reverter and the risk of it falling in. Note that the corollary of this provision is that a possibility of reverter is listed in sub-s (4)(*a*) as a legal interest in land owned separately from the determinable fee (see the Notes to that section).

10 This is the other main category of modified fee, where a fee simple is subject to a condition subsequent giving the grantor a right of entry or re-entry (see Lyall, *Land Law in Ireland* (2nd edn, Round Hall, 2000), pp 178–179; Wylie, *Irish Land Law* (3rd edn, Tottel Publishing, 1997), paras 4.048–4.050). Paragraph (*b*) recognises that the condition may take the form of either a right of entry or right of re-entry. These are often confused but there is a technical distinction between the two (see Note 84 to s 3). Most modified fees subject to a condition are subject to the latter, ie a provision whereby the owner of the fee simple is liable to forfeit it as a result of exercise of the right of re-entry. That at least is the position where the grantor has the right on the occurrence of the event triggering the right. Where the right is exercisable by a third party, it may be more appropriate to call it a right of entry by that person rather than a right of re-entry, but it again in that situation involves forfeiture of the interest of the holder of the modified fee. Paragraph (*b*) is designed to catch all these situations. Again the Law Reform Commission took the view that such modified fees should involve holding the legal title and not attract settlements legislation (or its replacement as provided for by Part 4) (see Note 9 above).

11 This is the other form of condition that may be attached to a modified fee (see Note 10 above). Note that both rights of entry and rights of re-entry are listed amongst legal interests in sub-s (4) (see Notes to that subsection).

12 This lists further categories where again the Law Reform Commission took the view that the owner of the fee simple should retain legal title and be free to deal with the land without having to comply with settlements legislation (or its replacement) (see LRC CP 34–2004, para 4.17). The word "only" indicates that in each of the cases listed the fee simple must be subject only to the provision in question. If there are other provisions involving a succession to the land, it will be subject to a trust of land within Part 4 and the power of dealing with it will reside in trustees and not the owner of the fee simple.

13 It is not uncommon for a fee simple to be subject to such a power exercisable by the grantor, usually on the occurrence of some event. Prior to the Act such a power was legal only if created by way of a limitation to uses executed by the Statute of Uses (Ireland) 1634 (see Wylie, *Irish Land Law* (3rd edn, Tottel Publishing, 1997), para 3.020). It may be registered as a burden on registered land (see Fitzgerald, *Land Registry Practice* (2nd edn, Round Hall Press, 1995), para 12.15). The 1634 Statute

is repealed by the Act (see Schedule 2) and the need for a limitation to uses is removed by s 62(2) and (3) (see the Notes to that section).

14 Again the Law Reform Commission took the view that the owner of a fee simple subject only to such minor charges (without any succession of interests such as a settlement or trust would usually involve) should retain legal title and the freedom to deal with it (see LRC CP 34–2004, para 4.17).

15 The Law Reform Commission recommended (see Note 14 above) adoption of the distinction which has emerged in case law and was recognised by the Registration of Title Act 1964 (s 81: see Fitzgerald, *Land Registry Practice* (2nd edn, Round Hall Press, 1995), pp 37, 208 and 247). If a right of residence is exclusive to a person and relates to the whole of the land in question, the owner has, in effect, a life interest and the owner of the fee simple is not in possession (see *National Bank v Keegan* [1931] IR 344). That creates a settlement situation and would create a trust of land within Part 4 of the Act (see the Notes to that Part). Any other type of right of residence, such as one where the right is shared or relates to part only of the land, is more likely to be regarded as a mere personal licence or lien or charge on the land (see *Kelaghan v Daly* [1913] 2 IR 328; *Re Shanahan* [1919] 1 IR 131; *Johnston v Horace* [1993] ILRM 594; see Lyall, *Land Law in Ireland* (2nd edn, Round Hall, 2000), pp 525–531; Wylie, *Irish Land Law* (3rd edn, Tottel Publishing, 1997), paras 20.13–20.24). In such cases the owner of the fee simple subject to the right retains legal title and can deal with it regardless of Part 4 of the Act.

16 To be distinguished from a freehold estate, which is dealt with by sub-s (2) (see Notes 1 and 2 above).

17 These sections introduce substantial changes to grants and leases involving leasehold estates (see the Notes to those sections).

18 See the definition of "tenancy" in s 3 (and Notes 88–90 to that section). Note that this provision makes it clear that under Irish law the grant of a tenancy does create an estate in the land. The Law Reform Commission was not convinced of the correctness of recent developments in England where it has been held that the relationship of landlord and tenant can be created without conferring an estate (so that a person holding a mere licence to occupy the land can nevertheless grant a tenancy to someone else: see *Bruton v London and Quadrant Housing Trust* [2001] 1 AC 406: see *Consultation Paper on General Law of Landlord and Tenant* (LRC CP 28-2003), para 1.18).

19 This covers both a fixed period of definite duration and a period of uncertain duration. It has long been the law in Ireland, at least since the enactment of s 3 of Deasy's Act, that a tenancy can be granted for a period of uncertain duration (see Wylie, *Landlord and Tenant Law* (2nd edn, Tottel Publishing, 1998), paras 2.23 and 5.27). The Irish courts do not seem to have had the same concerns on this issue which the English courts have had (see *Lace v Chantler* [1944] KB 368; *Prudential Assurance Co Ltd v London Residuary Body* [1992] 2 AC 386). See also paragraph (c) and Note 24 below.

20 This covers periodic tenancies, such as a tenancy from week to week or month to month. The word "any" confirms the position at common law that the recurring period can be any period (eg quarterly or three-monthly periods: see Wylie, *Landlord and Tenant Law* (2nd edn, Tottel Publishing, 1998), para 4.18).

21 The following paragraphs confirm that a tenancy will still create a legal estate even though, as is common, it is held subject to various qualifications and restrictions. This confirms the position at common law, that leasehold land was not subject to special legislation like the Settled Land Acts 1882–1890. Leasehold law was a much later development in the land law system and was not part of the feudal system (see Note 2 to s 9 above).

22 This confirms that it is possible to grant a tenancy on 1 January and provide that possession is not to be taken by the tenant until 1 July. It has long been the accepted view that since Deasy's Act the doctrine of *interesse termini* (that the tenant acquires no estate until possession is taken) does not apply to Ireland (see Wylie, *Landlord and Tenant Law* (2nd edn, Tottel Publishing, 1998), paras 2.24 and 4.08; Lyall, *Land Law in Ireland* (2nd edn, Round Hall, 2000), p 566).

23 By its very nature a leasehold estate is subject to another estate or interest, the landlord's reversionary interest at the very least.

24 This confirms that in Ireland a tenancy can be granted for a period of uncertain duration (see Note 19 above).

25 Such liability to termination by notice is inherent in a periodic tenancy (see Wylie, *Landlord and Tenant Law* (2nd edn, Tottel Publishing, 1998), paras 4.16, 4.19 and 23.01), but a tenancy for a fixed term may contain a "break" clause entitling the landlord or tenant to terminate it early by giving notice (see Wylie, *Landlord and Tenant Law* (2nd edn, Tottel Publishing, 1998), paras 20.14–20.16).

26 Most leases contain a "re-entry" clause entitling the landlord to forfeit the lease for breach of covenant by the tenant (see Wylie, *Landlord and Tenant Law* (2nd edn, Tottel Publishing, 1998), ch 24).

27 This covers situations where a tenancy is deemed to disappear automatically, eg as a result of a merger or surrender (see Wylie, *Landlord and Tenant Law* (2nd edn, Tottel Publishing, 1998), ch 25) or as a consequence of a process like bankruptcy (Wylie, *Landlord and Tenant Law* (2nd edn, Tottel Publishing, 1998), paras 25.03–25.07 and 25.15).

28 Such a provision used to be inserted in a mortgage by demise or sub-demise, so as to provide for termination on redemption of the mortgage. It is no longer strictly necessary because of intervention by statute, such as the Satisfied Terms Act 1845 and the provisions for automatic discharge in s 18 of the Housing Act 1988 (see Wylie, *Irish Land Law* (3rd edn, Tottel Publishing, 1997), para 13.125).

29 This recognises that, as with a freehold estate (see Note 9 above), there is no reason why a lease should not contain a provision that the term granted ceases on the occurrence of a specified event.

30 As explained earlier (see Note 1 above) the purpose of sub-s (4) is to identify the interests in land which fall short of being an estate coming within sub-ss (2) and (3) but can nevertheless be legal interests as opposed to equitable interests in land. They can, of course, be equitable interests as well (which they are depending on how they are created or arise), as sub-s (6) confirms (see Note 50 below), but if that is the case they suffer from the risk of losing priority which all equitable, as opposed to legal, interests run.

31 This refers to such interests' initial creation.

32 This refers to their subsequent disposal – note that this covers both *inter vivos* conveyances and leaving by will: see the definitions of "conveyance" and "disposition" in s 3 (and Notes 18–20 and 28 to that section).

33 This is a well-established category of incorporeal hereditament (see Bland, *The Law of Easements and Profits à Prendre* (Round Hall, 1997). See further Part 8, Chapter 1 and the Notes to that chapter).

34 Hitherto freehold covenants have been enforceable against successors in title to the covenant in equity only and even then subject to substantial limitations under the rule in *Tulk v Moxhay* (1848) 2 Ph 774 (see Lyall, *Land Law in Ireland* (2nd edn, Round Hall, 2000), ch 21; Wylie, *Irish Land Law* (3rd edn, Tottel Publishing, 1997), ch 19). That is all changed by Part 8, Chapter 4 (see the Notes to that Chapter). Under these provisions freehold covenants become fully enforceable and so, like easements and profits, join the category of legal interests.

35 This includes mortgages and charges (see the definition in s 3 and Note 36). As with all these categories listed in sub-s (4) some examples of an incumbrance may be equitable only (such as a portion or other charges existing under a trust) – it depends on how the interest is created (see Note 30 above).

36 This recognises that rent payable under a tenancy may be regarded as a separate interest in the land and may be disposed of separately from the landlord's reversion in favour of a third party (see *Inland Revenue Commissioners v John Lewis Properties plc* [2002] 1 WLR 35, aff'd [2003] Ch 513; *Clarence House Ltd v National Westminster Bank plc* [2009] EWHC 77 (Ch)). In the case of a fee farm grant creating the relationship of landlord and tenant, there is, of course, no reversion held by the grantor (the grantee has the fee simple) and the only interest owned by the grantor is the right to the rent (and to enforce any covenants in the grant) (see Wylie, *Irish Land Law* (3rd edn, Tottel Publishing, 1997), paras 4.083–4.086 and 4.097–4.101). (See also s 12(6) and Note 17 to that section.)

37 This is the interest held by the grantor of a determinable fee (see Note 9 above). There has been some controversy in the past as to whether a "bare possibility" should be treated as an interest in land and, therefore, disposable by will (see *Bath and Wells Diocesan Board of Finance v Jenkinson* [2003] Ch 89). Para (*e*) and sub-s (9) resolve any remaining doubts.

38 A *profit à prendre* is another well-established incorporeal hereditament (see Bland, *The Law of Easements and Profits à Prendre* (Round Hall, 1997). See further Part 8, Chapter 1 (and the Notes to that Chapter).

39 A mining right is really a category of profit but this was added to conform with the equivalent reference in s 69(1)(j) of the Registration of Title Act 1964 (burdens which may be registered as affecting registered land).

40 Public rights include rights of way dedicated to the public (see Lyall, *Land Law in Ireland* (2nd edn, Round Hall, 2000), pp 726–729 and 856; Wylie, *Irish Land Law* (3rd edn, Tottel Publishing, 1997), paras 6.041–6.042).

41 Local customary rights are usually owned by a section of the community, such as the inhabitants of a village or parishioners of a church (see Lyall, *Land Law in Ireland* (2nd edn, Round Hall, 2000), p 729; Wylie, *Irish Land Law* (3rd edn, Tottel Publishing, 1997), paras 6.043–6.045).

42 A rentcharge is to be distinguished from a rent "service" such as is created under a tenancy (the latter is covered by paragraph (*d*): see Note 36 above). Rentcharges used to be fairly common (eg, some fee farm grants used to create such charges instead of the relationship of landlord and tenant: see Wylie, *Irish Land Law* (3rd edn, Tottel Publishing, 1997), paras 4.104–4.110). Rentcharges were also sometimes created under settlements of land (see Lyall, *Land Law in Ireland* (2nd edn, Round Hall, 2000), pp 382 and 397; Wylie, *Irish Land Law* (3rd edn, Tottel Publishing, 1997), paras 6.015 and 6.134). Substantial changes to the law were introduced by Part 8, Chapter 2 (see the Notes to that Chapter).

43 These are rights attached to the other main category of a "modified" fee simple, a fee simple subject to a condition (see Notes 10 and 11 above),

44 Such rights are commonly held by utility bodies or companies which are given statutory powers to lay cables etc to facilitate the provision of the services they supply. They are sometimes referred to as "statutory" easements (see Bland, *The Law of Easements and Profits à Prendre* (Round Hall, 1997), paras 5.26 and 10.07–10.12).

45 This is a "catch-all" saving for any new legal interests which may be created by statute (as the Act did in respect of freehold covenants: see Note 34 above).

46 This qualification is made because of provisions such as those in ss 12–14 and 42 (see the Notes to those sections).

47 This confirms the principle that, although the Act abolishes feudal tenure, it preserves the concept of estates (see the Notes to ss 9 and 10 above).

48 This recognises another fundamental principle of land law, that a particular parcel of land may be subject to a variety of different estates and interests owned by different persons at the same time.

49 Again this qualification is necessary because of provisions in the Act which prohibit the creation of certain estates and interests, such as ss 12–14 and 41 (see the Notes to these sections).

50 For example a life interest, which since 1 December 2009, can operate only under a trust of land governed by Part 4 (see s 18(4) and the Notes to that Part).

51 This reiterates a point made earlier, that whether or not a particular interest is legal or equitable depends on how it is created or arises. Thus an interest which is capable of being a legal interest (because it comes within the list in sub-s (4)) may be an equitable interest only because the formalities for its creation have not been followed (eg use of a deed as required by s 62: see the Notes to that section).

52 This is express acknowledgement that the courts increasingly recognise the existence of an equitable interest in land by invoking doctrines such as those relating to resulting and constructive trusts and proprietary estoppel (see Delany, *Equity and the Law of Trusts in Ireland* (4th edn, Round Hall, 2007), chs 7, 8 and 17). The Act does not interfere with such jurisdiction.

53 This qualification is necessary because of the changes, albeit minor, made by Part 6 (see the Notes to that Part). Also in so far as powers previously required a conveyance to uses, that is no longer necessary by virtue of s 62(2) (see the Notes to that section). Part 4 of the Act also clearly affects powers of dealing with settled land

which a tenant for life had under the Settled Land Acts 1882–1890 (see the Notes to that Part).

54 This provision was added during the Bill's passage through the Seanad to clarify that such powers were not turned into equitable powers by not being listed in sub-s (4). Subsection (4) is concerned with legal interests which persons own in their own right. Powers are generally held by persons to enable them to dispose of someone else's interest. Subsection (8) preserves the effectiveness of such powers (subject to changes referred to in Note 53).

55 This comprehensive provision replaces the various old provisions scattered in different statutes, such as s 6 of the Real Property Act 1845. It also clarifies the provisions relating to interests like a possibility of reversion (se Note 37 above). It supplements provisions in other statutes, such as s 10 of the Conveyancing Act 1881 (as amended by s 2 of the Conveyancing Act 1911) (these provisions in the 1881 and 1911 Acts are not listed in Schedule 2 as they deal primarily with landlord and tenant law) and s 76 of the Succession Act 1965 (which replaced s 3 of the Wills Act 1837, as to which see *Bath and Wells Diocesan Board of Finance v Jenkinson* [2003] Ch 89).

---

[43]

Prohibition of fee farm grants.[1]

12.—(1) The creation of a fee farm grant at law or in equity is prohibited.[2]

(2) Any instrument[3] executed after the commencement of this Part[4] purporting to—

    (*a*)   create a fee farm grant, or

    (*b*)   grant a lease for life or lives renewable for ever or for any period which is perpetually renewable,[5]

vests[6] in the purported grantee or lessee a legal fee simple or, as the case may be, an equitable fee simple[7] and any contract for such a grant entered into after such commencement operates as a contract for such a vesting.[8]

(3) A fee simple which vests under *subsection (2)* is freed and discharged from any covenant or other provision relating to rent,[9] but all other covenants or provisions continue in force so far as consistent with the nature of a fee simple.[10]

(4) *Subsection (2)* does not apply to any contract[11] or instrument giving effect to a contract[12] entered into before the commencement of this Part.

(5)[13] Notwithstanding *section 11(2)*,[14] any fee simple held under a fee farm grant existing at law at the commencement of this Part continues as a legal estate and may be disposed of.[15]

(6) Notwithstanding *section 11(4)*,[16] any fee farm rent existing at law at the commencement of this Part continues as a legal interest and may be disposed of.[17]

Definitions

See s 3 for definitions of: "covenant"; "fee farm grant"; "instrument"; "lease"; "legal interest"; "lessee"; "rent".

Notes

1 The Law Reform Commission took the view that the primary objective of simplification of the law suggested that "hybrid" grants combining freehold and leasehold attributes should be removed from Irish law (see LRC CP 34–2004, paras 2.17–2.22). Fee farm grants were rarely made in recent times and where made it was usually to take advantage of leasehold law governing enforceability of covenants. The issue of enforceability of freehold covenants is resolved by Part 8, Chapter 4 (see the Notes to that Chapter). Section 12 deals with the position post-1 December 2009. It does not affect fee farm grants already in existence at that date – they continue in force (see sub-ss (5) and (6) and the Notes to them).

2 This prohibits the creation of a new fee farm grant from 1 December 2009. Note that the prohibition extends to equity, so that a contract for such a grant will not create an equitable one. The consequence of a purported grant or contract post-1 December is spelt out in sub-s (2). This prohibition extends to any type of fee farm grant (see the definition in s 3 and Notes 30 and 31 to that section). This general prohibition also deals with the recommendation by the Law Reform Commission that it should be made clear that the Landlord and Tenant (Ground Rents) Act 1978 prohibits creation of a ground rent in respect of a dwelling by way of a fee farm grant (see LRC CP 34–2004, paras 2.19–2.20). This point has never been entirely clear (see Wylie, *Landlord and Tenant Law* (2nd edn, Tottel Publishing, 1998), para 4.44).

3 This includes both an *inter vivos* grant and one made by will (see the definition in s 3 and the Notes 37–39 to that section).

4 That is 1 December 2009 (see SI 356/2009).

5 Such a grant made after 1849 was automatically converted into a fee farm grant by s 37 of the Renewable Leasehold Conversion Act 1849 (see Wylie, *Irish Land Law* (3rd edn, Tottel Publishing, 1997), para 4.176), but that Act is repealed by Schedule 2 (see the Notes to that Schedule). Paragraph (*b*) ensures that any attempt after 1 December 2009 to grant a perpetually renewable lease (whether involving lives or years) will create a fee simple shorn of any rent.

6 As a consequence of this provision there is an automatic vesting of the fee simple in the grantee. This is, of course, subject to the general law that the grantor must have title to make such a grant.

7 Whether or not a legal or equitable fee simple is vested depends on such factors as whether or not the formalities for creation of a fee simple have been completed (eg use of a deed as required by s 62: see the Notes to that section).

8 This concerns contracts entered into after 1 December 2009. As regards contracts entered into before that date see sub-s (4) below (and the Notes to it).

9   The consequence is that no rent will be payable under the purported grant nor will any provision relating to the rent (eg a rent review provision or forfeiture provision for non-payment of rent).

10 This includes freehold covenants rendered enforceable by Part 8, Chapter 4 (see the Notes to that Part), but not, eg, a covenant offending the rule against inalienability as it applies to freehold land (see Note 17 to s 9).

11 This confirms that a contract for the creation of a fee farm grant entered into before 1 December 2009 remains valid after that date.

12 This confirms that an instrument giving effect to such a pre-1 December 2009 contract and making the actual grant after 1 December 2009 is also valid.

13 This provision was not in the Bill as originally drafted and introduced in the Seanad but was added at the Dáil Select Committee Stage to clarify the position of a fee farm grantee holding under a fee farm grant in existence on 1 December 2009. Such grants continue in force.

14 This refers to the fact that the meaning of "freehold estate" given by s 11(2) does not include a fee simple held under a free farm grant. That section is concerned primarily with the post-1 December 2009 situation, when no new fee farm grant can be created (see sub-s (1) and Note 2 above).

15 Subsection (5) makes it clear that fee farm grants existing on 1 December 2009 continue in force and the grantee has a legal fee simple (provided, of course, the formalities for the creation of such an estate had been followed: see Wylie, *Irish Land Law* (3rd edn, Tottel Publishing, 1997), paras 4.061 and 4.093).

16 Again s 11(4) is concerned primarily to list the legal interests in land which may be created or disposed of after 1 December 2009 and so a fee farm rent is not included.

17 Subsection (6) makes it clear that the fee farm rent reserved in a legal fee farm grant existing on 1 December 2009 continues as a legal interest in the land (see Note 36 to s 11).

---

[44]

Abolition of the fee tail.[1]

13.—(1) The creation of a fee tail of any kind[2] at law or in equity[3] is prohibited.[4]

(2) Any instrument[5] executed after the commencement of this Part[6] purporting to create a fee tail in favour of any person vests in that person a legal fee simple[7] or, as the case may be, an equitable fee simple and any contract for such a creation entered into before or after[8] such commencement operates as a contract for such vesting.[9]

(3)[10] Where—

   (a) immediately before the commencement of this Part, a person was entitled to a fee tail at law or in equity,[11] or

   (b) after such commencement, a person becomes entitled to such a fee tail,[12] a legal or, as the case may be, an equitable fee simple vests in that person on such commencement or on that person becoming so entitled provided any protectorship has ended.[13]

(4) In *subsection (3)*[14] "fee tail" includes—

> (*a*) a base fee provided the protectorship has ended,[15]
>
> (*b*) a base fee created by failure to enrol the disentailing deed,[16]

but does not include the estate of a tenant in tail after possibility of issue extinct.[17]

(5) A fee simple which vests under *subsection (2)* or *subsection (3)*[18] is—

> (*a*) not subject to any estates or interests limited by the instrument creating the fee tail to take effect after the termination of the fee tail,[19]
>
> (*b*) subject to any estates or interests limited to take effect in defeasance of the fee tail which would be valid if limited to take effect in defeasance of a fee simple.[20]

Definitions

See s 3 for definition of: "instrument".

Notes

1   This section implements the recommendation that the fee tail estate should be abolished and existing entails should be barred automatically so as to produce the same result as a tenant in tail could achieve by executing a disentailing assurance under the Fines and Recoveries (Ireland) Act 1834 (see LRC CP 34–2004, paras 2.27–2.30). The fee tail was the creature of statute (De Donis Conditionalibus 1285) and designed to enable feudal landowners to ensure that land passed down through successive generations of their families. It continued to play an important role in family settlements in later centuries but was regarded by the Commission as belonging to a different era.

2   This makes it clear that the prohibition on creation of a fee tail after 1 December 2009 applies to any kind of such estate (see Lyall, *Land Law in Ireland* (2nd edn, Round Hall, 2000), pp 222–224; Wylie, *Irish Land Law* (3rd edn, Tottel Publishing, 1997), paras 4.112–4.142). Cf the definition in sub-s (3) (see Notes 10–13 below).

3   This makes it clear that a fee tail cannot be created either at law or in equity, so that a failed attempt to create one at law cannot be construed as creating one in equity.

4   Subsection (1) prohibits the creation of a fee tail after 1 December 2009. Subsection (2) deals with the consequence of trying to do so.

5   This includes both an *inter vivos* purported grant and a will (see the definition in s 3 and Notes 37–39 to that section).

6   That is 1 December 2009 (see SI 356/2009).

7 Whether or not a legal or equitable fee simple vests depends on factors such as whether the formalities for creation of a legal estate have been followed (eg use of a deed as required by s 62: see the Notes to that section). See also sub-s (5) as to the attributes of the fee simple which so vested (see Noted 18–20 below).

8 Note that, unlike in the case of contracts to create a fee farm grant entered into prior to 1 December 2009 (which remain valid: see s 12(4) and Note 11 to that section), a contract to create a fee tail entered into before that date also operates as a contract to create a fee simple. The likelihood of such a contract being entered into must be extremely remote and the view was taken that any uncompleted contract would have been entered into with the knowledge of likely impending legislation. The Law Reform Commission's initial draft Bill was published in its 2005 Report (LRC 74–2005) and the Government's Bill was initiated in 2006 and any contract entered into prior to 2005 would probably haven been completed by 1 December 2009. It would then be caught by sub-s (3) and converted into a few simple by it.

9 Thus both pre- and post-1 December 2009 contracts to create a fee tail operate as a contract to create a fee simple.

10 Subsection (3) is designed to implement the Commission's recommendation that existing fees tail should be automatically converted into fees simple where the tenant in tail could do this by executing a disentailing assurance under the Fines and Recoveries (Ireland) Act 1834 (see Note 1 above: see also Lyall, *Land Law in Ireland* (2nd edn, Round Hall, 2000), pp 233–241; Wylie, *Irish Land Law* (3rd edn, Tottel Publishing, 1997), paras 4.123–4.125). Note that there are exceptions to such automatic conversion specified in sub-s (4) (see Notes 14–17 below), as there are in sub-s (3) itself (see Note 13 below).

11 This covers fees tail existing on 1 December 2009.

12 This covers the case where some pre-condition or contingency had to be satisfied before the fee tail vests in a person and this does not occur until after 1 December 2009.

13 This reference to protectorship was added at the Seanad Committee Stage and is an important qualification to automatic conversion into a fee simple. Under the Fines and Recoveries (Ireland) Act 1834 a disentailing assurance would not be fully effective without the consent of the "protector" (see Lyall, *Land Law in Ireland* (2nd edn, Round Hall, 2000), pp 234–236; Wylie, *Irish Land Law* (3rd edn, Tottel Publishing, 1997), paras 4.128–4.138). The protector was either the owner of a prior estate (eg a life owner where the disentailing tenant held a remainder interest only) or someone specified in the settlement creating the fee tail. As a result of this amendment a fee tail existing on 1 December 2009 will not be converted into a fee simple until the protectorship ends (on the death of the life owner or the specified protector, unless the settlement made provision for succession to the protectorship). The view was taken that this would accord more with the Commission's view that automatic conversion should take place when the tenant in tail could achieve this on his or her own by executing a disentailing assurance. It was also felt that this amendment would allay doubts which might otherwise exist over the constitutionality of sub-s (3). (See Mee, "The Fee Tail: Putting Us Out of its Misery" (2005) 10(1) CPLJ 4 at 6–8). It is now simply doing automatically what an existing tenant in tail could do on his or her own. However, it would appear that such

conversion under s 13 is now the only way in which a fee tail will be barred in future because the Act repeals the 1834 Act (see Schedule 2), unless the power to execute a disentailing assurance could be construed as a "right, privilege" etc coming within s 27(1)(c) of the Interpretation Act 2005 (which the repeal of an enactment does not affect). On the other hand, repeal of that Act may mean that the protector could release the protectorship, so as to end it and trigger automatic conversion (s 34 of the Act rendered void anything attempting to control the protector and any contract to withhold consent). Apart from that, a prior tenant for life would also be able to end any protectorship attached to the life interest by releasing it. Unless the prior tenant for life takes such action, the life interest remains in force and there will be no conversion of the fee tail in remainder until it falls into possession on death of the life owner.

14 This clarifies further where an automatic conversion of a fee tail into a fee simple will occur under sub-s (3).

15 This deals with the usual case of a base fee, where a tenant in tail has failed to bar the entail fully because the consent of the protector was not obtained to the disentailing assurance. The principle outlined in Note 13 is followed here too, ie conversion will take place only when the protectorship ends.

16 This deals with the other category of base fee, where the failure to execute a fully effective disentailing assurance was merely a technical one, ie a failure to enrol the deed in the High Court within 6 months (as required by s 39 of the 1834 Act). Such a failure was common due to oversight and created a "voidable" or "determinable" base fee (see Lyall, *Land Law in Ireland* (2nd edn, Round Hall, 2000), p 234; Wylie, *Irish Land Law* (3rd edn, Tottel Publishing, 1997), para 4.123). The Law Reform Commission regarded this technical requirement as "excessive" (see LRC 30–1989, para 14) and so the view was taken that such a base fee should be automatically converted into a fee simple. The requirement goes in any event with the repeal of the 1834 Act.

17 This excludes conversion in the case of such an "unbarrable" fee tail. This arose in the case of a fee tail "special", where the issue entitled to succeed to the entail were designated as the children of a specified spouse. If that spouse predeceased the tenant in tail and they had no children, there could be no issue capable of succeeding to it – the surviving tenant became a tenant in tail "after possibility of issue extinct". The consequence is that the tenant in tail became, in effect, a tenant for life and those due to take on determination of the fee tail (as reversioners or remaindermen) had a vested interest (Wylie, *Irish Land Law* (3rd edn, Tottel Publishing, 1997), para 4.140). In view of that the view was taken that there should be no conversion of such a fee tail into a fee simple and the reversionary or remainder interests will remain vested and fall into possession on death of the tenant in tail.

18 Subsection (5) spells out the effect of construing purported creation of a fee tail after 1 December 2009 as creation of a fee simple under sub-s (2) and conversion of existing fees tail under sub-s (3).

19 This accords with the principle of the section, ie doing what the tenant in tail could do by executing a disentailing assurance. This barred not only the issue in tail but also reversioners and remaindermen designated in the instrument creating it as due to take the land when the fee tail interest determined (eg when the current owner

died without issue to succeed to it) (see Lyall, *Land Law in Ireland* (2nd edn, Round Hall, 2000), pp 233–236; Wylie, *Irish Land Law* (3rd edn, Tottel Publishing, 1997), paras 4.123–4.125). This effect of barring the entail had been recognised even before the Fines and Recoveries (Ireland) Act 1834 (through use of collusive actions like "levying a fine" or "suffering a common recovery") and arguably became an inherent feature of a fee tail. It is very doubtful, therefore, that such a well-established feature would have been open to a successful constitutional challenge (see Lyall, *Land Law in Ireland* (2nd edn, Round Hall, 2000), p 236).

20 This recognises that a fee tail might have been subject to a "defeasance" provision just as a fee simple might be, such as a provision that upon the occurrence of an event or upon satisfaction of a specified condition, the grantor or some third party had the right to re-enter or enter the land and put an end to the fee tail. Paragraph (*b*) preserves such a defeasance provision and applies it to the fee simple vesting under sub-ss (2) or (3), provided it is valid in respect of a fee simple. That would not be so if it offended the rule against inalienability (see s 9(4) and Note 17 to that section).

[45]

Prohibition of leases for lives.[1]

14.—The grant of a lease for[2]—

(*a*) a life or lives,[3]

(*b*) a life or lives combined with a concurrent or reversionary term of any period,[4]

(*c*) any term coming to an end on the death of a person or persons,[5]

and any contract for such a grant[6] made after the commencement of this Part[7] is void both at law and in equity.[8]

Definitions

See s 3 for definition of: "lease".

Notes

1 This section implements the recommendation of the Law Reform Commission that other, now extremely, rare combined freehold/leasehold estates should be prohibited in the interests of simplification of the law (see LRC CP 34–2004, paras 2.33–2.35). These sorts of leases derived from an era long past, when it was necessary to own a freehold interest in order to have the right to vote in elections and when succession to freeholds was different from leaseholds under the old law of inheritance (see *Duckett v Keane* [1903] 1 IR 409 at 413–441, *per* FitzGibbon LJ). A life estate was a freehold interest and so it became common to grant leases for lives or for lives combined with a term of years. Another example was leases for lives renewable for ever which were dealt with by the Renewable Leasehold Conversion Act 1849 (see s 12(2)(*b*) of the 2009 Act and Note 5 to that section above).

2 Section 14 covers various combinations of leases for lives, as specified by paragraphs (*a*)–(*c*).

3 This covers a straightforward "lease" for a life or lives (without any term of years involved). Such a lease creates a tenancy involving the relationship of landlord and tenant (see the definition in s 3 and Note 59 to that section) and should not be confused with a grant under a settlement or will of a freehold life estate not involving any such tenancy (see s 18(4) and the Notes to that section).

4 This covers the more common, though nowadays very rare, combination lease, involving a lease for a life or lives and a term (not necessarily "of years"). Difficult questions of construction used to arise as to whether the term ran concurrently with the lives or was reversionary (see Wylie, *Irish Land Law* (3rd edn, Tottel Publishing, 1997), paras 4.177–4.178).

5 This covers a lease for a term which is to determine early on the death of the tenant or some other person or persons. This is to be distinguished from paragraph (*a*) which does not involve a term. Note again that it can be any term, not necessarily a term "of years".

6 The section catches both grants of such leases and contracts for such grants.

7 The section catches only grants and contracts made after 1 December 2009. The view was taken that such grants were so rare nowadays that it was not worth dealing with existing leases or any contract entered into prior to that date. The Law Reform Commission took the view that these could be left to "wither on the vine" (see LRC CP 34–2004, para 2.35).

8 On the same basis it was felt more appropriate just to declare any attempts to create such leases void rather than have provisions declaring that the attempt created something else. In view of the different combinations any such provision would be likely to be complicated (cf s 149(6) of the English Law of Property Act 1925 and Article 37 of the Property (NI) Order 1997: see Wylie, *Irish Land Law* (3rd edn, Tottel Publishing, 1997), paras 4.178).

[46]

PART 3[1]

FUTURE INTERESTS[2]

Notes

1 This Part implements the recommendations made by the Law Reform Commission in its *Report on the Rule Against Perpetuities and Cognant Rules* (LRC 62–2000), but subject to a modification later recommended in the Commission's *Consultation Paper on Reform and Modernisation of Land Law and Conveyancing Law* (LRC CP 34–2004). The 2000 Report had recommended retention of the common law contingent remainder rules. Those rules were developed by the courts in order to facilitate the collection of feudal dues from those "seised" of the land (see Lyall, *Land Law in Ireland* (2nd edn, Round Hall, 2000), pp 227–290; Wylie, *Irish Land*

Law (3rd edn, Tottel Publishing, 1997), paras 5.012–5.030). In particular they were designed to ensure that it would always be clear who was seised of the land at any time, so that they did not allow an "abeyance" of seisin or arbitrary shifting of the seisin from one person to another. However, apart from the arcane nature of this subject, the Commission pointed out in its 2004 Consultation Paper that any lingering purpose to such rules would be removed by other reforms it was recommending in that Paper and which are implemented by the Act. The common law rules applied to freehold land only and under the Act any future freehold interests would be held under a trust of land coming within Part 4 (see the Notes to that Part). Under s 11 of the Act the legal title is always attached to a fee simple "in possession" held either by an individual or body without any future interests attached (other than in the case of a few exceptions listed in s 11(2)) and where there is a succession of interests that will exist under a trust, whereby the legal title will be vested in trustees or a trust corporation. There will, therefore, never be an "abeyance of seisin" the avoidance of which the Commission had thought in its earlier 2000 Report might still be a useful function for the rules in modern times. As the Act itself states, all future interests exist in equity only from 1 December 2009 (s 15(1) and see the Notes to that section). The Commission concluded in its 2004 Consultation Paper that the common law contingent remainder rules should be abolished along with the other rules recommended for abolition by the 2000 Report (see LRC CP 34–2004, paras 3.02–3.04).

2 This Part is concerned for the most part with abolition of various rules mostly developed by the courts over the centuries to deal with future interests. Although most of these rules were initially developed to deal with future interests in land it is important to note that some of them were given a wider scope. Thus the rule against perpetuities was extended to cover all kinds of property. The same applied to the statutory rule against accumulations. This illustrates a point made earlier (see Note 1 to s 1), that some of the Act's provisions apply to property other than land.

---

[47]

Operation of future inter-ests in land.[1]   **15.**—(1) Subject to *subsection (2)*,[2] all future interests in land,[3] whether vested or contingent,[4] exist in equity only.[5]

(2) *Subsection (1)* does not apply to[6]—

    (*a*)   a possibility of reverter,[7] or

    (*b*)   a right of entry or of re-entry attached to a legal estate.[8]

Definitions

See s 3 for definitions of: "land"; "right of entry"; "right of re-entry".

Notes

1 As explained above (see Note 1 to Part 3), this section states explicitly the consequences of other provisions in the Act, in particular, the provisions in s 11

relating to freehold estates and in Part 4 relating to trusts of land (see the Notes to that section and that Part).

2 This qualification is necessary because the future interests specified in sub-s (2) remain legal interests (see the Notes to it).

3 The provisions affecting future interests referred to in Note 1 above concern interests in land only.

4 For the distinction between vested and contingent interests see Lyall, *Land Law in Ireland* (2nd edn, Round Hall, 2000), pp 273–275; Wylie, *Irish Land Law* (3rd edn, Tottel Publishing, 1997), paras 5.008–5.011. This distinction had particular significance in relation to rules like the rule against perpetuities.

5 This, as indicated above (see Note 1), is the consequence of s 11 and Part 4 (see the Notes to that section and that Part).

6 This is because the interests specified in paragraphs (*a*) and (*b*) remain legal interests (see s 11(2)(*a*) and (*b*) and 4(*e*) and (*i*) (see Notes 9–11, 37 and 43 to that section).

7 This is the interest retained by the grantor of a determinable fee (see Note 9 to s 11).

8 This is the interest attached to a fee simple subject to a condition subsequent (see Note 10 to s 11).

---

[48]

16.—Subject to *section 17*,[2] the following rules are abolished:[3]

    (*a*)   the rules known as the common law contingent remainder rules;[4]

    (*b*)   the rule known as the Rule in *Purefoy v. Rogers*;[5]

    (*c*)   the rule known as the Rule in *Whitby v. Mitchell*[6] (also known as the old rule against perpetuities[7] and the rule against double possibilities);[8]

    (*d*)[9] the rule against perpetuities;[10]

    (*e*)   the rule against accumulations.[11]

Abolition of various rules.[1]

Notes

1 This section implements the recommendations of the Law Reform Commission for abolition of various rules which it viewed as either obsolete or no longer serving a useful purpose in modern times (see Notes 1 and 2 to Part 3 above).

2 This qualification is necessary because s 17 makes the abolition of the rules retrospective but subject to some limitations (see the Notes to that section).

3 Note again that under s 17 this operates retrospectively subject to some limitations.

4 As explained earlier, the Law Reform Commission concluded that, as a consequence of other changes made by the Act, these arcane rules should be abolished (see Note 1 to Part 3 above). As a consequence statutes like the Contingent Remainders Act 1877 are repealed by the Act (see Schedule 2).

5   This obscure and complicated rule was developed by the courts in connection with the common law contingent remainder rules (see Lyall, *Land Law in Ireland* (2nd edn, Round Hall, 2000), pp 283–285; Wylie, *Irish Land Law* (3rd edn, Tottel Publishing, 1997), paras 5.020–5.022) and is abolished along with these rules (see Note 4 above).

6   This obscure rule seemed to have different guises (see Notes 7 and 8 below) and there is some doubt whether it applied to Ireland (there is very little authority on the point: see Lyall, *Land Law in Ireland* (2nd edn, Round Hall, 2000), pp 299–303; Wylie, *Irish Land Law* (3rd edn, Tottel Publishing, 1997), paras 5.042–5.055) and again the Law Reform Commission took the view that it had no place in modern law.

7   This is one of its main guises (see Lyall, *Land Law in Ireland* (2nd edn, Round Hall, 2000), p 299; Wylie, *Irish Land Law* (3rd edn, Tottel Publishing, 1997), para 5.042).

8   This is another of its guises (see Lyall, *Land Law in Ireland* (2nd edn, Round Hall, 2000), pp 300–301; Wylie, *Irish Land Law* (3rd edn, Tottel Publishing, 1997), paras 5.043–5.044).

9   Far and away the most significant provision in s 16 is the abolition of the rule against perpetuities. This rule, as it was developed by the courts from a rule originally confined to future interests in land, extended to such interests in all kinds of property. In particular it was applied to interests held under settlements and trusts and to various interests in commercial property (such as options) and relating to conveyancing transactions (such grants of future easements and other rights vested once a new development was completed). The Law Reform Commission in a comprehensive review of the complications and often arbitrary operations of the rule concluded that its usefulness was outweighed by the difficulties it created for lawyers and their clients. Rather than follow what was done in England and Wales (see the Perpetuities and Accumulations Act 1964) and Northern Ireland (see the Perpetuities and Accumulations Act (NI) 1966), which was to keep the rule but introduce statutory reforms to remove many of the more absurd features, the Commission concluded that it would be more sensible simply to abolish it (see LRC 62–2000, ch 4). It should be noted that the Commission accompanied this recommendation with a recommendation that such abolition should not be implemented without the introduction of variations of trusts legislation (paras 4.31–4.32). When the Bill which became this Act was initially drafted it was contemplated that such legislation would be introduced separately (perhaps as part of reform of the general law of trusts), so that this Part of the Act might be commenced at a later date. However, during the Bill's passage through the Dáil the Government decided to bring forward variation of trusts provisions and Part 5 was added at the Dáil Select Committee Stage (see the Notes to that Part). As a consequence of this abolition of the rule the drafters of wills, settlements, trusts, conveyances and commercial documents no longer have to worry about the perpetuities problems. The trap for the unwary has been removed.

10   It should be noted that s 16 does not affect the rule against inalienability. Indeed, as indicated earlier, the Act confirms that rule as it applies to freehold land (see s 9(4) and Note 17 to that section). That rule applies also to personal property where it is sometimes referred to as the rule against perpetual trusts or trusts of undue duration (see Delany, *Equity and the Law of Trusts in Ireland* (4th edn, Round Hall, 2007),

ch 9). In this context the rule is often invoked by the courts to control "purpose" trusts and gifts to unincorporated bodies. In this application it is often confused with the rule against perpetuities (a confusion which is added to by the courts using the perpetuity period applicable when no "lives in being" are relevant, ie 21 years), but the two rules are fundamentally different. The rule against perpetuities is concerned with the "initial vesting" of property whereas the rule against inalienability is concerned with the "duration" of property which has already vested. The Law Reform Commission took the view that the latter was dealing with different situations and recommended no change at this stage (LRC 62–2000, paras 5.08–5.16).

11 The law relating to accumulations has always been somewhat anomalous. Apart from the rule against perpetuities there was no independent rule in Ireland. The Accumulations Act 1800 (which was passed in England in response to the notorious case of *Thelluson v Woodford* (1799) 4 Ves 227, (1805) 11 Ves 112) did not apply to Ireland, but curiously (presumably through oversight as to the 1800 Act) the amending Accumulations Act 1892 did! (See Lyall, *Land Law in Ireland* (2nd edn, Round Hall, 2000), pp 344–347; Wylie, *Irish Land Law* (3rd edn, Tottel Publishing, 1997), paras 5.150–5.153)). The Law Reform Commission recommended removal of this anomaly and abolition of the rule along with repeal of the 1892 Act (LRC 62–2000, paras 5.42–5.55) (see Schedule 2 and the Notes to that Schedule).

---

[49]

17.—*Section 16*[2] applies to any interest in property[3] whenever created[4] but does not apply[5] if, before the commencement of this Part,[6] in reliance[7] on such an interest being invalid by virtue of the application of any of the rules abolished by that section[8]—

Scope of section 16.[1]

   (*a*)   the property has been distributed or otherwise dealt with,[9] or

   (*b*)[10]any person has done or omitted to do any thing which renders the position of that or any other person[11] materially altered to that person's detriment[12] after the commencement of this Part.[13]

Definitions

See s 3 for definition of: "property".

Notes

1 This section has already proved to be controversial because, as recommended by the Law Reform Commission (see LRC 62–2000, paras 4.33–4.46 and 5.56–5.63), it provides that the abolition of the rules listed in s 16 applies to any interest in property "whenever created", ie including settlements, trusts, wills, conveyances and commercial transactions entered into and operative before 1 December 2009. This

retrospective effect of s 16 has been criticised by some academic writers as potentially offending the Constitution or the European Convention on Human Rights and Freedoms by interfering with vested rights (see Lyall, "Report on the Rule Against Perpetuities and Cognate Rules of the Law Reform Commission: A Comment" (2002) 7(1) CPLJ 2–5 and (2002) 7(3) 54–57; Mee, "From Here to Eternity? Perpetuities Reform in Ireland" (2000) 22 DULJ 91). Several points should be made in this context. First, the Law Reform Commission considered this issue in some detail and stressed that it was recommending "limited" retrospectivity only (see the paras in the 2000 Report cited above). Secondly, the draft Bill appended to that Report (see Appendix A) followed that recommendation, which was based on recommendations which had been made elsewhere (in particular South Australia and Manitoba). Thirdly, s 17 largely follows the Commission's draft in this respect. Fourthly, the Attorney General's Department is responsible for advising the Government on the constitutionality of Government Bills and will no doubt have satisfied itself as to the constitutionality of ss 16 and 17.

2   That is the abolition of the various rules listed in s 16.

3   This recognises that some of the rules listed in s 16 are not confined to land (see Note 2 to Part 3 and Note 9 to s 16).

4   This introduces the element of retrospectivity (see Note 1 above) but note that the section then goes on to qualify this.

5   In essence retrospectivity does not apply to someone who can claim to have "shifted their position on the basis that a gift was void" by virtue of application of one or more of the abolished rules (see LRC 62–2000, para 4.41). Or, to put it another way, any person who by 1 December 2009 "had already taken property under a gift over will not have this ownership disrupted" and any person who acted in reliance upon the applicability of the rules has their interests "protected" (see LRC 62–2000, para 4.46).

6   Note that the protection against retrospectivity applies only where a person received property through or acted in reliance on application of one of the rules abolished before 1 December 2009.

7   Protection from retrospectivity is based upon a person having a legitimate claim because of reliance upon application of the rules before 1 December 2009 (see LRC 62–2000, paras 4.44–4.45).

8   Note that the protection against retrospectivity applies in respect of application of any of the rules abolished by s 16 (see LRC 62–2000, paras 4.46 and 5.56–5.63).

9   This protects a person who had taken property before 1 December 2009 in reliance on application of one of the rules abolished rendered some other gift void (see LRC 62–2000, paras 4.40 and 4.44–4.45).

10   This protects persons who, before 1 December 2009 (see Notes 6 and 7 above), acted on the basis that one of the rules applied so as to render void a gift to some person or to determine who was entitled to the property. Such a person may then have assumed that they owned it and dealt with it in various ways, thereby involving third parties. Provided the condition laid down by paragraph (*b*) is satisfied (see Notes 12 and 13 below), that person and any third parties are protected and such dealings will stand post-1 December 2009.

11 This recognises that third parties may have been involved in dealings with a person who relied on application of one of the rules.

12 Again the protection is based upon a "shifting of position" to a person's detriment (see Notes 5, 6, 7 and 9 above). The phrase "that person's detriment" relates to the alteration of position and so covers both the person who acted on reliance of the application of one of the rules and any other person who may have dealt with the acting person.

13 Note that the requirements are (1) reliance *before* 1 December 2009 by a person on the applicability of one of the abolished rules (see Note 7 above) which (2) renders *after* 1 December 2009 the position of that person or any other person materially affected to their detriment.

---

[50]

PART 4[1]

TRUSTS OF LAND[2]

Notes

1 Part 4 of the Act implements the recommendation of the Law Reform Commission that the complicated and often confusing provisions of the Settled Land Acts 1882–1890 should be replaced with a more simple statutory regime governing trusts of land (see LRC CP 34–2004, ch 4).

2 The provisions in Part 4 cover all trusts of land, ie not just settlements of land (which may or may not include an express trust: see Note 2 to s 18 below) and express trusts (whether or not a trust for sale), but all situations where a trust may arise in relation to land, such as a bare trust or trust arising by implication or operation of law (see Note 16 to s 18 below). Part 4 adopts a completely different approach to that in the 1882–1890 Acts. Much of their provisions was taken up with conferring various statutory powers on a tenant for life and the trustees of the settlement. Part 4 confines the legal title to trustees and gives to them powers of dealing with the land that an absolute owner would have. There is, therefore, no need to spell out powers in either the Act or the instrument creating the settlement or trust. The only issue for the drafter of the instrument is whether to put some restriction on the full power to deal with the land. The Act does, however, reiterate that the trustees are subject to the general law of trusts and so must exercise their powers accordingly. It is also important to note that the provisions of Part 4 apply to settlements and trusts of land existing on 1 December 2009 (see the Notes to s 18). The view was taken that the provisions of Part 4 enhance the position of parties to a settlement, by conferring much greater and more flexible powers of dealing with the land. The more direct involvement of trustees is the one major change to the position of a "tenant for life" under the Settled Land Acts 1882–1890 (who, under those Acts, had the powers of dealing with the land). However, it was important to remember that the tenant for life did not have an entirely free hand in dealing with the land under those Acts. Any

capital money resulting from a dealing (eg the proceeds of a sale) had to be paid to the trustees of the settlement, or into court, if a good title was to pass to a purchaser or other person dealing with the tenant for life. Imposition of a trust under Part 4 recognises this practical reality. Furthermore, their position is, however, protected to a large extent by making the tenant for life under an existing settlement on 1 December 2009 one of the trustees (see s 19(1)(*a*) and the Notes to that section). In view of that protection and the general enhancement of existing settlements it was considered appropriate to make the provisions retrospective. This does, of course, avoid what could be a very lengthy period when two statutory regimes would apply to settlements and trusts of land.

---

[51]

Trusts of land.[1]

18.—(1) Subject to this Part,[3] where land[4] is—

[SLA 1882, ss. 2, 59, 60][2]

(*a*)[5] for the time being[6] limited[7] by an instrument,[8] whenever executed,[9] to persons by way of succession[10] without the interposition of a trust[11] (in this Part referred to as a "strict settlement"),[12] or

(*b*)[13] held, either with or without other property,[14] on a trust whenever it arises[15] and of whatever kind,[16] or

(*c*)[17] vested, whether before or after the commencement of this Part,[18] in a minor,[19]

there is a trust of land for the purposes of this Part.[20]

(2)[21] For the purposes of—

(*a*)[22] *subsection (1)(a)*, a strict settlement exists where an estate or interest in reversion or remainder is not disposed of and reverts to the settlor or the testator's successors in title,[23] but does not exist where a person owns a fee simple in possession,[24]

(*b*)[25] *subsection (1)(b)*, a trust includes an express, implied, resulting, constructive and bare trust and a trust for sale.[26]

(3) Subject to this Part,[27] a trust of land is governed by the general law of trusts.[28]

(4) Conversion of a life estate into an equitable interest only[29] does not affect a life owner's liability for waste.[30]

[LEA 1695]

(5)[31] Where, by reason of absence from the State or otherwise,[32] it remains uncertain for a period of at least 7 years[33] as to whether a person upon whose life an estate or interest depends[34] is alive, it shall continue to be presumed[35] that the person is dead.

(6) If such presumption is applied to a person but subsequently rebutted by proof to the contrary,[36] that person[37] may bring an action for damages[38] or another remedy[39] for any loss suffered.

(7) In dealing with an action under *subsection (6)*, the court may make such order as appears to it to be just and equitable in the circumstances of the case.[40]

(8)[41] Any party to a conveyance shall, unless the contrary is proved,[42] be presumed to have attained full age at the date of the conveyance.

(9)[43] This Part does not apply to land held directly[44] for a charitable purpose and not by way of a remainder.[45]

Definitions

See s 3 for definitions of: "conveyance"; "court"; "instrument"; "land"; "property".

Notes

1   This section defines the scope of Part 4.

2   In doing so it replaces some of the provisions in the Settled Land Act 1882, in particular those which defined a "settlement" coming within that Act (and who was a "tenant for life") (s 2) provided that an "infant" entitled to land was a tenant for life (s 59) but that the powers of dealing with the infant's land had to be exercised by the trustees of the settlement (s 60). See on these provisions Lyall, *Land Law in Ireland* (2nd edn, Round Hall, 2000), ch 14; Wylie, *Irish Land Law* (3rd edn, Tottel Publishing, 1997), ch 8.

3   Although Part 4 covers the vast majority of trusts involving land, it does not apply to land currently held by a charity (see sub-s (9) and the Notes to it).

4   Part 4 is concerned only with settlements and trusts involving land (but not necessarily land exclusively: see Note 14 below).

5   Paragraph (*a*) deals with the typical, traditional family settlement of land, under which the land would be settled on members of the family in succession to one another. This would involve use of life and entailed estates and would aim to tie up the land within the family for several generations (see Lyall, *Land Law in Ireland* (2nd edn, Round Hall, 2000), ch 14; Wylie, *Irish Land Law* (3rd edn, Tottel Publishing, 1997), ch 8). Often this would be done by limiting the land to the successive generations directly (using those "limited" freehold estates falling short of a fee simple) and without interposing an express trust: eg "to A for life, remainder to B in fee tail, remainder to C in fee simple" (instead of "to X and Y as trustees to hold on trust for A for life, remainder etc").

6   Part 4 applies only where the settlement or succession of interests still exists. It ceases to apply when the settlement has worked through, so that no further element of succession exists. Thus taking the example given in Note 5, it would cease to apply when A has died and succession to B's fee tail ceases (because there are no

issue capable of succeeding to it). When that happens the fee simple will vest in C or C's successor in title.

7   That is where a settlement or will "limits" the land to a succession of people.

8   As the definition in s 3 makes clear this covers a settlement created by both an *inter vivos* deed and a will.

9   This confirms that Part 4 applies to existing settlements, so that from 1 December 2009 it applies rather than the Settled Land Acts 1882–1890 (which are repealed: see Schedule 2).

10   It was this element of "succession" which defined a "settlement" within the meaning of the 1882–1890 Acts (see Lyall, *Land Law in Ireland* (2nd edn, Round Hall, 2000), pp 386–396; Wylie, *Irish Land Law* (3rd edn, Tottel Publishing, 1997), paras 8.018–8.027).

11   Paragraph (*b*) deals with a settlement involving interposition of a trust (on this distinction see Note 5 above).

12   This is the traditional description of such a settlement of land (see Wylie, *Irish Land Law* (3rd edn, Tottel Publishing, 1997), paras 8.004–8.010). See the further explanation in sub-s (2)(*a*) (and the Notes to it).

13   Paragraph (*b*) deals with the other way of creating a succession of interests, ie vesting land in trustees to be held on trust for persons in succession (instead of limiting it to those persons directly: see Notes 5, 7 and 11 above),

14   This makes it clear that Part 4 applies to a trust under which land is held on trust with other property.

15   This makes it clear that Part 4 applies to trusts existing on 1 December 2009 (see Note 2 to Part 4).

16   This makes it clear that Part 4 applies to any kind of trust, not just an express trust creating a succession of interests. Indeed, it covers any kind of express trust, including a discretionary trust (such trusts did not come within the Settled Land Acts 1882–1890: see Lyall, *Land Law in Ireland* (2nd edn, Round Hall, 2000), pp 398–399; Wylie, *Irish Land Law* (3rd edn, Tottel Publishing, 1997), para 8.029). It also applies to trusts arising by implication, such as resulting and constructive trusts found by a court through the application of equitable principles (note the saving in s 11(7) and Note 52 to that section). In such cases the legal owner holds the land for some other person usually without any element of succession. The same applies to a bare trust such as arises where a vendor holds the land for a purchaser who has paid the purchase price (see Keogan, Mee and Wylie, *The Law and Taxation of Trusts* (Tottel Publishing, 2007), para 2.007 and ch 25). (See further sub-s (2)(*b*) and the Notes to it).

Note, however, that Part 4 does not apply to land held by a charity (see sub-s (9) and the Notes to it).

17   Paragraph (*c*) deals with another situation where no succession of interests in the land may exist, ie where it is vested in a minor. The Settled Land Acts 1882–1890 nevertheless treated such land as if it created a settlement and the minor as a tenant for life within those Acts (even though the land was vested in the minor absolutely). Despite that, dealings with the land to be effective (ie not liable to be set aside by the minor on reaching majority) had to be made by trustees of the settlement (or under a

court order) (see Lyall, *Land Law in Ireland* (2nd edn, Round Hall, 2000), p 396; Wylie, *Irish Land Law* (3rd edn, Tottel Publishing, 1997), paras 8.026 and 25.00). The Act recognises the realities of this and so provides that in future a minor's land will be held on trust under Part 4, with the minor holding an equitable interest only (see further sub-s (8) and the Notes to it).

18 Again, Part 4 applies to land vested in a minor on 1 December 2009, so long as the minority lasts.

19 That is a person who has not yet reached the age of 18 years: Age of Majority Act 1985, ss 2(1) and 4(1).

20 This means that it attracts the provisions of Part 4, in particular the trustee powers conferred by s 20, the overreaching provisions of s 21 and the provisions for resolution of disputes in s 22.

21 Subsection (2) clarifies the provisions of sub-s (1).

22 Paragraph (*a*) deals with a subject which was far from clear under the Settled Land Acts 1882–1890, namely, when did a succession of interests exist (so that any dealing with the land would have to be carried out under those Acts) and when did it not exist (so that the current holder of the land was free to deal with it without regard to the restrictions or requirements of those Acts) (see Lyall, *Land Law in Ireland* (2nd edn, Round Hall, 2000), pp 386–398; Wylie, *Irish Land Law* (3rd edn, Tottel Publishing, 1997), paras 8.020–8.027).

23 This makes it clear that a succession of interests exists even though the deed or will does not expressly create one. For example, if land is conveyed or left by will by the owner of the fee simple simply "to A for life", there appears to be no succession of interests. However, because the owner in fee simple has disposed of a lesser estate only, there is an automatic reversionary interest held by A. That would be regarded as a strict settlement within sub-s (1)(*a*) and attracts the provisions of Part 4.

24 This is linked with s 11(2) (see the Notes to that section) and again determines who is entitled to deal with the land – the holder of the estate or interest in question or trustees under Part 4. Thus s 11(2) makes it clear that Part 4 (and the need for dispositions to be made by trustees) does not apply to the holder of modified fees (like a determinable fee or fee simple subject to a condition) or a fee simple subject only to powers like a power of revocation or certain rights of residence.

25 Paragraph (*b*) clarifies sub-s (1)(*b*) and makes it clear that Part 4 applies to most trusts involving land (see Note 16 above).

26 One of the difficulties with the Settled Land Acts 1882–1890 was the different treatment of trusts for sale, as opposed to "holding" trusts or, indeed, strict settlements without the interposition of a trust (see Lyall, *Land Law in Ireland* (2nd edn, Round Hall, 2000), pp 412–414; Wylie, *Irish Land Law* (3rd edn, Tottel Publishing, 1997), paras 8.043–8.049). Part 4 removes these difficulties by treating all settlements and trusts in the same way.

27 This qualification covers provisions in Part 4 extending or modifying the general law, eg s 20 (see the Notes to that section).

28 The point here is that Part 4 deals only with certain matters specific to trusts of land and leaves other more general matters to the general law, both as developed by the courts and as enshrined in statute law, such as the Trustee Act 1893 (see the Law

Reform Commission's *Report on Trust Law: General Proposals* (LRC 92–2008). This covers matters relating to the office of a trustee (appointment, removal, retirement, etc.), liabilities and various powers (such as investment, insurance and delegation). The view was taken that these matters should be the subject of review in the context of trusts as a whole and to be left to be dealt with by general reform such as proposed by the Commission in its 2008 Report. This position is reiterated by other provisions in Part 4 (eg ss 19(3) and 20(1): see the Notes to those sections).

29 Such conversion is, of course, the consequence of s 11(1) and (2) (see the Notes to that section).

30 The general law of waste governs owners of a limited interest in land (such as a tenant for life or leasehold tenant) and is designed to protect those entitled to the property in reversion or remainder (see Lyall, *Land Law in Ireland* (2nd edn, Round Hall, 2000), pp 245–248; Wylie, *Irish Land Law* (3rd edn, Tottel Publishing, 1997), paras 4.149–4.154). Subsection (4) confirms that where a tenant for life is in occupation of the land after 1 December 2009 (as the trustees may permit: see s 20(2)(a) and the Notes to that section) he or she must not commit waste.

31 Subsections (5)–(7) re-enact the substance of the Life Estates Act (Ir) 1695 (which is repealed by the 2009 Act: see Schedule 2). It is obviously vital to know when the holder of a life estate dies, because at that date reversionary or remainder interests vest. However, the holder of the life estate may have disappeared or not have been seen for some time, so that it is not known whether he or she is still alive. This was a particular problem in Ireland because of the many grants of leases for lives renewable for ever, with fines payable for renewing lives (see Lyall, *Land Law in Ireland* (2nd edn, Round Hall, 2000), p 254; Wylie, *Irish Land Law* (3rd edn, Tottel Publishing, 1997), para 4.170; also s 14 and the Notes to it), but the problem can also arise in respect of a freehold life estate created under a settlement or trust.

32 This makes it clear that it does not matter what the reason is for the uncertainty as to whether a person is alive.

33 The 7-year period for the presumption of death was contained in s 1 of the 1695 Act.

34 The object of the provision is to provide certainty for reversioners or remaindermen entitled to take on the death of the holder of a life interest.

35 Subsection (5) continues the presumption created by s 1 of the 1695 Act (see Note 33 above). Note that it is a presumption only which may be rebutted later by evidence establishing that the person presumed dead is still alive: see sub-ss (6) and (7) (and the Notes to them).

36 This confirms that the presumption of death after 7 years is a rebuttable one only.

37 This refers to the person to whom "the presumption is applied", ie the life owner whose whereabouts were unknown and who has been presumed dead.

38 Subsections (6) and (7) replace s 3 of the 1695 Act, but confer a wider jurisdiction on the court. Section 3 referred to re-instatement of the person presumed dead in the land in question and damages for loss of profits from the land.

39 Subsection (6) does not specify what another remedy might be – this is a matter for the court in exercise of the discretion conferred by sub-s (7) (see the Notes to that subsection). Such a remedy could involve re-instatement in the land, if the court thought that "just and equitable".

40 This confirms the wider jurisdiction conferred by the 2009 Act (see Notes 38 and 39 above). No doubt the court will consider first the remedy sought by the applicant under sub-s (6), but the wording of sub-s (7) is wide enough to enable the court to consider, and in its discretion grant, some other remedy.

41 Subsection (8) is a new provision designed to deal with what might otherwise be conveyancing difficulties arising from a minor no longer able to hold legal title to land (see Notes 17–19 above). Where a minor is entitled to land it must be dealt with by trustees under Part 4 – only they can sell, lease, mortgage or otherwise dispose of it. Were it not for the provision in sub-s (8) purchasers' solicitors might feel it necessary to raise enquiries or requisitions as to the age of the vendor. Instead, they can rely upon the presumption that any party to a conveyance is of full age at the date of the conveyance. This covers both past conveyances which may form part of the title deeds and the conveyance which the current vendor is to execute in order to complete the sale or other transactions with respect to the land.

42 Subsection (8) raises a presumption only which, like all presumptions, is rebuttable by evidence proving the contrary.

43 Subsection (9) contains an important exception to the provisions of Part 4 relating to trusts of land. The view was taken that charities are subject to a special statutory regime, now largely contained in the Charities Act 2009 (which amends the Charities Act 1961; see also the Charities Act 1973).

44 The exception from Part 4 applies only where the charity currently holds the land.

45 The exception does not apply where the charity holds a remainder interest. In such cases the land will currently be held by a non-charity and so long as that situation continues (ie until the prior interest ends and the charity's interest falls into possession) Part 4 will apply.

---

[52]

19.—(1) The following persons[3] are the trustees of a trust of land—

   (*a*)   in the case of a strict settlement,[4] where it—

      (i)   exists at the commencement of this Part,[5] the tenant for life within the meaning of the Settled Land Act 1882[6] together with any trustees of the settlement for the purposes of that Act,[7]

      (ii) is purported to be created after the commencement of this Part,[8] the persons who would fall within *paragraph (b)*[9] if the instrument creating it were deemed to be an instrument creating a trust of land,[10]

  (*b*)[11]   in the case of a trust of land created expressly[12]—

      (i)   any trustee nominated by the trust instrument,[13] but, if there is no such person,[14] then,

Trustees of land.[1]

[SLA 1882, ss. 38, 39][2]

(ii)   any person on whom the trust instrument confers a present or future power of sale of the land, or power of consent to or approval of the exercise of such a power of sale,[15] but, if there is no such person, then,

(iii)   any person who, under either the trust instrument[16] or the general law of trusts,[17] has power to appoint[18] a trustee of the land, but, if there is no such person, then,

(iv)   the settlor or, in the case of a trust created by will, the testator's personal representative or representatives,[19]

(c)   in the case of land vested in a minor before the commencement of this Part[20] or purporting so to vest after such commencement,[21] the persons who would fall within *paragraph (b)* if the instrument vesting the land were deemed to be an instrument creating a trust of land,[22]

(d)[23]in the case of land the subject of an implied, resulting, constructive or bare trust, the person in whom the legal title to the land is vested.[24]

(2) For the purposes of—

(a)   *subsection (1)(a)(ii)* and *(1)(c)*, the references in *subsection (1)(b)* to "trustee" and "trustee of the land" include a trustee of the settlement,[25]

(b)   *subsection (1)(b)(iii)* a power to appoint a trustee includes a power to appoint where no previous appointment has been made.[26]

(3) Nothing in this section affects the right of any person to obtain an order of the court appointing a trustee of land[27] or vesting land in a person as trustee.[28]

Definitions

See s 3 for definitions of: "court"; "instrument"; "land"; "personal representative"; "strict settlement"; "trust of land".

Notes

1   Section 19 identifies who are the trustees of any trust of land coming within Part 4. This is a vital matter because under Part 4 it is the trustees who hold legal title to the land and who must carry out any dealing with it. Since Part 4 covers also settlements and trusts existing on 1 December 2009 s 19, like s 18 (see the Notes to that section), contains provisions identifying who are the trustees for such settlements and trusts.

2   To some extent the provisions of s 19 are based on ss 38 and 39 of the Settled Land Act 1882, but the 1882 provisions had a much narrower scope, being confined to trustees of a settlement coming within that Act. Part 4 of the 2009 Act has a much wider scope (see s 18 and the Notes to it).

3   If, in the case of a particular trust of land (which includes settlements and trusts in existence on 1 December 2009: see Note 1 above), there are no such persons the fall-back position is that an application may be made to the court for appointment of trustees: see sub-s (3) (and the Notes to it).

4   This refers to the traditional family settlement limiting land to persons in succession without the interposition of trustees: see 18(1)(*a*) (and Notes 5–12 to that section).

5   That is 1 December 2009 (see Note 1 above).

6   This includes not only the holder of a life estate but holder of other limited freehold estates, such as a fee tail (see Lyall, *Land Law in Ireland* (2nd edn, Round Hall, 2000), pp 389–396; Wylie, *Irish Land Law* (3rd edn, Tottel Publishing, 1997), paras 8.028–8.030). This provision in sub-paragraph (i) was included to "compensate" the tenant for life of an existing settlement for losing the sole power of dealing with it under the 1882–1890 Acts. The tenant for life, instead, becomes one of the legal owners with full title to the land (instead of having only a limited interest and power to deal with the land as if the full owner) and full power to deal with it on that basis (rather than having only the powers conferred by the 1882–1890 Acts, with their substantial restrictions: see Lyall, *Land Law in Ireland* (2nd edn, Round Hall, 2000), pp 399–405; Wylie, *Irish Land Law* (3rd edn, Tottel Publishing, 1997), paras 8.028–8.030 and 8.057–8.091).

7   The tenant for life of a settlement existing on 1 December 2009 shares the trustees' role with any "trustees of the settlement" within the 1882 Act (see Lyall, *Land Law in Ireland* (2nd edn, Round Hall, 2000), pp 405–409; Wylie, *Irish Land Law* (3rd edn, Tottel Publishing, 1997), paras 8.092–8.103). Who these persons are was governed by s 2(8) of the 1882 Act and s 16 of the Settled Land Act 1890. The repeal of those Acts (see Schedule 2 to the 2009 Act) does not affect their operation in identifying those persons: see s 27(1)(b) of the Interpretation Act 2005.

8   Any purported creation of a strict settlement without the interposition of trustees after 1 December 2009 operates as a trust of land (see 18(1)(*a*) and the Notes to it) and should, instead, have been created as a trust with designated trustees holding the legal title to the land.

9   Note that where a post-1 December 2009 instrument purports to convey or leave the land to persons directly in succession but, as would be good practice prior to that date, nominates other persons as "trustees of the settlement" (see Note 7 above) those persons will be the trustees of the land under Part 4: see sub-s (2)(*a*).

10 This adapts the provisions of sub-s (1)(*b*) to post-1 December 2009 instruments purporting to create an "old-style" strict settlement.

11 Subsection (1)(*b*) deals with who are the trustees in the case of an express trust of land, which all post-1 December 2009 settlements should be created as. It adapts provisions in the Settled Land Act 1882 (ss 2(8), 38 and 39, as supplemented by s 16 of the Settled Land Act 1890).

12 The "descending" list of persons indicates the "first choice", then the "second choice" and so on. As under the 1882–1890 Acts, in default of any person coming within the paragraph (*b*) categories, an appointment of trustees can be made by the court (see sub-s (3) and the Notes to it).

13 Clearly it is good practice for the trust instrument to nominate the trustees.

14 This confirms the "descending" order in paragraph (*b*): see Note 12 above.

15 The inclusion of such powers is common in trust instruments, although that may become less so in view of the "plenary" statutory powers conferred by s 20 (see the Notes to that section).

16 Again it is common to include such a power of appointment in a trust instrument, especially because the statutory powers in s 10 of the Trustee Act 1893 are limited (see the Law Reform Commission's *Report on Trust Law: General Proposals* (LRC 92–2008), paras 2.39–2.103). In particular they can be exercised only to appoint a replacement for an existing trustee. Note that sub-s (2)(*b*) extends for the purposes of the 2009 Act the category of persons with a power of appointment to include someone with a power to make an initial appointment of a trustee and not just someone with a power to appoint a replacement of an existing trustee.

17 This includes statutory powers such as those contained in s 10 of the Trustee Act 1893 (see Note 16 above).

18 Note again the provision in sub-s (2)(*b*) (see Note 16 above).

19 This provision will usually be the "last resort" which will operate, so that there will be no need to apply to the court under sub-s (3). This will become less likely if the Law Reform Commission's recommendations for extending the statutory provisions relating to non-judicial appointment of trustees are implemented (see LRC 92–2008, ch 2).

20 Prior to 1 December 2009 a minor could hold legal title, but it was treated as settled land under the Settled Land Acts 1882–1890 (see Notes 17–19 to s 18). Any such land became a trust of land under Part 4: see 18(1)(*c*).

21 Post-1 December 2009 a conveyance of land to a minor will not vest legal title in the minor and, instead, will operate as a trust of land under Part 4.

22 This adapts the provisions of sub-s (1)(*b*) to both pre- and post-1 December 2009 conveyances or wills purporting to vest legal title in a minor. Note also that sub-s (2)(*a*) makes it clear that the persons who may be the trustees include persons who would have been the trustees of the settlement under the Settled Land Acts 1992–1890, had they continued to apply (see Note 9 above).

23 This deals with cases where a trust of land is not created expressly, but arises by implication or operation of law, or involves no succession of interests or other circumstances which previously would have attracted the provisions of the Settled Land Acts 1882–1890 (such as land being vested in a minor).

24 In such cases what usually occurs is that the trust is regarded as attaching to or is imposed upon the person who holds legal title to the land but ought to recognise the claim of some other person.

25 See Notes 9 and 22 above.

26 See Notes 16 and 18 above.

27 The court has both an inherent power to appoint trustees (see *Pollock v Ennis* [1921] 1 IR 181 and the Law Reform Commission's Report LRC 92–2008, paras 2.104–2.122) and under statutory provisions (see Trustee Act 1893, ss 25 and 36: see LRC 92–2008, paras 2.105–2.111).

28 As regards the court's power to make vesting orders see the Trustee Act 1893, ss 26 and 35 and *Re Heidelstone Co Ltd* [2006] IEHC 408.

---

[53]

20.—(1) Subject to[2]—

   (*a*) the duties of a trustee,[3] and

   (*b*) any restrictions imposed by any statutory provision[4] (including this Act)[5] or the general law of trusts[6] or by any instrument[7] or court order relating to the land,[8]

a trustee of land has the full power of an owner to convey or otherwise deal with it.[9]

(2) The power of a trustee under *subsection (1)* includes the power to[10]—

   (*a*)[11]permit a beneficiary to occupy or otherwise use[12] the land on such terms as the trustee thinks fit,[13]

   (*b*) sell the land and to re-invest the proceeds, in whole or in part, in the purchase of land, whether or not situated in the State,[14] for such occupation or use.

Powers of trustees of land.[1]

Definitions

See s 3 for definitions of: "instrument"; "land".

Notes

1 Section 20 deals with the powers of trustees of land and adopts the opposite approach to that in the Settled Land Acts 1882–1890. Those Acts contained numerous provisions setting out the various powers of the tenant for life and trustees of the settlement. Section 20, instead, gives the trustees full "plenary" powers to deal with the land, ie the power that an absolute owner would have, but subject to the vital qualification that in the exercise of such powers they must act as trustees (see Note 3 below).

2 These are qualifications on the powers of an absolute owner which the trustees would otherwise have.

3 This recognises that the trustees are trustees who, by virtue of their office, must act on behalf of their beneficiaries and not in their own interests. For discussion of the various duties which the courts have long recognised see Keane, *Equity and the Law of Trusts in the Republic of Ireland* (Tottel Publishing, 1998), ch 10; Delany, *Equity and the Law of Trusts in Ireland* (4th edn, Round Hall, 2007), ch 12. Note also the

Law Reform Commission's recommendation for introduction of a statutory duty of care: see LRC 92–2008, ch 3.

4 This would include, eg, restrictions of powers of investment contained in Part I of the Trustee Act 1893, as amended by the Trustee (Authorised Investments) Act 1958 (see Keane, *Equity and the Law of Trusts in the Republic of Ireland* (Tottel Publishing, 1998), paras 10.04–10.06; Delany, *Equity and the Law of Trusts in Ireland* (4th edn, Round Hall, 2007), p 430 *ff*).

5 This refers to the provisions in s 21 relating to overreaching on a conveyance to a purchaser. The purchaser will not obtain a clear title unless, eg, at least two trustees or a trust corporation makes the conveyance in certain cases (see s 21(2)(*a*) and the Notes to that section).

6 This recognises that in imposing various duties on the trustees in the administration of a trust, the courts will often regard various restrictions as applying to how they carry out their duties (see Note 3 above).

7 This recognises that it is open to a settlor or testator to impose express restrictions in the instrument setting up the trust. The result is that the drafter of a trust instrument relating to land must, since 1 December 2009, consider what restrictions, if any, to impose of the plenary powers the trustees will otherwise have. Prior to that date the essential consideration was whether to add to the limited powers contained in the Settled Land Acts 1882–1890 and Trustee Act 1893.

8 The courts have a discretion to impose conditions whenever making an order relating to land, eg, as to how a sale should be carried out (see Wylie and Woods, *Irish Conveyancing Law* (3rd edn, Tottel Publishing, 2005), paras 11.02–11.07).

9 This gives the trustees the powers of an absolute owner, but subject to the qualifications referred to in Notes 3–8 above. Such "plenary" powers would surely inlcude a power to insure trust property: see also *Re Kingham* [1897] 1 IR 170; cf Lyall, "Life Tenants and Insurance" (2008) 13(2) CPLJ 26.

10 Subsection (2) deals with points upon which there has been uncertainty in the past as to the extent of trustees' powers. Arguably the plenary powers conferred by sub-s (1) cover these points, but the view was taken that the qualifications to those powers meant that the points might still be in doubt. In essence, these doubts related to whether it was appropriate or authorised for trustees to use trust funds to allow particular beneficiaries (to the exclusion of others) to occupy trust land or to use trust funds to purchase land for occupation or use by a beneficiary (see *Robinson v Robinson* (1876) IR 10 Eq 189). The Law Reform Commission has recommended that statutory powers of investment should be extended to cover such matters (see LRC 92–2008, paras 8.36–8.38).

11 This not only enables the trustees to allow particular beneficiaries to occupy or use the trust land but also to set the terms of this (see Note 13 below).

12 Other use might be appropriate where the land is not wanted or needed for living in.

13 In allowing such occupation by a particular beneficiary the trustees should have regard to the interests of other beneficiaries and the risk of injustice or unfairness to them. Thus the occupying beneficiary might be required to pay rent or other compensation to be distributed to other beneficiaries.

14 The equivalent provision in England and Wales does not allow purchase of land outside the jurisdiction (see Trustee Act 2000, s 6(3)) whereas that in Northern Ireland (see Trustee Act (NI) 2001, s 8) contains no such restriction. This permits trustees in the North to purchase land in the Republic for occupation or use by beneficiaries. The Law Reform Commission recommended that this approach should be adopted here too: see LRC 92–2008, para 8.37).

---

[54]

21.—(1) Subject to *subsection (3)*,[2] a conveyance[3] to a purchaser[4] of a legal estate[5] or legal interest[6] in land by the person or persons specified in *subsection (2)*[7] overreaches[8] any equitable interest in the land so that it ceases to affect that estate or interest,[9] whether or not the purchaser has notice of the equitable interest.[10]

Overreaching for protection of purchasers.[1]

(2) For the purposes of *subsection (1)*,[11] the "person or persons specified"[12]—

    (*a*)[13] shall be at least two trustees[14] or a trust corporation[15] where the trust land comprises[16]—

        (i) a strict settlement,[17] or

        (ii)[18]a trust, including a trust for sale,[19] of land held for persons by way of succession, or

        (iii) land vested in or held on trust for a minor,[20]

    (*b*) may be a single trustee or owner of the legal estate or interest in the case of any other trust of land.[21]

(3) *Subsection (1)* does not apply to[22]—

    (*a*) any conveyance made for fraudulent purposes[23] of which the purchaser has actual knowledge[24] at the date of the conveyance[25] or to which the purchaser is a party,[26] or

    (*b*) any equitable interest[27]—

        (i) to which the conveyance is expressly made subject,[28] or

        (ii) protected by deposit of documents of title relating to the legal estate or legal interest,[29] or

        (iii) in the case of a trust coming within *subsection (2)(b)*,[30] protected by registration prior to the date of the conveyance[31] or taking effect as a burden coming within section 72(1)*(j)* of the Act of 1964[32] (or, in the case of unregistered land, which would take effect as such a burden if the land were registered land).[33]

(4) In *subsection (3)(b)(iii)*, "registration" means registration in the Registry of Deeds[34] or Land Registry,[35] as appropriate.

(5) Where an equitable interest is overreached under this section it attaches to the proceeds arising from the conveyance[36] and effect shall be given to it accordingly.[37]

(6) Nothing in this section affects the operation of the Act of 1976.[38]

Definitions

See s 3 for definitions of: "Act of 1964"; "Act of 1976"; "conveyance"; "court"; "land"; "Land Registry"; "legal estate"; "legal interest"; "notice"; "purchaser"; "registered land"; "Registry of Deeds"; "strict settlement"; "trust corporation"; "trust of land"; "unregistered land".

Notes

1   Section 21 is linked, in particular, to s 11 and the distinction it draws between legal estates and interests on the one hand and equitable interests (see the Notes to that section). This distinction was particularly important in determining the priorities between competing claims to land and was bound up with the equitable doctrine of notice. A central part of that doctrine was the principle that a *bona fide* purchaser for value of a legal estate or interest in land would take free of any prior equitable interest (or, to put it another way, a conveyance to such a purchaser would "overreach" any existing equitable interest). It is important to note, however, that the doctrine of notice did not have as much significance in Ireland as it did in other jurisdictions because of the operation of the registration of deeds system introduced by the Registration of Deeds Act (Ir) 1707 (now replaced by Part 3 of the Registration of Deeds and Title Act 2006). Under that system priority between interests in land (whether legal or equitable) is governed by whether or not the deed creating them was registered rather than the doctrine of notice. Furthermore, notice is generally irrelevant to registered land transactions, where priority is governed more by whether or not interests have been registered or, in the case of equitable interests, protected by a caution or inhibition entered in the register. If this has not been done, a transferee will take free of those interests (unless they are burdens affecting registered land without registration). (See Lyall, *Land Law in Ireland* (2nd edn, Round Hall, 2000), pp 145–150 and 872–877; Wylie, *Irish Land Law* (3rd edn, Tottel Publishing, 1997), paras 3.084–3.090; Fitzgerald, *Land Registry Practice* (2nd edn, Round Hall Press, 1995), chs 10 and 13.) Furthermore, the concept of "overreaching" was given a special significance by the Settled Land Acts 1882– 1890 (in fact, the actual expression was not used in the Acts), under which a sale of land carried out under those Acts would give the purchaser a clean title shorn of the interests created by the settlement or trust. Instead those interests would thereafter attach to the capital money raised by the sale (the purchase money). The crucial

point about this meaning of "overreaching" is that, provided the mechanism laid down by the Acts was used (payment of the purchase money to trustees of the settlement), the purchaser still obtained a good title to the land, even though he or she was fully aware of the various interests created by the previous settlement or trust. To that extent, the 1882–1890 Acts did away with the doctrine of notice – it was irrelevant to sales under those Acts (see Lyall, *Land Law in Ireland* (2nd edn, Round Hall, 2000), pp 410 and 870–871; Wylie, *Irish Land Law* (3rd edn, Tottel Publishing, 1997), paras 8.041–8.042). The Law Reform Commission took the view that overreaching in this sense should be extended to cover all conveyances or transfers of land, in order to facilitate conveyancing and give greater protection to purchasers against equitable interests which they might have difficulty in discovering. The Commission drew attention, in particular, to the risk that equitable interests would be undocumented or "hidden" because those entitled (who might themselves not even be aware of their entitlement) would be relying upon equitable doctrines like resulting or constructive trusts or proprietary estoppel (see *Consultation Paper on Reform and Modernisation of Land Law and Conveyancing Law* (LRC CP 34–2004), paras 4.23–4.24 and 6.17–6.20). The Bill attached to the Commission's subsequent Report (LRC 74–2005) and 2006 Bill introduced to the Seanad contained such a wide provision. However, as noted below, it was amended at the Dáil Select Committee Stage so as to restrict the overreaching provision (see Note 32 below).

2 Subsection (3) specifies situations where the general overreaching of equitable interests does not apply.

3 Note that a "conveyance" includes a transfer of registered land, as well as various transactions not involving a sale, such as leases and mortgages (see Notes 18–20 to s 3).

4 Note that, as with a conveyance (see Note 3 above), a "purchaser" includes other persons acquiring an interest in land, such as lessees and mortgagees (see Notes 75 and 76 to s 3). Furthermore, it means such a person acquiring the interest for "valuable consideration" (see Note 95 to s 3). Note that there is no reference to "good faith" or "notice" in the s 3 definitions. Those concepts are largely displaced by s 21, but not entirely (see Note 23 below).

5 As to the meaning of this, see s 11(1) and (2) (and the Notes to that section).

6 As to the meaning of this, see s 11(4) (and the Notes to that section).

7 Subsection (2) specifies the conveyances (and by whom they must be made) which will overreach equitable interests in favour of a purchaser of a legal estate of interest for valuable consideration (whether or not that purchaser has notice of those interests).

8 This introduces the concept of "overreaching" expressly (see Note 1 above).

9 This specifies what is meant by "overreaches" and there is further clarification in sub-s (5) (see Note 36 below).

10 This confirms that s 21 widens the scope of the concept of overreaching as it applied under the Settled Land Acts 1882–1890 (see Note 1 above) and thereby greatly reduces the significance of the doctrine of notice in conveyancing after 1 December 2009 (see Note 21 below).

11 That is for determining when equitable interests are overreached on a conveyance of land to a purchaser of a legal estate or interest for valuable considerable.

12 These are the grantors of conveyances which overreach equitable interests.

13 Paragraph (*a*) replaces the overreaching provisions in the Settled Land Acts 1882–1890 (see Note 1 above) and largely replicates them.

14 This was the essential requirement under the 1882–1890 Acts (see s 39(1) of the Settled Land Act 1882). Note, however, that s 39(1) allowed the settlement to authorise receipt of capital money by one trustee. Section 21 drops this but introduces the alternative of a conveyance by a trust corporation (see Note 15 below). The view was taken that protection of owners of equitable interests (particularly future interests) required at least two trustees to agree to the overreaching transaction (see the Law Reform Commission's Report LRC 92–2008, paras 2.16–2.22).

15 The Law Reform Commission recommended introduction of this alternative (see *Consultation Paper on Trust Law: General Proposals* (LRC CP 35-2005), paras 1.46–1.87 and the subsequent Report (LRC 92-2008), paras 2.16–2.22). A "trust corporation" has the meaning given by s 30(4) of the Succession Act 1965 and includes institutions like banks which are authorised to undertake trust business.

16 These categories largely comprise the situations where settled land would have existed for the purposes of the Settled Land Acts 1882–1890 or would have been caught by the provisions of those Acts (eg trusts for sale).

17 This was the traditional family settlement limiting land to persons in succession without the interposition of trustees (see s 18(1)(*a*) and Notes 5–12 to that section).

18 This category includes post-1 December 2009 trusts of land coming within Part 4, but only where they involve a "settlement", ie a succession of beneficial interests.

19 This confirms that the same rule applies to trusts for sale. One of the problems with the Settled Land Acts 1882–1890 was the inconsistent treatment of trusts for sale (see Lyall, *Land Law in Ireland* (2nd edn, Round Hall, 2000), pp 412–414; Wylie, *Irish Land Law* (3rd edn, Tottel Publishing, 1997), paras 8.011–8.015).

20 This was another case where the land was treated as settled land under the 1882–1890 Acts and involves a trust of land under Part 4 since 1 December 2009 (see s 18(1)(*c*) and Notes 17–19 to that section).

21 Paragraph (*b*) contains the important extension of the concept of overreaching equitable interests regardless of the doctrine of notice (see Notes 1, 4 and 7 above). It includes cases where a legal owner of the land is a constructive trustee or is regarded as holding it subject to an "equity" arising under the doctrine of estoppel. Such "hidden" equitable interests or equities will now be overreached unless they are protected by the provisions of sub-s (3) (see Note 1 above and Notes to that subsection below).

22 Subsection (3) lists situations where equitable interests will not be overreached on a conveyance of a legal estate or interest to a purchaser for valuable consideration.

23 Paragraph (*a*) recognises the long-established principle that "fraud unravels all". A purchaser will not obtain a good title, nor will equitable interests be overreached, where he or she is aware of the fraudulent purpose or a party to it. The courts have jurisdiction to set aside deeds on the ground of fraud (see in relation to fraud on

creditors s 74 and the Notes to that section). In the present concept fraud would amount to deliberate actions by trustees of land or the holder of the legal title to deprive beneficiaries or persons entitled to any equitable interest of their interest. An example would be where there is an intention from the outset to spend the proceeds of a sale on themselves or otherwise dispose of them instead of holding or investing them for the beneficiaries.

24 Note that for overreaching not to operate in favour of a purchaser he or she must have "actual knowledge" – constructive notice as defined by s 86 is not enough (see the Notes to that section).

25 Knowledge acquired after the date of the conveyance will not affect overreaching.

26 No overreaching will occur where the purchaser is a party to the fraud being perpetrated by the grantor or grantors of the conveyance (see Note 23 above).

27 Section 21 is concerned with overreaching equitable interests on a conveyance of a legal estate or interest in land (see Notes 1, 4, 7 and 10 above).

28 Clearly a purchaser should not take free of any interest to which the conveyance is expressly made subject – the assumption in such cases is that the purchaser will continue to be bound by that interest and the sale will be closed on that basis.

29 This recognises the longstanding practice in Ireland of creating equitable mortgages by deposit of title documents (title deeds in respect of unregistered land and the land certificate or a charge certificate in respect of registered land) (see Lyall, *Land Law in Ireland* (2nd edn, Round Hall, 2000), pp 783–785; Wylie, *Irish Land Law* (3rd edn, Tottel Publishing, 1997), paras 12.43–12.46). This practice is not as common as it used to be (in more recent times banks and other lending institutions have tended to confine it to employees) and has become even less common since s 73 of the Registration of Deeds and Title Act 2006 provided that the Property Registration Authority would cease to issue land certificates and charge certificates (this has operated since 1 January 2007: see Registration of Deeds and Title Act 2006 (Commencement) (No 2) Order 2006 (SI 511/2006)). Nevertheless, the view was taken that protection of existing deposits should be continued according to the previous law. Such a deposit would usually mean that the purchaser or purchaser's solicitor would have actual or constructive notice of the existence of the equitable mortgage (see Lyall, *Land Law in Ireland* (2nd edn, Round Hall, 2000), pp 125–126 and 146; Wylie, *Irish Land Law* (3rd edn, Tottel Publishing, 1997), paras 13.154–13.155). Under s 73(2) of the 2006 Act such certificates cease to have any force or effect on the expiration of 3 years after commencement of that provision, ie from 1 January 2010. In order to protect an equitable mortgage created by deposit of such certificates a lien should be registered by 31 December 2009 as a s 69 (of the Registration of Title Act 1964) burden: see s 73(3) of the 2006 Act.

30 Subparagraph (iii) is dealing with the extension of the principle of overreaching to all conveyances by a trustee or legal owner of land (apart from the traditional family settlement or trust situation formally covered by the Settled Land Acts 1882–1890: see Notes 1 and 21 above). The Law Reform Commission took the view that in such cases the burden should be put on those entitled to equitable interests to protect themselves by registration, so that the interests would no longer be "hidden" and purchasers would no longer run the risk of not discovering them. It is that risk which leads to open-ended enquiries or requisitions on title raised on behalf of purchasers

(see Wylie and Woods, *Irish Conveyancing Law* (3rd edn, Tottel Publishing, 2005), para 16.23). The expectation was that such enquiries or requisitions would no longer be necessary – instead purchasers' solicitors would simply have to make the appropriate registry search (see Note 31 below); if that did not disclose the interest in question, it would be overreached. This principle remains in s 21 but it was amended during the Bill's passage through the Oireachtas so as to insert an important qualification (see Note 32 below).

31 The equitable interest in question must have been protected by registration of the appropriate form in the Registry of Deeds (in the case of unregistered land) or Land Registry (in the case of registered land) (see sub-s (4) and the Notes to it), otherwise it will be overreached under sub-s (1). Such registration is not necessary, however, where the person entitled to the equitable interest is also in actual occupation of the land (see Notes 32 and 33 below).

32 The original Bill did not contain this exception and, as passed by the Seanad, actually provided for the repeal of s 72(1)(j) of the 1964 Act. It had long been settled that a person was not protected by virtue of being in actual occupation of the land unless they also had a "right" to the land, ie at the very least an equitable interest or claim to it (see Fitzgerald, *Land Registry Practice* (2nd edn, Round Hall Press, 1995), pp 223–226; Wylie and Woods, *Irish Conveyancing Law* (3rd edn, Tottel Publishing, 2005), para 16.23). The original view was that, instead, the requirement to protect the interest by registration should apply to such persons as it applied to other holders or claimants to equitable interests. However, strong representations were made by the Property Registration Authority for retention of s 72(1)(j) on the ground that it was not infrequently relied upon to rectify errors in registration (see *Boyle v Connaughton* [2000] IEHC 28; Breen, "Registration of Title and Overriding Interests – Another Crack in the Mirror?" (2000) 5(3) CPLJ 52; see also Mee, "The Land and Conveyancing Law Reform Bill 2006: Observations on the Law Reform Process and a Critique of Selected Provisions" (2006) 11 (3) CPLJ 67.) The result was that this amendment was made to subparagraph (iii) at the Dáil Select Committee Stage.

33 Once the decision was made to retain s 72(1)(j) of the 1964 Act, the view was taken that it was not appropriate to have a different rule for unregistered land. This means that any person entitled to an equitable interest in either registered or unregistered land who is also in "actual occupation" of the land continues to be protected by the doctrine of notice and does not have to register anything in order to prevent the interest being overreached on a conveyance to a purchaser for valuable consideration.

34 See Registration of Deeds (No 2) Rules 2009 (SI 457/2009).

35 See Land Registration (No 2) Rules 2009 (SI 456/2009).

36 This provision is the corollary of sub-s (1) and spells out the effect of overreaching. It adapts more generally the provisions relating to capital money in the Settled Land Acts 1882–1890 (see Note 1 above). The "proceeds" covers whatever form the valuable consideration for the purchase takes (note the definition of "purchaser" in s 3 and Notes 75, 76 and 95 to that section) so that in the case of a sale by exchange of lands, the equitable interest will attach to the exchanged land conveyed by the

purchaser to the trustee or legal owner conveying the land previously subject to the equitable interest.

37 This confirms that overreaching does not destroy the equitable interest or claim but rather transfers it to the proceeds of the sale or other disposition for valuable consideration. The trustee or vendor holds those proceeds (or property forming the consideration; see Note 36 above) subject to the equitable interest.

38 This is a saving relating to family homes protected by the Family Home Protection Act 1976, under which the consent of a "non-owning" spouse is needed to any conveyance by the "owning" spouse (see Wylie and Woods, *Irish Conveyancing Law* (3rd edn, Tottel Publishing, 2005), paras16.48–16.57).

[55]

22.—(1) Any person having an interest[2] in a trust of land,[3] or a person acting on behalf of such a person, may apply to the court in a summary manner[4] for an order to resolve a dispute[5] between the[6]—

Resolution of disputes.[1]

(*a*)   trustees themselves, or

(*b*)   beneficiaries themselves, or

(*c*)   trustees and beneficiaries, or

(*d*)   trustees or beneficiaries and other persons interested, in relation to any matter concerning the—

   (i)   performance of their functions by the trustees,[7] or

   (ii)   nature or extent of any beneficial or other interest in the land,[8] or

   (iii)   other operation of the trust.[9]

(2) Subject to *subsection (3)*,[10] in determining an application under *subsection (1)*[11] the court may make whatever order[12] and direct whatever inquiries[13] it thinks fit in the circumstances of the case.[14]

(3) In considering an application under *subsection (1)(i) and (iii)*[15] the court shall have regard to[16] the interests of the beneficiaries as a whole[17] and, subject to these,[18] to[19]—

(*a*)   the purposes which the trust of land is intended to achieve,[20]

(*b*)   the interests of any minor or other beneficiary subject to any incapacity,[21]

(*c*)   the interests of any secured creditor of any beneficiary,[22]

(*d*)   any other matter which the court considers relevant.[23]

(4) In *subsection (1)*, "person having an interest" includes a mortgagee or other secured creditor,[24] a judgment mortgagee[25] or a trustee.[26]

(5) Nothing in this section affects the jurisdiction of the court under section 36 of the Act of 1995.[27]

Definitions

See s 3 for definitions of: "Act of 1995"; "court"; "land"; "trust of land".

Notes

1 This section implements the Law Reform Commission's recommendation that there should be a mechanism for resolution of disputes concerning trusts of land coming within Part 4 (see *Consultation Paper on Reform of Land Law and Conveyancing Law* (LRC CP 34–2004), paras 4.25–4.26). It enables any person interested in such a trust to apply to the Circuit or High Court (depending on their jurisdictional limits: see the definition of "court" in s 3 and Notes 21–23 to that section).

2 This includes a wide range of persons: see sub-s (4) and the Notes to it below.

3 This is defined by s 18(1) (see the Notes to that section).

4 As to such applications rules of court will be made.

5 As to the court's discretion as to orders see sub-s (2) and the Notes to it below.

6 Paragraphs *(a)*–*(d)* list various scenarios in which disputes may arise as between different persons having interests in land held on trust, involving either just those directly interested (the trustees and the beneficiaries) or those directly interested and other persons interested. Section 22 does not apply to disputes confined to persons not directly involved, eg, as between creditors but not involving the trustees or beneficiaries.

7 This would include a dispute concerning how the trustees exercise their plenary powers under s 20(1) or powers in respect of occupation or use of the land by a particular beneficiary under s 20(2) (see the Notes to that section).

8 This would include resolution of a claim by a person to a beneficial interest under a resulting or constructive trust and the doctrine of proprietary estoppel. The latter doctrine, if successfully invoked, gives rise to an "equity" in respect of which the court has a discretion as to how it should be satisfied. That will often involve declaring that the successful claimant has a beneficial interest in the land in question, but sometimes the court will take the view that some "other interest" might be more appropriate (eg a personal right to remain on the land for a limited period amounting to a right of residence in the form of a licence to occupy) (see Delany, *Equity and the Law of Trusts in Ireland* (3rd edn, Round Hall, 2003), pp 651–656).

9 This is a "catch-all" provision for matters relating to operation of the trust not covered by paragraphs (i) and (ii). This would include disputes as between the beneficiaries themselves or disputes involving other persons, such as creditors, which do not relate to matters coming within these paragraphs.

10 The discretion conferred by sub-s (2) is qualified by sub-s (3) (see the Notes to it below) in the sense that, in exercising it, the court must have regard to the matters referred to in that subsection.

11 See Note 4 above.

12 What order is made will obviously depend upon the nature of the dispute, the parties to it and the remedy sought in the application. However, the court's discretion is wide and it is free to make an order giving a remedy other than any sought by the parties.

13 Given the wide range of matters which might give rise to a dispute and the different parties who might be involved it will often be the case that the court will require further information than that furnished initially in the proceedings.

14 This gives the court wide discretion, but subject to sub-s (3).

15 This does not now refer to paragraph (ii) of sub-s (1) because the view was taken during the Bill's passage through the Seanad that different considerations arise in respect of issues coming within that paragraph. It concerns whether an applicant has an interest of some kind in the land and its extent and that will be determined by application of the principles relating to doctrines like resulting and constructive trusts and proprietary estoppel. Some of the considerations which the court is obliged to have regard to under sub-s (3) would be inappropriate to such issues (eg, the interests of a secured creditor). This amendment was made at the Seanad Committee Stage.

16 The court is required to have regard to the specified matters, but, having done that, the weight to put on them in exercising its discretion as to the order to be made under sub-s (3) lies entirely with the court.

17 This is the overriding consideration which the court must have regard to.

18 This confirms the point made in Note 17 above.

19 The weight to be put on the matters listed here is a matter for the court (see Note 16 above).

20 This is particularly relevant to an express trust and to a dispute as between the trustees and beneficiaries relating to how the trust property is dealt with, particularly where that property is occupied or used by one or more beneficiaries as their home or place of business. It may also be relevant in cases of a trust arising by way of a constructive trust or proprietary estoppel, where the applicant is arguing that the legal owner (trustee) acquired property to be occupied or used by the applicant as well.

21 This recognises that special considerations may arise from the need to protect those lacking the capacity to protect themselves. Thus selling the home of children may not be appropriate. The word "any" indicates that there is obviously no need to consider this matter if there are no such persons.

22 Note that the interests of creditors are required to be taken into account only where they are secured on the beneficiary's interest in the land. A "beneficiary" must be one with an interest under the trust of land and a creditor's interest would only be relevant to a dispute concerning that beneficiary and the operation of the trust (see sub-s (1) and the Notes to it above) if the debt was secured on that interest. Note again the word "any" (see Note 21 above).

23 This makes it clear that the court is free to conclude that other matters should be considered in exercising its discretion, in addition to the matters listed in paragraphs (*a*)–(*c*).

24 This would include the holder of a lien or charge not amounting to a mortgage (see Lyall, *Land Law in Ireland* (2nd edn, Round Hall, 2000), pp 773–775; Wylie, *Irish Land Law* (3rd edn, Tottel Publishing, 1997), paras 12.14–12.20); Johnston, *Banking and Security Law in Ireland* (Tottel Publishing, 1998), ch 17).

25 This was not in the original Bill as introduced to the Seanad because the definition of "mortgage" in that version included a "judgment mortgage". The view was taken subsequently that this did not recognise sufficiently the nature of judgment mortgages (and the distinction from ordinary mortgages) and so the definition in s 3 was amended to delete the reference to a "judgment mortgage" at the Seanad Committee Stage. The consequential amendment to insert a reference to such mortgages in s 21 was made at the Dáil Committee Stage.

26 This recognises that a trustee may also have an equitable interest in the land. This is often the case where the legal owner of land is held to be subject to a constructive trust or an equitable interest in some other person who has invoked the doctrine of proprietary estoppel. The land is held on trust for both the legal owner and some other person for shares deemed appropriate by the court (see Keane, *Equity and the Law of Trusts in the Republic of Ireland* (Tottel Publishing, 1998), chs 13 and 28; Delany, *Equity and the Law of Trusts in Ireland* (4th edn, Round Hall, 2007), chs 8 and 17).

27 This is a saving for the jurisdiction of the court to determine questions between spouses in relation to property now contained in s 36 of the Family Law Act 1995.

[56]

PART 5[1]
VARIATION OF TRUSTS[2]

Notes

1 Part 5 implements the Law Reform Commission's recommendation for introduction of variation of trusts legislation similar to that which has existed for decades in other jurisdictions, including England and Wales (see Variation of Trusts Act 1958) and Northern Ireland (see Variation of Trusts Acts (NI) 1958): see *Report on Variation of Trusts* (LRC 63–2000). This recommendation was prompted by the Commission's recommendation made at the same time in another Report (*Report on the Rule against Perpetuities and Cognate Rules* (LRC 62–2000)), which was published at the same time, for the abolition of the rule against perpetuities. That other Report is implemented by Part 3 (see the Notes to that Part). The essential point being made by the Commission was that the abolition of that rule might encourage some settlors and testators to set up a trust likely to last for a very long time. Future generations of beneficiaries might then find themselves "locked into" an arrangement which proved

over time very unsuitable or inconvenient, if not positively harmful financially, socially or otherwise. As the scope for obtaining a variation under existing law was very limited the Commission recommended introduction of a new jurisdiction similar to that adopted in most other jurisdictions recognising trusts. Part 5 was not in the original Bill and it was contemplated that it would be included in separate legislation. For that reason, it was anticipated that Part 3 of the Act would not be brought into force until the separate legislation was also enacted and could be brought into force at the same time. In the event the decision was taken at a late stage to include the variation of trusts provision in the Bill and Part 5 was inserted at the Dáil Select Committee Stage. Both Parts 3 and 5 come into force on 1 December 2009 (see the Notes to s 2).

2   As the Commission pointed out, the circumstances where a variation of an existing trust could be made were strictly limited. Judicial powers were limited to special, and comparatively rare, cases such as where the court could exercise "salvage" or "compromise" jurisdiction or could direct maintenance out of income supposed to be accumulated. Statutory powers under the Trustee Act 1893 are very limited and powers to make property adjustment orders under family law legislation are confined to cases of separation and divorce. It is, of course, always possible for beneficiaries to vary the trust or even put an end to it altogether under the rule in *Saunders v Vautier* (1841) Cr & Ph 240, but there is a fundamental limitation to that rule. This is that the beneficiaries can only so act if they are all of full capacity and together are entitled to the entire beneficial interests under the trust. In so acting they must all agree to the variations. All too often, however, beneficiaries will not be of full capacity (and therefore not capable of giving binding consent to a variation) and some may not even be born yet or identified because some contingency still has to be met. Some beneficiaries may have disappeared. In all such cases it is impossible to invoke the rule in *Saunders v Vautier* and variation of trusts legislation is designed to get round this problem. The essential principle is that the court is given jurisdiction to approve a variation of a trust on behalf of those beneficiaries who, for some reason or other, cannot agree to it themselves. That is usually the limit of the court's jurisdiction. It follows that the variation must usually be agreed to by any beneficiary who is in a position to agree on his or her own behalf (see Notes 17–27 to s 23 below). If that agreement is not forthcoming there would be no point in making an application to the court under Part 5.

Although Part 5 is clearly based on the draft provisions appended to the Commission's Report (LRC 63–2000 Appendix A) it is important to note that there are some important differences in the enacted version. Attention is drawn to these in the Notes to ss 23 and 25 below. The most significant difference is that under s 24 a court here will not be able to approve a variation where the Revenue Commissioners satisfy it that substantial motivation is tax avoidance. This is in marked contrast to the legislation in the vast majority of other jurisdictions, where many applications are made for the purposes of tax planning (see further Note 37 to s 24 below). The Commission based its recommendations and draft legislation on the English Variation of Trusts Act 1958, but, in doing so, suggested a number of changes to deal with controversial points which have arisen in relation to that Act. Attention is drawn to these in the Notes below.

Finally, it should be noted that although the heading uses the word "Variation", Part 5 covers approval of arrangements relating to trusts that might be regarded as going beyond a "variation" as that word is commonly understood, eg, revoking the trust altogether or resettling it (see Notes 11–13 to 23 below).

---

[57]

Interpretation of *Part 5*.[1]

23.—In this Part—

> "appropriate person",[2] in relation to a relevant trust,[3] means—
>
> (*a*) a trustee[4] of, or a beneficiary[5] under, the trust,[6] or
>
> (*b*) any other person that the court, to which the application concerned under *section 24* is made, considers appropriate;[7]
>
> "arrangement",[8] in relation to a relevant trust,[9] means an arrangement[10]—
>
> (*a*) varying,[11] revoking[12] or resettling[13] the trust, or[14]
>
> (*b*) varying, enlarging, adding to or restricting[15] the powers of the trustees under the trust to manage or administer the property the subject of the trust;[16]
>
> "relevant person",[17] in relation to a relevant trust,[18] means[19]—
>
> (*a*)[20]a person who has a vested or contingent interest[21] under the trust but who is incapable of assenting[22] to an arrangement by reason of lack of capacity (whether by reason of minority or absence of mental capacity[23]),
>
> (*b*) an unborn person,[24]
>
> (*c*) a person whose identity, existence or whereabouts cannot be established by taking reasonable measures,[25] or
>
> (*d*)[26]a person who has a contingent interest under the trust but who does not fall within *paragraph (a)*;[27]
>
> "relevant trust"[28]—
>
> (*a*)[29]subject to *paragraph (b)*,[30] means a trust arising, whether before, on or after the commencement of this section,[31] under a will, settlement or other disposition,[32]
>
> (*b*) does not include[33]—

(i) a trust created for a charitable purpose within the meaning of the Charities Acts 1961 and 1973 and the Charities Act 2009,[34]

(ii) an occupational pension scheme within the meaning of the Pensions Act 1990 established under a trust,[35]

(iii)[36] a trust created by a British statute,[37]

(iv) a trust created by a Saorstát Éireann statute,[38] or

(v) a trust created by an Act of the Oireachtas, whether passed before, on or after the commencement of this section.

Definitions

See s 3 for definition of: "court".

Notes

1   This section, through its various definitions, deals with several aspects of the court's new jurisdiction to "vary" trusts, such as who can make an application to the court, the scope of an order the court can make on such an application, on whose behalf the court can approve the variation and what trusts are excluded from this jurisdiction.

2   This defines the persons entitled to apply to the court for approval of a variation "arrangement" under s 24 (see the Notes to that section). The Law Reform Commission took the view that the category of persons entitled to make applications should be an inclusive one, avoiding too much rigidity in any list (see LRC 63–2000, paras 7.10–7.11).

3   This is defined later in s 23 and excludes certain types of trust from the variation jurisdiction (see Notes 33–38 below).

4   This refers to any of the trustees of the trust sought to be varied and in respect of which an application for approval is made under s 24.

5   Similarly this refers to a beneficiary of such a trust (see Note 4 above). This is likely to be a beneficiary of full age and capacity seeking approval on behalf of other beneficiaries who cannot agree to the variation on their own behalf. However, an application might be made directly by a beneficiary lacking capacity acting through some other person not otherwise connected with the trust but who is authorised to act on that person's behalf, eg the committee of a ward of court (see LRC 63–2000, para 7.11).

6   This refers to the trust in respect of which an application under s 24 is made.

7   This gives the court jurisdiction to exercise its powers on the basis of an application by someone other than a trustee or beneficiary of the trust in question. Since the application must relate to a particular trust, the court will presumably have to be satisfied that the applicant has some connection with that trust (see Note 5 above). The Law Reform Commission drew attention to the case of a beneficiary who is physically or mentally incapacitated but is not a ward of court for whom the

committee can act (see Note 5 above). In such case a member of the family or carer may wish to make the application (see LRC 63–2000, para 7.11). Note that successive applications may be made (see Note 4 to s 24).

8 This is the expression used in s 24 to describe the variation proposal or scheme which must be specified in the application under that section (see Note 5 to that section). It adopts the expression used in the English 1958 Act (see LRC 63–2000, paras 3.06–3.07).

9 See Notes 3 above and 28–38 below.

10 The Commission pointed out that "arrangement" is wider than "agreement" and does not imply that all those interested in the trust necessarily agree with it, eg an application could be made by a beneficiary which the trustees do not approve of (see *Re Steed's Will Trusts* [1960] Ch 407). No doubt the court will take the trustees' view into account in exercising its discretion whether to approve the arrangement in such cases, especially where it involves varying their powers of management or administration (see Notes 15–16 below). Note that the definition here comprises two legs (paragraphs (*a*) and (*b*)) – the Commission recommended keeping these matters more clearly separate than was done in the English 1958 Act (see LRC 63–2000, paras 2.08–3.10).

11 It is clear from the wording which follows that the court's jurisdiction is not confined to "varying" in a narrow sense. The Law Reform Commission was anxious to avoid the limitations which English judges put on the wording "varying or revoking" in the 1958 Act. It was, perhaps, somewhat surprising that the reference to "revoking" was not taken to indicate that the court could approve an arrangement which involved substantial changes amounting to a "resettlement" or upsetting the basic "substratum" of the trust (see *Re Ball's Settlement Trusts* [1968] 1 WLR 899; *Allen v Distiller Co (Biochemicals) Ltd* [1974] 2 WLR 481). For this reason it recommended inclusion of a specific reference to resettling (see LRC 63–2000, paras 3.17–3.19 and Note 13 below).

12 This would involve putting an end to the existing trust, not necessarily with a view to setting up a new one. It has long been recognised that under the rule in *Saunders v Vautier* (1841) Cr & Ph 240 beneficiaries who collectively are entitled to the entire interest can call upon the trustees to hand the trust property over to them and thereby put an end to the trust (see Delany, *Equity and the Law of Trusts in Ireland* (4th edn, Round Hall, 2007), p 479). Part 5 is designed partly to enable the beneficiaries to do what they could under that rule if they were all of full capacity (see Note 2 to Part 5 above).

13 This makes it clear that the court may approve an arrangement which involves a substantial or fundamental change to the existing trust (see Note 11 above).

14 This makes it clear that an application may be made for a variation under this second limb as an alternative, ie relating to the trustees' powers of management or administration. As pointed out above, the Commission was keen not to conflate these alternatives (see Note 10). There is no reason why a particular application should not propose variations which come within both paragraph (*a*) and paragraph (*b*).

15 The English 1958 Act refers simply to "enlarging" which the Commission regarded as too restricting (eg it might be construed as referring to changes to existing powers

rather than adding news ones). It recommended the wider wording used here (see LRC 63–2000, paras 3.20–3.21).

16 The Commission took the view this was phraseology which had a "generally accepted meaning", as exhibited by English case law (such as *Re Steed's Will Trusts* [1960] Ch 407; *Re Lister's Will Trusts* [1962] 1 WLR 144; *Re Cooper's Settlement* [1962] Ch 826; see also *Re Downshire's Settlement Trusts* [1953] Ch 218). See LRC 63–2000, paras 3.22–3.23.

17 This definition indicates the categories of persons for the benefit of whom the court has jurisdiction to approve a variation arrangement. Any other category must agree to the variation on its own behalf and a refusal to do so will prevent any variation being made (see Note 9 to s 24 below). Note that all the persons covered are beneficiaries, actual or potential, entitled under a trust sought to be varied.

18 See further Notes 28–38 below.

19 Note that approval can be given where a person comes within any of these alternatives, but it is possible that a particular person may come within more than one, eg, a person who comes within both paragraphs (*c*) and (*d*). The Commission took the view that these provisions were designed to cover two broad categories of persons – (1) those whose consent could not be given by themselves because of their personal circumstances; and (2) those whose interests were so conditional that it was not worth the time and trouble of securing their consent and who should not have a veto on an arrangement others agreed to. Paragraphs (*a*)–(*c*) cover category (1); paragraph (*d*) covers category (2).

20 Paragraph (*a*) covers beneficiaries who cannot agree to a variation because they lack the capacity to enter into a binding agreement.

21 As to this distinction see Lyall, *Land Law in Ireland* (2nd edn, Round Hall, 2000), pp 273–275; Wylie, *Irish Land Law* (3rd edn, Tottel Publishing, 1997), paras 5.008–5.011.

22 The Commission preferred this to "consenting" on the basis that "assenting" does not preclude approval of an existing arrangement, whereas "consent" might be taken to suggest that no arrangement is possible without such consent: see LRC 63–2000, para 5.04 (fn 4).

23 Note that lack of capacity is limited to these – the Commission's draft used the phrase "infancy or other incapacity". However, other persons who may lack capacity to enter into a binding contract are unlikely to be relevant, such as corporations with limited powers or intoxicated persons (see McDermott, *Contract Law* (Tottel Publishing, 2001), ch 17). It is debatable whether prisoners are still subject to incapacity, especially following the repeal of the Forfeiture Act 1870 by the Criminal Law Act 1997 (see McDermott, paras 17.41–17.43).

24 Clearly such a potential beneficiary could not agree to a variation of a trust under which they would become entitled to an interest on birth.

25 The Commission recommended this extension of the English 1958 Act's provisions to cover "missing" or "unknown" beneficiaries, but was concerned to concentrate on their identity etc and to rule out the court acting where insufficient "industry, resources, etc." had been deployed in trying to find them (see LRC 63–2000, paras 5.03–5.04).

26 The Commission discussed at length how far the court should be able to approve a variation on behalf of a fully competent beneficiary who was being "recalcitrant" and, in effect, force through a variation against that individual's wishes. The Commission concluded that this could be justified only in the strictly limited case where the beneficiary's interest was contingent only, ie neither vested in possession nor vested in interest. Being contingent only such an interest may never materialise because the contingency is never satisfied. The Commission considered the convoluted provision in the English 1958 Act (s 1 (b)), which has given rise to much debate (see *Knocker v Youle* [1986] 2 All ER 914; *Re Moncrieff's Settlement Trusts* [1962] 1 WLR 1344) and rejected it, preferring the simple formulation in paragraph (*d*).

27 This makes it clear that paragraph (*d*) covers a fully competent beneficiary, ie an adult without any mental incapacity. Note that, as with all the categories of "relevant person", the court can only approve a variation if satisfied that it is for the benefit of that person (see Note 7 to s 24). Note also that the Commission took the view that there was no need in the Irish context for another category covered by the English 1958 Act – a person entitled to a discretionary interest under a "protective" trust (s 1(d)). Our law does not have the special legislation relating to such trusts as exists in England and Northern Ireland (Delany, *Equity and the Law of Trusts in Ireland* (4th edn, Round Hall, 2007), p 70; Wylie, *Irish Land Law* (3rd edn, Tottel Publishing, 1997), paras 9.083–9.084).

28 This definition specifies the trusts in respect of which an application can be made to the court for approval of a variation arrangement under s 24 and those which are excluded.

29 Paragraph (*a*) specifies the trusts in respect of which applications under s 24 can be made. Note that this paragraph excludes trusts arising by implication or operation of law, such as resulting and constructive trusts. The Commission took the view that it was inappropriate for the variation jurisdiction to extend to such trusts, as they usually involve situations and policy needs far removed from the "usual field" of trusts set up by a settlement or will (see LRC 63–2000, paras 6.01–6.03). On the other hand, the Commission took the view that there was no need to exclude any category of revocable trust (para 6.04).

30 Paragraph (*b*) specifies a number of other exclusions of trusts, ie trusts in respect of which an application cannot be made under s 24.

31 Note that Part 5 applies to trusts arising before or on 1 December 2009, as well as ones arising after that date. Since the basis on which an approval to a variation arrangement is given by the court under s 24 is that it is for the relevant person's benefit (see Note 7 to that section), the Commission took the view that there was no constitutional "flaw" in making the provisions retrospective (LRC 63–2000, paras 6.23–6.24). Note that the "benefit" rule applies equally to a case where the court approves on behalf of a "recalcitrant" beneficiary (see Note 26 above). On the same basis it is difficult to see how the legislation could be successfully challenged on human rights grounds.

32 This wording, as recommended by the Commission (LRC 63–2000, p 49), makes it clear that the jurisdiction conferred by Part 5 is confined to trusts created expressly and does not apply to those arising by implication or imposed by the courts through

application of equitable doctrines like constructive trusts and proprietary estoppel (see Note 29 above). The Commission also took the view that application of Part 5 to "strict settlements" (generally settlements creating a succession of interests in land *without* the interposition of a trust: see ss 18(1)(*a*) and 19(1)(*a*) of the Act and the Notes to those sections) was "superfluous" (LRC 63–2000, para 6.26). In fact, Part 4 of the Act converts such settlements into trusts of land, which, therefore, come within Part 5 (see again the Notes to ss 18 and 19).

33 Paragraph (*b*) contains a list of categories of trust to which the Part 5 jurisdiction does not apply.

34 The Commission discussed at length whether charitable trusts should be excluded. Such trusts are, of course, subject to *cy-près* jurisdiction (see Keane, *Equity and the Law of Trusts in the Republic of Ireland* (Tottel Publishing, 1998), paras 11.22–11.28; Delany, *Equity and the Law of Trusts in Ireland* (4th edn, Round Hall, 2007), pp 381–396), but the Commission concluded that they should also be subject to the variation jurisdiction (see LRC 63–2000, paras 6.13–6.22). This was not accepted by the Government and sub-paragraph (i) excludes them. Since the Commission's Report was published the regulation of charities has been overhauled by the Charities Act 2009 and they will be regulated by the Charities Regulatory Authority when it is established. The former Commissioners of Charitable Donations and Bequests for Ireland will be dissolved and its functions, including *cy-près* jurisdiction, will be transferred to the Authority s 82 of the 2009 Act). See also s 24(6)(*a*) (and Note 49 to that section).

35 After much discussion of the pros and cons the Commission concluded that pension schemes should also be included (see LRC 63–2000, paras 6.05–6.12), but again this was not accepted by the Government and sub-paragraph (ii) excludes them.

36 The Commission agreed that trusts created by statutes, including private Acts, should remain governed by their own special legislation and be excluded from the variation jurisdiction (see LRC 63–2000, para 6.27).

37 This refers to a pre-1922 statute enacted at Westminster: see Interpretation Act 2005, Schedule, Part 1.

38 See again the Schedule to the 2005 Act.

---

[58]

24.—(1) An appropriate person[2] may make, in respect of a relevant trust,[3] an application to the court[4] for an order to approve an arrangement[5] specified in the application[6] for the benefit[7] of a relevant person specified in the application[8] if[9] the arrangement has been assented[10] to in writing[11] by each other person[12] (if any) who[13]—

    Jurisdiction of court to vary, etc., trusts.[1]

  (*a*) is not a relevant person,[14]

  (*b*) is beneficially interested in the trust,[15] and[16]

  (*c*) is capable of assenting to the arrangement.[17]

(2)[18] The court shall not hear an application[19] made to it under *subsection (1)* in respect of a relevant trust unless it is satisfied[20] that the applicant has given notice in writing of the application—

    (*a*)   to the Revenue Commissioners,[21] and

    (*b*)   to such persons as may be prescribed by rules of court,[22]

at least 2 weeks[23] before the hearing[24] of the application.

(3) The court may hear an application made to it under *subsection (1)* otherwise than in public if it considers that it is appropriate to do so.[25]

(4) The court shall determine an application[26] made to it under *subsection (1)* in respect of a relevant trust[27]—

    (*a*)   subject to *paragraph (b)*,[28] by making an order approving the arrangement specified in the application[29] if it is satisfied[30] that the carrying out of the arrangement would be for the benefit[31] of—

        (i) the relevant person specified in the application,[32] and[33]

        (ii) any other relevant person,[34]

    (*b*)   by refusing to make such an order in any case where—

        (i)[35] the court is not satisfied as referred to in *paragraph (a)*,[36] or

        (ii)[37] the Revenue Commissioners have satisfied[38] the court that the application is substantially[39] motivated[40] by a desire to avoid,[41] or reduce the incidence of,[42] tax.

(5) In determining under *subsection (4)* whether an arrangement would be for the benefit of a relevant person,[43] the court may have regard to[44] any benefit or detriment,[45] financial or otherwise,[46] that may accrue to that person directly or indirectly in consequence of the arrangement.[47]

(6) Nothing in this section shall be construed as derogating from or affecting the operation of[48]—

    (*a*)   the Charities Acts 1961 and 1973 and the Charities Act 2009,[49]

    (*b*)   any power of a court, whether under an enactment or rule of law, to—

        (i) vary, revoke or resettle a trust (including a relevant trust),[50] or

        (ii) vary, enlarge, add to or restrict the powers of the trustees under a trust (including a relevant trust) to

> manage or administer the property the subject of
> the trust,⁵¹

(*c*) any rule of law relating to the termination or revocation
of a trust (including a relevant trust).⁵²

Definitions

Apart from s 23 (see the Notes to that section), see s 3 for definition of: "court".

Notes

1   Section 24 confers the new jurisdiction on the court to approve a "variation" arrangement to a trust on behalf of beneficiaries who cannot agree to this on their own behalf or any beneficiary who has a contingent interest only and may be holding up an arrangement which all the other beneficiaries agree to (see the Notes to s 23 above).

2   This is defined by s 23 (see Notes 2 and 3 to that section).

3   This is also defined by s 23 (see Notes 28–38 to that section).

4   This means the Circuit Court exercising concurrent jurisdiction with the High Court in accordance with the Third Schedule to the Courts (Supplemental Provisions) Act 1961 (see the amendment to reference 26 in that Schedule made by Schedule 1 to the 2009 Act and Notes to Schedule 1). This was recommended by the Commission (see LRC 63–2000, paras 7.01–7.03). Rules of court will be made for such applications. The Commission discussed whether an application in respect of a particular trust should be a "one-off" application leading to a "permanent" variation or whether further applications could be made later. It concluded that the latter should be the position, relying on the view that the word "any" used in conjunction with "arrangement" in the English 1958 Act supports this (see LRC 63–2000, paras 3.24–3.29). The Act uses "a" rather than "any" but this would seem to have the same effect. Thus a trust previously the subject of a court order approving a variation may be the subject of later applications for approval of further variations – the court is not being asked to vary the trust, it is only being asked to approve a variation agreed by the beneficiaries who are competent to agree on their own behalf (see *Goulding v James* [1997] 2 All ER 239 at 247 *per* Mummery J). The Commission also drew attention to the provision in the Interpretation Act (now the Interpretation Act 2005) that any power conferred by an Act of the Oireachtas may be exercised "from time to time as occasion requires" (see s 22(1) of the 2005).

5   This is defined in s 23 (see Notes 8–16 to that section).

6   The application must specify for consideration by the court the precise variation arrangement which the court is being asked to approve on behalf of the "relevant person" (see Note 29 below). That person must also be specified in the application (see Note 8 below).

7   The court can only approve of the arrangement if it is satisfied that it is for the benefit of the person on whose behalf it is being asked to give approval or other relevant person: see sub-s (4)(*a*) and Notes 31–34 below.

8   The application must clearly identify the person or persons on whose behalf the court is being asked to approve the arrangement (see Notes 17–27 to s 23 above).

9   The court cannot approve the arrangement unless it has been agreed in writing by the beneficiaries who are competent to agree to it on their own behalf. If they have not agreed to it there is no point in making an application to the court. Note the jurisdiction to approve an arrangement where a beneficiary entitled to a contingent interest refuses to agree (see Notes 26 and 27 to s 23).

10   Note the deliberate use of this word (see Note 22 to s 23).

11   This written confirmation of assent should be furnished with the application.

12   Each competent beneficiary must assent in writing for the application to be considered by the court.

13   Paragraphs (*a*)–(*c*) specify who is a competent beneficiary who must assent in writing to the arrangement before the court can give approval to it on behalf of other beneficiaries. Note that these paragraphs are cumulative, ie all the conditions must apply to the person assenting in writing (see Note 16 below).

14   Such a person is a person on whose behalf the court has to give approval (see Notes 17–27 to s 23).

15   It is only competent beneficiaries who have to assent in writing, not the trustees. This accords with the rule in *Saunders v Vautier* (see Note 2 to Part 5 and Note 12 to s 23; see also Note 17 below).

16   This confirms the cumulative operation of paragraphs (*a*)–(*c*) (see Note 13 above).

17   This confirms that an assent in writing is only necessary in the case of beneficiaries who are competent to agree to the arrangement on their own behalf (see Note 15 above).

18   This provision was not in the Commission's draft Bill (see LRC 63–2000, Appendix A), but then it did not have the provision relating to the Revenue Commissioners (see Note 2 to Part 5 above and Notes 37–40 below).

19   This provision is mandatory and if not complied with will prevent the application from proceeding.

20   Proof of written notice having been given should ideally be furnished with the application, but see Note 24 below.

21   The reason for this is to give the Revenue Commissioners the opportunity to make representations to the court in relation to tax avoidance or reduction (see sub-s 4(*b*)(ii) and Notes 37–40 below).

22   Rules of court will be made to cover this.

23   The 2-week period is a minimum period.

24   Note that it is not the date of lodging the application. Thus it is not fatal to an application that the notice was not given 2 weeks before its lodging, or has not even been given at all, so long as it has been given 2 weeks before the application is heard. The court may agree to postpone the hearing to allow that 2-week notice period to be met.

25   The Commission recommended that it be made explicit that the court has a discretion to hear applications *in camera*, since often they will involve minors and private matters relating to a family which should not be aired in public. The analogy

with s 117 applications under the Succession Act 1965 was drawn (see LRC 63–2000, paras 7.04–7.07).

26 Subsection (4) provides alternative determinations, in effect, an order approving the arrangement or a refusal to make an approval order. The Law Reform Commission recommended that the legislation should explicitly reserve a discretion for the court to refuse approval (citing the English 1958 Act's wording "may, if it thinks fit, approve") (see LRC 60–2000, para 4.16). Subsection (4) does not adopt this formula, but, arguably, achieves the same thing by paragraph (*b*)(i) (see Note 35 below). See also Note 47 below.

27 Paragraphs (*a*) and (*b*) set out the grounds upon which either an approval order or refusal should be made.

28 This qualification is made because, notwithstanding that the court is satisfied that the arrangement is for the benefit of the beneficiary on whose behalf approval is sought (and any other beneficiary for whom it can give approval: see Note 34 below), thereby satisfying paragraph (*a*), it may still have to refuse an order because the Revenue Commissioners intervene under paragraph (*b*)(ii).

29 The court can only approve the arrangement specified in the application (see Note 6 above), not substitute its own arrangement. Leave may, however, be given to amend the application or to submit a new application.

30 This is a pre-condition to the court making an order approving the arrangement specified in the application.

31 The test of "benefit" underpins the court's jurisdiction to approve arrangements. Following discussion of experiences in other jurisdictions the Commission concluded that the concept should be kept simple, without other elaboration or restriction (see LRC 63–2000, paras 4.02–4.15). In fact s 24 does not follow that policy: see sub-s (5) which does elaborate upon the concept (see Notes 43–47 below). Note also that paragraph (*b*)(ii) deals with tax matters which were also discussed by the Commission (see Notes 37–40 below).

32 This is the person on whose behalf the court's approval of the application is sought (see Notes 17–27 above).

33 Note the cumulative "and" here.

34 The court must also be satisfied that it is for the benefit of any other person on whose behalf an application could have been made but, presumably for whatever reason, was not specified in the application. It is not clear how the court will determine who such persons might be if they are not clearly identified as such persons in the documentation about the arrangement specified in the application. Note that such "other" relevant persons could include competent adult beneficiaries with a contingent interest (see Notes 26 and 27 to s 23). Note also that the court is *not* concerned with the benefit to other beneficiaries who can agree to the arrangement on their own behalf. It is left to them to make their own judgments as to benefit or otherwise to them and to decide whether to approve of the arrangement.

35 This makes it clear that the court must refuse to make an approval order where it is not satisfied that the "benefit" test has been met. On the face of it this leaves no discretion to the court (contrary to the recommendation of the Commission), but

there necessarily is inherent discretion in the sense that it is left to the court to decide in each case whether it is "satisfied".

36 That is as to whether the "benefit" test has been met (see Notes 31 and 34 above).

37 The Commission, after reviewing the "thorny" issue of whether a variation approval order could be made in respect of an arrangement designed to minimise tax liability (which is the case in several other jurisdictions, including England and Northern Ireland), concluded that there was no need for any special provision restricting the court's jurisdiction in such cases (LRC 63–2000, paras 4.17–4.21). It was pointed out that there already exists a "wide-ranging and sophisticated battery of laws" which the Revenue Commissioners can use to deal with tax avoidance (such as s 811 of the Taxes Consolidation Act 1997). Nevertheless, the Government decided to include sub-paragraph (ii) which imposes a substantial restriction on the court's variation jurisdiction as compared with other jurisdictions.

38 The onus is clearly on the Revenue Commissioners to satisfy the court about the tax "motivation" (see Note 40 below). The Commissioners must have been given 2 weeks' notice of the application (see Notes 18–24 above). Presumably, if they do not make representations at the hearing the court may disregard the issue of tax. This, however, depends on whether the court regards tax avoidance or reduction as a "benefit" so as to satisfy paragraph (*a*). This may not be the case (see the Law Reform Commission's comments on this point: LRC 63–2000, para 4.17). The courts may be influenced on this point by the existence of sub-paragraph (*b*)(ii) (as an indication of the Oireachtas' policy on the issue). On the other hand, if the Revenue Commissioners do not make representations following notice of the application, the court may take the view that it should give little, if any, weight to the tax issue and approve the arrangement on the basis of benefit generally. Note also the reference in sub-s (5) to "financial" benefit (see Note 46 below).

39 This suggests that the Commissioners must establish that tax avoidance or reduction is a major, if not the main, motivation for the variation application.

40 Presumably this "motivation" is to be discerned by the Commissioners from the terms of the arrangement specified by the application and the court may require it to be explained how the avoidance or reduction in tax will be the consequence of the rearrangement.

41 In view of the subsequent reference to "reduce" this presumably refers to avoiding a tax liability altogether.

42 This refers to a reduction falling short of total avoidance.

43 Note that the benefit to more than one relevant person may have to be considered by the court (see Notes 32–34 above).

44 Note that the court has a discretion whether to have regard to these matters and, *à fortiori*, even if it does so clearly may decide what weight to put on them.

45 Presumably the reference to "detriment" is made because this would go against the benefit test in sub-s (4) being satisfied.

46 This confirms that the benefit may take a variety of forms, not all of which are necessarily financial (see LRC 63–2000, paras 4.05–4.07).

47 The Law Reform Commission pointed out that the determination of benefit is a matter for the judgment of the court, acting objectively and not according to the

wishes of the beneficiary on whose behalf approval is being given by the court (see LRC 63–2000, para 4.05). The Act makes no provision for taking into account the wishes of those beneficiaries.

48 The Law Reform Commission recommended that the new variation jurisdiction should not be seen as necessarily rendering redundant existing, more limited, statutory or inherent powers to vary trusts (see LRC 63–2000, para 6.25).

49 This covers the *cy-près* jurisdiction relating to charitable trusts.

50 This covers jurisdiction such as "salvage" and "compromise" jurisdiction (see Note 2 to Part 5 above). It also covers the jurisdiction to make property adjustment orders under family law legislation.

51 A full discussion of existing powers and reform proposals is contained in the Law Reform Commission's *Report on Trust Law: General Proposals* (LRC 92–2008), especially chs 6–11.

52 This refers to the rule in *Saunders v Vautier* (see Note 2 to Part 5 above).

---

[59]

PART 6[1]

POWERS[2]

Notes

1 Part 6 implements the recommendations made by the Law Reform Commission in its *Consultation Paper on Reform and Modernisation of Land Law and Conveyancing Law* (LRC CP 34–2004; see also the draft Bill in the later Report LRC 74–2005). These recommendations related to powers of appointment, but Part 5 has wider scope (see Note 2 below).

2 Essentially Part 6 consolidates various pre-1922 statutory provisions relating to powers generally and, in doing so, clarifies some issues (as indicated in the Notes to particular sections). Two main types of powers are commonly created in respect of property (unlike most of the Act Part 6 applies also to property other than land). One is a power of appointment which is often created in a settlement, trust or will. This usually confers on one person (the "donee" of the power) power to "appoint" (ie select) from amongst a group of specified persons (the "objects" of the power) which of them (the appointees) should obtain specified property or shares (including what shares) in the property (see *Butler v Butler* [2006] IEHC 104; Lyall, *Land Law in Ireland* (2nd edn, Round Hall, 2000), pp 370–378; Wylie, *Irish Land Law* (3rd edn, Tottel Publishing, 1997), paras 11.06–11.27). Part 6 is concerned primarily with pre-1922 statutory provisions relating to such powers. The other main type of power commonly created is a power of attorney. The law relating to such powers, including previous statute law (such as the provisions in Part XI of the Conveyancing Act 1881) was overhauled by the Powers of Attorney Act 1996 (see Gallagher, *Powers of Attorney Act 1996* (1998); Wylie, *Irish Land Law* (3rd edn, Tottel Publishing, 1997), paras 11.29–11.43). The 1996 Act also introduced provisions relating to enduring

powers of attorney (see Part II of that Act) (as had been recommended by the Law Reform Commission: see *Report on Land Law and Conveyancing Law: (2) Enduring Powers of Attorney* (LRC 31–1989)). Part 6 does not affect the provisions of the 1996 Act (apart from a couple of minor consequential amendments and repeals set out in Schedules 1 and 2: see Notes to those Schedules). Finally, it should be noted that the Act does contain other provisions relating powers, such as s 11(8) (see Notes 53–54 to that section) and various provisions in Part 10 relating to mortgagor and mortgagee powers in relation to the mortgaged property (see the Notes to that Part).

[60]

Application of Part 6.[1] **25.**—Except where stated otherwise,[2] this Part applies to powers created or arising before or after the commencement of this Act.[3]

Notes

1 Section 25 specifies the application of Part 5 – in view of its largely consolidating purpose it has retrospective effect, for the most part.

2 See s 26(1) (and Note 5 to that section).

3 This confirms the largely retrospective effect of Part 6, ie its provisions replace existing provisions without substantial amendment.

[61]

Execution of non-testamentary powers of appointment.[1] **26.**—(1) Subject to *subsection (2)*,[2] an appointment[3] made by deed[4] after the commencement of this Part[5] under a power of appointment is valid provided the instrument making the appointment complies with *section 64*.[6]

[LPAA 1859, s. 12] (2)[7] *Subsection (1)* does not—

(*a*) prevent a donee of a power of appointment from making a valid appointment in some other way expressly authorised by the instrument creating the power,[8] or

(*b*)[9] relieve such a donee from compliance with any direction in the instrument creating the power that—

(i) the consent of any person is necessary to a valid appointment,[10] or

(ii) an act is to be performed having no relation to the mode of executing and attesting the deed of appointment in order to give validity to any appointment.[11]

Definitions

See s 3 for definitions of: "consent"; "deed"; "instrument".

Notes

1   Section 26 replaces the provisions in s 12 of the Law of Property Amendment Act 1859 (which is repealed by Schedule 2). It relates to execution of a "non-testamentary" power (ie not exercised by making a will). The provisions in the 1859 Act were designed to preserve the effectiveness of exercise when making the appointment by a deed, by stating when such an exercise would be valid despite the donee not following strictly the formalities for execution of the deed of appointment prescribed by the instrument creating the power (see Lyall, *Land Law in Ireland* (2nd edn, Round Hall, 2000), p 373; Wylie, *Irish Land Law* (3rd edn, Tottel Publishing, 1997), paras 11.14 and 11.16). However, the Law Reform Commission pointed out that there was an anomaly about s 12 of the 1859 Act. It required the donee when making the appointment to meet requirements not strictly necessary for execution of deeds generally prior to 1 December 2009, namely, attestation of the deed by 2 or more witnesses (although witnessing was not strictly necessary for execution of deeds (see *Fitzsimons v Value Homes Ltd* [2006] IEHC 144), the practice was for each signature to be attested by one witness: see Wylie and Woods, *Irish Conveyancing Law* (3rd edn, Tottel Publishing, 2005), paras 18.137–18.138). The contrast was drawn with testamentary powers, because s 79 of the Succession Act 1965 requires only that exercise by the donee of a power of appointment by making a will need comply only with the law relating to execution of wills generally (ie the exercise would be valid despite not complying with some "additional or other form of execution or solemnity" required by the instrument creating the power: see s 79(2) of the 1965 Act). The Commission recommended that a similar rule should be introduced for "non-testamentary" exercise of powers (see LRC CP 34–2004 paras 5.06–5.07).

2   Subsection (2) deals with situations where the donee is not required to execute a deed or is required to comply with other instructions in the instrument creating the power of appointment.

3   Section 26 relates to exercise of powers of appointment only (see Note 1 above).

4   That is not appointments made by will, which are governed by s 79 of the Succession Act 1965 (see Note 1 above).

5   Because sub-s (1) is changing the pre-1 December 2009 law (see Note 1 above) it operates only in respect of appointments made after that date. These include appointments made under instruments creating powers on or before that date.

6   This implements the change in the law recommended by the Law Reform Commission, to align the law relating to exercise of a power of appointment by an *inter vivos* deed with that relating to exercise of such a power by will (see Note 1 above). The exercise (appointment) will be valid provided the law relating to execution of deeds generally is followed and despite not complying with any additional or other formalities required by the instrument creating the power. Section 64 of the 2009 Act now sets out the requirements for execution of deeds generally and introduces considerable changes, particularly for execution by individuals: the

need for a seal is dropped but attestation by a witness becomes a requirement (see the Notes to that section).

7   Subsection (2) re-enacts provisions in s 12 of the 1859 Act with no change of substance.

8   Paragraph (*a*) makes it clear that subsection (1) is concerned only with exercise of a power of appointment by execution of a deed. It preserves the validity of an appointment made by a deed complying with s 64, despite the fact the instrument creating the power required the deed to meet additional requirements. Subsection (1) does not apply where the instrument creating the power did not specify that appointments had to be made by deed, but instead authorised them to be made in some way, eg in writing only. In such cases the donee of the power can exercise it in that way and does not have to make an appointment by deed.

9   Paragraph (*b*) also re-enacts provisions in s 12 of the 1859 Act making it clear that subsection (1) does not relieve a donee of a power of appointment with the need to comply with other directions in the instrument creating the power, ie ones not related to exercise of the power by making appointments by deed.

10 Note that "consent" includes "agreement, licence and permission" (see s 3).

11 Such an act might be a requirement to give notice of the making of the appointment to specified persons.

---

[62]

Release of powers.[1]
[CA 1881, s. 52]

27.—(1) Subject to *subsection (2)*,[2] a person to whom any power,[3] whether coupled with an interest or not,[4] is given may release[5] or contract not to exercise the power by deed[6] or in any other way in which the power could be created.[7]

(2)[8] *Subsection (1)* does not apply[9] to a power in the nature of a trust or other fiduciary power.[10]

Definitions

See s 3 for definition of: " deed".

Notes

1   Section 27 largely re-enacts the provisions of s 52 of the Conveyancing Act 1881. That provision related to what it called powers "simply collateral", ie where the donee of the power has no interest in the property in respect of which he or she can exercise the power (eg a power to appoint the property, or shares in it, to some other person). The rule at common law was that such a power could not be released by the donee (see *Re Dunne's Trusts* (1879) 5 LR Ir 76; *Re Radcliffe* [1892] 1 Ch 227; see Lyall, *Land Law in Ireland* (2nd edn, Round Hall, 2000), p 373; Wylie, *Irish Land Law* (3rd edn, Tottel Publishing, 1997), paras 11.07–11.08).

2   Subsection (2) deals with cases where the donee of a power is not entitled to release it (see Notes 8–10 below).

3 This section applies to any power and, unlike s 26, is not confined to power of appointment.

4 This makes it clear that subsection (1) applies to powers simply collateral (see Note 1 above).

5 This does not include a disclaimer which is governed by s 28 (see the Notes to that section). A release involves giving up a power which the donee has already accepted; a disclaimer is a refusal to accept from the start a power which someone has purported to confer on the donee.

6 Note that, as in s 52 of the 1881 Act, both a release and a contract not to exercise the power must be by deed (which means complying with s 64 of the Act: see the Notes to it). Normally, contracts relating to land do not have to be by deed (see s 51 and the Notes to it).

7 This wording does not appear in s 52 of the Act and was designed to recognise that a power may be released by implication, arising from the conduct or actions of the donee (see *Stewart v Marquis of Donegal* (1845) 8 Ir Eq R 621; *Stuart v Kennedy* (1852) 3 Ir Jur 305). However, the word "created" should read "released".

8 Subsection (2) implements the Law Reform Commission's recommendation that the position as regards fiduciary powers should be clarified (see LRC CP 34–2004, paras 5.08–5.09).

9 That is release of the power is not possible in such cases.

10 It has long been established that such a power cannot be released because this would amount to a breach of trust and the same rule probably applied to any other power which attached a fiduciary obligation on the donee to exercise the power (see *Re Eyre* (1883) 49 LT 259; *Saul v Pattison* (1886) 55 LJ Ch 831; *Re Somers* [1896] 1 Ch 250; *Re Will's Trust Deeds* [1964] Ch 219; *Re Hay's Settlement Trusts* [1982] 1 WLR 202; *Turner v Turner* [1984] Ch 100). Subsection (2) confirms the position.

---

[63]

28.—(1) A person to whom any power,[2] whether coupled with an interest or not,[3] is given may by deed[4] disclaim the power[5] and, after disclaimer, may not exercise or join in the exercise of the power.[6]

Disclaimer of powers.[1]
[CA 1882, s. 6]

(2) On such disclaimer, the power may be exercised by any other person or persons, or the survivor or survivors of any other persons, to whom the power is given, subject to the terms of the instrument creating the power.[7]

Definitions

See s 3 for definition of: "deed".

Notes

1 Section 28 re-enacts the provisions of s 6 of the Conveyancing Act 1882. It confers a general right on donees of a power to disclaim it, ie refuse to accept it in the first place; cf a release which is governed by s 27 (see the Notes to that section). Note that the marginal note refers to powers generally. Section 6 of the 1882 Act referred to disclaimer of powers "by trustees", but it was clear from that section's substantive provisions that it applied to "any power" (see Note 2 below). Once a trustee has accepted the office of trustee, he or she cannot, of course, disclaim that office but may retire (see *Doyle v Blake* (1804) 2 Sch & Lef 231; *Plunket v Smith* (1844) 8 Ir Eq R 523; *Re Somerville* (1878) 1 LR Ir 293; Delany, *Equity and the Law of Trusts in Ireland* (4th edn, Round Hall, 2007), p 415).

2 This confirms that the section applies to any person (not just a trustee: see Note 1 above) holding any power, not just a power of appointment.

3 That is it covers the case where the donee of the power has no other interest (other than the power itself) in the property over which the power may be exercised.

4 That is which complies with the requirements of s 64 (see the Notes to that section). It had been held that this enables a power to be disclaimed on the same basis upon which an estate or interest in land may be disclaimed (see *Re Fisher and Haslett* (1884) 13 LR Ir 546).

5 Such a disclaimer does not necessarily destroy the power; it merely prevents the disclaiming donee from exercising it (see Note 6 below). Note also subsection (2) (see Note 7 below).

6 This confirms the effect of a disclaimer (see Note 5 above). The reference to "join" covers the situation where there is a joint power held by more than one donee and only one or some disclaim.

7 This confirms that a disclaimer affects only the position of the donee disclaiming, so that in the case of a joint power, the other donees may continue to exercise the power (see *Burnaby v Baillie* (1889) 42 Ch D 282).

---

[64]

Validation of appointments.[1]

[IAA 1830]
[PAA 1874]

29.—(1) No appointment made in exercise of any power to appoint[2] any property[3] among two or more persons[4] is invalid on the ground that—

    (*a*) an insubstantial, illusory or nominal share only is appointed to or left unappointed to devolve on any one or more of those persons,[5] or

    (*b*) any such person is altogether excluded, whether by way of default of appointment or otherwise.[6]

(2) This section does not affect any provision in the instrument creating the power which specifies the amount of any share from which any such person is not to be excluded.[7]

Definitions

See s 3 for definitions of: "instrument"; "property".

Notes

1   Section 29 implements the recommendation of the Law Reform Commission that the somewhat confusing provisions in the Illusory Appointments Act 1830 and the Powers of Appointment Act 1874 should be consolidated and clarified as was done for England and Wales by s 158 of the Law of Property Act 1925 (see LRC CP 34–2004, paras 5.02–5.05). Prior to 1830 the courts were concerned that in the case of a "non-exclusive" power (ie one where the settlor had made it clear in the instrument creating the power that each object should be allocated some property by the donee when exercising the power), the donee might attempt to thwart the settlor's wishes by cutting off a particular object "with a shilling" – hence the expression "illusory appointment" (see *Gibson v Kinven* (1682) 1 Vern 66; *Vanderzee v Aclom* (1799) 4 Ves 771; Lyall, *Land Law in Ireland* (2nd edn, Round Hall, 2000), pp 373–374; Wylie, *Irish Land Law* (3rd edn, Tottel Publishing, 1997), para 11.20). The 1830 Act provided that the appointment of a nominal sum was not to invalidate the exercise of a power (unless the instrument creating it indicated otherwise). Confusion was then created by the 1874 Act which provided that every power of appointment should be construed as "exclusive", so that, in effect, the donee had a complete discretion as regards exercise of the power, including the discretion not to exercise at all (unless again the instrument creating it provided otherwise) (see *Re Walsh's Trusts* (1878) 1 LR Ir 320; *Wybrants v Maude* [1895] 1 IR 214; *Re Staples* [1933] IR 126; *Re Dolan* [1970] IR 94). As another author put it pithily: "The Act of 1830 enabled an appointor to cut off any object of a power with a shilling; the Act of 1874 enables him to cut off the shilling also" (see Farwell, *Powers* (3rd edn, 1916), p 427). Section 29 consolidates the 1830 and 1874 provisions as recommended by the Commission.

2   Section 29, unlike ss 27 and 28, but like s 26, is confined to powers of appointment.

3   As with the rest of Part 6 the section applies to powers concerning any kind of property, not just land.

4   The section is concerned with powers to appoint (select) who is to take the property and in what shares.

5   Paragraph (*a*) re-enacts the substance of the 1830 Act (see Note 1 above).

6   Paragraph (*b*) re-enacts the substance of the 1874 Act.

7   Subsection (2) confirms the position under both the 1830 and 1874 Acts: the donee of a power of appointment cannot get away with cutting off an object of the power "with a shilling" only or cutting the object off altogether, if the instrument creating the power makes it clear that the object is not to be excluded from a specified share.

[65]

PART 7[1]
Co-Ownership[2]

Notes

1   Part 7 implements the Law Reform Commission's recommendation for reform of various aspects of the law of co-ownership, ie where land (or, indeed, other property) is owned by one of more persons or bodies concurrently (see *Consultation Paper on Reform and Modernisation of Land Law and Conveyancing Law* (LRC CP 34–2000), ch 6 and Part 6 of the draft Bill appended to Report LRC 74–2005; these recommendations incorporated proposals made in earlier reports: see *Report on Land Law and Conveyancing Law: (1) General Proposals* (LRC 30-1989), pp 11–12; *Report on Land Law and Conveyancing Law: (7) Positive Covenants over Freehold Land and Other Proposals* (LRC 70–2003), para 5.02; *Consultation Paper on Judgment Mortgages* (LRC CP 30–2004), paras 6.12 and 6.16).

2   It is important to note that Part 7 does not include the substantial change in the law relating to co-ownership of land introduced in England and Wales by the Law of Property Act 1925 (ss 34–36; see Megarry and Wade, *The Law of Real Property* (7th edn, Sweet & Maxwell, 2008), ch 13). This was concerned with the so-called "fragmentation of ownership" which can occur when the legal title to land is held by tenants in common. Each such tenant is regarded as having a distinct share which they are free to leave by will to as many successors as they please (unlike in the case of a joint tenancy where the right of survivorship operates on death to leave the legal title to the land vested in the surviving joint tenants). The result may be that over time the title to land held under a tenancy in common may become vested in a very large number of persons, all of whom would have to join in executing any instruments necessary to dispose of the land (see Lyall, *Land Law in Ireland* (2nd edn, Round Hall, 2000), ch 16; Wylie, *Irish Land Law* (3rd edn, Tottel Publishing, 1997), ch 7; Conway, *Co-Ownership of Land: Partition Actions and Remedies* (Tottel Publishing, 2000)). The English provisions prohibit the legal title to land being held under a tenancy in common and require it always to be held on a joint tenancy (but a tenancy in common can exist in equity). The Law Reform Commission took the view that it was not appropriate to introduce such provisions here. They have proved to be controversial in England and the evidence of practitioners consulted was to the effect that the conveyancing difficulties perceived to arise from fragmentation of the legal title did not seem to arise in practice. It was also pointed out that in recent times it had become very common for large groups of investors to acquire commercial property and hold it as tenants in common, because each would wish to have a distinct share. It would not be acceptable to such co-owners to have the legal title vested in a small number of them only (the English legislation limits the number of joint tenants holding the title on trust for themselves and other co-owners to 4). See LRC 70–2003, para 5.04; LRC CP 34–2004, paras 6.02–6.05. Finally, it should be noted that another aspect of the law of co-ownership, namely "commorientes" (persons dying together, usually in some accident, when it

is uncertain which survives the other), which the Commission recommended should be amended (in effect, changing the operation of s 5 of the Succession Act 1965) (see LRC 70–2003, ch 3) was dealt with by s 68 of the Civil Law (Miscellaneous Provisions) Act 2006.

[66]

30.[2]—(1) From the commencement of this Part,[3] any—

    (*a*)   conveyance,[4] or contract for a conveyance,[5] of land held in a joint tenancy,[6] or

    (*b*)   acquisition of another interest in such land,[7]

by a joint tenant without the consent[8] referred to in *subsection (2)* is void both at law and in equity[9] unless such consent is dispensed with under *section 31(2)(e).*[10]

(2) In *subsection (1)* "consent" means the prior[11] consent in writing of the other joint tenant or, where there are more than one other, all the other joint tenants.[12]

(3)[13] From the commencement of this Part,[14] registration of a judgment mortgage[15] against the estate or interest in land of a joint tenant does not sever the joint tenancy[16] and if the joint tenancy remains unsevered, the judgment mortgage is extinguished upon the death of the judgment debtor.[17]

(4)[18] Nothing in this section affects the jurisdiction of the court to find that all[19] the joint tenants by mutual agreement or by their conduct have severed the joint tenancy in equity.[20]

Unilateral severance of a joint tenancy.[1]

Definitions

See s 3 for definitions of: "consent"; "court"; "conveyance"; "judgment mortgage"; "land".

Notes

1   Section 30 implements a radical change to the law governing "severance" of a joint tenancy ie the process whereby a joint tenancy is converted to a tenancy in common, thereby giving each co-owner a distinct share and destroying the right of survivorship (see Lyall, *Land Law in Ireland* (2nd edn, Round Hall, 2000), pp 435–443; Wylie, *Irish Land Law* (3rd edn, Tottel Publishing, 1997), paras 7.22–7.32). The Law Reform Commission concluded that, because this would often have the effect of destroying an expectation to become the sole owner of the land, such a severance should no longer be possible by the unilateral action of one joint tenant. Instead, the rule should be that severance should be based upon the consent of all the joint tenants (see LRC 70–2003, ch 5; LRC CP 34–2004, paras 6.06–6.07). This recommendation has since proved to be controversial with some commentators

pointing out that the need to obtain consent may prove troublesome for some owners (particularly the elderly or incapacitated and co-owners in a relationship which has broken down) and that it might have been sufficient to have a requirement that a joint tenant intending to sever should notify the other join tenants (see Mee, "The Land and Conveyancing Law Reform Bill 2006: Observations on the Law Reform Process and a Critique of Selected Provisions – Part II" (2006) 11 (4) CPLJ 91). It has also been pointed out that the "right" to survivorship is a misnomer – at most each joint tenant has an expectation but, in reality, only a hope that he or she will outlive the other joint tenants (see Conway, "When is a Severance Not Actually a Severance?" (2009) 16 Aust PLJ 278). However, this change has also been welcomed as appropriate, especially in the family law context where parties should be encouraged to resolve disputes by consent. Unilateral severance is "quite an aggressive way to resolve the issues which arise on the breakdown in the relationship between co-owners" (see Woods, "Unilateral Severance of Joint Tenancies – The Case for Abolition" (2007) 12(2) CPLJ 47). This section is based on the draft legislation in the Commission's Report LRC 70–2000, para 5.19, but note the amendment referred to in Note 10 below.

2   Note that s 30 does not deal with another aspect of the law of severance the Commission recommended should be reformed. This was the cumbersome method of severing a joint tenancy of freehold land which, until 1 December 2009, involved having to use the medieval device of a conveyance to a third party by way of a "use" executed by the Statute of Uses (Ireland) 1634 (see LRC 30–1989, para 29 and LRC 70–2003, paras 5.03–5.19). The Commission recommended that it ought to be possible to sever by a simple deed of conveyance. In fact the Act achieves this through other provisions. The 1634 Statute is repealed (see Schedule 2) and s 62(2) provides that a deed is fully effective without the need of a conveyance to uses (see also ss 66 (conveyance to oneself) and 69 (reservations) and the Notes to these sections).

3   The new rule re unilateral severance operates only from 1 December 2009, but applies to co-owners already in existence at that date.

4   Section 30 does not apply to wills because it has never been possible to sever a joint tenancy by will – this would be inconsistent with the right of survivorship which operates on the death of a joint tenant and distinguishes it from a tenancy in common (see Lyall, *Land Law in Ireland* (2nd edn, Round Hall, 2000), pp 423–424; Wylie, *Irish Land Law* (3rd edn, Tottel Publishing, 1997), para 7.04). "Alienation" by a joint tenant was a common method of severance (see Lyall, *Land Law in Ireland* (2nd edn, Round Hall, 2000), p 438; Wylie, *Irish Land Law* (3rd edn, Tottel Publishing, 1997), paras 7.28–7.31).

5   Note that s 30 also renders void even a "contract" for conveyance. This is not defined; cf the definition of "conveyance" in s 1 of the Family Home Protection Act 1976 (see Wylie and Woods, *Irish Conveyancing Law* (3rd edn, Tottel Publishing, 2005), paras 3.40 and 16.49). A contract would effect a severance in equity only (see Lyall, *Land Law in Ireland* (2nd edn, Round Hall, 2000), p 442; Wylie, *Irish Land Law* (3rd edn, Tottel Publishing, 1997), para 7.32).

6   Severance relates to a joint tenancy only. Tenants in common have distinct shares which they are free to dispose of both *inter vivos* and by will (see Lyall, *Land Law in*

Ireland (2nd edn, Round Hall, 2000), p 429; Wylie, *Irish Land Law* (3rd edn, Tottel Publishing, 1997), paras 7.08–7.09).

7　This was a common way in which a severance would be brought about (eg one joint tenant buying out another's interest or acquiring a remainder interest held by a third party) (see Lyall, *Land Law in Ireland* (2nd edn, Round Hall, 2000), pp 436–438; Wylie, *Irish Land Law* (3rd edn, Tottel Publishing, 1997), paras 7.25–7.27).

8　It does not have to be referred to as "consent" in the written document giving it: see the definitions in s 3.

9　That is no severance at all will have taken place, not even in equity (the word used is "void" not "voidable"). The co-owners will have remained joint tenants. There is an analogy with s 3 of the Family Home Protection Act 1976 (see Wylie and Woods, *Irish Conveyancing Law* (3rd edn, Tottel Publishing, 2005), para 16.49).

10　This wording did not appear in the Bill as originally drafted and introduced to the Seanad but was added at the Seanad Committee Stage to mitigate what some feared might result in hardship to joint tenants who, because of their relationship with other joint tenants, might find it very difficult to secure consent (see Note 1 above).

11　This word was also added at the Seanad Committee Stage to avoid the argument that consent could be given later so as to validate retrospectively a conveyance or acquisition previously thought invalid (see Mee, "The Land and Conveyancing Law Reform Bill 2006: Observations on the Law Reform Process and a Critique of Selected Provisions – Part II" (2006) 11 (4) CPLJ 91). Again the analogy with s 3 of the Family Home Protection Act 1976 was followed (see Note 9 above).

12　This makes it clear that a joint tenant wishing to sever must get the consent of all the other joint tenants. If that is not forthcoming an application can be made to the court under s 31(2)(*e*) (see Note 12 to that section).

13　As originally drafted and introduced to the Seanad the Bill also contained in this subsection a provision relating to the effect of insolvency of a joint tenant but this was dropped at the Seanad Committee Stage on the ground that the Bill was not the appropriate place for amending insolvency law.

14　Again this provision operates only from 1 December 2009.

15　This matter is now dealt by Part 11, which replaces the provisions of the Judgment Mortgage (Ireland) Acts 1850 and 1858 (which are repealed: see Schedule 2) (see the Notes to that Part).

16　This resolves what appeared to be an anomaly in the previous law. The position seemed to be that registration of a judgment mortgage severed a joint tenancy in *unregistered* land (see *McIlroy v Edgar* (1881) 7 LR Ir 521; *Containercare v Wycherley* [1982] IR 143; *Murray v Diamond* [1982] ILRM 113) but not in *registered* land (see *Judge Mahon v Lawlor* [2008] IEHC 284; *Irwin v Deasy* [2006] IEHC 25). The Commission took the view that severance in such cases offended the new rule against unilateral severance without consent and recommended adoption of the position as regards registered land (see *Consultation Paper on Judgment Mortgages* (LRC CP 30–2004), paras 6.09–6.16). Subsection (3) implements this.

17　This confirms the consequence of there being no severance. The judgment mortgage attaches only to the estate or interest of the joint tenant against whom a judgment has been obtained (the judgment debtor) and so if the judgment creditor does not seek to enforce the registered judgment mortgage (by applying for an order under s 31: see the Notes to that section), the risk will be run that it will become extinguished on death of the judgment debtor. The reason is, of course, that on death of a joint tenant, his or her estate or interest in the land ceases and the right of survivorship operates in favour of the surviving joint tenant or tenants (see the judgments of Laffoy J in *Irwin v Deasy* [2006] IEHC 254 and *Judge Mahon v Lawlor* [2008] IEHC 284).

18 Subsection (4) recognises that it has long been the position that the courts, exercising equitable jurisdiction, will recognise that the parties by their words or actions have treated themselves as if they have ceased to be joint tenants and have become tenants in common with distinct shares (this is sometimes referred to as the principle in *Williams v Hensman* (1861) 1 J & H 546 at 557 *per* Page-Wood VC; see also *Burgess v Rawnsley* [1975] 1 Ch 429; Lyall, *Land Law in Ireland* (2nd edn, Round Hall, 2000), pp 439–441; Wylie, *Irish Land Law* (3rd edn, Tottel Publishing, 1997), para 7.32). This is consistent with the Law Reform Commission's policy so long as such severance is based on the words and actions to which all the joint tenants are parties or subscribe (see Note 19 below).

19 It is important to note that the saving for severance in equity is confined to situations where *all* the joint tenants are a party to it or are regarded by the court as subscribing to it or otherwise accepting that they are bound by it. This limitation is important to comply with the new rule against *unilateral* severance introduced by subsection (1).

20 Since the severance takes effect in equity only, the legal title will remain in a joint tenancy. Thus on death of a joint tenant, the surviving tenant or tenants will hold the legal title, but on trust for whoever has succeeded to the share of the deceased tenant (as to that tenant's share in equity) and the trustee's or trustees' (surviving joint tenant or tenants in law) own share or shares in equity.

---

[67]

Court orders.[1]

31.—(1) Any person having an estate or interest in land[2] which is co-owned[3] whether at law or in equity[4] may apply to the court[5] for an order under this section.[6]

(2) An order under this section includes[7]—

[PA 1868]
[PA 1876]

(*a*) an order for partition of the land amongst the co-owners,[8]

(*b*) an order for the taking of an account of incumbrances affecting the land, if any, and the making of inquiries as to the respective priorities of any such incumbrances,[9]

(*c*) an order for sale of the land and distribution of the proceeds of sale as the court directs,[10]

[AJA 1707, s.23]

(*d*) an order directing that accounting adjustments be made as between the co-owners,[11] (*e*) an order dispensing with consent to severance of a joint tenancy as required by *section 30* where such consent is being unreasonably withheld,[12]

(*f*)[13] such other order relating to the land as appears to the court to be just and equitable in the circumstances of the case.[14]

(3)[15] In dealing with an application for an order under *subsection (1)* the court may[16]—

(*a*) make an order with or without conditions or other requirements attached to it, or

(*b*) dismiss the application without making any order, or

(*c*) combine more than one order under this section.[17]

(4) In this section—

(*a*) "person having an estate or interest in land" includes a mortgagee or other secured creditor,[18] a judgment mortgagee[19] or a trustee,[20]

(*b*) "accounting adjustments" include[21]—

(i) payment of an occupation rent by a co-owner who has enjoyed, or is continuing to enjoy, occupation of the land to the exclusion of any other co-owner,[22]

(ii) compensation to be paid by a co-owner to any other co-owner who has incurred disproportionate expenditure in respect of the land (including its repair or improvement),[23]

(iii) contributions by a co-owner to disproportionate[24] payments made by any other co-owner in respect of the land (including payments in respect of charges, rates, rents, taxes and other outgoings[25] payable in respect of it),

(iv) redistribution of rents and profits received by a co-owner disproportionate to his or her interest in the land,[26]

(v) any other adjustment necessary to achieve fairness between the co-owners.[27]

(5)[28] Nothing in this section affects the jurisdiction of the court under the Act of 1976,[29] the Act of 1995[30] and the Act of 1996.[31]

(6)[32] The equitable jurisdiction of the court to make an order for partition of land which is co-owned whether at law or in equity is abolished.

Definitions

See s 3 for definitions of: "Act of 1976"; "Act of 1995"; "Act of 1996"; "consent"; "court"; "incumbrance"; "judgment mortgage"; "land"; mortgagee"; "rent".

Notes

1   The primary purpose of s 31 is to implement the Law Reform Commission's recommendation that the complicated, and sometimes uncertain, provisions of the Partition Acts 1868 and 1876 should be replaced (see LRC CP 34–2004, paras 6.10–6.12 and LRC 74–2005, Appendix A, p 109). In essence s 31 introduces a new exclusive statutory jurisdiction (the 1868 and 1876 Acts are repealed: see Schedule 2) giving the court a wide discretion to deal with disputes which may arise between co-owners. This is designed to avoid difficulties the courts have had in the past in interpreting and applying the Partition Acts (see eg *ACC Bank plc v Markham* [2005] IEHC 437; *Irwin v Deasy* [2006] IEHC 25; *Sheehy v Talbot* [2008] IEHC 207; Conway, *Co-Ownership of Land: Partition Actions and Remedies* (Tottel Publishing, 2000)).

2   Note that sub-s (1) does not draw any distinction between the different estate or interest or the size of shares held by the applicant. This often gave rise to issues as to jurisdiction of the court under the Partition Acts (see Note 1 above). Note also the broad category of persons who may apply, as having an interest in the land specified, in sub-s (4)(*a*) (see Notes 18–20 below).

3   Section 31 is confined to co-owned land. As regards property other than land, partition actions rarely, if ever, are made in respect of such property. In future, with the repeal of the Partition Acts 1868 and 1876, co-owners of such property would have to invoke equitable jurisdiction (s 31 replaces this only in respect of land: see sub-s (6)) (see Conway, *Co-Ownership of Land: Partition Actions and Remedies* (Tottel Publishing, 2000), ch 6).

4   Often co-ownership exists under a trust, where a legal owner is regarded as holding legal title to land on trust for himself or herself and some other person who has acquired an equitable interest in it, eg by way of a constructive trust. It would also arise where there is a severance of a joint tenancy in equity only (see Notes 18–20 to s 30).

5   The Circuit Court has concurrent jurisdiction with the High Court: see the definition of "court" in s 3 and Note 23 to that section).

6   This does not affect the jurisdiction of the court under family related legislation: see sub-s (5) (and Notes 28–31 below).

7   Subsection (2) lists a variety of orders which the court may make in its discretion and note the discretion to make others as it sees fit: see paragraph (*f*) (and Notes 13–14 below). Note also the power to make conditional orders and combine orders in particular cases: see sub-s (3) (and Notes 15–17 below).

8   Paragraph (*a*) continues statutory jurisdiction to order partition if the court thinks this appropriate. Often, of course, physical division of the land in question (especially where it comprises a building with limited facilities, eg, one kitchen, one bathroom etc) is simply not practicable.

9   Paragraph (*b*) was not in the Bill as originally drafted and introduced to the Seanad but was added at the Dáil Report Stage to deal with cases where a mortgagee or judgment mortgagee applies to the court (see Notes 18–19 below). See also s 117(2) (and the Notes to that section).

10 This continues the jurisdiction, which was an important feature of the Partition Acts 1868 and 1876, to order a sale instead of physical partition of the land. Section 31 makes this available in all cases and leaves it open to the court to decide when it is appropriate to order a sale, without imposing any presumptions based on the nature of the applicant's interest or size of his or her share (see Notes 1 and 2 above).

11 Paragraph (*d*) continues the jurisdiction under s 23 of the Administration of Justice (Ireland) Act 1707 (which is repealed: see Schedule 2) to order "accounting adjustments" as between the co-owners (see Conway, *Co-Ownership of Land: Partition Actions and Remedies* (Tottel Publishing, 2000), ch 11). The apparent repeal of s 23 by s 3 of the Common Law Procedure Amendment Act (Ir) 1853 related only to its procedural aspects and the jurisdiction remained (see *Kearney v Kearney* (1861) 13 ICLR 314 at 322–323, *per* Fitzgerald J; see also Dowling, "The Baby and the Bathwater: The Administration of Justice Act (Ireland) 1707, s 23" (1996) 47 NILQ 428; Conway, *Co-Ownership of Land: Partition Actions and Remedies* (Tottel Publishing, 2000), paras 6.23–6.25). Subsection (4)(*b*) gives further guidance as to what sort of adjustments these might be (see Notes 21–27 below)

12 Paragraph (*e*) was added at the Seanad Committee Stage to deal with cases where a joint tenant wishing to sever cannot secure the consent of the other joint tenants which is required under s 30 (see Notes 1, 10 and 12 to that section). It is left to the court to decide in a particular case whether a joint tenant's consent is being "unreasonably withheld". The obvious analogy is the court's power to declare that a landlord's consent is being unreasonably withheld from a tenant wishing to alienate: Landlord and Tenant (Amendment) Act 1980, ss 66–69 (see Wylie, *Landlord and Tenant Law* (2nd edn, Tottel Publishing, 1998), chs 18, 19, 21 and 22).

13 This makes it clear that it is open to the court to make an order not listed in paragraphs (*a*)–(*e*).

14 This bases the court's jurisdiction entirely in the court's discretion, to make whatever order appears to it to be "just and equitable". It has been left to the courts to develop the principles to be adopted in such cases (see Woods, "Property Disputes Between Co-owning Cohabitees – A Conveyancer's Perspective" (2007) 12 (1) CPLJ 18). Subsection (5) contains a saving for jurisdiction in family co-ownership cases and, at the time the Bill was being drafted, the Law Reform Commission was also conducting a review of the law relating to cohabitees (see *Consultation Paper on Rights and Duties of Cohabitees* (LRC CP 32–2004): see Fox, "Property Rights of Co-habitees: The Limits of Legislative Reform" (2005) 1 IJFL 2; Mee, "A Critique of the Law Reform Commission's Consultation Paper on the Rights and Duties of Cohabitees" (2004) 36 Ir Jur (ns) 74). The view was taken that the need for further legislative interference or guidance on such matters should be considered in that wider context. The Commission's subsequent Report (LRC 82–2006) recommended jurisdiction to make property adjustment orders in respect of

"qualified cohabitants" (see the draft Cohabitants Bill appended to the Report; Civil Partnership Bill 2009 (No 44 of 2009).

15 Subsection (3) makes it clear that the court has a free hand in deciding what the appropriate order is.

16 Use of this word reiterates the court's discretion (see Notes 14 and 15 above).

17 Thus the court in many cases is likely to order the taking of an account under sub-s (2)(*b*) before a sale under an order made under sub-s (2)(*c*).

18 For example the owner of a lien or charge not amounting to a mortgage (see Lyall, *Land Law in Ireland* (2nd edn, Round Hall, 2000), pp 773–775; Wylie, *Irish Land Law* (3rd edn, Tottel Publishing, 1997), paras 12.15–12.20).

19 Section 31 relates to a judgment mortgage relating to co-owned land. It ties in with the provisions relating to enforcement of a judgment mortgage generally in s 117(2) (see the Notes to that section).

20 This ties in with Part 4, especially s 22 which recognises that disputes may arise between trustees and beneficiaries in respect of land held on trust. Where the land is co-owned either at law or in equity, it may be that it is more appropriate for a trustee to seek a specific order under s 31 than referring a dispute under s 22. Thus both beneficiaries and trustees may agree that accounting adjustments are needed, but cannot agree on what basis or how they should be applied, and so the trustees might seek an order under sub-s (2)(*d*) (see Note 21 below).

21 Paragraph (*b*) lists the sort of adjustments that could be ordered under sub-s (2)(*d*) and, in doing so, clarifies and extends the jurisdiction introduced by s 23 of the 1707 Act (see Note 11 above). To a large extent it is declaratory of the law developed by the courts (see the discussion in Conway, *Co-Ownership of Land: Partition Actions and Remedies* (Tottel Publishing, 2000), ch 11). Note, in particular, the wide discretion confirmed by subparagraph (v) (see Note 27 below). Essentially such adjustments are made to "even up" the position of the various co-owners in respect of the co-owned land.

22 Note that subparagraph (i) requires that the other co-owners have been "excluded", which involves an element of refusal by the occupying co-owner to allow others to exercise their equal right to possession (see *Dennis v McDonald* [1982] Fam 63; *Glass v McManus* [1996] NI 401; Conway, *Co-Ownership of Land: Partition Actions and Remedies* (Tottel Publishing, 2000), paras 11.14–11.20). Subject to that the matter is left to the discretion of the court.

23 The key element in subparagraph (ii) is that compensation should be paid only where one co-owner has incurred "disproportionate" expenditure (see *Leigh v Dickeson* (1884) 15 QBD 60; Conway, *Co-Ownership of Land: Partition Actions and Remedies* (Tottel Publishing, 2000), paras 11.28–11.42). Subject to that again the matter is left to the discretion of the court.

24 Again the key element is "disproportionate" payments justifying contributions from other co-owners (see Conway, *Co-Ownership of Land: Partition Actions and Remedies* (Tottel Publishing, 2000), paras 11.43–11.44).

25 They must be other outgoings payable in respect of the land, such as mortgage and insurance payments (see Conway, *Co-Ownership of Land: Partition Actions and Remedies* (Tottel Publishing, 2000), paras 11.45–11.54).

26 Section 23 of the 1707 Act (see Notes 11 and 21 above) referred specifically to an action of account against a co-owner who has received more than his share of rents and profits issuing from the land (see *Kearney v Kearney* (1861) 13 ICLR 314; Dowling, "The Baby and the Bathwater: The Administration of Justice Act (Ireland) 1707, s 23" (1996) 47 NIQ 428; Conway, *Co-Ownership of Land: Partition Actions and Remedies* (Tottel Publishing, 2000), paras 6.23, 11.08 and 11.58–11.61).

27 Subparagraph (v) confirms that subparagraphs (i)–(iv) are simply illustrative as to the sort of accounting adjustment order which the court can make under sub-s (2)(*d*). The court retains a complete discretion as to what other order it thinks necessary to achieve fairness between the co-owners.

28 Subsection (5) contains a saving for other statutory jurisdiction which the court has in respect of land held in co-ownership.

29 Under the Family Home Protection Act 1976 the court may be asked to dispense with consent of a "non-owning" spouse to alienation of the family home (see s 4), but the "owning" spouse may be holding it on trust for that spouse because he or she has a claim to an equitable share (eg under a constructive trust). The equitable or beneficial interest in the home is, therefore, co-owned.

30 The Family Law Act 1995 gives the court wide powers to make property adjustment orders in respect of property (which may be co-owned) on separation of spouses (see s 9).

31 The Family Law (Divorce) Act 1996 gives power to make such property adjustment orders on divorce (see s 14).

32 Subsection (6) was added at the Seanad Committee Stage. It was a matter of some controversy whether the equitable jurisdiction in the court to order partition of co-owned property survived the repeal by the statute law revision Acts (eg Statute Law Revision (Pre-Union Irish Statutes) Act 1962) of the legislation originally creating statutory jurisdiction (the Act for Jointenants 1542, 33 Hen 8 c 10 (Ir)) (see *O'D v O'D* [1983] IEHC 82; cf *F v F* [1987] ILRM 1). The clear view of the commentators was that the equitable jurisdiction survived (see Pearce, "The Right to Partition and Sale Between Co-owners" (1987) 5 ILT (NS) 36; Mee, "Partition and Sale of the Family Home" (1993) 15 DULJ 78; Lyall, *Land Law in Ireland* (2nd edn, Round Hall, 2000), p 446; Wylie, *Irish Land Law* (3rd edn, Tottel Publishing, 1997), para 7.35; Conway, *Co-Ownership of Land: Partition Actions and Remedies* (Tottel Publishing, 2000), paras 6.26–6.44). Subsection (6) now makes it clear that this is no longer the case with respect to co-owned land – s 31 contains the sole jurisdiction. However, equitable jurisdiction with respect to other co-owned property is untouched.

---

[68]

32.[2]—(1) A body corporate may acquire and hold any property[3] in a joint tenancy in the same manner as if it were an individual.[4]   **Bodies corporate.**[1]

(2) Where a body corporate and an individual or two or more bodies corporate become entitled to any property in   **[BC(JT)A 1899]**

circumstances or by virtue of any instrument which would, if the body or bodies corporate had been an individual or individuals, have created a joint tenancy, they are entitled to the property as joint tenants.[5]

(3) On the dissolution of a body corporate which is a joint tenant of any property, the property devolves on the other surviving joint tenant or joint tenants.[6]

Definitions

See s 3 for definitions of: "instrument"; "property".

Notes

1   Section 32 implements the Law Reform Commission's recommendation that the Bodies' Corporate (Joint Tenancy) Act 1899 should be replaced without substantial amendment (it is now repealed: see Schedule 2) (see LRC CP 34–2004, paras 6.15–6.16).

2   The 1899 Act was enacted to facilitate banks and other corporate bodies to hold land as joint tenants with other persons. The common law found difficulty with this concept because of the right of survivorship which is inherent in that form of co-ownership – a corporation is a body which "never dies" and so the courts tended to construe a transfer to a corporation and other persons as creating a tenancy in common (see *Law Guarantee, etc Society v Bank of England* (1890) 24 QBD 406).

3   Note that, unlike ss 30 and 31, s 32 applies to "any property", as did the 1899 Act.

4   This confirms that a body corporate can be a joint tenant with another such body or individual.

5   This confirms that a disposition in favour of a body corporate makes it a joint tenant if that would be the case in such a disposition to an individual.

6   This confirms that the right of survivorship operates in respect of a body corporate as it does in respect of an individual. Normally on dissolution of a body corporate its assets (which would include its share in property held under a tenancy in common) vest in the State under s 28 of the State Property Act 1954 (see s 9(3)(*a*)(i) and Note 11 to that section).

[69]

PART 8[1]
APPURTENANT RIGHTS[2]

Notes

1   Part 8 implements changes to the law relating to "appurtenant" rights over land which the Law Reform Commission had suggested over the years (see Note 2 below). Such rights do not confer the substantial ownership over land which estates

like freehold and leasehold estates do, but, generally, minor rights in respect of someone else's land. They comprise mostly rights which a landowner has over a neighbour's land (hence the description "appurtenant"). The classic example is an easement, such as a right of way, and many *profits à prendre*, such as the right to fish or hunt and the right to cut timber or turf (turbary). However, it is important to note that the heading to Part 8 is slightly misleading in that it covers some rights which strictly are not appurtenant in this sense. Some *profits* are held "in gross" in the sense that they are not owned by a neighbouring landowner, indeed, they may be held by someone who owns no other land at all (ie other than the *profit* itself) (see generally Lyall, *Land Law in Ireland* (2nd edn, Round Hall, 2000), ch 22; Wylie, *Irish Land Law* (3rd edn, Tottel Publishing, 1997), ch 6; Bland, *The Law of Easements and Profits à Prendre* (Round Hall, 1997)). However, they do share with easements the fundamental feature that they comprise rights over someone else's land and the law governing them is largely the same. They both form part of the law of "incorporeal hereditaments", ie, rights that do not confer the rights to possess or occupy the land (the "corpus") over which they are exercisable, unlike an estate or interest which usually confers that right (which are "corporeal" hereditaments). The view was taken that it was appropriate to treat such rights together in the same Part. For the same reason it was considered appropriate to deal with another category of incorporeal hereditament – rentcharges.

Similar explanations can be given for the treatment of other subjects in Part 8. One is the law relating to "party structures" which concern only neighbouring landowners. The other concerns the law relating to freehold covenants and their enforceability as between neighbouring landowners.

2   The provisions in Part 8 are based on recommendations contained in two major Reports of the Law Reform Commission: *Report on Acquisition of Easements and Profits à Prendre by Prescription* (LRC 66–2002) and *Report on Land Law and Conveyancing Law: (7) Positive Covenants over Freehold Land and Other Proposals* (LRC 70–2003), ch 1. Further recommendations were made in the *Consultation Paper on the Reform and Modernisation of Land Law and Conveyancing Law* (LRC CP 34–2004), ch 7 (see also the draft Bill (Part 7) appended to Report LRC 74–2005). The Consultation Paper also recommended a number of things which are dealt with elsewhere by the Act. It pointed out that a number of incorporeal hereditaments had become obsolete and that various pre-1922 statutes relating to them should be repealed without any replacement. These included statutes relating to tithe rentcharges, former Crown rents and similar rents no longer collected by the State (see LRC CP 34–2000, paras 7.05–7.10). These statutes are repealed (see Schedule 2 and the Notes to that Schedule). Part 8 radically changes the law relating to rentcharges (which have ceased to have much practical significance), but some other provisions in the Act affect these (eg s 73 (see the Notes to that section) and Schedule 2 again lists as repealed other provisions (see LRC CP 34–2000, paras 7.13–7.14)).

[70]

CHAPTER 1[1]

Easements and profits à prendre[2]

Notes

1   It is important to note that Chapter 1 is confined to reforming only those aspects of the law relating to easements and *profits à prendre* which the Law Reform Commission considered in need of reform or modernisation (see Note 2 to Part 8 above). It does not, eg, cover an issue which frequently arises, namely, whether a particular right claimed constitutes an easement. For example, there has been much controversy over the years whether the right to park vehicles on land (which often will come close to possession or occupation and, therefore, more than an "incorporeal" hereditament (see Note 1 to Part 8 above) (see *Redfont Ltd v Custom House Dock Management Ltd* [1998] IEHC 206; *Moncrieff v Jamieson* [2007] 1 WLR 2620) is an easement. The view was taken that the law on such issues should continue to be developed by the courts.

2   Essentially, Chapter 1 overhauls the law relating to prescription (ss 33–39) and rationalises and clarifies the law relating to acquisition of easements and *profits à prendre* by implied grant. As regards prescription it rids the law of the complications of "common law" prescription and the notorious (and unedifying in modern times) doctrine of "lost modern grant". It replaces the Prescription Act 1832, which was applied to Ireland by the Prescription (Ir) Act 1858 and had the unenviable reputation of being "one of the worst drafted Acts on the Statute Book" (see English Law Reform Committee's 14th Report *Acquisition of Easements and Profits à Prendre* (1966 Cmnd 3100), quoted in LRC 66–2002, para 2.25). The English Committee debated at length whether the doctrine of prescription should be retained and by a majority concluded that it should, but that the law should be radically simplified and reformed. The Law Reform Commission came to the same conclusion and, further, that acquisition of easements and *profits à prendre* (including profits in gross) should not be distinguished (see LRC 66–2002, ch 2). The provisions in Chapter 1 are largely based on the draft Bill attached to the Report (see Appendix A to the Report) (for a critique see Mee, "Reform of the Law on the Acquisition of Easements and Profits à Prendre by Prescription" (2005) 12 (1) DULJ 86). It is important to note that, unlike the Prescription Act 1832, Chapter 1 does not, for the purposes of acquisition by prescription, distinguish between easements and profits or, indeed, between different easements and different profits. They are all treated alike, subject to the same rules and same prescriptive periods. This introduces a considerable simplification in the law (see Bland, *The Law of Easements and Profits à Prendre* (Round Hall, 1997), chs 13–17).

[71]

33.—In this Chapter, unless the context otherwise requires[2]—

"dominant land"[3] means land benefited by an easement or *profit à prendre* to which other land is subject, or in respect of which a relevant user period has commenced;[4] and "dominant owner" shall be read accordingly and includes that owner's predecessors and successors in title;[5]

"foreshore" has the meaning given to it by section 2(1) of the Act of 1957;[6]

"interruption"[7] means interference[8] with, or cessation of,[9] the use or enjoyment of an easement or *profit à prendre* for a continuous period of at least one year,[10] but does not include an interruption under *section 37(1)*;[11]

"period of non-user" means a period during which the dominant owner ceases to use or enjoy the easement or *profit à prendre*;[12]

"relevant user period"[13] means a period of user[14] as of right[15] without interruption[16] by the person claiming to be the dominant owner[17] or owner of *profit à prendre* in gross[18]—

(*a*) where the servient owner is not a State authority, for a minimum period of 12 years,[19] or

(*b*) where the servient owner is a State authority,[20] for—

(i) a minimum period of 30 years,[21] or

(ii) where the servient land is foreshore, a minimum period of 60 years;[22]

"servient land"[23] means land subject to an easement or *profit à prendre*, or in respect of which a relevant user period has commenced;[24] and "servient owner" shall be read accordingly and includes that owner's predecessors and successors in title;[25]

"State authority" means a Minister of the Government or the Commissioners of Public Works in Ireland;[26]

"user as of right"[27] means[28] use or enjoyment without force,[29] without secrecy[30] and without the oral or written[31] consent[32] of the servient owner.

Interpretation of Chapter 1.[1]

Definitions

See s 3 for definitions of: "Act of 1957"; "consent"; "land".

Notes

1   Section 33 contains various definitions of concepts which underpin the new law of prescription contained in Chapter 1. These concepts are referred to in the following sections of the Chapter.

2   For example, the running of the "relevant user period" may be suspended under s 37.

3   This recognises that all easements and many profits (ie those other than profits "in gross": see Note 1 to Part 8 above and Note 18 below) belong to a neighbouring landowner. It utilises the long-recognised concepts of "dominant" and "servient" lands (tenements) (see Bland, *The Law of Easements and Profits à Prendre* (Round Hall, 1997), ch 1).

4   This is an important extension of the meaning. Strictly an easement or profit does not benefit dominant land until it has been acquired. Chapter 1 is concerned with the process of acquisition by prescription, ie long use or enjoyment of a *quasi*-right which will not ripen into a full right until the relevant user period has been successfully completed (see Bland, *The Law of Easements and Profits à Prendre* (Round Hall, 1997), ch 13). The definition covers both an acquired easement or profit and one still in the process of being acquired (see also Note 24 below).

5   This recognises the position under the previous law, that a claim to acquisition of an easement or profit by prescription can be based on user or enjoyment of successive landowners. Thus prescription "at common law" (see Note 3 to s 34) was based on theoretical continuous user or enjoyment since the year 1189!

6   This is relevant to the "relevant user period" (see Note 13 below). The definition in the Statute of Limitations 1957 was adopted because it too is concerned with time running against persons (the law of adverse possession). Note that the new general statutory period for prescription is the period for adverse possession under the 1957 Statute (see Note 19 below).

7   This adapts a concept which was incorporated in the Prescription Act 1832 (applied in Ireland by the Prescription (Ir) Act 1858) (both Acts are now repealed: see Schedule 2 and the Notes to that Schedule). The "continuous" running of the "relevant user period" (see Note 13 below) is only interrupted (so as to prevent a claim based on prescription succeeding) where the interruption lasts for a minimum period of one year (see Bland, *The Law of Easements and Profits à Prendre* (Round Hall, 1997), paras 13.10–13.12).

8   Under the 1832 Act this related to action by the servient owner submitted to or acquiesced in by the dominant owner (Bland, *The Law of Easements and Profits à Prendre* (Round Hall, 1997), para 13.11).

9   This wording in the Commission's draft extends the 1832 Act's concept of interruption to action by the dominant owner, but the change may not be that significant. Even under the 1832 Act the user had to be "continuous" and a failure to use or enjoy the right for a continuous period of one year would usually negate that

(see Bland, *The Law of Easements and Profits à Prendre* (Round Hall, 1997), 13.42–13.43).

10 Note that the period of interference or cessation must be for a "continuous" period – intermittent cessation (such as is caused by holidays, illness and similar occurrences in every day life) do not count (even though if added together from a period of years they would amount to one year).

11 The reference to "interruption" in this cross-reference to s 37(1) should probably be to "suspension". The point is that the running of the user period is only suspended during a period of mental incapacity and resumes when the incapacity ceases (ie, a period of user before the incapacity of the servient owner can be added to a period of user after the incapacity ceases to make up the requisite user period for a prescriptive claim). An interruption, on the other hand, stops the user period running altogether and the requisite user period can only start afresh after the interruption ceases (there is no question of tacking on to it any user period prior to the interruption). The Bill as introduced to the Seanad used "interruption" in what is now s 37 (it was s 35 in that Bill) and a new version was substituted at the Dáil Select Committee Stage, substituting "suspended" for "interrupted" in s 37(1). This, in fact, restored the wording of the equivalent provision in the Bill attached to the Commission's Report LRC 66–2002 (s 5(2)). A similar consequential amendment could have been made to the cross reference in this definition in s 33.

12 This is relevant to s 39 (extinguishment of easements and profits) (see the Notes to that section).

13 This is the key concept for acquisition of easements and profits by prescription – as under the previous law, a person acquires such an interest by purporting to exercise it over someone else's land (the "servient land") for the requisite period. The reference is to the "relevant" period because of the different periods in paragraphs (*a*) and (*b*). However, such user is only the basis for a claim to acquisition under Chapter 1, as s 35 requires that claim to be established in court and, if successful, for the court order to be registered (see the Notes to that section).

14 As under the previous law, the "user" comprises use or enjoyment of a *quasi*-right only until the relevant user period has been completed and other formalities are completed (see Note 4 above and the Notes to s 35 below).

15 See Notes 27–32 below.

16 See Notes 7–11 above.

17 See Notes 3–5 above.

18 Chapter 1 applies to acquisition by prescription of all easements and profits including a profit "in gross" (see Note 1 to Part 8 above).

19 Paragraph (*a*) introduces from 1 December 2009 a new, single statutory period for all prescriptive claims (apart from those against State land), in contrast to the complicated provision for shorter (20 years for easements, 30 years for profits) and longer periods (40 and 60 respectively) in the Prescription Act 1832 (see Bland, *The Law of Easements and Profits à Prendre* (Round Hall, 1997), ch 13). As pointed out earlier (see Note 6 above), the single period is the same as the period for a claim to ownership by adverse possession under the Statute of Limitations 1957 (see s 13(2)) – 12 years (see Brady and Kerr, *The Limitation of Action* (2nd edn, 1994), ch 4;

Lyall, *Land Law in Ireland* (2nd edn, Round Hall, 2000), ch 25; Wylie, *Irish Land Law* (3rd edn, Tottel Publishing, 1997), ch 23). This was recommended by the Law Reform Commission in its Report LRC 66–2002, paras 3.02–3.03.

20 The Law Reform Commission recognised that, as in the case of adverse possession claims (see s 13(1) of the Statute of Limitations 1957), the State, which owns large tracts of land over which it would be unreasonable to expect it to keep a close eye, needs special protection against acquisition of easements and profits of land belonging to it (see LRC 66–2002, paras 3.12–3.14). Paragraph (*b*) reflects its recommendation. Note also the "long stop" period of 30 years where the servient owner is mentally incapacitated (see Note 15 to s 37 below).

21 This is also the period for adverse possession claims: see s 13(1)(*a*) of the 1957 Statute.

22 This is also the period under the 1957 Statute. Note that this applies only where the State is still the owner of the foreshore. If it has ceased to be that owner (because a private individual has acquired title to it by adverse possession: see Note 21 above), the prescriptive period against that individual is, of course, 12 years only under paragraph (*a*). The Commission's original draft Bill had the provision relating to foreshore as a separate one (which would have meant that 60 years applied regardless of who owned it: see Mee, "Reform of the Law on the Acquisition of Easements and Profits à Prendre by Prescription" (2005) 12 (1) DULJ 86 at 91, fn 36). The Bill subsequently introduced to the Seanad contained this change.

23 This again utilises the long-established concepts relating to easements and profits (see Note 3 above). Even in the case of a profit in gross, where there is no "dominant land" (see Notes 3 and 18 above), there is always "servient land", ie land over which the profit can be exercised or, to put it another way, land which is subject to the profit held by someone else.

24 Again the extended meaning is used of land in respect of which an easement or profit is in the course of being acquired (but the process has not yet been completed) (see Note 4 above).

25 Again a prescriptive claim may be established on the basis of user or enjoyment against successive servient owners (see Note 5 above).

26 See Note 20 above.

27 This retains a fundamental principle which has long underpinned the law of prescription, both under the common law (and doctrine of lost modern grant) and the Prescription Act 1832 (see Bland, *The Law of Easements and Profits à Prendre* (Round Hall, 1997), paras 13.28–13.41).

28 What follows is declaratory of the general law (see Note 21 above). The Law Reform Commission thought there should be a statutory expression in the interest of clarity (see LRC 66–2002, para 3.32).

29 *Nec vi* is one long-established element (see Bland, *The Law of Easements and Profits à Prendre* (Round Hall, 1997), para 13.29).

30 *Nec clam* is another such element (see Bland, *The Law of Easements and Profits à Prendre* (Round Hall, 1997), paras 13.30–13.33).

31 This clarifies the previous law, especially under the Prescription Act 1832, which seemed to treat oral and written consent differently (see Bland, *The Law of*

Easements and Profits à Prendre (Round Hall, 1997), para 13.36), as recommended by the Law Reform Commission (LRC 66–2002, paras 13.33–13.34).

32 Note the definition in s 3 which includes "agreement, licence and permission". For a recent illustration of the *nec precario* (without permission) principle in relation to a claim to a profit (fishing rights) see *Agnew v Barry* [2009] IESC 45.

[72]

34.—Subject to *section 38*,[2] acquisition of an easement or *profit à prendre* by prescription at common law[3] and under the doctrine of lost modern grant[4] is abolished and after the commencement of this Chapter acquisition by prescription shall be in accordance with *section 35*.[5]

Abolition of certain methods of prescription.[1]

Notes

1   Section 34 implements the Law Reform Commission's recommendation that in order to simplify and clarify the law there was no virtue in retaining prescription at common law (based on user or enjoyment "from the time whereof the memory of man runneth not to the contrary" – in fact, by statute, from the year 1189) or the doctrine of "lost modern grant" (once described judicially as a "revolting fiction" – *Dalton v Angus* (1877) 3 QBD 85 at 94 *per* Lush J) (see LRC 66–2002, paras 2.21–2.24).

2   Section 38 contains transitional provisions governing cases where a user period had commenced on or before 1 December 2009 (see the Notes to that section).

3   See Bland, *The Law of Easements and Profits à Prendre* (Round Hall, 1997), para 13.03.

4   See Bland, *The Law of Easements and Profits à Prendre* (Round Hall, 1997), paras 13.04–13.05.

5   Section 35 instituted after 1 December 2009 a new, single statutory-based law of prescription to replace the methods abolished and the regime previously operating under the Prescription Act 1832 (see the Notes to that section).

[73]

35.—(1) An easement or *profit à prendre*[2] shall be acquired at law[3] by prescription only on registration of a court[4] order under this section.[5]

(2) Subject to *subsection (3)*,[6] in an action to establish or dispute[7] the acquisition by prescription[8] of an easement or *profit à prendre*, the court shall[9] make an order declaring the existence of the easement or *profit à prendre* if it is satisfied that there was a

Acquisition of easements and *profits à prendre* by prescription.[1]
[PA 1832]
[PA 1858]

relevant user period[10] immediately before the commencement of the action.[11]

(3)[12] The court may make an order under *subsection (2)* where the relevant user period was not immediately before the commencement of the action if it is satisfied that it is just and equitable to do so in all the circumstances of the case.[13]

(4) An order under *subsection (2)* shall be registered in the Registry of Deeds or Land Registry, as appropriate.[14]

Definitions

In addition to those in s 33, see s 3 for definitions of: "court"; "Land Registry"; "Registry of Deeds".

Notes

1 Section 35 implements the Law Reform Commission's recommendation that, in future, a prescriptive claim to an easement or profit should be based on a statutory system similar to, but with various simplifications such as those noted under s 33, that which previously operated under the Prescription Act 1832. As it was often put, that Act "aided only the litigant", ie, in order to obtain legal title to an easement or profit by prescription the claimant had to apply to the court for an order confirming the claim (see Bland, *The Law of Easements and Profits à Prendre* (Round Hall, 1997), paras 13.06–13.27). The Bill attached to the Commission's Report LRC 66–2002 followed this (see s 4) but the Bill subsequently introduced to the Seanad added the requirement that the court order should be registered. This was added in furtherance of the policy of improving the conveyancing process and ensuring that as many rights over land as possible are registered and do not stay hidden from purchasers of land (see Mee, "Reform of the Law on the Acquisition of Easements and Profits à Prendre by Prescription" (2005) 12 (1) DULJ 86).

2 Note that the new statutory method of acquisition applies to all easements and profits, including profits in gross (see Note 1 to Part 4 and Notes 3, 18 and 23 to s 33).

3 The requirements to obtain a court order and register it concern only the acquisition of legal title to the easement or profit by prescription. Where a claimant has completed the "relevant user period" to establish a claim, but has not yet completed the formality of applying to the court under s 35, it is possible that an "equitable" easement or profit could be claimed to exist on the long-established principle that a court, in equity, "will not allow a statute to be used as an instrument of fraud". This principle underpins the doctrine of part performance which mitigates a failure to comply with formalities relating to contracts for sale (see s 51 and the Notes to it) (see Keane, *Equity and the Law of Trusts in the Republic of Ireland* (Tottel Publishing, 1998), paras 16.13–16.17; Delany, *Equity and the Law of Trusts in Ireland* (4th edn, Round Hall, 2007), pp 623–627; Farrell, *Irish Law of Specific Performance* (Tottel Publishing, 1994), ch 6). It is also always possible that the servient owner could be held to be subject to an equitable claim on the basis of a

constructive trust or proprietary estoppel (see Bland, *The Law of Easements and Profits à Prendre* (Round Hall, 1997), ch 14). Such matters are obviously relevant where a sale of either the dominant or servient land is being entered into before a court order has been obtained and registered. It was not uncommon for sales to be closed on the basis of statutory declarations confirming long user of such rights, but, even before the new Act, such closings, even if backed up by Counsel's Opinion, proceeded on the basis that the purchaser was prepared to assume that a "good holding title" existed. There was never any guarantee that this was so and it could only be confirmed, if challenged subsequently, by court action. As pointed out above, the Prescription Act 1832 aided only the litigant and even the common law doctrine and doctrine of lost modern grant were grounded in what a court would rule on the evidence put before it. In that sense the new Act does not change the position. A purchaser may still be prepared to close on the basis of a judgment as to whether the evidence furnished shows that a claim would be likely to succeed under s 35. It is, however, a matter of judgment whether the risk of closing without clear legal title acquired by prescription should be run. Many purchasers and their solicitors may take the view that the risk is too high and insist that s 35 is invoked.

4   The Circuit Court has concurrent jurisdiction with the High Court (see Note 23 to s 3).

5   Subsection (2) provides for actions to establish or dispute acquisition by prescription (see the Notes to it).

6   Subsection (3) was added during the Bill's passage through the Oireachtas (see Note 12 below).

7   This confirms that it is open to both a dominant and servient owner to bring an action. As regards such actions rules of court will be made.

8   Section 35 is concerned only with acquisition of easements and profits by prescription.

9   The court must make the declaratory order if the evidence establishes the necessary requirements.

10 This is the new 12-year prescriptive period, unless the servient land is owned by the State (in which case longer periods apply) (see Notes 13–22 to s 33 above).

11 The Law Reform Commission recommended retention of this feature of the Prescription Act 1832 on the grounds that evidence before the court is likely to be fresher and easier to establish (see LRC 66–2002, paras 3.04–3.11) (see also *Orwell Park Management Ltd v Henihan* [2004] IEHC 27; Bland, *The Law of Easements and Profits à Prendre* (Round Hall, 1997), paras 13.13–13.14). Note, however, the change made during the Bill's passage through the Oireachtas (see Note 12 below).

12 During the Bill's passage the view was taken that the requirement to establish user right up to the date of the action might work hardship in some cases. Although this was a requirement under the Prescription Act, it was not for a claim based on the common law or under the doctrine of lost modern grant (which is partly why it was not uncommon to plead all three in an action) (see *Tehidy Minerals Ltd v Norman* [1971] 2 QB 528; *Smith v Brudenell-Bruce* [2002] 2 P & CR 4). Subsection (3) was added at the Dáil Report Stage.

13 Presumably in exercising this discretion the court will take into account the policy behind sub-s (2) (relating to fresh evidence: see Note 11 above). In cases where claims succeeded in the past under the doctrine of lost modern grant there was no user "as of right" for 16 out of the immediate past 20 years (see *Hulbert v Dale* [1909] 2 Ch 570) and 19 out of the past 30 years (*Tehidy Minerals Ltd v Norman* [1971] 2 QB 528).

14 See Registration of Deeds (No 2) Rules 2009 (SI 457/2009); Land Registration (No 2) Rules 2009 (SI 456/2009).

[74]

Tenancies.[1]
[PA 1832, s. 8]

36.[2]—(1) Where the dominant owner acquiring an easement or *profit à prendre* under *section 35* owns a tenancy[3] only in the dominant land, the easement or *profit à prendre* attaches to that land and when the tenancy ends, passes to the landlord.[4]

(2)[5] Where an easement or *profit à prendre* is acquired under *section 35* against a servient owner who owns a tenancy only in the servient land, it ends when that tenancy ends,[6] but if the servient owner—

    (*a*)   acquires a superior interest in the land, the easement or *profit à prendre* attaches to the superior interest,[7]

    (*b*)   obtains an extension or renewal of the tenancy, the easement or *profit à prendre* continues to attach to the land for the period of that extension or renewal.[8]

(3) Nothing in *subsection (2)* prevents the subsequent acquisition of an easement or *profit à prendre* under *section 35* on the basis of a new relevant user period against a landlord who takes possession of the servient land after the tenancy ends.[9]

Definitions

In addition to those in s 33, see s 3 for definitions of: "land"; "landowner"; "tenancy".

Notes

1 Section 8 of the Prescription Act 1832 contained some obscure provisions requiring "deductions" from the user period where the servient land was held under a tenancy, but only in certain cases (see Bland, *The Law of Easements and Profits à Prendre* (Round Hall, 1997), paras 13.18–13.21). The Law Reform Commission concluded that these were an "unnecessary complication" and should not be repeated in new legislation (see LRC 66–2002, paras 3.28–3.29). Instead the Commission recommended that the Irish case law (departing from English law: see Megarry and Wade, *The Law of Real Property* (7th edn, Sweet & Maxwell, 2008), paras 28.040–28.042) ruling that prescription can operate in favour of and against tenants should

be confirmed (see LRC 66–2002), paras 3.30–3.31; see Bland, *The Law of Easements and Profits à Prendre* (Round Hall, 1997), paras 13.47–13.52. In fact the draft Bill appended to the Commission's Report referred to holders of a "limited interest" (defined as an interest "for the duration of a life or lives or for a period certain": see ss 2 and 4). Leases for lives are prohibited by s 14 (see the Notes to that section). Section 36 implements the Commission's recommendation with respect to tenancies.

2   Section 36 deals with both dominant and servient owners who are tenants. The provisions are largely declaratory of the voluminous case law on the subject and avoid some of the odd distinctions which have been made from time to time, often depending upon the basis of the prescriptive claim (eg, under the common law or the Prescription Act 1832) (see Delany, "Lessees and the Doctrine of Lost Grant" (1958) 74 LQR 82; Chua, "Easements: Termors in Prescription in Ireland" (1964) 15 NILQ 489; Lyall, *Land Law in Ireland* (2nd edn, Round Hall, 2000), pp 753–755; Wylie, *Irish Land Law* (3rd edn, Tottel Publishing, 1997), para 6.079).

3   Note the definition of "tenancy" in s 3, which excludes a tenancy at will or at sufferance (see Notes 88–90 to that section).

4   Subsection (1) confirms that where the dominant owner is a tenant only, any easement or profit (this is a case where the profit is not "in gross": see Note 1 to Part 4 above) acquired by prescription attaches to the dominant land and so, when the tenancy ends, passes to the landlord as an appurtenance to that land.

5   Subsection (2) deals with the converse situation, where the easement or profit is acquired by prescription against land held by a tenant.

6   The general rule is that the prescriptive right attaches to the interest of the person against whom the user or enjoyment was exercised and who should have been aware of it and could have taken steps to interrupt it. So long as the tenancy existed the landlord would have no right to possession and so would be unlikely to be aware of the dominant owner's user or enjoyment.

7   The principle at play in paragraph (*a*) is that the tenant should not be able to extinguish the easement or profit he or she has acquiesced in or allowed to be acquired over the servient land by acquiring the landlord's superior interest.

8   Paragraph (*b*) makes it clear that again an easement or profit which the tenant has allowed to be acquired by prescription in respect of the servient land continues to attach to that land if that tenancy is extended or renewed.

9   Subsection (3) makes it clear that the general rule that an easement or profit acquired against a tenant of the servient land attaches only to the tenant's interest (and so ends with the tenancy) does not prevent acquisition of a new easement or profit against the landlord when he or she resumes possession at the end of the tenancy. As a new claim, it must be based on a new relevant user period running after the end of the tenancy.

---

[75]

37.—(1) Subject to *subsection (2)*,[2] where the servient owner is incapable, whether at the commencement of or during the

Incapacity.[1]
[PA 1832, s. 7]

141

relevant user period,[3] of managing his or her affairs[4] because of a mental incapacity,[5] the running of that period is suspended[6] until the incapacity ceases.[7]

(2) *Subsection (1)* does not apply[8] where—

(a)[9] the court considers that it is reasonable, in the circumstances of the case, to have expected some other person,[10] whether as trustee,[11] committee of a ward of court,[12] an attorney under an enduring power of attorney[13] or otherwise,[14] to have acted on behalf of the servient owner during the relevant user period, or

(b) at least 30 years have elapsed since the commencement of the relevant user period.[15]

Definitions

In addition to those in s 33, see s 3 for definition of: "court".

Notes

1   Section 37 implements the Law Reform Commission's recommendation that the extensive provisions in s 7 of the Prescription Act 1832 relating to incapacity should not be repeated, particularly those relating to married women, life owners and minors (see LRC 66–2002, paras 3.20–3.23; Bland, *The Law of Easements and Profits à Prendre* (Round Hall, 1997), para 13.17). Married women have long since ceased to lack capacity, life owners acquired capacity under the Settled Land Acts 1882–1890 and minors usually have parents or guardians to look after their interests. In fact the latter two groups no longer hold legal title to the land because under Part 4 of the Act it will be vested in trustees charged with protecting the land (see the Notes to that Part). The result is that s 37 is limited to mental incapacity and stops the user period running against a servient owner for the period of the incapacity, but subject to a "long-stop" period of 30 years (see Note below).

2   Subsection (2) qualifies the provisions of sub-s (1) in two ways (see Notes 8–15 below).

3   Note that the suspension operates in both circumstances, ie in effect the incapacity may prevent the user period from starting to run because, when the dominant owner starts using or enjoying the easement or profit, the servient land is vested in an incapacitated person.

4   The mental incapacity must be sufficiently severe to have this effect. Note also sub-s (2)(a) (see Note 9 below).

5   Section 37 is confined to this. The Bill appended to the Commission's Report LRC 66–2002 also covered "disease or impairment of ... physical ... condition" (see s 5(2)), but that was dropped from the Bill introduced to the Seanad as inappropriate (see the Commission's *Consultation Paper on Vulnerable Adults and the Law: Incapacity* (LRC CP 37–2005)).

6 The Bill as introduced to the Seanad had the word "interrupted" here but this was changed to "suspended" at the Dáil Select Committee Stage (see Note 11 to s 33 above). Incapacity simply stops the user period running during the period of incapacity and, unlike an interruption, the user period resumes (if it had already started before the incapacity: see Note 3 above) running once the incapacity ceases (eg on death of the servient owner and succession by an owner who is not incapacitated).

7 When the user period starts running again (see Note 6 above).

8 That is a suspension of the user period does not operate.

9 Paragraph (*a*) was not in the Commission's Bill attached to its Report LRC 66–2002, but was added to the Bill introduced to the Seanad. It empowers the court to rule out a suspension where some other person could reasonably have been expected to protect the incapacitated servient owner's interests.

10 By implication someone who is not himself or herself also incapacitated.

11 That will apply in the case of an incapacitated servient owner who is entitled to a life interest or is a minor (see Note 1 above).

12 See Wylie, *Irish Land Law* (3rd edn, Tottel Publishing, 1997), para 25.18.

13 Created under the Powers of Attorney Act 1996.

14 For example, relatives or other persons acting as carers for an incapacitated person not made a ward of court.

15 This imposes a maximum "long-stop" period for a suspension under s 37 as recommended by the Law Reform Commission in its Report LRC 66–2002 (see para 3.23).

[76]

38.—In relation to any claim to an easement or *profit à prendre* made after the commencement of this Chapter,[2] *sections 34* to *37*—

Application of *sections 34* to *37*.[1]

(*a*) apply to any claim based on a relevant user period[3] notwithstanding that it is alleged that an additional user period occurred before that commencement,[4]

(*b*) do not apply to any claim based on a user period under the law applicable prior to the commencement of this Chapter and alleged to have commenced prior to such commencement where the action in which the claim is made is brought within 3 years of such commencement.[5]

Notes

1 Section 38 explains how the new prescription rules apply where a user period commenced before 1 December 2009. The Law Reform Commission's original Bill

appended to Report LRC 66–2002 provided that the new regime would operate prospectively only (see s 7), but this was reconsidered because it would have meant that the old law would apply for many years to come. So the Commission later decided to "ripen" claims in the process of maturing under the old law on 1 December 2009 much earlier (see Mee, "Reform of the Law on the Acquisition of Easements and *Profits à Prendre* by Prescription" 2005 12(1) DULJ 86). The Bill appended to the Commission's later Report LRC 74–2005 instead contained the provision which is now s 38 (see s 39 of the appended Bill).

2   The transitional provisions relate only to claims made after 1 December 2009 (which would involve applying to the court under s 35), but which are based on a user period which commenced before that date.

3   This means a claim based on the 12-year period laid down by s 33 (see Note 19 to that section) which must be the period immediately before the date of an action brought under s 35 (see Note 11 to that section).

4   What paragraph (*a*) achieves for someone who had commenced user before 1 December 2009 is the opportunity to claim the easement rather earlier than would be the case if ss 34–37 applied only to user commencing after that date (as the Commission proposed originally). Take someone who commenced user of a path running through a neighbour's land (who ultimately would wish to claim a right of way) on 2 December 2004. Under the Commission's original proposal that person could not claim an easement under the Prescription Act 1832 (its repeal by the 2009 Act does not affect any rights accrued under it: Interpretation Act 2005, s 27(1)(*c*)) until 2 December 2024 (ie 20 years later, taking the shorter of the periods under that Act; such a period is also what is usually sought to establish a claim under the old common law system and doctrine of lost modern grant abolished by s 34: see the Notes to that section). But under paragraph (*a*) that person can apply to court under s 35 12 years after 1 December 2009, ie 2 December 2021; in effect, 17 years after the user began rather than 20 years. In the case of a profit (where the minimum period under the 1832 Act is longer, 30 years) the claim could be made in an even shorter time than would be required if the claimant had to continue to rely upon the old law.

5   Paragraph (*b*) deals with two scenarios. One is where prior to 1 December 2009 a person has already completed the user period required under the old law. Such a person can continue to rely upon that but must bring an action to establish the claim within 3 years of 1 December 2009. The other is where, again prior to 1 December 2009, a person was very close to completing the new period required under the old law (in effect, was, on that date, within 3 years of completing the period). Such a person has again three years in which to bring a claim relying upon the old law (when in that period the action should be brought depends on when under the old law the period is completed). It is important to note that, because ss 34–37 do *not* apply to such cases, there is *no* requirement that the court order in such actions brought within the transitional period of 3 years is registered (note, however, the need to protect against extinguishment by non-user under s 39: see the Notes to it). Once, however, this transitional period expires (ie 1 December 2012) all claims to an easement will have to be made under s 35 and be based on 12 years' user commencing after 1 December 2009 (ie 2 December 2021 will be the earliest date

for claims to new easements and profits by prescription). Practitioners will have to be alert to these transitional provisions. For example someone who has completed prior to 1 December 2009 a substantial period of user (but not enough to come within 3 years of completing the period under the old law), say 15 years, could not utilise the 3-year transitional period in paragraph (*b*) to rely upon the old law (at the end of that transitional period only 18 years' user could be shown, whereas the old law required a minimum of 20 years.) Instead, paragraph (*a*) applies and such a person has to show a minimum of 12 years commencing after 1 December 2009, which means that on 2 December 2021 a claim could be made under s 35, which actually involves 27 years (12 after and 15 before 1 December 2009). However, it is important to remember that under both the old and new laws these periods were and are minimum periods only and it is very rare for a claim to be made immediately after the minimum period. In practice it is usually made after a much longer period and only when a dispute or query arises between the dominant and servient owner or when it becomes necessary to resolve the issue as part of a transaction with respect to the dominant or servient land.

[77]

39.—(1)[2] On the expiry of a 12 year continuous period[3] of non-user[4] of an easement or *profit à prendre* acquired by[5]— **Extinguishment.**[1]

  (*a*) prescription,[6] or

  (*b*) implied grant or reservation,[7]

the easement or *profit à prendre* is extinguished except where it is protected by registration in the Registry of Deeds[8] or Land Registry, as appropriate.[9]

(2) This section applies to extinguishment of an easement or *profit à prendre* notwithstanding that it was acquired before the commencement of this Chapter,[10] provided at least 3 years of the period of non-user occur after such commencement.[11]

(3)[12] Nothing in this section affects the jurisdiction of the court to declare that an easement or *profit à prendre*, however acquired,[13] has been abandoned or extinguished.[14]

Definitions

In addition to those in s 33 see s 3 for definitions of: "court"; "Land Registry"; "Registry of Deeds".

Notes

1 Section 39 modifies the Law Reform Commission's recommendation that there should be a corresponding presumption of abandonment of an easement or profit acquired by prescription (based on 12 years' user) where 12 years' non-user has elapsed (see LRC 66–2002, paras 3.38–3.40). Instead, the Commission later decided

that conveyancing practice would be simplified by introducing a rule that easements and profits so acquired would be extinguished after such a period of non-user, unless protected by registration. The point about easements and profits so acquired under pre-1 December 2009 was that they are not evidenced by any documentation which will be furnished along with title documents to a prospective purchaser. In the case of registered land they are burdens which affect the land *without* registration (see s 72(1)(*h*) of the Registration of Title Act 1964). In the future, of course, any claimed under the new regime will be registered under s 35, so the provisions of s 39 apply primarily to easements and profits acquired by prescription before 1 December 2009 or acquired during the transitional 3-year period under s 38(*b*) (see Note 5 to that section). The Commission concluded that the same reasoning should be applied to easements and profits arising by *implied* grant or reservation (see on implied grant of easements s 40 and the Notes to that section) (see Mee, "Reform of the Law on the Acquisition of Easements and *Profits à Prendre* by Prescription" (2005) 12(1) DULJ 86). These also are not documented and are again burdens which affect registered land without registration (s 72(1)(*h*) of the 1964 Act applies to all easements and profits unless they are created by *express* grant and, therefore, documented). The result was that the Bill subsequently appended to the Commission's Report LRC 74–2005 contained what is now s 39.

2   Subsection (1) introduces the new rule of extinguishment for existing easements and profits (and those acquired under the old law in the 3-year transitional period post-1 December 2009) as a consequence of 12 years' non-user (see Note 1 above).

3   This mirrors the new period for acquisition of easements and profits introduced by Chapter 1 (see the notes to ss 33–35). Note that, as with the period of user for acquisition (which must be "without interruption": see Note 11 to s 33), it must be a "continuous" period.

4   See the definition in s 33 (and Note 12 to that section). Neither s 33 nor sub-s (1) limits the period of non-user to a period occurring after 1 December 2009, so it applies where such non-user commenced before that date. However, there is a 3-year transitional period in which the dominant owner can protect the right, either by resuming user or by registration: see sub-s (2) (and Note 11 below).

5   Paragraphs (*a*) and (*b*) limit the new extinguishment provisions to easements and profits acquired other than by express grant or reservation.

6   This is what the Law Reform Commission originally proposed (see Note 1 above). Note again that there will be no application of this section to easements and profits acquired in the future under s 35, since it will require a court order and registration (see Notes 1 and 3 to that section).

7   This was the provision added subsequently by the Commission (see Note 1 above). Note that the risk of extinguishment by non-user, and need to protect by registration, will continue indefinitely in the case of easements and profits arising by implication, because there is no equivalent of s 35 for such cases (ie there is otherwise no requirement to register such rights). Since sub-s (1) provides that on expiry of a 12-year period of continuous non-user they are extinguished, they cease to be easements or profits and so are no longer burdens affecting registered land under s 72(1)(*h*) of the Registration of Title Act 1964. Until such expiry, they, of course, remain such burdens.

8   See Registration of Deeds (No 2) Rules 2009 (SI 457/2009).

9   See Land Registration (No 2) Rules 2009 (SI 456/2009).

10 Subsection (2) makes it clear that extinguishment as a consequence of non-user applies to easements and profits already acquired before 1 December 2009. However, there was no extinguishment where 12 years' non-user had already occurred before that date – that would involve an interference with vested rights which would probably be unconstitutional or violate the European Convention on Human Rights and Fundamental Freedoms. Instead, extinguishment will occur only if a further 3-year period of non-user continues after 1 December 2009.

11 The result is that a person who had not been using an easement or profit for a continuous period of at least 9 years prior to that date has a 3-year period running from 1 December 2009 in which to protect it from extinguishment by either resuming user or registering it under sub-s (1).

12 Subsection (3) is a saving for the general law governing extinguishment or "abandonment" of easements and profits by implication – often referred to as "implied release" (see Lyall, *Land Law in Ireland* (2nd edn, Round Hall, 2000), pp 755–757; Wylie, *Irish Land Law* (3rd edn, Tottel Publishing, 1997), para 6.105). This is based on the intention to do so by the dominant owner and the courts have long made it clear that mere non-user, even for a long time, does not necessarily indicate such an intention; at most it may raise a presumption of abandonment (see *Carroll v Sheridan* [1984] ILRM 451; *Orwell Park Management Ltd v Henihan* [2004] IEHC 27). Section 39 does not interfere with this jurisdiction which applies to all easements and profits, however created. Over time s 39 will only have an impact on easements acquired by prescription or implication because it provides for statutory extinguishment regardless of issues relating to intention and in such cases there will be no point in invoking the general law.

13 The saving is important with respect to easements and profits created by *express* grant – s 39 applies only to extinguishment of those acquired by prescription or by implied grant or reservation (see Notes 1 and 12 above).

14 Or what is often referred to as "implied release" (see Note 12 above).

---

[78]

40.—(1) The rule known as the Rule in *Wheeldon v. Burrows*[2] is abolished[3] and replaced by *subsection (2)*.[4]   **Implied grant.**[1]

(2)[5] Where the owner of land disposes[6] of part of it[7] or all of it in parts,[8] the disposition creates by way of implication[9] for the benefit of such part or parts[10] any easement[11] over the part retained,[12] or other part or parts simultaneously disposed of,[13] which[14]—

    (*a*)[15] is necessary to the reasonable enjoyment[16] of the part disposed of, and[17] (*b*) was reasonable[18] for the parties, or would have been if they had adverted to the matter,[19] to assume at the date the disposition[20] took effect as being included in it.

(3) This section does not otherwise[21] affect—

(*a*) easements arising by implication as easements of necessity[22] or in order to give effect to the common intention of the parties to the disposition,[23]

(*b*) the operation of the doctrine of non-derogation from grant.[24]

Definitions

See s 3 for definitions of : "disposition"; "land".

Notes

1   Section 40 implements the Law Reform Commission's recommendation that the rule in *Wheeldon v Burrows* should be abolished and replaced by a statutory provision based on the doctrine of non-derogation from grant (see LRC CP 34–2004, paras 7.22–7.23). It is important to note that the new provision has a limited operation in this respect and that it does not otherwise affect rules governing acquisition of an easement by implied grant (see Notes 21–33 below). In this context the Commission also recommended clarification of the operation of s 6 of the Conveyancing Act 1881, which is often invoked by a grantee to argue that an easement or profit has passed despite not being referred to expressly in the conveyance (see LRC CP 34–2004, paras 7.24–7.27). This is dealt with in the replacement of s 6 (see s 71 and the Notes to that section). The provision originally drafted by the Commission and introduced to the Seanad was amended somewhat to make it clearer at the Seanad Committee Stage (see critique in Mee, "The Land and Conveyancing Law Reform Bill 2006: Observations on the Law Reform Process and a Critique of Selected Provisions" (2006) 11 (3) CPLJ 67).

2   This rule applied only to easements and, as developed by the courts, enabled grantees of land disposed of in parts to claim that they had acquired by implication easements over land retained by the grantor or other parts disposed of by the grantor (see Bland, *The Law of Easements and Profits à Prendre* (Round Hall, 1997), paras 12.05–12.11). It is usually regarded as part of a wider doctrine, namely, that a grantor must not derogate from the grant (see *Head v Meara* [1912] 1 IR 262 at 265 *per* Ross J). The Supreme Court recently approved the application of that doctrine in the context of implied easements (see *William Bennett Construction Ltd v Greene* [2004] IESC 15, approving Barron J in *Connell v O'Malley* [1983] IEHC 17). The essential problem with the rule in *Wheeldon v Burrows* was that there was uncertainty as to its formulation and, therefore, application (it was largely dependent on what were strictly *obiter dicta* of Thesiger LJ in the case itself). The Commission recommended a new statutory formulation more firmly based on the non-derogation principle.

3   This makes it clear that the rule cannot be invoked since 1 December 2009.

4 Instead in cases which might have involved an appeal to the rule prior to 1 December 2009, the provisions of sub-s (2) can be invoked since that date. Note that in such cases the parties are not necessarily restricted to those provisions: see sub-s (3) (and Notes 20–23 below).

5 The formulation of sub-s (2) was expanded somewhat at the Seanad Committee Stage to clarify the operation of the new provision (see Note 1 above).

6 This recognises that the former rule applied (and the new provision applies) to both *inter vivos* conveyances and dispositions by will (see *Phillips v Low* [1892] 1 Ch 47; *Milner's Safe Co Ltd v Great Northern and City Railway* [1907] 1 Ch 208).

7 The classic situation for application of the former rule and the new provision is where the owner of land disposes of part of it only and the grantee argues that an easement arises by implication in his or her favour over the land retained by the grantor.

8 This recognises that the former rule applied (and the new provision applies) also to the situation where an owner of land makes simultaneous dispositions of different parts of the land to different grantees who each claim mutual easements of the others' parts (see *Broomfield v Williams* [1897] 1 Ch 602; *Milner's Safe Co Ltd v Great Northern and City Railway* [1907] 1 Ch 208; *Hansford v Jago* [1921] 1 Ch 322).

9 These words were inserted to make it clear that, just like the former rule, the new provision relates only to easements arising by implication.

10 See Note 8 above.

11 The new provision, like the former rule, is concerned with easements. In so far as profits can arise by implication (which will be rare, given the nature of such rights) reliance will continue to have to be made on other doctrines, such as common intention or the wider doctrine of non-derogation from grant (see Bland, *The Law of Easements and Profits à Prendre* (Round Hall, 1997), paras 12.04 and 12.21–12.22).

12 See Note 7 above.

13 See Note 8 above.

14 Paragraphs (*a*) and (*b*) ground the new provision firmly on the doctrine of non-derogation from grant, as discussed by Barron J in *Connell v O'Malley* [1983] IEHC 17 and the Supreme Court in *William Bennett Construction Ltd v Greene* [2004] IESC 15 (see Note 2 above).

15 Paragraph (*a*) adopts one of the elements of the former rule which was relatively uncontroversial.

16 As under the former rule, it is important to emphasise that "necessary for reasonable enjoyment" is not the same as an easement "of necessity" (see sub-s (3)(*a*) and Note 21 below), ie an easement which must be implied otherwise the land cannot be enjoyed *at all* (eg a right of way necessary to provide access to a property which would otherwise be landlocked). What is required to be established under sub-s (2) is much less than that, that it is necessary for "reasonable" enjoyment (see *McDonagh v Mulholland* [1931] 1 IR 110; *Wheeler v JJ Saunders Ltd* [1996] Ch 19).

17 This makes it clear that both paragraphs (*a*) and (*b*) must be established under the new provision.

18 This makes it clear that the test in paragraph (*b*) is an objective one, ie the court must be satisfied that it was reasonable for the parties to make the assumption as to an easement arising as a consequence of the disposition. This is a matter for the court to judge in the light of the evidence and despite what will often be conflicting views expressed by the disputing parties.

19 This recognises that in many cases which come to court the parties and their legal advisers overlooked the question of easements and the purpose of the provision is to deal with an issue they never adverted to.

20 This provision, like the former rule, is dealing with implied "grant", so the time at which to consider what the parties should be taken to have arranged, had they adverted to the issue, is the date of the grant (see *Re St Clement's, Leigh-on-Sea* [1988] 1 WLR 720).

21 The new provision obviously has an effect on the non-derogation doctrine, in so far as it is based on that doctrine (see Notes 2, 11 and 14 above and 23 below).

22 This is another basis upon which an easement can arise by implication (see Note 16 above). Unlike the rule in *Wheeldon v Burrows*, and its replacement in sub-s (2) (which related and relate only to easements arising by implied *grant* in favour of the *grantee*), an easement of necessity can arise also by way of implied *reservation* in favour of the *grantor* (see *Maguire v Browne* [1921] 1 IR 148; *Maude v Thornton* [1929] IR 455; Bland, *The Law of Easements and Profits à Prendre* (Round Hall, 1997), paras 12.17–12.20).

23 An easement, and also profits, may be held by a court to arise where it is satisfied that this was the "common intention" of the parties (see *Rudd v Rea* [1921] 1 IR 223; *Jeffers v Odeon (Ireland) Ltd* (1953) 87 ILTR 187; Bland, *The Law of Easements and Profits à Prendre* (Round Hall, 1997), paras 12.21–12.22).

24 This preserves the wider doctrine of non-derogation from grant recognised by the Supreme Court in *William Bennett Construction Ltd* case (see Note 2 above) (see Lyall "Non-derogation from Grant" (1988) 6 ILT 143; Bland, *The Law of Easements and Profits à Prendre* (Round Hall, 1997), para 12.04).

[79]

CHAPTER 2[1]

Rentcharges[2]

Notes

1 Chapter 2 implements the Law Reform Commission's recommendation that rentcharges should be regarded as essentially obsolete, so that their future creation should be prohibited, subject to some exceptions (see LRC CP 34–2004, paras 7.11–7.12). Note that the Act does contain other provisions relating to rentcharges existing on 1 December 2009: see ss 11(4)(*h*) and 73 (see the Notes to those sections).

2 Rentcharges are to be distinguished from leasehold rents – there is no relationship of landlord and tenant between rentchargor and rentchargee (see the definition in s 3

and Notes 81–83 to that section). Essentially a rentcharge arises where an annual or periodic sum is "charged" on land (see Lyall, *Land Law in Ireland* (2nd edn, Round Hall, 2000), pp 757–764; Wylie, *Irish Land Law* (3rd edn, Tottel Publishing, 1997), paras 6.015 and 6.131–6.145). They used to be commonly created under family settlements in order to provide "pin money" or annuities for younger members of the family not given a substantial interest in the land, such as a fee tail or life estate (see Lyall, *Land Law in Ireland* (2nd edn, Round Hall, 2000), p 382; Wylie, *Irish Land Law* (3rd edn, Tottel Publishing, 1997), paras 6.015 and 6.134). But this belongs to a different era of landowning and the Commission concluded that there was no need for such charges in modern times.

---

[80]

41.—(1) Subject to *subsection (2)*,[2] the creation of a rentcharge at law or in equity is prohibited.[3]

(2) *Subsection (1)* does not apply to the creation of a rentcharge under—

    (*a*)   a contract entered into before the commencement of this Chapter,[4]

    (*b*)   an order of the court,[5] or

    (*c*)   any statutory provision.[6]

Prohibition of certain rent-charges.[1]

Definitions

See s 3 for definition of: "rentcharge".

Notes

1   Section 41 implements the Law Reform Commission's recommendation for the prohibition of the creation of future rentcharges (see Notes 1 and 2 to Chapter 2 above). Note the word "certain"; see the exceptions in sub-s (2) (see Notes 4–6 below).

2   Subsection (2) permits a limited class of rentcharges still to be created.

3   Note that the prohibition applies to both legal and equitable rentcharges.

4   This is the usual saving for obligations entered into before the Act commenced on 1 December 2009; cf s 12 (4) (see Notes 11 and 12 to that section).

5   This saving was thought appropriate but it must be doubtful whether a court would order the creation of a rentcharge nowadays, as there are probably better ways of arranging income payments. However, the courts' power under legislation like the Family Law Act 1995 (see ss 8 and 9) and Family Law (Divorce) Act 1996 (see ss 13 and 14) to make secured periodical payments orders and property adjustment orders are very wide.

6   It used to be common for statutes to create rentcharges. The Commission drew attention to those created in respect of land drainage and improvement schemes promoted under legislation like the Landed Property Improvement (Ireland) Act

1847 (see LRC CP 34–2004, para 7.11). In fact the numerous pre-1922 Acts dealing with such matters are repealed by the Act (see Schedule 2) because such schemes nowadays operate under post-1922 statutes like the Arterial Drainage Acts 1945 and 1955 (see LRC CP 34–2004, paras 13.12–13.13). See also s 81(5)(*b*) and Note 13 to that section.

[81]

Enforcement of rentch-arges.[1]
[CA 1881, s. 44]

42.—Subject to any other statutory provision,[2] from the commencement of this Chapter,[3] a rentcharge is enforceable as a simple contract debt only.

Definition

See s 3 for the definition of: "rentcharge".

Notes

1 The Law Reform Commission originally proposed that, so far as existing rentcharges were concerned, the provisions in s 44 of the Conveyancing Act 1881 relating to enforcement of rentcharges should be re-enacted without substantial amendment. This was subject to deletion of references to the obsolete right of distress (see LRC CP 34–2004, paras 7.15–7.16). The other remedies in s 44 were a right of entry to take possession until arrears are paid off and the right to devise the land to a trustee to enable the trustee to mortgage the lease and thereby raise money to pay off arrears. In the end it was decided that such cumbersome remedies were obsolete and not worth re-enacting, so the Bill introduced to the Seanad contained what is now s 42. Section 44 of the 1881 Act is repealed (see Schedule 2).

2 This saving is designed to cover any other statutory provision which relates to enforcement of rentcharges, particularly statutes creating rentcharges (see Note 6 to s 41 above).

3 That is 1 December 2009.

[82]

CHAPTER 3[1]

Party structures[2]

Notes

1 Chapter 3 implements the Law Reform Commission's recommendation that the long-forgotten provisions in the Boundaries Act (Ireland) 1721 (which is repealed: see Schedule 2) (see Wylie, *Irish Land Law* (3rd edn, Tottel Publishing, 1997), para 7.57) relating to disputes between neighbouring landowners should be replaced by a

modern system of statutory regulation. It was also envisaged that this would extend the provisions of the private and local Dublin Corporation Act 1890 (the 2009 Act does not repeal this rarely invoked Act: see Wylie, *Irish Land Law* (3rd edn, Tottel Publishing, 1997), paras 7.58–7.62). In addition it was recommended that another matter which often arises as between neighbouring landowners should be dealt with, namely, the need to access neighbouring land in order to be able to carry out work to a building so close to the boundary line, that access can only be gained from the neighbouring land (see LRC CP 34–2004, paras 6.23–6.26). Precedents for such legislation existed in England and Wales: the Party Wall, etc Act 1996 and Access to Neighbouring Land Act 1992. However, those Acts have given rise to some difficulties of interpretation and seem to overlap in a not very satisfactory way (see Megarry and Wade, *The Law of Real Property* (7th edn, Sweet & Maxwell, 2008), paras 30.035–30.045).

2   Chapter 3 introduces the new statutory regime which covers the matters referred to in Note 1 above in an integrated way. In essence it is designed to cover a wide variety of situations where a landowner wishes or needs to carry our works to "structures" dividing neighbouring properties or situated so close to a neighbouring property that access is needed in order to carry out the works. It provides a mechanism to resolve disputes or difficulties which may arise from an uncooperative or recalcitrant neighbour – an application can be made to the District Court for a "works order", but there are various protections for the neighbour against abuse by a domineering landowner.

[83]

43.—In this Chapter, unless the context otherwise requires—

Interpretation of Chapter 3.[1]

"adjoining" includes adjacent;[2]

"adjoining owner" means the owner of any estate or interest in a building or unbuilt-on land[3] adjoining[4] that of the building owner;[5]

"building" includes part of a building;[6]

"building owner" means the owner for the time being of any estate or interest[7] in a building or unbuilt-on land who wishes to carry out works[8] to a party structure;[9]

"the court" means the District Court;[10]

"party structure"[11] means any arch, ceiling, ditch, fence, floor, hedge, partition, shrub, tree, wall or other structure[12] which horizontally, vertically or in any other way[13]—

(*a*) divides adjoining[14] and separately owned[15] buildings,[16] or (*b*) is situated at or on or so close to the boundary line between adjoining and separately owned buildings or between such buildings and unbuilt-on lands that it is impossible or not reasonably practical to carry out works to the structure without access to the adjoining building or unbuilt-on land,[17]

and includes any such structure which is—

(i) situated entirely in or on one of the adjoining buildings or unbuilt-on lands,[18] or

(ii) straddles the boundary line between adjoining buildings or between such buildings and unbuilt-on lands and is either co-owned by their respective owners or subject to some division of ownership between them;[19]

"works"[20] include[21]—

(*a*) carrying out works of adjustment, alteration, cutting into or away, decoration, demolition, improvement, lowering, maintenance, raising, renewal, repair, replacement, strengthening or taking down,

(*b*) cutting, treating or replacing any hedge, tree or shrub,

(*c*) clearing or filling in ditches,

(*d*) ascertaining the course of cables, drains, pipes, sewers, wires or other conduits and clearing, renewing, repairing or replacing them,

(*e*) carrying out inspections, drawing up plans and performing other tasks requisite for, incidental to or consequential on any works falling within *paragraphs* (*a*) to (*d*);

"works order" means an order under *section 45(1)*.[22]

Definitions

In addition to the definitions in this section, see s 3 for definition of: "land".

Notes

1 Section 43 contains definitions of several keys concepts used in the remaining provisions of Chapter 3. These define the scope and operation of the new provisions.

2 The point about this is that "adjoining" means, literally, joined onto, as in the case of a semi-detached building with different owners owning the two parts. Chapter 3 deals with disputes over not only a "party wall" separating the two halves of such a

building but also buildings and other structures which are not so joined onto a neighbouring building or land, but are so close to the neighbouring building or land that works can be carried out only by access from that neighbouring building or land (see Notes 1 and 2 to Chapter 3 above).

3   In most cases a dispute will concern works to be carried out to a building, but this definition encompasses works, such as new building work, on what is still unbuilt-on land: see the wide definition of "works" (and Notes 20 and 21 below).

4   See Note 2 above.

5   See Notes 7–9 below.

6   The person who wishes to carry out the work may own or occupy only part of a building, eg a tenant occupying part of a building who may be in dispute with tenants of other parts of the building or the owner of a neighbouring building.

7   Chapter 3 thus applies to tenants as well as freehold owners (see Note 6 above).

8   See Notes 20–21 below.

9   See Notes 11–17 below.

10 Unlike the general provision for the Act, which gives jurisdiction to the Circuit Court concurrently with the High Court (see s 3 and Notes 21–23 to that section). The view was taken that it was more appropriate to give jurisdiction over what will often be a minor dispute to the District Court, which already has jurisdiction under the Dublin Corporation Act 1890 (see s 5 of that Act). But note s 44(4) (and Notes 18 and 19 to that section).

11 This is a key concept in Chapter 3. It is works in relation to such a structure which may give rise to a dispute with a neighbour and which may have to be resolved by applying to the District Court for a "works order" under s 45 (see the Notes to that section).

12 This is a very wide list of items which may comprise a "structure" which adapts the provisions in the replaced Boundaries Act (Ireland) 1721 (see especially the items referred to in s 1 of that Act) and the definition of "party structure" in s 6 of the Dublin Corporation Act 1890. Note that it covers both built structures and growing items like hedges, trees and shrubs.

13 This recognises that divisions between buildings and parts of buildings may not be strictly horizontal or vertical (see Notes 45, 50 and 55 to s 3).

14 See Note 2 above.

15 See Note 6 above.

16 See again Note 6 above.

17 This refers to the issue referred to in Notes 1 and 2 to Chapter 3 above and Note 2 above.

18 This covers the situation where the structure is not a "party" structure.

19 This covers a "party" structure. It recognises that such a structure (which may not be necessarily a "wall") may be the subject of different ownership arrangements (see Lyall, *Land Law in Ireland* (2nd edn, Round Hall, 2000), p 726; Wylie, *Irish Land Law* (3rd edn, Tottel Publishing, 1997), paras 7.53–7.56).

20 This defines the sort of works which a landowner may carry out under s 44 and, if there is a dispute, in respect of which he or she may seek a "works order" under s 45 (see the Notes to that section).

21 The matters listed in paragraphs (*a*)–(*e*) are a huge range of works which reflect the wide definition of "party structure" (see Note 12 above). Note that it is not exhaustive – it is an "including" definition and so other matters of a similar nature may fall within the definition despite not being referred to specifically. Note also the "ancillary" or "consequential" matters covered by paragraph (*e*).

22 See the Notes to that section.

---

[84]

Rights of building owner.[1]

44.—(1) Subject to *subsection (2)*,[2] a building owner[3] may carry out works[4] to a party structure[5] for the purpose of—

(*a*) compliance with any statutory provision or any notice or order under such a provision,[6] or

(*b*) carrying out development which is exempted development or development for which planning permission has been obtained or compliance with any condition attached to such permission, or

(*c*) preservation of the party structure or of any building or unbuilt-on land of which it forms a part, or

(*d*) carrying out any other works which—

(i) will not cause substantial damage or inconvenience to the adjoining owner, or

(ii) if they may or will cause such damage or inconvenience, it is nevertheless reasonable to carry them out.[7]

(2) Subject to *subsection (3)*,[8] in exercising any right under *subsection (1)* the building owner shall—

(*a*) make good all damage caused to the adjoining owner as a consequence of the works, or reimburse the adjoining owner the reasonable costs and expenses of such making good,[9] and[10]

(*b*) pay to the adjoining owner—

(i) the reasonable costs of obtaining professional advice with regard to the likely consequences of the works,[11] and[12]

(ii) reasonable compensation for any inconvenience caused by the works.[13]

(3)[14] The building owner may—

(*a*) claim from the adjoining owner as a contribution to, or deduct from any reimbursement of, the cost and expenses of making good such damage under *subsection (2)(a)*, or

(*b*) deduct from compensation under *subsection (2)(b)(ii)*, such sum as will take into account the proportionate use or enjoyment[15] of the party structure which the adjoining owner makes or, it is reasonable to assume, is likely to make.[16]

(4)[17] If—

(*a*) a building owner fails within a reasonable time to—

(i) make good damage under *subsection (2)(a)*, the adjoining owner may apply to the court for an order requiring the damage to be made good and on such application the court may make such order as it thinks fit, or

(ii) reimburse costs and expenses under *subsection (2)(a)* or to pay reasonable costs or compensation under *subsection (2)(b)*, the adjoining owner may recover such costs, expenses or compensation as a simple contract debt in a court of competent jurisdiction.[18]

(*b*) an adjoining owner fails to meet a claim to a contribution under *subsection (3)(a)*, the building owner may recover such contribution as a simple contract debt in a court of competent jurisdiction.[19]

Definitions

Apart from those in s 43, see s 3 for definitions of: "development"; "exempted development"; "planning permission".

Notes

1 Section 44 sets out the rights of a landowner to carry out works to a party structure for a variety of specified purposes, but subject to various provisions designed to protect the neighbouring (adjoining) landowner. (See also the further protection provided for by s 46(2)(*b*) and (3) (see Notes 5–9 to that section.) It adapts provisions in the Dublin Corporation Act 1890 (see ss 11–20 of that Act).

2 This contains the protection for the neighbouring landowner (see Notes 9–13 below).

3 See the definition in s 43 (and Notes 7–9 to it).

4 See the definition in s 43 (and Notes 20–21 to it).

5 See the definition in s 43 (and Notes 11–19 to it).

6   For example under the Building Control Act 1990, Fire Services Act 1981 or environmental protection legislation (see Wylie and Woods, *Irish Conveyancing Law* (3rd edn, Tottel Publishing, 2005), paras 16.67–16.78).

7   In the event of a dispute referred to the District Court under s 45 it would be up to the Judge to determine if it was "reasonable" to allow the works to be carried out.

8   Subsection (3) permits the building owner to make "accounting adjustments" in certain circumstances (see Note 14 below).

9   It is left open to the building owner which option to go for, but, if the adjoining owner refuses to co-operate, the matter may have to be referred to the District Court which, in making a works order, can lay down various terms and conditions (see s 46 and the Notes to it).

10 Note that both paragraphs (*a*) and (*b*) must be complied with.

11 Subparagraph (i) is an important protection for an adjoining owner, since it will often be only after obtaining such advice that a decision will be made to agree to or oppose the works.

12 Note again that both subparagraphs (i) and (ii) must be complied with.

13 This is over and above making good the damage or reimbursing the cost of making it good. It would cover disruption to the adjoining owner's business conducted on the adjoining land.

14 Subsection (3) recognises that both the building owner and adjoining owner may share the benefits of the party structure and so it may be fair to make accounting adjustments to payments which the building owner would otherwise have to make under subsection (2).

15 The adjustments should reflect the use or enjoyment of the party structure which the parties have had in the past and will continue to have following the works.

16 See Note 15 above.

17 Subsection (4) enables either party to sue the other in the event that various actions, payments or claims under the previous provisions are not met.

18 Note that, in this instance, the court is not necessarily the District Court (see Note 10 to s 43 above).

19 Note again that this is not necessarily the District Court.

---

[85]

Works orders.[1]

45.—(1) A building owner[2] who is in dispute with an adjoining owner[3] with respect to exercise of rights under *section 44* may apply to the court[4] for an order authorising the carrying out of specified works[5] (a "works order").

(2) In determining whether to make a works order and, if one is to be made,[6] what terms and conditions should be attached to it, the court shall have regard[7] to *section 44* and may take into account any other circumstances which it considers relevant.[8]

Notes

1　Section 45 enables a building owner to apply to the District Court to resolve a dispute with an adjoining owner over works to a party structure. Only the building owner may apply. The adjoining owner may simply refuse to co-operate, in which case the building owner is the one who has to force the issue.

2　See the definition in s 43 (and Notes 7–9 to it).

3　See the definition in s 43 (and Notes 3–5 to it).

4　The District Court (see s 43 and Note 10 to it). As to applications rules will be made for these.

5　See the definition of "works" in s 43 (and Notes 20–21 to it).

6　The District Judge has a discretion whether to make an order and, if making one, as to what terms and conditions to impose, but that discretion must be exercised after having regard to the provisions of s 44 (which sets out what a building owner is entitled to do and on what basis: see the Notes to that section).

7　This is mandatory. The District Judge cannot exercise his or her discretion without considering this matter.

8　But what other circumstances are taken into account is left to the District Judge – it is for him or her to consider what else is relevant.

[86]

46.—(1) Subject to *subsection (3)*,[2] a works order shall authorise the carrying out of the works specified, on such terms and conditions (including those necessary to comply with *section 44*)[3] as the court thinks fit in the circumstances of the case.

Terms and conditions of works orders.[1]

(2) Without prejudice to the generality of *subsection (1)*, a works order may—

(*a*)[4]　authorise the building owner, and that owner's agents, employees or servants, to enter on an adjoining owner's building or unbuilt-on land for any purpose connected with the works,

(*b*)[5]　require the building owner to indemnify or give security to the adjoining owner for damage, costs and expenses caused by or arising from the works or likely so to be caused or to arise.

(3)[6] A works order shall not authorise any permanent[7] interference with, or loss of, any easement of light or other easement[8] or other right[9] relating to a party structure.

Notes

1 Section 46 gives the District Judge a wide discretion as to the terms and conditions to be attached to a works order made under s 45. Note, however, that this discretion must be exercised by having regard to the rights and obligations of a building owner set out in s 44 (see s 45(2) and Notes 7 and 8 to that section).

2 This contains an important saving with respect to easements and other rights (see Note 6 below).

3 This would include the provisions for making good damage, payments, claims and deductions in sub-ss (3) and (4) of s 44 (see Notes 8–16 to that section).

4 Paragraph (*a*) facilitates the building owner in carrying out the works.

5 Paragraph (*b*) gives further protection to the adjoining owner, over and above that given by s 44(2) and (4) (see the Notes to that section).

6 This again gives extra protection to an adjoining owner and imposes an important restriction on building owners' rights under s 44. If any such interference would be the consequence of the works, the building owner will have to negotiate a release of the easement or other right.

7 This qualification is important – often the works will cause temporary interference when they are being carried out.

8 For example an easement of support.

9 For example wayleaves similar to easements to run pipes, wires and cables through the party structure.

[87]

Discharge or modification of works orders.[1]   **47.**—On the application of any person affected[2] by a works order, the court may discharge or modify the order, on such terms and conditions as it thinks fit.[3]

Notes

1 Section 47 enables "any person" affected by a works order (including, therefore, both the building owner who obtained it and the adjoining owner) to apply for it to be discharged or modified. Note that the Act does *not* contain a provision for registration of works orders which was in the Bill appended to the Law Reform Commission's Report LRC 74–2005 (see s 49). The view was taken subsequently that this was neither necessary nor appropriate in respect of what would normally be temporary works carried out on land, so that the relevance of a works order would have a very limited lifespan.

2 Apart from the building owner and adjoining owner (see Note 1 above), this might include other occupants of a tenanted building or its landlord or management company.

3 Again the District Judge is given a wide discretion.

[88]

CHAPTER 4[1]

Freehold covenants[2]

Notes

1   Chapter 4 implements the recommendations by the Law Reform Commission that the law relating to *freehold* covenants, especially their enforceability, should be overhauled (see *Report on Land Law and Conveyancing Law: (7) Positive Covenants over Freehold Land and Other Proposals* (LRC 70–2003), ch 1). The main problem with that law was that it never developed properly, so that often a freehold covenant would not bind successors in title. In particular, the running of the burden of a freehold covenant (ie against successors of the original covenantor) was restricted by the rule in *Tulk v Moxhay* (1848) 2 Ph 774 to "negative" or "restrictive" covenants (eg a covenant restricting the use of land to certain purposes) and did not extend to "positive" covenants (those involving expenditure of money or other positive action, eg a covenant to build or repair) (see Lyall, *Land Law in Ireland* (2nd edn, Round Hall, 2000), ch 21; Wylie, *Irish Land Law* (3rd edn, Tottel Publishing, 1997), ch 19). This was in marked contrast to leasehold covenants where as a result of statutory intervention centuries ago both the benefit and burden of all types of covenant found in leases, and entered into by both landlords and tenants, pass to their respective successors in title (see Wylie, *Landlord and Tenant Law* (2nd edn, Tottel Publishing, 1998), ch 21). In addition the Commission recommended introduction of jurisdiction, which has long existed in England and Wales (introduced by s 84 of the Law of Property Act 1925: see Megarry and Wade, *The Law of Real Property* (7th edn, Sweet & Maxwell, 2008), paras 32.084–32.093), to discharge or modify covenants which have become obsolete or involve an "unreasonable interference" with the use and enjoyment of land. Both these matters are covered by Chapter 4. The provisions are largely based on the draft legislation contained in the Commission's Report (LRC 70–2003, para 1.20), but a number of amendments were made to the Bill introduced to the Seanad to meet points raised during its passage (see Mee and Murphy, "Reform of the Law of Covenants" (2007) 12(3) CPLJ 100). Those amendments were made at the Dáil Select Committee Stage.

2   It is important to emphasise that Chapter 4 is confined to *freehold* covenants and does not affect the law relating to leasehold covenants (see Note 1 above). The defects in the law relating to enforceability of freehold covenants had been judicially noted, especially because of its impact on conveyancing practice (see *Metropolitan Properties Ltd v O'Brien* [1995] 2 ILRM 383; *Cardiff Meats Ltd v McGrath* [2007] IEHC 219). It explains why multi-unit developments (like apartment buildings and office blocks) have hitherto been leasehold developments (see Wylie and Woods, *Irish Conveyancing Law* (3rd edn, Tottel Publishing, 2005), paras 19.11–19.22; Laffoy, *Irish Conveyancing Precedents* (Bloomsbury Professional), Division C; Law Reform Commission's *Report on Multi-Unit Developments* (LRC 90–2008)). The changes introduced by Chapter 4 may well cause a change in conveyancing practice in the future with respect to such developments (note also the Multi-Unit

Land and Conveyancing Law Reform Act 2009, s 48

Development Bill (No 32 of 2009) recently introduced by the Government). A consequence of the new provisions is that provisions relating to covenants in the Conveyancing Act 1881 (ss 58 and 59) and Conveyancing Act 1911 (s 11) could be repealed.

The mechanism for getting the benefit of the law relating to leasehold covenants for a freehold interest by using a fee farm grant (see Wylie, *Irish Land Law* (3rd edn, Tottel Publishing, 1997), paras 4.099–4.101) ceased to be available after 1 December 2009 by virtue of s 12 (see Notes to that section).

[89]

Interpretation of Chapter 4.[1]

48.—In this Chapter, unless the context otherwise requires—

"developer"[2] means the person who creates a scheme of development[3] and that person's successors in title;

"dominant land"[4] means freehold land with the benefit of a covenant to which other freehold land is subject;[5] and "dominant owner" shall be read accordingly and includes persons deriving title from or under that owner;[6]

"freehold covenant"[7] means a covenant attaching to dominant land[8] and servient land[9] which has been entered into after the commencement of this Chapter;[10]

"persons deriving title"[11] include[12]—

(*a*) a person who has acquired title to the land by possession under the Act of 1957;[13]

(*b*) a mortgagee, or receiver appointed by a mortgagee, in possession of the land;[14]

"scheme of development"[15] means a development of land under which[16]—

(*a*) the land is, or is intended to be, subdivided into 2 or more parts for conveyance in fee simple to each owner of a part;[17]

(*b*) there is an intention as between the developer and the owners of parts to create reciprocity of covenants in accordance with *section 49(3)*;[18]

(*c*) that intention is expressed in each conveyance to the owners of parts or implied from the covenants in question as they relate to the parts and the proximity of the relationship between their owners;[19]

"servient land"[20] means freehold land which is subject to a covenant benefiting other freehold land;[21] and "servient owner" shall be read accordingly and includes—

(a) persons deriving title from or under that owner,[22] but not a tenant for a period less than 5 years,[23]

(b) in the case of a covenant which is restrictive in substance, a licensee or other person in occupation of the land with or without the consent of that owner.[24]

Definition

In addition to the definitions in this section, see s 3 for definitions of: "Act of 1957"; "consent"; "conveyance"; "development"; "land"; "mortgagee"; "possession".

Notes

1   Section 48 defines various concepts which are fundamental to the substantive provisions in ss 49 and 50.

2   This is relevant to the definition of "scheme of development" (see Notes 15–19 below).

3   This is referred to in s 49(3) (see Notes 14–16 to that section).

4   This is referred to in the definition of "freehold covenant" (see Notes 7–10 below). In essence, what s 49 does is turn a freehold covenant into a *legal* interest in land, like an easement or *profit à prendre*. (Note that it is now included with those interests in the list of legal interests set out in s 11(4): see paragraphs (a), (b) and (f) and Notes 33, 34 and 38 to that section). Previously, owing to the fact that the burden of a freehold covenant (where it did run: see Note 1 to Chapter 4 above) ran in equity only under the rule in *Tulk v Moxhay* (1848) 2 Ph 774 it created an equitable interest only (see Lyall, *Land Law in Ireland* (2nd edn, Round Hall, 2000), p 694; Wylie, *Irish Land Law* (3rd edn, Tottel Publishing, 1997), paras 19.44–19.45). This has obvious consequences for the priority of freehold covenants created after 1 December 2009 – legal interests bind the whole world and are not, like equitable interests, vulnerable to losing priority to a *bona fide* purchaser of a legal interest (under the doctrine of notice: see s 86 and the Notes to that section): see LRC 70–2003, para 1.16. Note also that, like easements and profits created by express grant (see s 69(1)(j) of the Registration of Title Act 1964), freehold covenants affecting registered land must be registered as burdens on the folio relating to the *servient* land in order to preserve their enforceability against that land. Section 129 adds a new paragraph (kk) to s 69(1) of the 1964 Act (see the Note to s 129). The *benefit* of a freehold covenant can be noted on the folio relating to the *dominant* land under s 82 of the 1964 Act (as a right "appurtenant" to that land). The language of "dominant" and "servient" owner is, of course, the traditional language of the law of easements (see s 33 and Notes 3–5 and 23–25 to that section) and Chapter 4 adapts it to the new status of freehold covenants.

5   This confirms the new general rule that freehold covenants bind successors in title of the original covenantee (and also covenantors – see definition of "servient owner" and Notes 20–24 below).

6   Note that the definition not only covers a direct successor of the freehold estate owned by the original covenantee, but also someone who derives title "under" either the original freehold covenantee or such a successor, eg a tenant to whom the freehold land has been leased or a mortgagee (see Note 14 below). This change was made in England and Wales by s 78 of the Law of Property Act 1925 (see *Smith v River Douglas Catchment Board* [1949] 2 KB 500; *Federated Homes Ltd v Mill Lodge Properties Ltd* [1980] 1 WLR 594). Such persons will, in future, also be able to enforce a freehold covenant so long as they hold their interest in the benefited land.

7   This definition (combined with the definition of "servient land") confirms that Chapter 4 is concerned only with enforceability of freehold covenants (although as pointed out in Note 5 above and Note 23 below it deals with enforceability of *freehold* covenants by or against *lessees*). Because s 48 is concerned with "freehold" covenants the covenants must be created by a deed (see s 62 and the Notes to it) and so the definition of "covenant" in s 3 does not apply. It is not concerned with the enforceability of *leasehold* covenants, ie those contained in a lease. Those are governed by leasehold law, especially statutory provisions like ss 12 and 13 of the Landlord and Tenant Law Amendment Act, Ireland 1860 (Deasy's Act) and ss 10 and 11 of the Conveyancing Act 1881 (which remain in force and are *not* repealed by the 2009 Act: see Schedule 2 and the Notes to it). For this reason the rule in *Tulk v Moxhay* is *not* abolished altogether (see Note 4 to s 49).

8   See Notes 4–6 above.

9   See Notes 20–24 below.

10 This emphasises that the new law relating to enforceability of freehold covenants applies only to those entered into after 1 December 2009. Note, however, that the provisions of s 50 apply to existing covenants (see Note 8 to that section).

11 This relates to the definitions of "dominant owner" (see Note 6 above) and "servient owner" (see Notes 20–24 below).

12 This word is significant for the reason explained in Note 13 below relating to paragraph (*a*). A squatter who has already acquired title to the dominant land can enforce the covenant, but a squatter still in the course of doing so cannot (cf such a squatter on the servient land: see Note 24 below).

13 This makes it clear that someone who has become the owner of the dominant land by adverse possession can enforce the freehold covenant and someone who has by the same means become owner of the servient land takes subject to the covenant (this largely reflects existing law: see *Re Nisbet and Potts' Contract* [1906] 1 Ch 386). Since a freehold covenant will, in future, be a legal interest (provided, in the case of registered land, it is registered as a s 69(1)(*kk*) burden on the servient land: see Note 4 above) it will, of course, bind everyone on the servient land, even a squatter who has not yet acquired title by adverse possession. As the *Nisbet* case illustrated this was even the position under the previous law, when the dominant owner had an equitable interest only, because such an interest was enforceable against anyone who was not a "purchaser" of a legal interest. However, under the definition here a

squatter who has not acquired title by adverse possession to the *dominant* land will not be able to enforce the *benefit* of the freehold covenant until he has acquired the title.

14 This confirms that a mortgagee (or receiver appointed by the mortgagee) who is in possession of the dominant or servient land can enforce the freehold covenant or is subject to it.

15 This relates to s 49(3) (see Notes 14–16 to that section).

16 Paragraphs (*a*)–(*c*) extend what was often referred to as the rule in *Elliston v Reacher* [1908] 2 Ch 374, which was applied by the Irish courts (see *Fitzpatrick v Clancy* High Court, 1964 No 1879P; *Belmont Securities Ltd v Crean* [1988] IEHC 20; Lyall, *Land Law in Ireland* (2nd edn, Round Hall, 2000), pp 701–705; Wylie, *Irish Land Law* (3rd edn, Tottel Publishing, 1997), paras 19.34–19.37). That rule dealt with cases, such as housing estates and other large developments, where, because houses or units tend to be sold off as soon as they are completed, often when later one owner of a house or unit wished to enforce a covenant they had all entered into when they bought their houses or units against a neighbour, it would not be possible because the person claiming the benefit was not a successor to land to which the benefit of the neighbour's covenant was attached. However, it is important to note that this rule applied only to enforce the *benefit* of covenants, not the *burden*. The original draft of the Bill and as introduced to the Seanad referred specifically to the rule, but that was dropped in the amendments made at the Dáil Select Committee Stage (see Note 1 to Chapter 4 above). The revised provisions make it clear, in order to conform with the primary purpose of s 49 of making both the benefit and burden of freehold covenants as fully enforceable as possible, that the "reciprocity" principle enshrined in the rule in *Elliston v Reacher* applies to enforceability of both the benefit and burden. On the other hand, Chapter 4 is concerned only with enforceability of freehold covenants (see Note 7 above). The rule in *Elliston v Reacher* also applies to leasehold developments (such as apartment or office blocks: see *Alexander v Mansions Proprietary* (1900) 16 TLR 431; *Gedge v Bartlett* (1900) 17 TLR 43; *Kelly v Battershell* [1949] 2 All ER 830; see as regards units in a shopping centre *Belmont Securities Ltd v Crean* [1988] IEHC 20). This aspect of the rule remains untouched.

17 This reflects the scenario which the scheme of development (or, rather misleadingly, since the rule applied to subdivisions of land not necessarily involving building (see *Brunner v Greenslade* [1971] Ch 993) the building scheme) principle was concerned with, ie a developer dividing up land in several plots for sale to different persons (see *Baxter v Four Oakes Properties Ltd* [1965] Ch 816; *Re Dolphin's Conveyance* [1970] Ch 654).

18 This intention to create reciprocity was central to the scheme of development principle enshrined in the rule in *Elliston v Reacher* – "community of interest necessarily ... requires and imports reciprocity of obligation" (*per* Lord Macnaghten in *Spicer v Martin* (1888) 14 App Cas 12 at 25).

19 This reflects the idea that a sort of "local law" for the development is intended to be created (see *Reid v Bickerstall* [1909] 2 Ch 305 at 319 (*per* Cozeus-Hardy MR), adopted by O'Hanlon J in *Belmont Securities Ltd v Crean* [1988] IEHC 20).

20 This is referred to in the definition of "freehold covenant" (see Note 7 above).

21 This reiterates that Chapter 4 is confined to enforceability of *freehold* covenants (see Note 7 above).

22 See Notes 12–14 above.

23 This qualification was added at the Dáil Select Committee Stage. Since the new law in s 49 provides for general enforceability of both positive and negative covenants, so that it would relate to covenants which might involve considerable expenditure of money (eg on building or repair work), the view was taken that such a covenant should not *automatically* bind a tenant with such a limited interest in the land. A tenant would have to covenant expressly in the lease to be bound by covenants affecting the landlord's freehold title to the servient land.

24 On the other hand, paragraph (*b*) reflects the previous law, that the burden of a restrictive covenant affecting freehold land bound, under the rule in *Tulk v Moxhay*, any person in occupation of the servient land who was not a "purchaser", including a squatter (whether or not title has been acquired by adverse possession: see Notes 12 and 13 above).

---

[90]

Enforceabil-
ity of freehold
covenants.[1]

49.—(1) Subject to *subsection (6)*,[2] the rules of common law and equity (including the rule known as the rule in *Tulk v. Moxhay*) are abolished[3] to the extent that they relate to the enforceability of a freehold covenant.[4]

[CA 1881,
ss. 58 and 59]

(2) Subject to *subsections (3)* to *(6)*, any freehold covenant which imposes in respect of servient land an obligation to do or to refrain from doing any act or thing[5] is enforceable[6]—

  (*a*) by[7]—

   (i) the dominant owner for the time being,[8] or

   (ii) a person who has ceased to be that owner but only in respect of any breach of covenant occurring during the period when that person was such owner,[9]

  (*b*) against[10]—

   (i) the servient owner for the time being in respect of any breach of covenant by that owner[11] or which occurred before and continued unremedied after that person became the servient owner,[12] or

   (ii) a person who has ceased to be that owner, but only in respect of a breach of covenant which occurred during the period when that person was such owner.[13]

(3) Where there is a scheme of development[14] *subsection (2)* applies so as to render covenants which are capable of

reciprocally benefiting and burdening the parts of land within the scheme[15] enforceable by and against the owners for the time being of such parts or persons referred to in *subsection (2)(a)(ii) and (2)(b)(ii)*.[16]

(4)[17] Where the servient land has been subdivided any obligations, whether to do or to refrain from doing any act or thing, relating to that land—

    (*a*)   are apportioned, as appropriate to the subdivided parts of the land, between those parts,

    (*b*)   are enforceable accordingly by or against the persons in whom the subdivided parts are vested,

as if those obligations had originally been entered into separately in respect only of each such part.

(5)[18] Any dispute as to the application of *subsection (4)* to a particular case may be referred to the court[19] for determination and, on such application,[20] the court may order such apportionment as it thinks fit.

(6) This section—

    (*a*)   does not affect—

        (i)   the enforceability of a covenant under the doctrine of privity of contract[21] or a covenant for title under *section 80*,[22] or

        (ii) the application to a freehold covenant of the Act of 1957,[23]

    (*b*)   takes effect subject to the terms of the covenant or the instrument containing it.[24]

Definitions

Apart from the definitions in s 48, see s 3 for definitions of: "Act of 1957"; "court"; "covenant"; "instrument"; "land".

Notes

1   Section 49 introduces the new law relating to enforceability of freehold covenants, as explained in the Notes to Chapter 4 and s 48 above. Note that because this law is so comprehensive there was no need to re-enact ss 58 and 59 of the Conveyancing Act 1881 (which are repealed: see Schedule 2 and the Notes to it).

2   Subsection (6) contains various savings and also makes it clear that parties can "contract out" of s 49. This means that it continues to be the case that the instrument creating the covenant can indicate that it is purely personal to the original covenantor or covenantee, so that the benefit or burden or neither passes to their respective successors in title (see *Renals v Cowlishaw* (1879) 11 Ch D 866; *Rogers v*

Hosegood [1900] 2 Ch 388; *Federated Homes Ltd v Mill Lodge Properties Ltd* [1980] 1 WLR 594; *Roake v Chadha* [1984] 1 WLR 40; see also *Power Supermarkets Ltd v Crumlin Investments Ltd* (22 June 1981) HC).

3   This makes it clear that from 1 December 2009 (see Note 10 to s 48 above) the law governing the enforceability is contained within ss 48 and 49.

4   This reiterates the point made several times above, that Chapter 4 is concerned only with the enforceability of *freehold* covenants (see Notes 1 and 2 to Chapter 4 and Notes 7 and 16 to s 48). In so far as the rules abolished apply to the enforceability of *leasehold* covenants they remain in force. Thus the rule in *Tulk v Moxhay* can continue to be invoked by a head-landlord to enforce covenants in the head-lease against a sub-tenant (with whom there is neither privity of contract nor privity of estate) (see *Craig v Greer* [1899] 1 IR 258; *Whelan v Cork Corporation* [1991] ILRM 19 (aff'd by SC, *ex tempore*, [1994] 3 IR 367; *Northern Ireland Carriers Ltd v Larne Harbour Ltd* [1981] NI 171; Wylie, *Landlord and Tenant Law* (2nd edn, Tottel Publishing, 1998), paras 22.08–22.09).

5   This makes it clear that s 49 applies to both positive and negative covenants.

6   The provisions of paragraphs (*a*) and (*b*) render freehold covenants enforceable fully against successors in title like leasehold covenants have been for centuries.

7   Paragraph (*a*) deals with the enforcement of the benefit of a freehold covenant.

8   The general rule is that the benefit can be enforced by whoever is currently entitled to the freehold land benefited by the freehold covenant at the time of enforcement. Note, however, that this may not be the owner of the freehold, because persons deriving title under that owner (eg tenants) can also enforce the covenant (see Notes 6 and 11–14 to s 48).

9   Note that a previous owner can sue only in respect of a breach which occurred when he or she was the owner. To some extent this reflects the position with respect to leasehold covenants (see s 14 of the Landlord and Tenant Law Amendment Act, Ireland 1860 (Deasy's Act); Wylie, *Landlord and Tenant Law* (2nd edn, Tottel Publishing, 1998), para 21.27).

10 Paragraph (*b*) deals with the enforcement of the burden of a freehold covenant.

11 The general rule is that the burden can be enforced against the person entitled to the freehold land subject to the freehold covenant who breached the covenant while so entitled, though again other persons deriving title from that person or in occupation may also be liable (see Notes 11–14 and 20–24 to s 48).

12 This involves liability for continuing breaches of covenant, where they are not remedied after the person becomes the servient owner (again as widely defined: see Note 11 above).

13 This mirrors subparagraph (*a*)(ii) and provides that a servient owner will remain liable for breaches occurring while he or she was the owner of the servient land. This is different from leasehold law under ss 14 and 16 of the Landlord and Tenant Law Amendment Act, Ireland 1860 (Deasy's Act), but those provisions deal with a situation where the person entitled to enforce the covenant (the landlord) consents to the assignment of the lease which relieves the tenant or assignor from liability (see Wylie, *Landlord and Tenant Law* (2nd edn, Tottel Publishing, 1998), paras 21.27 and 21.30). A freehold owner is free to convey or transfer the freehold without

restriction (eg under the rule against inalienability: see s 9(4) and Note 17 to that section).

14 See the definition in s 48 (and Notes 15–19 to that section).

15 On the element of reciprocity see Notes 16–18 to s 48.

16 This extends the rule in *Elliston v Reacher* (see Note 16 to s 48).

17 Subsection (4) supplements sub-s (3) and provides for apportionment of covenants where the servient land is subdivided. This is particularly important where the covenant is a positive one, involving expenditure of money or repairs or other building work. In essence it provides that a servient owner is liable only for an apportioned expenditure or works which relate to his or her part of the servient land.

18 Subsection (5) makes provision for resolution of disputes relating to operation of the apportionment provisions in sub-s (4). These subsections were added at the Dáil Select Committee Stage (see Note 1 to Chapter 4).

19 The Circuit Court has concurrent jurisdiction with the High Court (see Note 23 to s 3).

20 For such applications rules of court will be made.

21 That is as between the original covenantor and covenantee. Note also the saving in s 70(2) (see Note 5 to that section).

22 Such enforceability is governed by sub-s (5) to s 80 (see Note 22 to that section). Note also s 81(4) (and Note 11 to that section).

23 This is a saving for the law of limitation of actions (see s 5(*a*) of the Statute of Limitations 1957).

24 This confirms that it is open to the parties to a freehold covenant to vary the terms of s 49 or to restrict it severely, eg by making it enforceable only as between themselves (ie personal to one or other of them or both of them) (see Note 2 above).

---

[91]

50.—(1) A servient owner[2] may apply to the court[3] for an order discharging[4] in whole or in part[5] or modifying[6] a freehold covenant[7] (whether created before or after the commencement of this Chapter[8]) on the ground that continued compliance with it would constitute an unreasonable interference[9] with the use and enjoyment of the servient land.[10]

Discharge and modification.[1]

(2) In determining whether[11] to make an order under *subsection (1)* and, if one is to be made, what terms and conditions should be attached to it,[12] the court shall have regard[13] as appropriate[14] to the following matters[15]—

   (*a*) the circumstances in which, and the purposes for which,[16] the covenant was originally entered into and the time which has elapsed since then,[17]

   (*b*) any change in the character of the dominant land and servient land or their neighbourhood,[18]

(c)   the development plan for the area under the Act of 2000,[19]

(d)   planning permissions granted under that Act in respect of land in the vicinity of the dominant land and servient land or refusals to grant such permissions,[20]

(e)   whether the covenant secures any practical benefit to the dominant owner and, if so, the nature and extent of that benefit,[21]

(f)   where the covenant creates an obligation on the servient owner to execute any works or to do any thing, or to pay or contribute towards the cost of executing any works or doing any thing, whether compliance with that obligation has become unduly onerous compared with the benefit derived from such compliance,[22]

(g)   whether the dominant owner has agreed, expressly or impliedly, to the covenant being discharged or varied,[23]

(h)   any representations made by any person interested in the performance of the covenant,[24]

(i)   any other matter which the court considers relevant.[25]

(3) Where the court is satisfied that compliance with an order under *subsection (1)* will result[26] in a quantifiable loss[27] to the dominant owner or other person adversely affected[28] by the order, it may[29] include as a condition in the order a requirement by the servient owner to pay the dominant owner or other person such compensation[30] as the court thinks fit.[31]

(4) An order under *subsection (1)* shall be registered in the Registry of Deeds or Land Registry, as appropriate.[32]

Definitions

Apart from the definitions in s 48, see s 3 for definitions of: "Act of 2000"; "court"; "development plan"; "land"; "Land Registry"; "planning permission"; "Registry of Deeds".

Notes

1   As explained earlier (see Note 1 to Chapter 4 above) s 50 introduces jurisdiction to deal with discharge or modification of freehold covenants which have become obsolete or involve an "unreasonable interference" with the enjoyment of land. Such jurisdiction was introduced in England and Wales by s 84 of the Law of Property Act 1925 (and extended by s 28 of the Law of Property Act 1969: see Megarry and Wade, *The Law of Real Property* (7th edn, Sweet & Maxwell, 2008), paras 32.084–32.093) to remove the opportunity of those entitled to enforce such covenants to "blackmail" those subject to covenants into paying substantial sums as a "ransom"

to secure release of what are often "obsolete" covenants. The point is that such covenants will often have been imposed several decades, if not centuries, ago when the circumstances relating to the land (both dominant and servient lands) were quite different. The Commission also drew attention to the comprehensive provisions dealing with "impediments" in Part II of the Northern Ireland Property (NI) Order 1978 (see Dawson, "Modification and Extinguishment of Land Obligations under the Property (NI) Order 1978" (1989) 29 NILQ; Shaw, "Modification of Restrictive Covenants under Statute" (1981) 32 NILQ 289). Those provisions cover also easements and profits and *leasehold* covenants (but not in the first 21 years of the term unless special permission for an application to such covenants is granted). The Commission took the view that there was no need to extend its proposal so widely and so s 50 is confined to *freehold* covenants (see LRC 70–2003, para 1.19). The Commission also recommended that an application should not be made even in the case of freehold covenants until it had been in existence for at least 20 years (see LRC 70–2003, para 1.19). However the Bill subsequently drafted and introduced to the Seanad did not contain this restriction. It does not exist with respect to freehold covenants in the North's provisions and the view was taken that the various factors which the court is obliged to consider under sub-s (2) (note in this context, in particular, paragraph (*a*): see Note 17 below), plus the provision for compensation in sub-s (3), adequately protected the interest of the dominant owner of a relatively new covenant.

2   See the definition in s 48 (and Notes 20–24 to that section). Notwithstanding the extension of that definition to cover persons like licensees and other persons in occupation (including squatters) it must be doubted whether such persons would be interested in making such an application. Even if such a person did, it must be doubted whether the court would regard it as appropriate to exercise its discretion in favour of such a person with a limited or tenuous interest in the land, especially if the freehold owner did not join in the application. It could also be argued that, in the context of s 50, this is an instance in respect of a s 48 definition where "the context otherwise requires".

3   The Circuit Court has concurrent jurisdiction with the High Court (see s 3 and Notes 21–23 to that section). The Law Reform Commission had recommended that this jurisdiction be exercised by county registrars (see LRC 70–2003), but the view was taken that the general position under the Act should be applied here. Substantial issues concerning the rights of landowners may arise under the section (see Notes 7–8 below). Rules of Court will provide for such applications.

4   A "discharge" means that the covenant ceases to be enforceable.

5   The court might take the view that it was appropriate to have the covenant cease to be enforceable against only part of the servient land in order, eg, to facilitate building on or a change of use of that part.

6   A "modification" should be distinguished from a "discharge" and means an amendment or change which falls short of a discharge. Thus it might involve relaxing a restrictive covenant to allow some uses it prohibits, but retaining others. The covenant will continue to operate, but as amended or changed.

7   See the distinction in s 48 (and Notes 7–10 to that section). Thus s 50 does not apply to leasehold covenants, not even those enforceable against sublessees or other

persons under the rule in *Tulk v Moxhay* as discussed by Murphy J in *Whelan v Cork Corporation* [1991] ILRM 19 (see also the Supreme Court at [1994] 3 IR 367). As originally drafted, this section used simply this definition, which meant that it would apply only to freehold covenants entered into after 1 December 2009. However, it was later noted that the Northern Ireland provisions, upon which the Law Reform Commission had put considerable weight (see LRC 70–2003, paras 1.18–1.19), applied to both existing and future covenants when introduced in 1978 (see Property (NI) Order 1978, Article 3(1); the same applied to s 84 of the English Law of Property Act 1925: see sub-s (7)). The view was taken that the same should apply to s 50 and the amendment noted below was made during the Bill's passage (see Note 8 below). It is doubtful whether s 50 applies to a covenant under a fee farm grant existing on 1 December 2009 (s 12 prohibits grants after that date: see the Notes to that section). Under such a grant the grantee holds the freehold land and the grantor has no fee simple – at most the grantor has a right to the fee farm rent and to enforce covenants, but these do not necessarily benefit other adjoining land which was a necessary requirement under the previous law relating to enforceability of freehold restrictive covenants under the rule in *Tulk v Moxhay* (see Lyall, *Land Law in Ireland* (2nd edn, Round Hall, 2000), p 695; Wylie, *Irish Land Law* (3rd edn, Tottel Publishing, 1997), paras 19.31–19.32). In this, as in other respects, covenants in fee farm grants are more like leasehold covenants (see Note 2 to Chapter 4, Note 7 to s 48 and Note 4 to s 49). Many of the factors which the court has to take into account under sub-s (2) also assume that the person entitled to the benefit of the covenant owns neighbouring land and so has an interest in protecting it (see the Notes to that subsection below).

8   These words in brackets were added at the Dáil Select Committee Stage (see Note 7 above). The result is that s 50 applies to freehold covenants created before 1 December 2009. In view of the various factors which the court is obliged (see Note 13 below) to take into account (see out in sub-s (2): see Notes 15–25 below) before exercising its discretion to order a discharge or modification *and* the jurisdiction to order payment of compensation under sub-s (3), it is extremely unlikely that there are any constitutional or human rights difficulties with this provision. The court is clearly required to balance the respective interests of the dominant and servient owners, in the light of various considerations which seem rational and in no way arbitrary or discriminatory, and thus the Oireachtas's solution to the problems created by "obsolete" or no longer useful covenants would seem to be proportionate (the key principle which the European Human Rights Court's Grand Chamber emphasised in its ruling in *JA Pye (Oxford) Ltd v UK* (2007) 46 EHRR 1083 (see the Introduction para 28 above). In fact the Northern Ireland provisions (which are also retrospective) were upheld by the European Court of Human Rights (see *Scott v United Kingdom* (1984) 41 DR 226, (see Application No 10741/84).

9   This is the fundamental concept which must be established to persuade the court to exercise its discretion to make an order discharging or modifying a freehold covenant (see Note 11 below). The Northern Ireland 1978 Order (see Notes 1 and 7 above) uses the expression "unreasonably impedes the enjoyment of land" (see Article 5(1)). The burden of establishing this must be on the applicant (the servient owner). In practice that will mean that in most cases at least one of the factors listed

in sub-s (2) will have to be established to the satisfaction of the court. Note, however, that it is open to the court to consider other factors which it considers relevant (see Note 25 below).

10 See the definition in s 48 (and see Notes 20–24 to that section), but see the remarks in Note 2 above.

11 This confirms that the court has a wide discretion in dealing with an application under s 50, including a discretion to refuse the application altogether.

12 This reiterates the wide discretion the court has.

13 This confirms that the discretion is not totally unfettered. In exercising it the court must have regard to the matters listed in paragraphs (a)–(i).

14 It is up to the court to decide what weight, if any, to give to the listed factors according to the circumstances of the particular application.

15 These factors are all relevant to determining whether the "continued compliance" with the covenant "would constitute an unreasonable interference with the use and enjoyment of the servient land" (see Notes 9 and 10 above).

16 These factors obviously go to the issue whether the covenant should be considered "obsolete" (but note also paragraph (b) (see Note 18 below).

17 Paragraph (a) clearly requires the court to consider when the covenant was created and it is likely that a court would be very reluctant to discharge, or even modify, a covenant which was freely entered into by the parties comparatively recently. This meets a point the Law Reform Commission raised (see Note 1 above).

18 Paragraph (b) again goes to the issue of whether the covenant is "obsolete" (and, therefore, an "unreasonable interference"): see on similar wording in s 84 of the Law of Property Act 1925 *Re Quaffers Ltd's Application* (1988) 56 P & CR 142; *Re Wards Construction (Medway) Ltd's Application* (1994) 67 P & CR 379.

19 Paragraph (c) could be regarded as, in the words of Article 43.2.2° of the Constitution, introducing a "public interest" element into the court's consideration, which serves to emphasise that, in enacting s 50, the Oireachtas was delimiting the exercise of property rights "with a view to reconciling their exercise with the exigencies of the common good" (see discussion in Hogan and Whyte, *JM Kelly: The Irish Constitution* (4th edn, Tottel Publishing, 2003), ch 7.7). The Strasbourg Court's Grand Chamber in *JA Pye (Oxford) Ltd v UK* (2007) 46 EHRR 1083 also emphasised that individual States have a wide margin of appreciation in such matters as control of the use of land and do not infringe the European Convention on Fundamental Rights and Freedoms if they adopt a proportionate approach. See on a similar provision in the English legislation *Re Martin's Application* (1988) 57 P & CR 119; *Re Beech's Application* (1990) 59 P & CR 502.

20 Paragraph (d) also relates to the public interest consideration, but, unlike paragraph (c), is linked more closely to the particular parcels of land directly affected by the covenant which forms the subject-matter of the application: see *Re Ghey and Gallon's Application* [1957] 2 QB 650.

21 Case law in England on the similar concept suggests that "practical benefit" may include enjoyment of a nice view (see *Re Bushells' Application* (1987) 54 P & CR 386), even one enjoyed by others as well (see *Gilbert v Spoor* [1983] Ch 27) or preservation of the peaceful character of the neighbourhood (see *Stannard v Issa*

[1987] AC 175). On the other hand, mere loss of the opportunity to bargain a price for agreeing to release the covenant would not come within the concept – that would defeat the object of the provisions (see Note 1 above) (see *Stockport MBC v Alwiyah Developments* (1983) 52 P & CR 278; *Re Hydeshire Ltd's Application* (1993) 67 P & CR 93).

22 Paragraph *(f)* does recognise that in such cases there may still be *some* benefit, however disproportionate, and that may be considered to be a case where some compensation should be paid as a condition of the servient owner obtaining a discharge or modification in accordance with sub-s (3) (see Notes 26–31 below).

23 It is unlikely that an application to the court will be necessary in the case of an express agreement, unless there are difficulties in securing, eg, a deed of release to complete the agreement, such as where a company has been struck off or the owner has gone abroad and there are difficulties in making contact. In the case of an alleged implied agreement evidence will have to be furnished to show that the dominant owner really did have an intention to discharge or modify the covenant. Cf implied release of an easement or profit: see s 39 (and Note 12 to that section).

24 Such representations, if acted upon by the servient owner to his or her detriment, might give rise to a claim under the doctrine of proprietary estoppel, but that confers an equitable right only until a court determines how the "equity" arising from the estoppel should be satisfied. An order under s 50 may be an appropriate way to do that.

25 This makes it clear that the court is not restricted to having regard to the factors listed in paragraphs *(a)*-*(h)*.

26 It is important to note that sub-s (3) comes into play only *after* the court has decided that an order under sub-s (1) is appropriate and that involves having regard to the factors listed in sub-s (2). Subsection (3) does not allow a dominant owner, such as a developer who has acquired land with a view to redeveloping, to force a dominant owner to sell the benefit of a covenant on the basis that price (compensation) is the only consideration. The court must first be satisfied that there are other grounds for making the order and only then consider whether some quantifiable loss would result from the order.

27 The dominant owner will have to adduce evidence quantifying the loss if compensation is going to be payable under sub-s (3).

28 For an "other" person to be adversely affected he or she must have some interest in the covenant, such as neighbouring landowners on a housing estate or other development protected by a common scheme of covenants (see Notes 15–19 to s 48 and 14–16 to s 49).

29 The court has a discretion whether to order compensation.

30 And a discretion as to the amount.

31 This confirms the court's discretion.

32 See Registration of Deeds (No 2) Rules 2009 (SI 457/2009); Land Registration (No 2) Rules 2009 (SI 456/2009).

[92]

PART 9[1]
CONTRACTS AND CONVEYANCES[2]

Notes

1 Part 9 implements the Law Reform Commission's recommendations in Chapter 8 of its *Consultation Paper on Modernisation of Land Law and Conveyancing Law* (LRC CP 34–2004) (see Part 8 of the draft Bill appended to its later Report LRC 74–2005). The Consultation Paper drew attention to the numerous earlier Reports which had been issued by the Commission but which had not been acted upon (see the Introduction to this book, paras 7–9). The Commission saw this subject as very much bound up with its examination of the possible development of an electronic (paperless) conveyancing system. However, it accepted that it would take some time to devise such a system and have it operating universally and so there was a need to continue statutory provisions which have underpinned the conveyancing system for over 100 years. What Part 9 is concerned with, essentially, is replacing such provisions (in particular the Conveyancing Acts 1881–1911) with more up-to-date provisions.

2 Part 9 deals in particular with contracts relating to land transactions and the conveyancing process (see generally Wylie and Woods, *Irish Conveyancing Law* (3rd edn, Tottel Publishing, 2005). Apart from replacing the 1881–1911 Acts, so far as they deal with such matters, it also replaces various other pre-1922 statutes which relate to this subject, such as the Statute of Frauds (Ireland) 1695 (but only s 2 so far as it relates to land transactions: see Note 1 to s 51 below), Statute of Uses (Ireland) 1634, Conveyancing Act (Ireland) 1634, Real Property Act 1845 and Vendor and Purchaser Act 1874. The Notes to individual sections identify in each instance the pre-1922 provisions being replaced. Part 9 also deals with various points to do with the general law which the Commission had over the years recommended as in need of reform.

---

[93]

CHAPTER 1[1]
Contracts relating to land[2]

Notes

1 Chapter 1 contains various provisions relating to the early stage of the conveyancing process – the contract stage (see Wylie and Woods, *Irish Conveyancing Law* (3rd edn, Tottel Publishing, 2005), chs 6–13). It deals with formation of a binding contract and the position of the parties under such a contract pending completion by conveyance or transfer of legal title to the purchaser.

2   Note that the heading does not refer to contracts "for sale". The point is that the provisions of Chapter 1 (like the provisions of the replaced s 2 of the Statute of Frauds (Ir) 1695) apply to a contract for any disposition of land, ie not just for a sale, but also for the grant of a lease or some other lesser interest (such as an easement) or for a mortgage or charge (see Note 6 to s 51). As originally drafted by the Law Reform Commission the Bill included provisions designed to replace, with substantial amendments, the Sale of Land by Auction Act 1867 (see Draft Bill appended to LRC 74–2005, s 55); this was recommended by LRC CP 34–2004, paras 8.08–8.09. However this was dropped from the Bill subsequently introduced to the Seanad because this matter was to be dealt with by the Property Services (Regulation) Bill 2009 (No 28 of 2009) (see s 57 of that Bill).

[94]

Evidence in writing.[1]
[SF 1695, s. 2]

51.[2]—(1) Subject to *subsection (2)*,[3] no action[4] shall be brought to enforce any contract[5] for the sale or other disposition[6] of land[7] unless the agreement on which such action is brought, or some memorandum or note[8] of it,[9] is in writing[10] and signed[11] by the person against whom the action is brought[12] or that person's authorised agent.[13]

(2) *Subsection (1)* does not affect the law relating to part performance[14] or other equitable doctrines.[15]

(3) For the avoidance of doubt,[16] but subject to an express provision in the contract to the contrary, payment of a deposit in money or money's worth is not necessary for an enforceable contract.

Definitions

See s 3 for the definitions of: "disposition"; "land".

Notes

1   Section 51 replaces s 2 of the Statute of Frauds (Ir) 1695, but only so far as it relates to contracts relating to land (see Schedule 2). Section 2 remains in force in respect of, eg, contracts of guarantee and in consideration of marriage (see McDermott *Contract Law* (Tottel Publishing, 2001), ch 4). Section 2 did not require that land contracts should be in writing, but only that they should be *evidenced* in writing. The Law Reform Commission reviewed this subject extensively in the context of "gazumping" in the 1980s and concluded that it was not appropriate to adopt the change made for England and Wales by s 2 of the Law of Property (Miscellaneous Provisions) Act 1989 (which had proved to be very controversial: see Megarry and Wade, *The Law of Real Property* (7th edn, Sweet & Maxwell, 2008), paras 15.014–15.045), which provided that no contract at all would exist unless put, with all its terms, in writing and signed by both parties (see *Report on Gazumping* LRC 59–

1989, paras 3.18–3.21; see also the Commission's *Report on Land Law and Conveyancing Law: (6) Further General Proposals Including the Execution of Deeds* (LRC 56–1998), ch 3). The Commission later took the view that the whole issue of the formalities for formation of a contract would have to be reviewed as part of the development of a paperless eConveyancing system (see Note 1 to Part 9 above). Pending that development it was considered more appropriate to retain the existing position under the 1695 Statute, especially since the Supreme Court had given a number of judgments bringing much needed clarification (such as *Boyle v Lee* [1992] ILRM 65; *Supermacs Ireland Ltd v Katesan (Naas) Ltd* [2000] 2 IR 273: see LRC CP 34–2004, para 8.03). Instead it was recommended that the provisions of s 2 (so far as relating to land contracts) should be recast in modern language, as was done for England and Wales by s 40 of the Law of Property Act 1925 (subsequently replaced by s 2 of the 1989 Act, as mentioned above). As regards the problem of "gazumping" (which is, of course, usually a temporary one depending on the state of the market) the Commission took the view that this subject (including the Commission's earlier recommendations concerning a statutory form of receipt for booking deposits and regulating advertisements relating to sales of new properties) would be best dealt with by a new power to make regulations by statutory instrument. Such a power is contained in s 88, which as originally drafted referred expressly to such matters. However that section was limited later restricted because the view was taken that they were better dealt with by the Property Services (Regulation) Bill 2009 (No 28 of 2009) (see Part 6 of that Bill) (see the Notes to s 88 below).

2   Section 51, as recommended by the Law Reform Commission, is based on s 40 of the Law of Property Act 1925 (see Note 1 above), but adds clarifications (see Notes 15–16 below).

3   Subsection (2) confirms the position under the Statute of Frauds, that absence of the written evidence required is not necessarily fatal if some other way of establishing the existence of the contract can be found, eg, by reference to equitable doctrines like part performance (see generally Farrell, *Irish Law of Specific Performance* (Tottel Publishing, 1994)).

4   Section 51 is concerned only with the evidence necessary for successful enforcement of contracts by action in court. A contract unsupported by such evidence may nevertheless be valid and enforceable in some other way, eg the vendor may forfeit the deposit for breach by the purchaser: see *Siebel v Kent* [1976–77] ILRM 127 at 128 (*per* Finlay J); also *Monnickendam v Leanse* (1923) 39 TLR 445. *Cf* money not paid as a deposit: see *Mayson v Clouet* [1924] AC 980; *Lowis v Wilson* [1949] IR 347. Similarly a vendor's lien may be invoked in relation to an oral agreement: see *Munster & Leinster Bank Ltd v McGlashan* [1937] IR 525 at 528 (*per* Meredith J) (aff'd SC at 531); *Re Aluminium Shop Fronts Ltd* [1987] IR 419 at 422 (*per* Murphy J). It is not so clear that a purchaser's lien can be invoked in relation to an oral agreement – clearly it can not if there is no agreement at all: see *Re Barrett Apartments Ltd* [1985] IR 350.

An oral agreement is enforceable even by action if the Statute is not pleaded as a defence, though leave to amend the pleadings may be given: see *Broughton v Snook* [1938] Ch 505. It is too late to plead the Statute in later proceedings between the same parties, on the *res judicata* principle: see *Humphries v Humphries* [1910] 2 KB 531. *Cf White v Spendlove* [1942] IR 224. An oral contract for the sale of land may also be enforced by an action if the plaintiff can counter a defence based on s 51 by a successful plea of part performance: see *Hope v Lord Cloncurry* (1874) IR 8 Eq 555; *Lowry v Reid* [1927] NI 142; *Steadman v Steadman* [1976] AC 536; *Mackey v Wilde* [1998] 1 ILRM 449. See Wylie and Woods, *Irish Conveyancing Law* (3rd edn, Tottel Publishing, 2005), para 6.48 *et seq*. See also Farrell, *Irish Law of Specific Performance* (Tottel Publishing, 1994), Ch 6.

Other contracts relating to land which are not caught by s 51 include: (1) court sales: see Wylie and Woods, *Irish Conveyancing Law* (3rd edn, Tottel Publishing, 2005), paras 6.08 and 11.02 *et seq*; (2) a contract coming into force as a result of a compulsory purchase under statutory powers: see *Re Green Dale Building Co Ltd* [1977] IR 256 at 265 (*per* Mc Mahon J) (aff'd SC); *Munton v GLC* [1976] 2 All ER 815; Wylie and Woods, *Irish Conveyancing Law* (3rd edn, Tottel Publishing, 2005), para 8.14 *et seq*.

5 Section 51 applies only to agreements relating to the grant of an interest in land and not to the actual grant itself. The grant itself will usually have to be by deed in accordance with s 64 (see the Notes to that section). In the typical conveyancing context this distinction between the contract for sale and the deed of conveyance is clear. In other contexts, eg a leasehold agreement, it may not be so clear, but nevertheless the distinction between a contract (for a lease) and the grant (of the lease) is still valid: see *McCausland v Murphy* (1881) 9 LR Ir 9 and Wylie, *Landlord and Tenant Law* (2nd edn, Tottel Publishing, 1998), para 5.01 *et seq*.

It would appear that s 51 does not apply to collateral contracts, ie an agreement collateral to the main contract (which does have to comply): see *Anom Engineering Ltd v Thorton* [1983] IEHC 3 and *Riordan v Carroll* [1996] 2 ILRM 263; also the English Court of Appeal decision on "lock-out" agreements, *Pitt v PHH Asset Management Ltd* (1993) 40 EG 149. *Cf* a unilateral agreement, or contract to contract: see *Daulia v Four Millbank Nominees Ltd* [1978] Ch 231. As regards "side letters" or "letters of comfort" see Wylie, *Landlord and Tenant Law*, (2nd edn, Tottel Publishing, 1998), para 5.13. Sometimes the main contract for the sale of land comprises several elements, some of which may be severed into separate parts not caught by s 51 because they do not constitute land, eg a sale of a pub and its stock (see *Godley v Power* (1957) 95 ILTR 135 at 146, *per* Kingsmill Moore J; *Cf Carthy v O'Neill* [1981] ILRM 443 at 445, *per* Henchy J) or of a farm and the farm implements and tools (see *Buckley v Irwin* [1960] NI 98). It is a matter of construction of the particular contract whether it can be so severed and, if it cannot be severed, the whole contract must comply with s 51: see *Bentham v Hardy* (1843) 6 Ir LR 179. Of course failure to comply with a collateral contract may affect enforcement of the main contract: see *Kennedy v Wrenne* [1981] ILRM 81.

6 See s 3 for the wide definition of "disposition". This confirms what was the position under the 1695 Statute, as interpreted by the courts. Thus s 51 covers contracts relating, *inter alia*, to granting and surrender of leases (see *Waldron v Jacob* (1870) IR 5 Eq 131; *Ronayne v Sherrard* (1877) IR 11 CL 146; *McCausland v Murphy* (1881) 9 LR Ir 9); *Cosmoline Trading Ltd v DH Burke & Son Ltd* [2006] IEHC 38; creation of mortgages or charges on land (see *Cloncurry v Laffan* [1924] 1 IR 78 at

81, *per* Molony CJ; *Bank of Ireland v Purcell* [1989] IR 333; also *Driver v Broad* [1893] 1 QB 744); creation of rights like easements and profits (see *Bayley v Marquis of Conyngham* (1865) 15 ICLR 406; *McGillicuddy v Joy* [1959] IR 189); compromises of proceedings relating to land (see *Alpine Investments Ltd v Elliot* (26 November 1980), HC; *O'Mahony v Gaffney* [1986] IR 36; *Taylor v Smyth* [1990] ILRM 377. Nor is the section confined to contracts for a "sale" in the narrow sense of a transaction with a purchaser; thus it applies to a contract (there must, of course, be consideration for the contract) to leave property by will to the other party: see *McCarron v McCarron* (13 February 1997), SC. It does not, however, apply to a contract to erect a building (*Black v Kavanagh* (1974) 108 ILTR 91 at 96 (*per* Gannon J), nor to a contract to submit the assessment of compensation for damage done to land.

7   Section 51 does not apply to contracts relating to property other than land (but see n 5 above on the question of severance of a contract into different parts). Land clearly includes "fixtures" which have become part of the land, but not fixtures which are removable, eg so-called "tenant's fixtures": see *Lombard and Ulster Banking Ltd v Kennedy* [1974] NI 20 and Wylie, *Landlord and Tenant Law* (2nd edn, Tottel Publishing, 1998), Ch 9. In England it has been held to apply to a contract for the sale of building materials in a house to be demolished (*Lavery v Purcell* (1888) 39 Ch D 508) and for the removal of slag from land (*Morgan v Russell & Sons* [1909] 1 KB 357).

There has been much discussion in the courts as to the position of a contract relating to crops or other items growing on land (eg timber). If the contract is that the property is not to pass until the items are severed from the land, it relates to "goods" rather than land and comes within the Sale of Goods Act 1893 (see the definition of "goods" in s 62): *Scully v Corboy* [1950] IR 140; see also *Washbourn v Burrows* (1847) 1 Exch 107; *Marshall v Green* (1875) 1 CPD 35. If, however, the property is to pass before the items are severed from the land, the English courts have drawn a distinction between natural produce of land like timber and grass (*fructus naturales*), which is regarded as part of the land and, therefore, within s 51 (see *Rodwell v Phillips* (1842) 9 M & W 501; *Carrington v Roots* (1837) 2 M & W 248), and produce dependent upon work and labour like corn and potatoes (*fructus industriales*) which is regarded as goods and, therefore, not within s 51 (see *Parker v Staniland* (1809) 11 East 362; *Mayfield v Wadsby* (1824) B & C 357). The applicability of some of the cases to Ireland may be doubted, especially where the arrangement comprises one well-known in rural communities such as a conacre or agistment contract: see below. *Cf Rhodes v Baker* (1851) 1 ICLR 488; *McKenna v Herlihy* (1920) TC 620. And see Wylie and Woods, *Irish Conveyancing Law* (3rd edn, Tottel Publishing, 2005), para 6.09.

Section 51 also covers contracts relating to all kinds of interests in land, of whatever size and whether legal or equitable. It applies to an undivided share in land held by co-owners – there is no statutory trust for sale in Ireland such as was created by the English Law of Property Act 1925, and gave rise to controversy there: see *Cooper v Critchley* [1955] Ch 431; *First National Securities Ltd v Hegarty* [1984] 1 All ER 139. There must, however, be an interest in *land*, so that it is questionable whether conacre and agistment arrangements come within the section. Under many of these the holder does not even have "possession" of the land: see Wylie, *Landlord and Tenant Law* (3rd edn, Toottel Publishing, 2005), para 3.20 *et seq*. However, it has been pointed out that each case must be looked at in the light of its own circumstances and many modern arrangements confer on the holder greater rights than has been the tradition and so many confer an interest in land: see *Maurice E Taylor (Merchants) Ltd v Commissioner of Valuation* [1981] NI 236. See also *McKenna v Herlihy* (1920) 7 TC 620. For the same reason many licence arrangements relating to land may not create a sufficient interest to come within the section: see *King v David Allen & Sons, Billposting, Ltd* [1915] 2 IR 448, affd [1916] 2 AC 54; *Whipp v Mackey* [1927] IR 372. Similarly a caretaker's agreement (see *Lambert v McDonnell* (1864) 15 ICLR 137; *Musgrave v McAvey* (1907) 41 ILTR 230), agreements relating to lodgers (see *Waucob v Reynolds* (1850) 1 ICLR 142) and hotel guests (see *Carroll v Mayo County Council* [1967] IR 364) and hiring arrangements (see *Kelly v Woolworth & Co* [1922] 2 IR 5; *Boylan v Dublin Corporation* [1949] IR 60; *MacGinley v National Aid Committee* [1952] Ir Jur 43; *Kenny Homes & Co Ltd v Leonard* (18 June 1998), SC. An intoxicating liquor licence is inalienable separately from the premises (*Macklin v Graecin & Co* [1983] IR 61 at 66, *per* Griffin J; *Re Sherry-Brennan* [1979] ILRM 113 at 118, *per* Henchy J) and so any valid sale must include the premises to which it relates, the contract thereby coming within s 51: see *Irish Industrial Building Society v O'Brien* [1941] 1 IR 1.

A sale of company shares is not within s 51 even though the main or only substantial asset of the company is its land: see *Guardian Buildings Ltd v Sleecon Ltd* (18 August 1988) HC. *Cf* a sale of shares in a partnership: see *Boyce v Greene* (1826) Batty 608.

8   This wording repeats the provision in s 2 of the 1695 Statute and confirms (see Note 1 above) that s 51 does *not* require the contract to be in writing; it is sufficient if there is some written *evidence* of the contract which can be produced to the court: *McQuaid v Lynam* [1965] IR 564 at 573 (*per* Kenny J). This written evidence may come into existence after the agreement is made (see *Powell v Dillon* (1814) 2 Ba & B 416), but must exist by the time the action to enforce the agreement is commenced (see *Lindsay v Lynch* (1804) 2 Sch & Lef 1; *Cf Grindell v Bass* [1920] 2 Ch 487): see also n 9 below.

It is settled by many cases that the parties need not intend that the written evidence in question should constitute the s 51 *note* or *memorandum*: see *Cloncurry v Laffan* [1923] 1 IR 127 at 134–135 (*per* O'Connor MR) (aff'd [1924] 1 IR 78): *Murphy v Harrington* [1927] IR 339 at 342 (*per* Meredith J); *McQuaid v Lynam* [1965] IR 564 at 569 (*per* Kenny J). The result is that relatively informal documentation such as letters may be construed as a sufficient memorandum or note. There have been numerous cases where solicitors' correspondence has been so construed: see *Godley v Power* (1961) 95 ILTR; *Lavan v Walsh* [1964] IR 87; *Black v Kavanagh* (1974) 108 ILTR 91. Hence the need to qualify such correspondence with the time-honoured "subject to contract" formula, see below. Other documents which have been held to constitute the memorandum or note include: an entry in a solicitor's instruction book (*Murphy v Harrington* [1927] IR 339); a note in an auctioneer's sale book (*McMeekin v Stevenson* [1917] 1 IR 348; *Cf Crane v Naughton* [1912] 2

IR 318); a cheque for a deposit (*Doherty v Gallagher* (9 June 1975) HC; a receipt for a deposit together with an application for a building society loan (*Murphy v Harrington* [1927] IR 339). Even a document intended to repudiate the contract may constitute the memorandum or note: see *Tradax (Ir) Ltd v Irish Grain Board Ltd* [1984] ILRM 471 (decided on s 4 of the Sale of Goods Act 1893).

The Supreme Court has made it clear that the memorandum or note must directly or by necessary implication recognise not only the terms of the alleged agreement, but also the existence of a concluded contract, so that any term or expression in the memorandum or note which negates this, such as "subject to contract", disqualifies that document as the memorandum or note: *Boyle v Lee* [1992] ILRM 65 at 77 (*per* Finlay CJ, Hederman J concurring). What was not so clear from the judgments was whether there were any exceptions to this rule. A majority (Finlay CJ, Hederman and McCarthy JJ) seemed to rule out any exceptions and, in doing so, overruled *Kelly v Park Hall School Ltd* [1979] IR 340 and cast severe doubts on the authority of *Casey v Irish Intercontinental Bank* [1979] IR 364, both of which suggested that a "Subject to Contract" formula might be ignored in a particular case where the evidence established that it was not part of the original concluded oral agreement. O'Flaherty and Egan JJ seemed to be prepared to contemplate exceptions and to accept the earlier decisions as being decided on their own special facts. See also the views of Keane J in *Mulhall v Haren* [1981] IR 364 and Henchy J in *Carthy v O'Neill* [1981] ILRM 443; *Cf McInerney Properties v Roper* [1979] ILRM 119. More recently the courts have emphasised that it is important to distinguish two questons: (1) did the parties ever conclude an agreement? (2) if so (and the second question arises only if the first is answered positively), is that agreement sufficiently evidenced as required by statute? The expression "Subject to Contract" may be relevant to both questions: see *Shirley Engineering Ltd v Irish Telecommunications Investments plc* [1999] IEHC 204; *Supermacs Ireland Ltd v Katesan Ltd* [2000] 4 IR 273; *Higgins v Argent Developments Ltd* [2002] IEHC 171 (aff'd *ex tempore*) (13 May 2003) SC); (see the discussion in Wylie and Woods, *Irish Conveyancing Law* (3rd edn, Tottel Publishing, 2005), paras 6.18–6.19 and 7.06–7.12). *Cf* the discussion in the English cases (decided on s 40 of the Law of Property Act 1925, since repealed and replaced by s 2 of the Law of Property (Miscellaneous Provisions) Act 1989: *Law v Jones* [1974] Ch 112; *Tiverton Estates Ltd v Wearwell Ltd* [1975] Ch 146. Since the *Boyle* decision it would have to be a very exceptional case to persuade a court to disregard the disqualifying effect of the "Subject to Contract" formula. See the discussion in Farrell, *Irish Law of Specific Performance* (1994), Ch 4.

It is settled that it is not necessary to insert the "Subject to Contract" formula in every item of writing which might be produced in evidence to satisfy the requirements of s 51, though there is no harm in doing so as a precautionary measure. What is important is to do so with the first item (eg a letter) to be written, so that this may act as an "umbrella" to protect subsequent items: see *Mulhall v Haren* [1981] IR 364 at 375 (*per* Keane J); also the English cases: *Tevanan v Norman Brett (Builders) Ltd* (1972) 223 EG 1945; *Sherbrooke v Neesdale Ltd* [1982] 2 All ER 97. It is also clear that it is not necessary to use the "Subject to Contract" formula; any form of words will do, provided they clearly negate the suggestion that a concluded agreement has been entered into: see *Dyas v Stafford* (1882) 9 LR Ir 520; *Irish Mainport Holdings Ltd v Crosshaven Sailing Centre Ltd* (16 May 1980) HC; *Devlin v Northern Ireland Housing Executive* [1982] NI 337; *Silver Wraith Ltd v Siuicre Éireann Cpt* [1989] IEHC 34. Similarly, if a condition precedent to a binding contract is specified, eg, exchange of formal contracts (see *Kelly v Irish Nursery and Landscape Co Ltd* [1981] ILRM 433; *Donnelly v O'Connell* (1924) 58 ILTR 164); or the drawing up of a formal written agreement (see *Brien v Swainson* (1877) 1 LR Ir 135; *Lowis v Wilson* [1949] IR 347; *Arnold v Veale* (28 July 1977) HC; *Cf Godley v Power* (1957) 95 ILTR 135; *UsiTravel Ltd v Freyer* (29 May 1973) (Cir App). See also *Walker v Glass* [1979] NI 129; *Barry v Buckley* [1981] IR 306.

It has been long settled that the written evidence adduced as the memorandum or note must contain all the "essential" or "material" terms of the parties' agreement, in particular an indication of the parties, the property, the price and any other essential provisions: see *Carrigy v Brock* (1871) IR 5 CL 501 at 504 (*per* Palles CB); *Crane v Naughten* [1912] 2 IR 318 at 324 (*per* Gibson J). As regards "other provisions" it is a matter of determining in each case their importance to the parties: see *Law v Roberts & Co* [1964] IR 292; *Barratt v Costelloe* (1973) 107 ILTSJ 239; *Black v Kavanagh* (1974) 108 ILTR 91. The descriptions do not have to be very precise, so long as the court can identify from the writing the necessary information – *id cestum est quod certum reddi potest*: see *Viscount Massereene v Finlay* (1850) 13 LR Ir 496; *Waldron v Jacob* (1870) IR 5 Eq 131; *Murphy v Harrington* [1927] IR 339. In the case of a contract for the grant of a lease the memorandum or note must, in addition, specify the date of commencement of the term to be granted and the duration of the term: see *Wyse v Russell* (1882) 11 LR Ir 173; *Phelan v Tedcastle* (1885) 15 LR Ir 165; *White v McMahon* (1886) 18 LR Ir 460; *Erskine v Armstrong* (1887) 20 LR Ir 296; *Williams v Kenneally* (1912) 46 ILTR 292; *Kerns v Manning* [1935] IR 869; *White v Spendlove* [1942] IR 224; *Murphy v Harrington* [1927] IR 339; *O'Flaherty v Arvan Properties Ltd* (21 July 1977) SC; *Silver Wraith Ltd v Siuicre Éireann Cpt* [1989] IEHC 34.

It is also clear that the memorandum or note may comprise more than one document, so that several documents (eg letters) may be joined together to meet the s 51 requirements: see *McQuaid v Lynam* [1965] IR 564 at 570 (*per* Kenny J). It is easier to persuade the courts to read together documents which are all signed by the party to be charged and which contain cross-references to each other. It is more difficult where only one or some are signed; here the traditional rule is that the court will first look at the signed document or documents and will only join with it or them other documents to which it or they cross-refer: see *Waldron v Jacob* (1870) IR 5 Eq 131; *Crane v Naughten* [1912] 2 IR 318; *Cf* the leading English case *Timmins v Moreland Street Property Co Ltd* [1958] Ch 110. There can be no joinder without such a cross-reference; express or implied: see *Clinan v Cooke* (1802) 1 Sch & Lef 22 at 33 (*per* Lord Redesdale). Thus there can be no joinder to the signed document of a document not in existence at the date of signature: see *Boyce v Greene* (1826) Batty 608. Parol evidence cannot be adduced to make the link between the documents sought to be joined, but once the link or cross-reference is shown such evidence may be adduced further to explain the documents so joined: see *Clinan v Cooke* (1802) 1 Sch & Lef

22; *Craig v Elliot* (1885) 15 LR Ir 257; see also *Howlin v Power (Dublin) Ltd* (5 May 1978) HC.

9 The words "of it" indicate that normally the concluded agreement must either precede or, at least, be entered into contemporaneously with the creation of the memorandum or note: see *Dyas v Stafford* (1882) 9 LR Ir 520 at 523 (*per* Law C). There is, however, a long-established apparent exception to this rule whereby the courts may enforce a written offer which is accepted orally: see *Swan v Miller* [1919] 1 IR 151 and the English cases *Parker v Clark* [1960] 1 All ER 93; *Tiverton Estates Ltd v Wearwell Ltd* [1975] Ch 146.

10 By virtue of Part 1 of the Schedule to the Interpretation Act 2005 this includes "printing, typewriting, lithography, photography and other modes of representing or reproducing words in visible form and any information kept in non-legible form, whether stored electronically or otherwise, which is capable by any means of being reproduced in a legible form".

11 The courts have interpreted this requirement fairly broadly, so that it is not necessary for there to be a hand-written signature in the usual form: see *Halley v O'Brien* [1920] 1 IR 330 at 339 (*per* O'Connor LJ). What is required is that the "signature" in whatever form it took was intended to authenticate the document of which it forms a part: see *McQuaid v Lynam* [1965] IR 564 at 569 (*per* Kenny J). This does not necessarily mean that it has to appear at the foot or end of the document in question: see *Dyas v Stafford* (1882) 9 LR Ir 520. It has been held to be sufficient if the party's name appears in some form on the document in question, even without a hand-written signature, eg where the writing appears on printed headed notepaper containing the party's name: see *Casey v Irish Intercontinental Bank* [1979] IR 364 at 369 (*per* Kenny J). Similarly use of a stamp embossed with the party's or the agent's name: see *Hudson v O'Connor* (1947) Ir Jur 21; see also *Henry Forde & Son Finance Ltd v Forde* (13 June 1981) HC.

Once the agreement has been concluded it would appear that any alterations or amendments to the memorandum or note must be authenticated by a fresh signature or, at least, by initialling in the same way: see the discussion by Goulding J in *New Hart Builders v Brindley* [1975] 1 All ER 1007.

12 The memorandum or note has to be signed only by the party to be charged or his agent, ie the plaintiff in an action for specific performance need not have signed: see *Lord Ormond v Anderson* (1813) 2 Ba & B 363 at 370–371 (*per* Lord Manners). If there are co-owners each must sign (see *Re Hayes' Estate* [1920] 1 IR 207) or be named in the memorandum or note and have it signed by an agent for them all (see *Carthy v O'Neill* [1981] ILRM 443 and *Mulhall v Haren* [1981] IR 364).

13 Several points may be made about this provision. First, the authorisation does not have to be in writing: see *Callaghan v Pepper* (1840) 2 Ir Eq R 399 at 401 (*per* Pennefather B); *McLaughlin v Duffill* [2009] EWCA Civ 1627. Oral authority is enough so long as it is clear: *Clinan v Cooke* (1802) 1 Sch & Lef 22; *McCausland v Murphy* (1881) 9 LR Ir 9. Secondly, authority may be implied from the circumstances of the particular case: see *Field v Boland* (1837) 7 ICLR 37; *Sheridan v Higgins* [1971] IR 291; *Guardian Builders Ltd v Kelly* [1981] ILRM 127. Thirdly, the authority required is authority to sign the memorandum or note, not to conclude the agreement (which is normally for the parties themselves to do): see on this

distinction the discussion by Gannon J in *Black v Kavanagh* (1974) 108 ILTR 91; see also *Lord Cloncurry v Laffan* [1924] 1 IR 78 at 84 (*per* O'Connor LJ) and *Kerns v Manning* [1935] IR 869 at 881 (*per* Meredith J). The courts have long recognised that an auctioneer has implied authority to sign a memorandum or note on behalf of *both* parties to the agreement concluded at the auction: see *Gardiner v Tate* (1876) IR 10 CL 460; *McMeekin v Stevenson* [1917] 1 IR 348. *Cf* an estate agent selling by private treaty: see *Law v Roberts & Co* [1964] IR 292; also *Wilde v Watson* (1878) 1 LR Ir 402. The position of a solicitor has given rise to much dispute in the courts: see, eg the differing views expressed in *Lord Cloncurry v Laffan* [1924] 1 IR 78. It will be a rare case where the court will accept that a solicitor has implied authority to conclude an agreement on behalf of his client, but the courts are more likely to accept that there is authority to sign the memorandum or note so as to render enforceable an agreement already concluded by the client: *Kerns v Manning* [1935] IR 869 at 881 (*per* Meredith J). See also *Black v Kavanagh* (1974) 108 ILTR 91.

Where an agent signs without authority it may be rendered effective by subsequent ratification by his principal, in accordance with the general law of agency: see *Sheridan v Higgins* [1971] IR 291. Such ratification may be oral (see *Callaghan v Pepper* (1840) 2 Ir Eq R 399; *Dyas v Cruise* (1845) 8 Ir Eq R 407 or by conduct (see *Barclays Bank v Breen* (1956) 96 ILTR 179).

In signing the memorandum or note the agent should make his agency clear by signing "as agent" or "for" his principal, otherwise he runs the risk of being held liable personally on the contract: see *Lavan v Walsh* [1964] IR 87; *Cf* a signature "on trust": see *United Yeast Co Ltd v Cameo Investments Ltd* (1977) 111 ILTR 13; *Starling Securities Ltd v Woods* (24 May 1977) HC.

14 This confirms what was long held to be the position under the Statute of Frauds: see Farrell, *Irish Law of Specific Performance* (Tottel Publishing, 1994), ch 6; Wylie and Woods, *Irish Conveyancing Law* (3rd edn, Tottel Publishing, 2005), paras 6.48–6.60.

15 This clarifies a matter which has been the subject of some controversy in England, even under s 2 of 1989 Act (see Note 1 above), namely, how far other equitable doctrines, especially proprietary estoppel may be invoked (see *Yaxley v Gotts* [2000] Ch 162; cf *Yeoman's Row Management Ltd v Cobbe* [2008] 1 WLR 1752; Dixon, "Invalid Contracts, Estoppel and Constructive Trusts" [2005] Conv 207; McFarlane, "Proprietary Estoppel and Failed Contractual Negotiations" [2005] Conv 501). Subsection (2) is unqualified and leaves it open to the courts to invoke any equitable doctrines: see *Greenband Instruments v Bruton* [2009] IEHC 67.

16 Subsection (3) was included in the Bill to remove any lingering doubts that might have remained from some statements made by the Supreme Court in *Boyle v Lee* [1992] 1 IR 555 (especially remarks by Finlay CJ at 571) with respect to a deposit which is normally payable under a contract for the sale of land. These seemed to suggest that there could be no concluded contract unless the deposit had been agreed expressly by the parties. In fact later cases indicated that this was probably a misinterpretation of the statements. These later cases seem to establish that the parties may agree that *no* deposit is payable and conclude their agreement on that basis or may conclude an agreement subject to an *implied* term that the deposit will be the "usual" amount for such a transaction (eg 10%): see *Shirley Engineering Ltd v*

Irish Telecommunications Investments plc [1999] IEHC 204; *Supermacs Ltd v Katesan (Naas) Ltd* [2000] 4 IR 273 (see the discussion in Wylie and Woods, *Irish Conveyancing Law* (3rd edn, Tottel Publishing, 2005), para 6.18). It follows that in either of those circumstances it is *not* necessary for the note or memorandum in writing required by sub-s (1) to specify any deposit. The position has always been that the written evidence need only specify terms which the parties regarded as "essential" (see *Higgins v Argent Developments Ltd* [2002] IEHC 171, aff'd *ex tempore* (13 May 2003) SC); (see Wylie and Woods, *Irish Conveyancing Law* (3rd edn, Tottel Publishing, 2005), paras 6.25 and 7.06–7.120). Subsection (3) nails these points once and for all.

[95]

52.—(1)[2] Subject to *subsection (2),*[3] the entire beneficial interest[4] passes to the purchaser[5] on the making,[6] after the commencement of this Chapter,[7] of an enforceable[8] contract for the sale or other disposition of land.[9]

Passing of beneficial interest.[1]

(2) *Subsection (1)* does not affect[10]—

(*a*) the obligation of the vendor to maintain the land so long as possession of it is retained,[11] or

(*b*) the liability of the vendor for loss or damage under any contractual provision dealing with such risk,[12] or

(*c*) the vendor's right to rescind the contract for failure by the purchaser to complete or other breach of the contract,[13] or

(*d*) any provision to the contrary in the contract.[14]

Definitions

See s 3 for definitions of: "disposition"; "land"; "possession"; "purchaser".

Notes

1 Section 52 implements the Law Reform Commission's recommendation made on a number of occasions that the majority decision of the Supreme Court in *Tempany v Hynes* [1976] IR 101 should be reversed: see *Report on Land Law and Conveyancing Law: (1) General Proposals* (LRC 30–1989), paras 24–27; *Report on Interests of the Vendor and Purchaser in Land During the Period Between Contract and Completion* (LRC 49–1995), para 4.18. The majority of the Court (Kenny J, with O'Higgins J concurring) took a different view of what had previously been considered to be the position of a vendor and purchaser under a contract for the sale or other disposition of land. The traditional view was that from entering into an enforceable contract, ie a contract of which the court would grant an equitable decree of specific performance, the vendor was regarded as holding the land as trustee for the purchaser (who from the contract had the equitable or beneficial

interest) (this view was adhered to by the dissenting judge, Henchy J: see [1976] IR 101 at 109). The majority, however, took the view that the beneficial interest passed only to the extent that the purchase price was paid, so that, if as is usual, a deposit (say 10%) was paid, the purchaser obtained only a 10% beneficial interest. If no deposit was paid, the entire beneficial interest, as well as the legal title, would remain vested in the vendor. This decision proved to be extremely controversial because it gave rise to all sorts of practical difficulties (see Wylie and Woods, *Irish Conveyancing Law* (3rd edn, Tottel Publishing, 2005), paras 12.02–12.10). In particular it raised questions as to the effect on the purchaser of a judgment mortgage registered against the vendor's interest *after* the contract but *before* completion. If the purchaser received no beneficial interest or the vendor retained some beneficial interest, then any judgment mortgage registered against the vendor's interest might survive completion and the purchaser would have to insist upon it being discharged on or before closing (or on the basis of an undertaking to do so out of the proceeds of sale after closing): see Law Reform Commission's *Consultation Paper on Judgment Mortgages* (LRC CP 30–2004), paras 2.41–2.48. Even the judiciary subsequently hinted that the decision in *Tempany v Hynes* might have to be revisited: see *Hamilton v Hamilton* [1982] IR 466; *Re Grange Developments Ltd* [1987] IR 733; *Murnaghan Bros v Ó Maoldomhnaigh* [1991] 1 IR 455.

2 It is important to reiterate that subsection (1) seeks to restore the law as it was understood prior to *Tempany v Hynes* and has been consistently applied in England and Wales for over 100 years (see Megarry and Wade, *The Law of Real Property* (7th edn, Sweet & Maxwell, 2008), paras 15.052–15.065; the irony is that Kenny J in *Tempany v Hynes* based the majority view on an apparent conflict in 19th century English cases: see Wylie and Woods, *Irish Conveyancing Law* (3rd edn, Tottel Publishing, 2005), para 12.02).

3 Subsection (2) both clarifies the effect of sub-s (1) and makes it clear that the parties to the contract can contract out of it (see Note 14 below).

4 Note that it is the "entire" beneficial interest, which gets rid of the complications of *Tempany v Hynes* ie part only of the purchase price being paid (see Note 1 above). This means that the purchaser acquires an interest which will have priority over any judgment mortgage registered *after* the contract. Even Henchy J in *Tempany v Hynes* took the view that, notwithstanding the traditional principle that the beneficial interest passed to the purchaser on the entering into of the contract, the vendor retained a substantial interest, pending completion, capable of being charged with a judgment mortgage ([1976] IR 101 at 109; see also *Re Kissock and Currie's Contract* [1916] 1 IR 376). In the case of registered land, s 71(4) of the Registration of Title Act 1964 made it clear that any registered judgment mortgage is subject to "all unregistered rights subject to which the judgment debtor held [his interest] at the time of registration of the affadavit" (see now s 71(3)(*c*), as substituted by s 130 below). As Henchy J pointed out in *Tempany v Hynes* once the purchaser completes and becomes registered as full owner "the *post*-contract judgment mortgages will no longer affect the lands and he will be entitled to have them cancelled from the folios" ([1976] IR 101 at 109). This had previously been held by the Supreme Court to be the position: see *Re Strong* [1940] IR 382, following *Re Murphy and McCormack* [1930] IR 322. So far as unregistered land is concerned it had

previously been established that a judgment mortgagee, who is a volunteer and not a purchaser for value, takes subject to prior equitable interests whether or not he or she has notice of them and without the necessity to protect that prior interest by registering the document creating it in the Registry of Deeds: see *McAuley v Clarendon* (1858) 8 Ir Ch R 121; *Eyre v McDowell* (1861) 9 HLC 620; Madden, *Registration of Deeds, Conveyances and Judgment Mortgages* (2nd edn, 1901) ch 8; LRC CP 30–2004, para 2.45. As Henchy J put it in *Tempany v Hynes* the vendor's interest against which the judgment mortgage is registered after the context is a "transient" one only which passes out of existence once the purchaser becomes the full owner of the land on completion ([1976] IR 101 at 109). The purchaser, therefore, obtains a title from the conveyance which is no longer subject to the judgment mortgage.

5   It must be reiterated that s 52 was not intended to affect other laws relating to contracts. It had been suggested that it might have implications for VAT purposes and move the tax point from completion to the date of the contract. It was not intended to do so. The VAT regime pre-dates *Tempany v Hynes* (decided in 1976), being introduced by the Value Added Tax Act 1972. The Revenue Commissioners confirmed in November 2009 that s 52 made "no change in the existing position for the determination of the time of supply for property transactions" (e-Brief Issue 75/09). Supply will remain being regarded as taking place on completion. It has no implications for stamp duty since it is conveyances rather than contracts which are stampable (Wylie and Woods, *Irish Conveyancing Law* (3rd edn, Tottel Publishing, 2005), paras 18.108–18.116). Special rules apply to building agreements: see Wylie and Woods, *Irish Conveyancing Law* (3rd edn, Tottel Publishing, 2005), para 11.10.

6   That is, it is the making of the contract which is important, not, as held by the majority in *Tempany v Hynes*, the payment of the purchase price (see Note 1 above).

7   The reversal of *Tempany v Hynes* operates only in respect of contracts entered into after 1 December 2009.

8   It is vital to understand that the passing of the entire beneficial interest only operates where the contract is an "enforceable" one, ie one in respect of which a court would grant specific performance. It is the availability of this equitable remedy which led to the traditional *pre-Tempany v Hynes* view that the contract gave the purchaser an equitable interest. This means that the contract must comply with s 51 (written evidence) or be enforceable, alternatively, through doctrines like part performance or proprietary estoppel (see the Notes to s 51). If the contract is not so enforceable, the purchaser does not obtain an equitable interest. The result would be, therefore, that he or she would take on completion subject to any judgment mortgage registered against the vendor's interest after the contract but before completion (see Note 4 above).

9   Like s 51, s 52 applies to any contract relating to a land transaction (see Note 6 to s 51).

10 Paragraphs (*a*)–(*c*) were included to confirm that the reversal of *Tempany v Hynes* by sub-s (1) was not intended to affect other aspects of the general law relating to the position of the vendor and purchaser under a contract (see Henchy J in that case [1976] IR 101 at 109; there was nothing explicit in Kenny J's judgment in that case which cast doubt on these aspects of the general law). See Law Reform

Commission's *Report on Interests of Vendor and Purchaser in Land During the Period Between Contract and Completion* (LRC 49–1995); Wylie and Woods, *Irish Conveyancing Law* (3rd edn, Tottel Publishing, 2005), ch 12).

11 See Wylie and Woods, *Irish Conveyancing Law* (3rd edn, Tottel Publishing, 2005), paras 12.21–12.24.

12 See Wylie and Woods, *Irish Conveyancing Law* (3rd edn, Tottel Publishing, 2005), paras 12.36–12.43. The Law Society's *General Conditions of Sale (2001 Edition)* reiterate this duty and the risk of damage remaining with the vendor (see Condition 43).

13 A remedy of rescission exists under both the general law and the Law Society's *General Conditions of Sale (2001 Edition)*: see Wylie and Woods, *Irish Conveyancing Law* (3rd edn, Tottel Publishing, 2005), paras 13.58–13.75.

14 Paragraph (*d*) makes it clear that the parties can contract out of sub-s (1). This might be desirable, on occasion, for tax reasons or where the contract is part of a complex series of transactions.

---

[96]

Abolition of the Rule in *Bain v. Fothergill.*[1]

53.—(1) The rule of law restricting damages recoverable[2] for breaches of contract occasioned by defects in title[3] to land (known as the Rule in *Bain v. Fothergill*) is abolished.

(2) *Subsection (1)* applies only to contracts made after the commencement of this Chapter.[4]

Definitions

See s 3 for definition of: "land".

Notes

1 Section 53 implements the Law Reform Commission's recommendation that this very controversial rule should be abolished: see *Report on Land Law and Conveyancing Law: (1) General Proposals* (LRC 30–1989), paras 24–27; *Report on Interests of Vendor and Purchaser in Land During the Period Between Contract and Completion* (LRC 49–1995), para 4.18). In essence the rule devised by the English courts in the 19th century restricted a purchaser's right to claim damages against the vendor for breach of contract – a claim could not be made where it turned out that the vendor could not show a good title to the land contracted to be sold. The rule is of greater antiquity than the case which gave rise to its name (it probably dates from *Flureau v Thornhill* (1776) 2 Wm Bl 1078; see O'Connor MR in *Kelly v Duffy* [1922] 1 IR 62; O'Driscoll, "A Note on the Rule in *Bain v Fothergill*" (1975) 9 Ir Jur (ns) 203). Although followed by Irish courts, it was much criticised and viewed by judges on both sides of the Irish Sea as "anomalous" (see Wylie and Woods, *Irish Conveyancing Law* (3rd edn, Tottel Publishing, 2005), paras 13.81–13.88). It was abolished in England and Wales by s 3 of the Law of Property Act 1969.

2   In essence a purchaser, where the rule applied, was restricted to recovery of the deposit paid (with interest) and conveyancing costs up to the date of discovering the defect in title: see *Re McDermott and Kellett's Contract* (1904) 4 NIJR 89; *McMahon v Gaffney* [1930] IR 576; *McQuaid v Lynam* [1965] IR 564. There was no entitlement to damages for loss of bargain: see *Nolan v Feely* (1899) 33 ILTR 132; *McDonnell v McGuinness* [1939] IR 223.

3   The *rationale*, in so far as there was one, for the rule was the complexity of titles to land which excused a vendor not being able to show good title: see *Engell v Fitch* (1869) LR 4 QB 659 at 666 (*per* Kelly CB); *Bain v Fothergill* (1874) LR 7 HL 158 at 210–211 (*per* Lord Hatherley).

4   The abolition operates only in respect of contracts entered into after 1 December 2009.

---

[97]

54.—Where the court refuses to grant specific performance of a contract for the sale or other disposition of land,[2] or in any action for the return of a deposit,[3] the court[4] may, where it is just and equitable to do so,[5] order the repayment of the whole or any part[6] of any deposit, with or without interest.[7]

Order for return of deposit.[1]

Definitions

See s 3 for definitions of: "court"; "disposition"; "land".

Notes

1   Section 54 implements a recommendation by the Law Reform Commission that an anomalous rule developed by the English courts should be reversed. This related to the jurisdiction of the court to order return of the purchaser's deposit in cases where the vendor is refused an order of specific performance of the contract for sale. Normally where the vendor fails to honour the contract the purchaser can rescind and is entitled to his deposit back (and now clearly damages for loss of bargain even in cases of a defect in title: see s 53 and the Notes to it). However, the English courts doubted whether they could order the deposit to be returned where technically the vendor had not been in breach of the contract. For example, the contract may have contained a condition preventing the purchaser from raising requisitions on or objections to the title (see, eg, Condition 11(a) of the Law Society's *General Conditions of Sale (2001 Edition)*; Wylie and Woods, *Irish Conveyancing Law* (3rd edn, Tottel Publishing, 2005), paras 15.25–15.26). If in due course it emerged that the vendor had no title or there is a serious defect in title, the court might refuse the vendor an order "to force a bad title on the purchaser". This would be particularly the case if the vendor knew this and the object of the condition was to disguise it: see *Geoghegan v Connolly* (1858) 8 Ir Ch R 598 at 607 (*per* Smith MR); *Re Davys and Verdon and Saurin's Contract* (1886) 17 LR Ir 334 at 337 (*per* Chatterton VC); *Re White and Hague's Contract* [1921] 1 IR 138 at 145–146 (*per* O'Connor MR).

However, notwithstanding that the vendor was refused specific performance, he would not have been in breach of the contract because of the protection afforded by the condition. In *Re Scott and Alvarez's Contract* [1895] 2 Ch 603 the English Court of Appeal ruled that in such a case the court had no jurisdiction to order return of the deposit. That decision was subjected to much criticism by Irish judges subsequently (see *Re Lyons and Carroll's Contract* [1896] 1 IR 383; *Re Turpin and Ahern's Contract* [1905] 1 IR 85), but doubts as to the status of the principle had continued (see *White v Spendlove* [1942] IR 224; *Cregan v Taviri Ltd* [2008] IEHC 159; Wylie and Woods, *Irish Conveyancing Law* (3rd edn, Tottel Publishing, 2005), paras 13.34–13.36). It was reversed in England and Wales by s 49(2) of the Law of Property Act 1925 (see Megarry and Wade, *The Law of Real Property* (7th edn, Sweet & Maxwell, 2008), paras 15.080 and 15.111). Section 54 now does the same here.

2   This is the usual situation where the *Re Scott and Alvarez's Contract* ruling applies.

3   This wording appears also in s 49(2) of the Law of Property Act 1925 and clearly contemplates that the jurisdiction arises also where the purchaser sues for return of the deposit. The result is that the jurisdiction is not confined to the *Re Scott and Alvarez's Contract* scenario. A purchaser may invoke it in any case where the purchaser considers that forfeiture of the deposit would be grossly unfair – that is certainly how the English courts have interpreted s 49(2) of the 1925 Act: see *Universal Corporation v Five Ways Properties Ltd* [1979] 1 All ER 552; *Schindler v Pigault* (1975) 30 P & CR 328. However, the English cases suggest that exceptional circumstances must be established by a purchaser to justify exercise of the discretion where the purchaser is unable to complete: see *Safehaven Investments Inc v Springbok Ltd* (1996) 71 P & CR 59; *Omar v El-Wakil* [2002] 2 P & CR 36. Such circumstances might be where the vendor is perceived as acting unconscionably or where the vendor has resold the land at a substantial profit *without* taking into account the forfeited deposit (see *Dimsdale Developments (South East) Ltd v De Haan* (1983) 47 P & CR 1; *Tennero Ltd v Majorarch Ltd* [2003] EWHC 2601 (Ch); *Midill (97 PL) Ltd v Park Lane Estates Ltd* [2008] 46 EG 114 (CS).

4   The Circuit Court has concurrent jurisdiction with the High Court (see Notes 21–23 to s 3). There is no provision in s 54 for contracting-out and so the general rule applies that a contract cannot oust the jurisdiction of the court: see on s 49(2) of the 1925 Act *Aribisala v St. James' Homes (Grosvenor Dock) Ltd* [2007] EWHC 1694 (Ch).

5   This makes it clear that the matter lies entirely at the discretion of the court (see Note 3 above and Note 6 below).

6   This wording is wider than s 49(2) and confirms that the order may require repayment of part only of the deposit if that is what the court considers more "just and equitable".

7   Nor does this wording appear in s 49(2).

[98]

55.—(1) Any party[2] to a contract for the sale or other disposition of land[3] may apply to the court[4] in a summary manner[5] for an order determining a question relating to the contract.[6]

Vendor and purchaser summons.[1]

(2) On such an application the court may make such order, including an order as to costs, as it thinks fit.[7]

[VPA 1874, s. 9]

(3)[8] A question in respect of which an application may be made under *subsection (1)* includes[9] a question relating to any requisition, objection,[10] claim for compensation[11] or other question arising out of or connected with the contract,[12] but does not include a question affecting the existence or validity of the contract.[13]

Definitions

See s 3 for definitions of: "court"; "disposition"; "land".

Notes

1   Section 55 implements the Law Reform Commission's recommendation that the special procedure for dealing with disputes over contracts relating to land transactions contained in s 9 of the Vendor and Purchaser Act 1874 should be retained (see LRC CP 34–2004, paras 8.16–8.17). This summary procedure has ceased to be used much in England and Wales (it is now provided for by s 49(1) of the Law of Property Act 1925) (see *Practice Directions* [1967] 1 All ER 656; [1970] 1 All ER 671; *Walia v Michael Naughton Ltd* [1985] 1 WLR 1115). However, it has remained much availed of here: see Farrell, *Irish Law of Specific Performance* (Tottel Publishing, 1994), paras 8.53–8.59. Section 9 is recast in more simple language.

2   Both the vendor and purchaser may apply, but the courts are reluctant to determine the rights of third parties on such an application: see *Re Carolan and Scott's Contract* [1899] 1 IR 1; *Re Brown and Mitchells' Contract* (1902) 2 NIJR 106. The court may agree, however, to a third party being joined in the action: see *Re Antrim County Land, Building and Investment Co Ltd* (1909) 43 ILTR 120.

3   Like s 9 of the 1874 Act the jurisdiction is confined to land contracts.

4   Under s 9 of the 1874 Act the jurisdiction was conferred on the High Court, but under s 3 the Circuit Court has concurrent jurisdiction (see Notes 21–23 to that section).

5   Under s 9 of the 1874 Act applications were made to the High Court by special summons: see Rules of the Superior Courts, Ord 3, item (12) and Farrell, *Irish Law of Specific Performance* (Tottel Publishing, 1994), para 8.54. Further rules, also covering the Circuit Court, no doubt will be issued to cover s 55.

6   This is clarified by sub-s (3) (see Notes 8–13 below).

7   This gives a wide discretion to the court. However, it has been held in relation to s 9 of the 1874 Act that the procedure cannot be used to seek orders like specific

performance (see *Re Ford and Ferguson's Contract* [1906] 1 IR 607) or rectification (see *Re McDermott and Kellett's Contract* (1904) 4 NIJR 89). However, in making an order under the procedure the court can grant ancillary relief, such as an order for return of the deposit or reimbursement of the costs of the investigation of title (see again *Re McDermott and Kellet's Contract* (1904) 4 NIJR 89).

8   Subsection (3) is declaratory of the guidance which the Irish courts have given as to the appropriate types of questions which can be put to the court under this summary procedure (see further Farrell, *Irish Law of Specific Performance* (Tottel Publishing, 1994), paras 8.56–8.57; Wylie and Woods, *Irish Conveyancing Law* (3rd edn, Tottel Publishing, 2005), paras 13.27–13.28).

9   The questions specifically referred to are not, therefore, exclusive (see Note 12 below).

10 As to such questions concerning title, see *Molphy v Coyne* (1919) 53 ILTR 177; *Re Cummins and Hanafy's Contract* (1905) 5 NIJR 111; *Lyons v Thomas* [1986] IR 666; *Kiely v Delaney* [2008] IEHC 69.

11 This must be connected with the contract and would include a claim to an abatement in the purchase price by reason of some misdescription: see *Molphy v Coyne* (1919) 53 NIJR 177; *Re Terry and White's Contract* (1886) 32 Ch D 14. It probably would not include an action for damages because this will usually put the validity of the contract in issue (see Note 13 below): *Re Hargreaves and Thompson's Contract* (1886) 82 Ch D 454; *Barber v Wolfe* [1945] Ch 187.

12 Such as the validity of a completion notice: see *Tyndarius Ltd v O'Mahony* (3 March 2003), SC; *Hegarty v Fusano Properties Ltd* [2006] IEHC 54; *Byrnes v Meaktown Construction Ltd* [2009] IEHC 123.

13 This limitation has long been established under s 9 of the 1874 Act: *Re Scott* (1879) 13 ICLR 139 at 140 (*per* Chatterton VC). Cf whether a particular clause is a nullity: see *Re Mitchell and McElhinney's Contract* [1902] 1 IR 83. Thus it cannot be used to seek rescission for fraud (*Re Delaney and Deegan's Contract* [1905] 1 IR 602) or misrepresentation (*Re Flynn and Newman's Contract* [1948] IR 104); cf where determination of a question properly put (re requisitions or an alleged defect in title) gives rise to a contractual right of rescission (*Re Cummins and Hanafy's Contract* (1905) 5 NIJR 111; *Re Turpin and Ahern's Contract* [1905] 1 IR 85).

[99]

CHAPTER 2[1]

Title[2]

Notes

1   Chapter 2 implements the Law Reform Commission's recommendations that various pre-1922 statutory provisions relating to deduction and investigation of title should be re-enacted, but with some modifications (see LRC CP 34–2004, paras 8.10–8.16).

2   As the sidenotes to various sections indicate Chapter 2 collects together provisions previously scattered in statutes such as the Vendor and Purchaser Act 1874,

Conveyancing Acts 1881–1911 and Law of Property Amendment Acts 1859 and 1860. The provisions in those statutes are repealed (see Schedule 2 and the Notes to that Schedule).

[100]

56.—(1) Subject to *subsections (2)* and *(3)*, after the commencement of this Chapter,[2] a period of at least[3] 15 years[4] commencing with a good root of title[5] is the period for proof of title which the purchaser may require.[6]   **Root of title.**[1]

(2) Where the title originates with a fee farm grant or lease, *subsection (1)* does not prevent the purchaser from requiring production of the fee farm grant or lease.[7]   [VPA 1874, s. 1]

(3) *Subsection (1)* takes effect subject to the terms of the contract for the sale or other disposition of the land.[8]

Definitions

See s 3 for definitions of: "disposition"; "fee farm grant"; "land"; "lease"; "purchaser".

Notes

1   This section replaces s 1 of the Vendor and Purchaser Act 1874 and reduces the period of title which a vendor must show under an "open" contract, ie where the title to be shown is not specified in the contract. In practice it is usually specified in the Special Conditions: see Wylie and Woods, *Irish Conveyancing Law* (3rd edn, Tottel Publishing, 2005), paras 14.54–14.55. The provision operates, therefore, as a "default" provision only: see sub-s (3).

2   The new rule operates only in respect of obligations in respect of deduction of title arising after 1 December 2009, which can arise only under a contract entered into after that date.

3   It has long been settled that the statutory period is a *minimum* one. It will be a rare transaction where a good root (see Note 5 below) will exist in a deed exactly 15 years old and, as an English judge once put it, title "cannot commence *in nubibus*": *Re Cox and Neve's Contract* [1891] 2 Ch 109 at 118 (*per* North J). The rule is, therefore, that, if there is no good root exactly 15 years old, title must be deduced from the first good root going back further from 15 years ago: Wylie and Woods, *Irish Conveyancing Law* (3rd edn, Tottel Publishing, 2005), para 14.70.

4   The period under the 1874 Act (s 1) was 40 years but the Law Reform Commission recommended that it be reduced to 20 years (see *Report on Land Law and Conveyancing Law: (1) General Proposals* (LRC 30–1989), paras 8–9; LRC CP 34–2004, para 8.11). It was reduced in England and Wales to 30 years (Law of Property Act 1925, s 44(1)), but was later reduced further to 15 years (Law of Property Act 1969, s 23). The Commission took the view that 15 years was "uncomfortably close" to the 12-year limitation period for actions to recover land (which can be extended in

cases of fraud or disability). The result was that the Bill originally drafted (see Bill appended to LRC 74–2005, s 60) and introduced to the Seanad specified 20 years. However, following representations by the Law Society, 15 years was substituted at the Dáil Select Committee Stage. There appear to have been no difficulties in England and Wales arising from the change made there in 1969 (see Megarry and Wade, *The Law of Real Property* (7th edn, Sweet & Maxwell, 2008), para 15.077).

5   As to what constitutes a "good root" see Wylie and Woods, *Irish Conveyancing Law* (3rd edn, Tottel Publishing, 2005), para 14.56.

6   But only if there is no contrary provision in the contract: see sub-s (3) and Note 8 below.

7   This confirms what has long been taken to be the position at common law – the purchaser (assignee) of a fee farm grant or lease is always entitled to see the original grant or lease however old it is – that is what is being acquired. There appears to be little or no direct authority on the point, but it is the implication in some older cases: see, eg, *Williams v Spargo* [1893] WN 100. Subsection (2) puts the point beyond doubt. It should be noted that this provision relates to the conveyance or assignment by a fee farm grantee or lessee, not the making of the original grant or lease, where the statutory rule was always that the title of the grantor or lessor could not be called for (see Wylie and Woods, *Irish Conveyancing Law* (3rd edn, Tottel Publishing, 2005), paras 14.68–14.70). However note the provisions of s 57 (and the Notes to that section). Although fee farm grants cannot be made since 1 December 2009 (see s 12 and the Notes to that section) ones existing on that date survive and will feature in investigation of titles for the foreseeable future.

8   This confirms what was also the position under the 1874 Act, the statutory period of title is a "default" provision only and solicitors must continue to consider whether to rely upon it or insist on inserting a Special Condition dealing with the title to be shown. There remains the risk that if the contract specifies *less* than 15 years' title the purchaser may nevertheless be fixed with constructive notice of interests which would have been discovered if at least the 15 years had been insisted upon (see Wylie and Woods, *Irish Conveyancing Law* (3rd edn, Tottel Publishing, 2005), para 16.60). Note, however, that the rule in *Patman v Harland* has been abolished by s 57(4) (see Notes 13–17 to that section).

---

[101]

Tenancies.[1] [VPA 1874, s. 2]	**57.**—(1) Subject to *subsections (2)* and *(5)*, under a contract to grant or assign[2] a tenancy or subtenancy of land, the intended grantee or assignee is not entitled to call for the title to[3]—
[CA 1881, ss. 3 and 13] [CA 1882, s. 4]	(*a*) the fee simple, or (*b*) any tenancy superior to that out of which the subtenancy is, or is to be, immediately derived.
	(2)[4] Subject to *subsection (5)*, under a contract made after the commencement of this Chapter[5] to grant[6] a tenancy or

subtenancy for a term exceeding 5 years[7] the intended grantee may call for—

>   (*a*)   in the case of a tenancy to be derived immediately out of the fee simple, a copy of the conveyance of that estate to the grantor,[8] or
>
>   (*b*)   in the case of a subtenancy, a copy of the superior lease out of which it is to be immediately derived and, if any, of the immediate assignment of the superior lease to the grantor,[9]

and, where the tenancy or subtenancy is granted for the full market rent, taking into account any premium also paid by, but disregarding any concessions or inducements made to, the intended grantee,[10] that grantee may also call for 15 years' title as a purchaser under *section 56(1)*.[11]

(3) For the purpose of the deduction of title to an intended assignee, no preliminary contract for or relating to the tenancy forms part of the title, or evidence of the title, to the tenancy.[12]

(4)[13] Where by reason of *subsection (1)*[14] an intended grantee or assignee is not entitled to call for the title to the fee simple or a superior tenancy, that person, where the contract is made after the commencement of this Chapter,[15] is not affected with notice[16] of any matter or thing of which, if the contract had specified that such title should be furnished, that person might have had notice.[17]

(5) *Subsections (1)* and *(2)* take effect subject to the terms of the contract for the grant or assignment of the tenancy or subtenancy.[18]

Definitions

See s 3 for definitions of: "land"; "lease"; "notice"; "tenancy".

Notes

1   Section 57 pulls together various provisions relating to the title to be shown on the grant or assignment of a tenancy, previously to be found in the Vendor and Purchaser Act 1874 and Conveyancing Acts 1881 and 1882 (see Wylie and Woods, *Irish Conveyancing Law* (3rd edn, Tottel Publishing, 2005), paras 14.68–14.73). However, some modifications have been made as recommended by the Law Reform Commission in order to make them accord more with the Law Society recommendations and actual practice (see LRC CP 34–2004, paras 8.13–8.14). It must be emphasised again that these provisions operate only in respect of an "open" contract – they are "default" provisions which give way to express provisions in the contract: see sub-s (5) (and Note 18 below).

2 Subsection (1) applies to both the original grant and subsequent assignments of a tenancy or subtenancy; cf s 56 (see Note 7 to that section). Note that s 57 adopts the terminology of the Act, as indicated by the definitions in s 3 and the provisions of s 11. The generic terms used to cover all cases where the relationship of landlord and tenant exists are: "landlord", "tenant", and "tenancy". The terms "lessor", "lessee" and "lease" are used only where the tenany has been created by a written document (see Notes 58, 59, 62, 63 and 87–91 to s 3). Section 57 covers both leases and other grants or assignments of tenancies.

3 Paragraphs (*a*) and (*b*) re-enact the rules in the 1874 and 1881 Acts that the grantee or purchaser of a leasehold interest cannot call for the title to the freehold nor the title to any superior leasehold reversion (which would apply in the case of sub- and sub-sub-tenancies) (see Wylie and Woods, *Irish Conveyancing Law* (3rd edn, Tottel Publishing, 2005), para 14.70 for examples of the operation of these provisions). However, sub-s (2) contains an important qualification to this general rule.

4 Subsection (2) changes the longstanding general rule in sub-s (1) as recommended by the Law Reform Commission (see Note 1 above).

5 Since it changes the previous law sub-s (2) relates only to deduction of title under contracts entered into after 1 December 2009.

6 Subsection (2) relates only to the original grant of a tenancy or subtenancy, not to its subsequent assignment, where the general rules in sub-s (1) and s 56 apply.

7 The view was taken that the change in the statutory rule should apply only where the tenancy being granted is a reasonably substantial one – in many cases a prospective tenant taking a short-term tenancy will not be bothered with investigating the landlord's title. However, where the prospective tenant consults a solicitor, the solicitor must, as always, consider whether it is appropriate to rely on the statutory rule. The risk is reduced by abolition of the rule in *Patman v Harland* by sub-s (4) (see Notes 13–17 below). However risks may remain whatever the length of the lease where, eg, the lessor may be subject to restrictions on the power to lease, such as a mortgagor: see *ICC Bank v Verling* [1995] 1 ILRM 123 and Wylie, *Landlord and Tenant Law* (2nd edn, Tottel Publishing, 1998), para 5.43. However, note that the position of a lessee taking a lease from a mortgagor is improved by s 112 (see the Notes to that section).

8 This entitles the intended grantee of a lease directly from the freehold owner to see the deed whereby that owner acquired the title. Under the last part of the subsection, where that is a very recent conveyance, the intended tenant may see previous conveyances of the freehold title under the 15-year rule in s 56 (see Note 11 below).

9 This entitles the intended sub-tenant (or sub-sub-tenant) to see the grantor's (sub- or sub-sub-landlord's) lease (ie the superior lease under which the landlord or sub- or sub-sub-landlord holds), plus the immediate assignment of that lease to him or her where he or she was not the original tenant or sub-tenant. Again under the last part of the subsection the intended sub- or sub-sub tenant may be entitled to see more than that assignment if it was very recent (see Note 11 below).

10 The view was taken that this additional provision should apply only to intended tenants or sub-tenants paying the full market price for the tenancy or subtenancy.

11 Under s 56(1) the intended tenant or sub-tenant may be entitled to more than 15 years' title because it is necessary to go back further to find a "good root", in this instance an assignment of the tenancy or of the subtenancy (see Note 3 to s 56). Thus if the assignment to the vendor (the intended landlord or sub-landlord) was very recent, the purchaser (the intended tenant or sub-tenant) may see previous assignments also made during or even before the 15-year title period.

12 Subsection (3) re-enacts the provision in s 4 of the Conveyancing Act 1881. In essence it means that the purchaser of an existing lease (ie one previously granted) cannot, as part of the deduction and investigation of title, call for production of any contract for or relating to the original grant of the tenancy. The general rule is that a contract merges in the conveyance giving effect to it (see Wylie and Woods, *Irish Conveyancing Law* (3rd edn, Tottel Publishing, 2005), paras 21.02–21.04).

13 Subsection (4) implements the Law Reform Commission's recommendation that the rule in *Patman v Harland* (1881) 17 Ch D 353 should be abolished (see LRC CP 34–2004, paras 8.15–8.16). In essence this rule stated that a purchaser of leasehold property (the rule was so confined) who relied upon the statutory title he or she was entitled to under an "open" contract could nevertheless be fixed with constructive notice of (and, therefore, would take subject to) interests created by documents which were part of the superior freehold or leasehold title (see Wylie and Woods, *Irish Conveyancing Law* (3rd edn, Tottel Publishing, 2005), paras 14.71–14.73). The reasoning behind this rule was that the purchaser could have contracted to see *more* than the statutory title (see *Leathem v Allen* (1850) 1 Ir Ch R 683 at 690). This has often been regarded as an anomalous rule which ran counter to the point of having "default" statutory rules as to title and it was abolished in England and Wales by the Law of Property Act 1925 (see s 44(5)). Note, however, that the significance of the abolition is reduced by the provisions of sub-s (2), which allow prospective tenants and sub-tenants to call for more of the superior freehold or leasehold title (see Note 14 below). Note also that the Act implements the Commission's recommendation that the confusing provisions of s 66 of the Conveyancing Act 1881 (as to which see Wylie and Woods, *Irish Conveyancing Law* (3rd edn, Tottel Publishing, 2005), para 14.73) should *not* be re-enacted (see LRC CP 34–2204, p 135).

14 This must be read as qualified by sub-s (2), see the wording at the beginning of sub-s (1).

15 The abolition of the rule operates only in respect of deduction and investigation of title under contracts entered into after 1 December 2009.

16 In effect usually "constructive" notice (see s 86 and the Notes to that section).

17 That is, if the contract had specified deduction of *more* title than s 57 allows for (see Note 13 above).

18 This confirms, as under previous statutory provisions, that s 57 contains "default" provisions operating with respect to "open" contracts only.

---

[102]

58.—(1)[2] Subject to *subsection (2)*, a purchaser of land is not entitled to require—

Other conditions of title.[1]

(a) the production of an instrument dated or made before the period referred to in *section 56*,[3] or stipulated in the contract for sale,[4] for the commencement of the title, even though the instrument creates a power subsequently exercised by an instrument produced to the purchaser,[5] or

(b) any information, or make any requisition, objection or inquiry with respect to any instrument referred to in *paragraph (a)* or the title prior to that period, notwithstanding that any instrument, or that prior title, is recited, agreed to be produced or noticed,[6]

and the purchaser shall assume, unless the contrary appears,[7] that—

(i) the recitals contained in the instruments produced, relating to any instrument forming part of that prior title are correct, and give all the material contents of the instrument so recited,[8] and

(ii) every instrument so recited was duly executed by all necessary parties, and perfected, if and as required, by any act required or permitted by law.

(2)[9] *Subsection (1)* does not deprive a purchaser of the right to require the production of any—

(a) power of attorney under which any instrument which is produced is executed,[10] or

(b) instrument creating or disposing of an interest, power or obligation which is not shown to have ceased or expired, and subject to which any part of the land is disposed of by an instrument which is produced, or a copy of which is produced,[11] or

(c) instrument creating any limitation or trust by reference to which any part of the land is disposed of by an instrument which is produced.[12]

(3)[13] On a sale of land, the purchaser, where the purchaser requires the vendor to carry out such matters, shall bear the expenses (except where such expenses should be borne by the vendor in compliance with the obligation to deduce title[14]) of—

(a) production and inspection of all instruments, letters of administration, probates, proceedings at courts, records, statutory provisions and other documents not in the possession of the vendor,[15] or the vendor's mortgagee or trustee,[16]

(b)   making, procuring, producing, searching for and verifying all certificates, declarations, evidence and information, and all attested, office, stamped or other copies or abstracts of, or extracts from, any statutory provisions or other documents, not in the possession of the vendor or the vendor's mortgagee or trustee,[17]

(c)   making any copy, whether attested or unattested, of any document retained by the vendor, or the vendor's mortgagee or trustee, required to be delivered by the purchaser.[18]

(4)[19] On a sale of land in lots, a purchaser of two or more lots held wholly or partly under the same title is entitled to no more than one abstract of the common title, nor to more than one copy of any document forming part of the common title,[20] except at the purchaser's own expense.

(5)[21] The inability[22] of a vendor to furnish the purchaser with an acknowledgment of the right to production and delivery of copies of documents of title[23] is not an objection to title where the purchaser will, on the completion of the contract, have an equitable right to the production of such documents.[24]

(6)[25] Such acknowledgments and such undertakings for the safe custody of documents as the purchaser requires[26] shall be furnished at the purchaser's expense, and the vendor shall bear the expense of perusal and execution on behalf of or by the vendor, and on behalf of and by necessary parties other than the purchaser.

(7)[27] A vendor may retain a document of title where—

(a)   the vendor retains any part of the land to which the document relates, or

(b)   the document comprises an instrument—

(i)   creating a trust which still exists, or

(ii) relating to the appointment or discharge of a trustee of an existing trust.

(8) This section takes effect subject to the terms of the contract for the sale or other disposition of the land.[28]

(9) Nothing in this section is to be read as binding a purchaser to complete the purchase in any case where, on a contract made without reference to this section but containing stipulations similar to any of its provisions, specific performance would not be granted by the court against the purchaser.[29]

(10)[30] In this section—

    (*a*)   "instrument" includes a copy or abstract,

    (*b*)   "production" includes furnishing a copy or abstract and cognate words shall be read accordingly.

Definitions

See s 3 for definitions of: "instrument"; "land"; "mortgage"; "purchaser".

Note also the additional definitions for the purposes of s 58 in sub-s (10) (see Note 30 below).

Notes

1   Section 58 re-enacts without substantial amendments various provisions in s 2 of the Vendor and Purchaser Act 1874 and s 3 of the Conveyancing Act 1881. These laid down several rules relating again to deduction and investigation of title: see Wylie and Woods, *Irish Conveyancing Law* (3rd edn, Tottel Publishing, 2005), chs 14 and 15. It aims to pull them together in a logical format. Note that it is possible to contract out of the provisions: see sub-s (8) and Note 28 below.

2   Subsection (1) re-enacts s 3(3) of the 1881 Act and confirms the general rule that a purchaser cannot insist upon investigating the "pre-root" title or raise objections or requisitions in respect of that title: see Wylie and Woods, *Irish Conveyancing Law* (3rd edn, Tottel Publishing, 2005), paras 14.59, 15.24 and 18.29. Notwithstanding this provision, it is open to a purchaser to show *aliunde* that there is a defect in the title, eg through information gained from third parties: see *Leathem v Allen* (1850) 1 Ir Ch R 683 at 691 (*per* Brady LC); *Re Cox and Neve's Contract* [1891] 2 Ch 109. It is not clear whether the very widely worded Condition 11(a) in the Law Society's *General Conditions of Sale (2001 Edition)* prevents this. A court might rule that this Condition does not relieve a vendor of the duty to disclose latent defects in title of which he or she is aware: see *Nottingham Patent Brick and Tile Co v Butler* (1886) 16 QBD 777; Wylie and Woods, *Irish Conveyancing Law* (3rd edn, Tottel Publishing, 2005), para 14.59. (See also s 60 and the Notes to that section.) Apart from that, whatever the provisions of s 58 or conditions in the contract, a vendor is likely to be refused specific performance where this would involve forcing a "bad title" on the purchaser: see *Re McDermott and Kellett's Contract* (1904) 4 NIJR 89; *Re Hogan and Murnell's Contract* [1919] 1 IR 422; *Re Geraghty and Lyon's Contract* (1919) 53 ILTR 57; see Wylie and Woods, *Irish Conveyancing Law* (3rd edn, Tottel Publishing, 2005), paras 13.53, 14.10 and 14.15. See sub-s (9) (and Note 29 below).

3   That is a "pre-root" instrument outside the s 56 statutory rules as to title to be shown.

4   That is a "pre-root" instrument before the root specified in the contract.

5   But note the exceptions in sub-s (2) (see the Notes to that subsection).

6   Paragraph (*a*) prevents a purchaser from making objections to or raising requisitions in respect of the pre-root tile.

7   This raises a presumption only, which may be rebutted by evidence to the contrary.

8 This is one of the advantages of putting recitals in a deed of conveyance: see Wylie and Woods, *Irish Conveyancing Law* (3rd edn, Tottel Publishing, 2005), para 18.29. See also s 59(1) (and see Note 3 to that section).

9 Subsection (2) is a new provision similar to one in the English Law of Property Act 1925 (see s 45(1): Megarry and Wade, *The Law of Real Property* (7th edn, Sweet & Maxwell, 2008), para 15.080). It is largely declaratory of the common law, as developed by the courts.

10 The validity of any such *post*-root instruments produced as part of the title obviously depends on the *pre*-root power of attorney: see *Re Copelin's Contract* [1937] 4 All ER 447; *Re Holmes and Cosmopolitan Press Ltd's Contract* [1994] Ch 53.

11 Paragraph (*b*) covers *pre*-root instruments relating to interests, etc which are not shown to have ceased or expired but which a *post*-root instrument shows the land being conveyed is subject to, eg, leases, mortgages, easements and covenants.

12 Paragraph (*c*) covers again interests created by *pre*-root instruments by reference to which the land being sold was disposed of by a *post*-root instrument, eg, the post-root instruments produced as part of the title documents might record that the land was conveyed by a trustee under powers conferred by a *pre*-root trust instrument (a case where the trust has not been kept "off the title": see Wylie and Woods, *Irish Conveyancing Law* (3rd edn, Tottel Publishing, 2005), paras 14.64, 15.19 and 18.36).

13 Subsection (3) re-enacts the substance of s 3(6) of the 1881 Act. It requires the purchaser to bear the cost of production of certain types of title documentation, generally that not in the vendor's possession but which is nevertheless necessary to confirm good title, eg a statutory declaration to verify a statement in an abstract of title: see *Re Conlon and Faulkener's Contract* [1916] 1 IR 241. The 1881 provision was enacted at a time when abstracts of title were commonly furnished and that is never done in modern practice, under which full copies of title documents are furnished. Furthermore it has long been settled that it did not apply to title documentation from which the vendor is obliged to deduce title and to hand over on closing: see *Re Johnson and Tustin* (1885) 30 Ch D 42; *Re Duthy and Jesson's Contract* [1898] 1 Ch 419; see Wylie and Woods, *Irish Conveyancing Law* (3rd edn, Tottel Publishing, 2005), paras 14.48–14.49 and 20.34 (see also Note 14 below). Furthermore, the subsection takes effect subject to the terms of the contract (see sub-s (8) and Note 28 below). Under the Law Society's *General Condition of Sale (2001 Edition)* the vendor is obliged to furnish various documents at his or her own expense, eg tax certificates (Condition 8(b)) and searches (Condition 19). See also the Law Society's *Objections and Requisitions on Title (2001 Edition)* Nos 16, 27, 28 and 35 (tax certificates and other certificates relating to planning, building control and multi-storey buildings: see Wylie and Woods, *Irish Conveyancing Law* (3rd edn, Tottel Publishing, 2005), paras 16.25, 16.62, 16.67 and 16.83. The result is that sub-s (3) is likely to operate as a "default" provision only where a transaction is conducted on an informal basis not using the Law Society's documentation.

14 The words in brackets were added to the original Bill drafted by the Law Reform Commission and introduced to the Seanad to confirm the interpretation given to the 1881 Act by the courts (see Note 13 above). In fact the courts often drew a distinction between verification of matters of *title* (which remain the responsibility

of the vendor) and mere matters of *conveyance* (the expense of which should be borne by the purchaser): see *Re Conlon and Faulkener's Contract* [1916] 1 IR 241; *Hopkins v Geoghegan* [1931] IR 135; see Wylie and Woods, *Irish Conveyancing Law* (3rd edn, Tottel Publishing, 2005), para 14.18.

15 This is a very important limitation on the purchaser's expenses which appeared in the 1881 Act.

16 This adds a further limitation which was introduced in the English equivalent (see s 45(5)(*a*) in the Law of Property Act 1925). It reverses *Re Willett and Argenti* (1889) 60 LT 735 and *Re Ebworth and Tidy's Contract* (1889) 42 Ch D 23.

17 Note again the substantial limitations on purchaser's expenses: see Notes 15 and 16 above).

18 This would cover the case where the vendor is disposing of part only of the land and so retaining the title documents relating to the whole, hitherto undivided, land: see also sub-s (4) and Note 19 below.

19 Subsection (4) re-enacts s 3(7) of the 1881 Act, but adds the reference to more than one copy of title documents relating to a common title, because abstracts are never furnished in practice nowadays (see Note 13 above).

20 See Note 19 above.

21 Subsection (5) re-enacts the provisions in the 3rd rule in s 2 of the 1874 Act, as amended by s 9(8) of the 1881 Act. The general rule was that a vendor had to use best endeavours to procure an acknowledgment with respect to documents not in his possession: see *Re Pursell and Deakin's Contract* [1893] WN 152. This provision was designed to relieve the vendor where the best endeavours proved to be unsuccessful. See also sub-s (6) and Note 25 below.

22 For example because they are lost or outside the jurisdiction: see *Re Halifax Commercial Banking Co Ltd and Wood* (1878) 79 LT 536; *Halkett v Earl of Dudley* [1907] 1 Ch 590.

23 As regards this acknowledgment see s 84 (and the Notes to that section).

24 It would appear that, where ownership of land held under one title is divided, and title documents remain in the possession of an owner of part only, the owners of the other parts have an "equitable" right to production of the documents where needed to prove title: see *Fain v Ayers* (1826) 2 Sim & St 533; *Re Jenkins and Commercial Electric Theatre Co's Contract* (1917) 61 Sol Jo 283; Wylie and Woods, *Irish Conveyancing Law* (3rd edn, Tottel Publishing, 2005), paras 2.43 and 18.103.

25 Subsection (6) re-enacts the substance of the 4th rule in s 2 of the 1874 Act.

26 See again s 84 and the Notes to that section.

27 Subsection (7), paragraph (*a*) re-enacts the substance of the 5th rule in s 2 of the 1874 Act (see *Re Williams and Newcastle's Contract* [1897] 2 Ch 144; *Re Lehmann and Walker's Contract* [1906] 2 Ch 640), but paragraph (*b*) extends its provisions to what was probably the position at common law (as was done in s 45(9) of the English Law of Property Act 1925): see *Clayton v Clayton* [1930] 2 Ch 12 (trustees still duties to perform).

28 This confirms the position under the 1874 and 1881 provisions – s 58 is subject to the provisions of the contract for sale.

29 Subsection (9) re-enacts s 3(11) of the 1881 Act and confirms the stance long held by the courts: see Note 2 above.

30 Subsection (10) supplements the general definitions in s 3 for the purposes of s 58. It enabled the wording of the section to be kept more simple than it might otherwise have been the case, by avoiding repetition of phrases like "or copy or abstract", as occurred in s 3 of the 1881 Act.

[103]

59.—(1)[2] Recitals, statements and descriptions of facts, matters and parties contained in instruments,[3] statutory provisions or statutory declarations 15 years old at the date of the contract are, unless and except so far as they are proved to be inaccurate, sufficient evidence[4] of the truth of such facts, matters and parties.

Protection of purchasers.[1]
[VPA 1874, s. 2]
[CA 1881, s. 3]

(2)[5] Where land sold is held under a tenancy (other than a subtenancy), the purchaser shall assume, unless the contrary appears,[6] that the tenancy was duly granted; and, on production of the receipt for the last payment due for rent under the tenancy before the date of the actual completion of the purchase, the purchaser shall assume, unless the contrary appears,[7] that all the covenants and provisions of the tenancy have been duly performed and observed up to the date of actual completion of the purchase.

(3)[8] Where land sold is held under a subtenancy, the purchaser shall assume, unless the contrary appears,[9] that the subtenancy and every superior tenancy were duly granted; and, on production of the receipt for the last payment due for rent under the subtenancy before the date of the actual completion of the purchase, the purchaser shall assume, unless the contrary appears,[10] that all the covenants and provisions of the subtenancy have been duly performed and observed up to the date of actual completion of the purchase, and also that all rent due under, and all covenants and provisions of, every superior tenancy have been paid and duly performed and observed up to that date.

Definitions

See s 3 for definitions of: "covenant"; "instrument"; "land"; "purchaser"; "rent"; "tenancy".

Notes

1 Section 59 re-enacts provisions in the Vendor and Purchaser Act 1874 and Conveyancing Act 1881 designed to protect purchasers of land in investigation of title and purchasing leasehold land.

2 Subsection (1) re-enacts a provision in the 2nd rule under s 2 of the 1874 Act, but modifies it to align it with the new period for title introduced by s 56(1) (see Note 4 to that section). In fact s 2 of the 1874 Act provided for 20 years in this context (as against 40 years for the period of title provided by s 1 to the 1874 Act: see Notes 1 and 4 to s 56 above). When the amendment to s 56(1) was made at the Dáil Select Committee Stage to reduce the period of title to 15 years, the view was taken that the same period should apply to s 59(1).

3 This again shows the usefulness of recitals and other statements in deeds in deducing and investigating title: see *Re Marsh and Earl Granville* (1882) 24 Ch D 1; Wylie and Woods, *Irish Conveyancing Law* (3rd edn, Tottel Publishing, 2005), paras 14.51, 14.52 and 18.28.

4 Note that they are only "sufficient" evidence, not "conclusive": see Note 6 below.

5 Subsection (5) re-enacts a provision in s 3(4) of the 1881 Act and raises presumptions in respect of previous compliance with the terms of a tenancy which is being bought (sub-s (6) deals with subtenancies: see Note 8 below).

6 The statutory provision raises a rebuttable presumption only: see *Becker v Partridge* [1966] 2 Ch 155 at 169 (*per* Dankwerts LJ).

7 Note that where the Law Society's *General Conditions of Sale (2001 Edition)* are used, Condition 10(b)(iii) makes the rent receipt *conclusive* evidence of compliance (see Wylie and Woods, *Irish Conveyancing Law* (3rd edn, Tottel Publishing, 2005), para 14.76). Thus subsection (5) applies only where the *General Conditions* are not used and there is no equivalent extending provision in the contract.

8 Subsection (6) re-enacts s 3(5) of the 1881 Act and contains an equivalent provision where a subtenancy is being purchased.

9 See Note 6 above.

10 Again Condition (b)(iii) makes the receipt *conclusive* evidence of compliance: see Note 7 above.

---

[104]

Fraudulent concealment and falsification.[1]

[LPAA 1859, s. 24]

[LPAA 1860, s. 8]

60.—(1) Any person disposing of land to a purchaser, or the solicitor or other agent of such a person, who with intent to defraud[2]—

   (*a*) conceals from the purchaser any instrument or incumbrance material to the title, or

   (*b*) falsifies any information or matter on which the title may depend in order to induce the purchaser to accept the title offered or produced,

is guilty of an offence under this Act.[3]

(2)⁴ Any such person or the person's solicitor or agent is also liable to an action for damages by the purchaser, or persons deriving title under the purchaser, for any loss sustained by reason of—

(*a*)   the concealment of the instrument or incumbrance, or

(*b*)   any claim made by a person whose title to the land was concealed by such falsification.

(3) In estimating damages, where the land is recovered from the purchaser or persons deriving title under the purchaser,⁵ regard shall be had to any expenditure by them on improving the land.⁶

(4) Nothing in this section affects the provisions of the Criminal Justice (Theft and Fraud Offences) Act 2001.⁷

Definitions

See s 3 for definitions of: "incumbrance"; "instrument"; "land"; "purchaser".

Notes

1   Section 60 re-enacts, with a recasting of the language, the substance of the provisions in s 24 of the Law of Property Amendment Act 1859, as amended by s 8 of the Law of Property Amendment Act 1860 (which was couched in very convoluted terms). It renders it a *criminal* offence for a vendor, or his solicitor or agent, fraudulently to conceal instruments or incumbrances or falsify information or matters relating to the title being deduced to the purchaser. They are also open to a damages claim for loss suffered by the purchaser as a consequence: see Wylie and Woods, *Irish Conveyancing Law* (3rd edn, Tottel Publishing, 2005), paras 9.31 and 14.61.

2   This intention will have to be proved on the part of any person prosecuted under this section. In *Smith v Robinson* (1879) 13 Ch D 148, Fry J questioned whether a solicitor would be liable for concealing an incumbrance in the *pre*-root title. *Sed quaere*: if there was a clear intention to defraud, though that might be very difficult to prove in respect of pre-root documents.

3   As regards offences see s 6 and the Note to that section.

4   Subsection (3) provides the purchaser with a remedy in damages, which, although linked to the criminal offence, is an independent remedy which can be pursued whether or not a criminal prosecution is brought.

5   The point is that some third party may prove to have a better title to the land and on that basis may recover it from the defrauded purchaser.

6   This provides some compensation for such a purchaser for expenditure on improvements before the purchaser recovered it. Presumably a court would disallow any expenditure incurred after the defrauded purchaser became aware of the fraud.

7   This saving was added to the Bill as introduced to the Seanad. The 2001 Act deals with various offences involving theft and fraud. Section 11 creates a general offence

of suppression of documents, the penalty for which is a fine or imprisonment for a term not exceeding 10 years; cf the penalty under s 6(1) of the 2009 Act.

[105]

Notice of rights on common title.[1] **[CA 1911, s. 11]**	**61.**—(1) Where land having a common title[2] with other land is conveyed to a purchaser (other than a tenant or mortgagee) who does not hold or obtain possession of the documents forming the common title, the purchaser, notwithstanding a stipulation to the contrary in the contract or conveyance,[3] may require[4] that a memorandum giving notice of any provisions in the conveyance restricting user of or conferring rights over[5] any other land comprised in the common title is endorsed on or permanently annexed to some document selected by the purchaser but retained in the possession or control of the vendor and being or forming part of the common title.

(2) The title of any person omitting to require an endorsement or annexation under this section is not affected or prejudiced merely by such omission.[6]

(3) This section does not apply to registered land.[7]

Definitions

See s 3 for definitions of: "conveyance"; "land"; "mortgage"; "purchaser"; "registered land"; "tenant".

Notes

1   Section 61 re-enacts the substance of s 11 of the Conveyancing Act 1911. It applies to unregistered land only (see sub-s (3) and Note 7 below) and deals with the situation where a purchaser is acquiring part only of a larger parcel of land, the title deeds to which are being kept by the vendor. If the purchaser is obtaining the benefit of restrictive covenants or other rights (such as easements) over other land (the side note to s 11 of the 1911 Act was misleading in referring to notice of "restrictive covenants") held under the common title, he or she can insist upon a memorandum of this being endorsed on or annexed to one of the title deeds retained by the vendor. In fact this is rarely done in practice and there is no obligation on a purchaser to insist upon it. Whether the increased enforceability of freehold covenants (including positive ones) under s 49 (see the Notes to that section) will lead to the practice remains to be seen. Such covenants become legal rights binding all successors and such an endorsement or annexation helps to warn such successors of their existence. Cf the provisions of s 84 relating to an acknowledgment for production of title documents.

2   See Note 1 above.

3   The vendor cannot insist on contracting out of this provision.

4 Conversely the purchaser is not obliged to invoke the provision.

5 These are not restricted and clearly cover a wide variety of rights other than a restrictive covenant (see Note 1 above).

6 This confirms that the purchaser is under no obligation to invoke the section and his or her title is not prejudiced by not invoking it.

7 The Registration of Title Act 1964, as amended by Part 13 of the 2009 Act (see the Notes to that Part), makes provision for registration of burdens like covenants and easements on the folio relating to the burdened land: see s 69(1)(*j*), (*k*) and (*kk*) (added by s 129 of the 2009 Act: see the Note to that section).

---

[106]

CHAPTER 3[1]

Deeds and their operation[2]

Notes

1 Chapter 3 implements various recommendations made by the Law Reform Commission over the years (see LRC CP 34–2004, paras 8.19–8.45).

2 To some extent the provisions of Chapter 4 replace provisions in pre-1922 statutes governing deeds and their operation, such as the Statute of Uses (Ireland) 1634, Real Property Act 1845, Law of Property Amendment Act 1859 and Conveyancing Act 1881. However, it also contains substantial changes to the formalities for execution of deeds: see s 64 (and the Notes to that section).

---

[107]

62.—(1) Subject to *section 63*,[2] a legal estate or interest[3] in land may only be created or conveyed by a deed.[4]

(2) A deed executed after the commencement of this Chapter is fully effective for such purposes[5] without the need for any conveyance to uses[6] and passes possession or the right to possession of the land, without actual entry,[7] unless subject to some prior right to possession.

(3) In the case of a voluntary conveyance executed after the commencement of this Chapter, a resulting use[8] for the grantor is not implied merely because the land is not expressed to be conveyed for the use or benefit of the grantee.[9]

(4)[10] A bargain and sale, covenant to stand seised, feoffment with livery of seisin or any combination of these are no longer effective to create or to convey a legal estate or legal interest in land.

Conveyances by deed only.[1]

[SU 1634]
[RPA 1845, ss. 2 and 3]

Definitions

See s 3 for definitions of: "conveyance"; "deed"; "land"; "legal estate"; "legal interest"; "possession".

Notes

1   Section 62 implements the Law Reform Commission's recommendation that the Statute of Uses (Ireland) 1634 should be repealed and no longer govern conveyances of land, that old feudal forms of conveyance should be abolished and that the modern deed should become the sole method of conveying land: see LRC CP 34–2004, paras 8.20–8.21 and 8.29–8.31.

2   Section 63 sets out various transactions relating to land which do not have to be carried out by execution of a deed (see the Notes to that section).

3   See further s 11 (and the Notes to that section). This does apply to *equitable* interests which may be created informally and where assignments need be in writing only: see s 6 of the Statute of Frauds (Ireland) 1695 (which section remains in force) and Delany, *Equity and the Law of Trusts in Ireland* (4th edn, Round Hall, 2007), pp 74–75; Wylie, *Irish Land Law* (3rd edn, Tottel Publishing, 1997), para 9.025.

4   What constitutes a deed since 1 December 2009 is set out in s 64(2) (see the Notes to that section).

5   That is the creation or conveyance of a legal estate or interest as referred to in sub-s (1).

6   This follows up the repeal of the Statute of Uses (Ireland) 1634 (see Schedule 2) (see also Note 1 above) with getting rid of any continuing need for conveyances "to uses" (see on the previous law Lyall, *Land Law in Ireland* (2nd edn, Round Hall, 2000), pp 92–108; Wylie, *Irish Land Law* (3rd edn, Tottel Publishing, 1997), paras 3.007–3.022). Instead, conveyances which prior to 1 December 2009 would have needed to include a "use" are, after that date, "fully effective" to achieve the same purpose without any "use".

7   This gets rid of any remaining vestiges of the ancient doctrine of *interesse termini*, the notion that a grantee did not acquire an estate in the land until he or she had actually entered and taken physical possession (see Lyall, *Land Law in Ireland* (2nd edn, Round Hall, 2000), pp 110 and 566–567; Wylie, *Irish Land Law* (3rd edn, Tottel Publishing, 1997), paras 3.023 and 17.006).

8   The need for a conveyance to uses prior to 1 December 2009 stemmed from the danger of such a resulting use being "executed" by the Statute of Uses (Ireland) 1634, thereby rendering the conveyance a nullity (see Lyall, *Land Law in Ireland* (2nd edn, Round Hall, 2000), pp 96–97 and 102–103; Wylie, *Irish Land Law* (3rd edn, Tottel Publishing, 1997), paras 3.017–3.019). Subsection (3) ensures that no longer including in voluntary conveyances since 1 December 2009 the formula "unto and to the use of" will not run the risk of a resulting use being implied.

9   The word "use" was substituted at the Seanad Committee Stage for "trust" which was used in the English equivalent (s 60(3) of the Law of Property Act 1925). That gave rise to the suggestion that a presumed resulting trust could no longer arise in the case of a gift of land (see *Hodgson v Marks* [1971] Ch 892 at 933 (*per* Russell

LJ); *Tinsley v Milligan* [1994] 1 AC 340 at 371 (*per* Lord Browne-Wilkinson; but see *Lohia v Lohia* [2001] WILR (HC) 101 (cf CA [2001] EWCA Civ 1691). It is unlikely that the English provision was intended to affect the more modern equitable doctrine of resulting trusts and the presumption of such a trust arising in the case of a voluntary conveyance of land will continue to operate here after 1 December 2009: see Keane, *Equity and the Law of Trusts in the Republic of Ireland* (Tottel Publishing, 1998), para 12.07; Delany, *Equity and the Law of Trusts in Ireland* (4th edn, Round Hall, 2007), pp 150–153; Mee, "A Stake Through the Heart of the Statute of Uses" (1996) 47 NILQ 367 and "The Land and Conveyancing Law Reform Bill: Observations on the Law Reform Process and a Critique of Selected Provisions: Part 2" (2006) 11(2) CPLJ 91.

10 Subsection (4) gets rid of the old feudal methods of conveying land and various developments around the Statute of Uses which survived the recognition of the modern deed of conveyance by the Real Property Act 1845 (ss 2 and 3) (see Lyall, *Land Law in Ireland* (2nd edn, Round Hall, 2000), pp 108–112; Wylie, *Irish Land Law* (3rd edn, Tottel Publishing, 1997), paras 3.023–3.030). They were abolished in England and Wales by s 51 of the Law of Property Act 1925.

[108]

63.—*Section 62(1)* does not apply to[2]—

(a)   an assent by a personal representative,[3]

(b)   a surrender or other conveyance taking effect by operation of law,[4]

(c)   a disclaimer not required to be by deed,[5]

(d)   a grant or assignment of a tenancy not required to be by deed,[6]

(e)   a receipt not required to be by deed,[7]

(f)   a vesting order of the court or other competent authority,[8] or

(g)   any other conveyance which may be prescribed.[9]

Exceptions to deeds.[1]

Definitions

See s 3 for definitions of: "assent"; "conveyance"; "tenancy".

Notes

1   Section 63 qualifies s 62 (1) and specifies various land transactions where it is not necessary to use a deed to transfer legal title. What constitutes a deed since 1 December 2009 is set out in s 64 (see the Notes to that section).

2   Paragraphs (a)–(f) recognise existing law.

3   Under s 53 of the Succession Act 1965 an assent need be in writing only.

4 As regards a surrender, eg of a tenancy, by "operation of law", see Wylie, *Landlord and Tenant Law* (2nd edn, Tottel Publishing, 1998), paras 25.10–25.15. The expression is used in s 7 of Deasy's Act (Landlord and Tenant Law Amendment Act, Ireland 1860): see also *Lynch v Lynch* (1863) 6 Ir LR 131 at 138 (*per* Brady CB); *McSweeney v McKeown* (7 December 1970), HC.

5 A disclaimer of "onerous" property by the Official Assignee (see Bankruptcy Act 1988, s 56) or the liquidator of a company (see Companies Act 1963, s 290) need be in writing only.

6 Leases and assignments of leases in certain cases need be in writing only, or, in some instances, can be carried out orally, under ss 4 and 9 of Deasy's Act 1860: see Wylie, *Landlord and Tenant Law* (2nd edn, Tottel Publishing, 1998), paras 5.26–5.40 and 21.04–21.06.

7 Generally receipts may be given in writing only. Sometimes they are endorsed on deeds, without themselves being executed as a deed, eg on discharge of a mortgage (see s 18 of the Housing Act 1988).

8 Such orders respecting land are governed by ss 33–40 of the Trustee Act 1893 and rules of court.

9 This reserves a power to exempt other documents relating to land from the requirement to use a deed.

---

[109]

Formalities for deeds.[1]

64.—(1) Any rule of law which requires—

    (*a*) a seal for the valid execution of a deed by an individual,[2] or

    (*b*) authority to deliver a deed to be given by deed,[3]

is abolished.

(2) An instrument executed after the commencement of this Chapter[4] is a deed[5] if[6] it is[7]—

    (*a*)[8] described at its head[9] by words such as "Assignment", "Conveyance", "Charge", "Deed", "Indenture", "Lease", "Mortgage", "Surrender" or other heading[10] appropriate to the deed in question, or it is otherwise[11] made clear on its face[12] that it is intended by the person making it,[13] or the parties to it, to be a deed, by expressing it to be executed or signed as a deed,[14]

    (*b*)[15] executed in the following manner:

        (i) if made by an individual[16]—

            (I) it is signed by the individual in the presence of a witness who attests the signature,[17] or

(II)   it is signed by a person at the individual's direction given in the presence of a witness who attests the signature,[18] or

(III)   the individual's signature is acknowledged by him or her in the presence of a witness who attests the signature;[19]

(ii)   if made by a company registered in the State, it is executed under the seal of the company in accordance with its Articles of Association;[20]

(iii)   if made by a body corporate registered in the State other than a company, it is executed in accordance with the legal requirements governing execution of deeds by such a body corporate;[21]

(iv)   if made by a foreign body corporate, it is executed in accordance with the legal requirements governing execution of the instrument in question by such a body corporate in the jurisdiction where it is incorporated,[22] and

(c)   delivered as a deed by the person executing it or by a person authorised to do so on that person's behalf.[23]

(3) Any deed executed under this section has effect as if it were a document executed under seal.[24]

(4)[25] A deed, whenever created, has the effect of an indenture although not indented or expressed to be an indenture.[26]

Definitions

See s 3 for definitions of: "conveyance"; "instrument"; "lease"; "mortgage".

Notes

1   Section 64 implements the Law Reform Commission's recommendations for reform of the law relating to execution of deeds, especially by individuals: see *Report on Land Law and Conveyancing Law: (6) Further General Proposals Including the Execution of Deeds* (LRC 56–1998), ch 2. Such changes had been made in England and Wales by s 1 of the Law of Property (Miscellaneous Provisions) Act 1989 (see Megarry and Wade, *The Law of Real Property* (7th edn, Sweet & Maxwell, 2008), paras 8.049–8.053). The section is based closely on the draft legislation included in the Commission's Report (see para 2.81) (but see Note 16 below). It is important to appreciate that, as with the English provisions, s 64 is based on continuance in the law of the distinction between a deed, on the one hand, and a document which is not a deed on the other (see LRC 56–1998, paras 2.72–2.73). Thus ss 62 and 63 of the 2009 Act retain this distinction (see the Notes to those sections), so that it remains important to determine in many situations whether a deed was executed. If it was not, the document may not be effective to carry out the intended transaction. Since 1

December 2009 that determination has to be made according to whether the requirements of s 64 have been met.

2   This introduces one of the major changes recommended by the Commission, the removal of the need for an *individual* (cf corporate bodies: see Notes 20–21 below) to use a seal in order to make the document a deed (see Wylie and Woods, *Irish Conveyancing Law* (3rd edn, Tottel Publishing, 2005), para 18.126). Since 1 December 2009 a document executed by an individual will be a deed provided it complies with sub-s (2). It is important to note that subsection (1) simply abolishes the "rule of law" which prior to that date "require[d]" use of a seal. It does not say that an individual is prohibited from using a seal nor does sub-s (2) say that a deed executed by an individual using a seal is invalid (see Note 16 below). The most that sub-s (2) does is to specify "other" requirements which have to be met after 1 December 2009; the addition of a seal does not prevent those other requirements being met. On the other hand, simply sealing without meeting those other requirements (in terms of, eg, witnessing) will not be enough – such a document, notwithstanding the seal, is not a deed coming within sub-s (2): see the definition of "deed" in s 3, which applies throughout the Act.

3   The Commission recommended that the common law rule that an agent being given authority to deliver a deed had to be given it also by deed (see *Powell v London and Provincial Bank* [1893] 2 Ch 555 at 563 (*per* Bowen LJ); *Re Seymour* [1913] 1 Ch 475 at 481 (*per* Joyce J) be abolished (LRC 56–1998, paras 2.70–2.71). This change had already been made by s 15 of the Powers of Attorney Act 1996 in respect of powers of attorney: see Wylie, *Irish Land Law* (3rd edn, Tottel Publishing, 1997), para 11.30.

4   That is after 1 December 2009.

5   This means that a document which does *not* comply with sub-s (2) is *not* a deed (see Note 2 above).

6   This is a word of "condition", ie what follows must be complied with (see Note 5 above).

7   Paragraphs (*a*)–(*c*) introduce the three new requirements for a deed, *all* of which (note the "and" after paragraph (*b*)) must be met.

8   Paragraph (*a*) introduces a new requirement recommended by the Commission, namely, some description or wording in the document to indicate an intention that it is a deed (see LRC 56–1998, para 2.73). It specifies two ways (alternatives) of doing this (see Note 14 below).

9   The first alternative specified by paragraph (*a*) is to use an "appropriate" heading for the document. Note that several examples are given but any other heading will do provided it is appropriate to the transaction being effected by the document in question. There is no need to use the time-honoured "Indenture" (note the change to Division E precedents recently made in *Laffoy's Irish Conveyancing Precedents* (Bloomsbury Professional): this is confirmed by sub-s (4) (see Note 25 below). If a conveyancer is in doubt, however, a "neutral" heading should be used, like "conveyance" or "deed".

10 This confirms that the headings specified are not exhaustive (see Note 9 above).

11 This introduces the alternative to using an appropriate heading (see Notes 8–9 above).

12 That is in the document itself and the wording indicates that it should be done in the execution part (see Note 13 below).

13 It is not necessary that both parties execute a deed unless they are doing something under it, such as conveying the land (which is why the grantor must execute it but not necessarily the grantee: see s 60 and the Notes to it) or entering into covenants (which is why the grantee must also execute it): see Wylie and Woods, *Irish Conveyancing Law* (3rd edn, Tottel Publishing, 2005), paras 18.77 and 18.123.

14 This is an alternative to using an appropriate heading (as was made clear by the Commission: see LRC 56–1998, para 2.73). The revised precedents of Division E recently issued for *Laffoy* (see Note 9 above) have opted for a heading and the execution clauses simply use the wording "**SIGNED**" and "**DELIVERED**" without the time-honoured introductory wording –"**IN WITNESS**" etc. This clearly complies with paragraph (*a*). The alternative would be use wording such as "**SIGNED** and **DELIVERED** as a **DEED**" (with or without an "**IN WITNESS**" introductory clause). If this is done the likelihood is that the document will adopt *both* alternatives, because in most instances it will also have an appropriate heading. There is nothing in paragraph (*a*) which rules out using both alternatives in the same document.

15 Paragraph (*b*) specifies the second requirement for a deed executed after 1 December 2009. It sets out several alternatives depending on the person or body executing the document, as recommended by the Commission.

16 Subparagraph (i) deals with individuals. There is no need to use a seal because of sub-s (i)(*a*) (see Note 2 above). The Commission's draft contained a fourth sub-clause (see LRC 56–1998, para 2.81) and this was in the Bill as introduced to the Seanad and read: "(IV) signed and sealed by an individual". This was intended to enable individuals to continue to use seals if they wanted to (notwithstanding abolition of the requirement to do so), but it was pointed out by the Law Society during the Bill's passage that it was inconsistent with the rest of s 64 and its general policy: in particular it did not require compliance with the new provisions in sub-clauses (I)–(III) for signing and witnessing (see Notes 17–18 below). Sub-clause (IV) was deleted at the Seanad Committee Stage. It should be reiterated that this does not prevent an individual using a seal after 1 December 2009 *provided* sub-clauses (I), (II) or (III) are *also* complied with. Simply signing and sealing without such compliance is not enough to make the document a deed (see Note 2 above).

17 Sub-clause (I) deals with the case of execution by the individual himself or herself and introduces for the first time *requirements* of both signing and attestation by a witness who must be present when the individual signs. At common law all that was required for a deed was sealing and delivery: see *Blennerhasset v Day* (1813) Beat 468 at 470 (*per* Lord Manners LC). However it has long been the practice to having the deed also signed, with the time-honoured execution clause beginning: "**SIGNED, SEALED** and **DELIVERED**" (see Wylie and Woods, *Irish Conveyancing Law* (3rd edn, Tottel Publishing, 2005), para 18.124). Although such attestation by witnesses was also common practice, it was not required at common law in order to validate the deed (unlike in the case of a will: see s 78 of the

Succession Act 1965): see the judgment of Clark J in *Fitzsimons v Value Homes Ltd* [2006] IEHC 144). It was held in a recent case in Northern Ireland that the witnesses do not have to be "independent", so that the common practice of a solicitor's employees witnessing the signature of a client is valid, as is a bank's employees witnessing the fixing of its seal: see *Northern Bank Ltd v Rush* [2009] NI Ch 6.

18 Sub-clause (II) introduces the requirement of attestation by a witness present when some other person signs the document on behalf of the individual who is party to the deed (see LRC 56–1998, para 2.62). The Commission took the view that this provides a safeguard against undue influence by the person signing on behalf of a party to the document intended to be a deed.

19 The Commission wished to cover the situation where the individual was incapable of signing in the normal way owing to "physical infirmity" and could, at most, place a mark on the document and acknowledge this in the presence of a witness attesting that this was his or her signature (see LRC 56–1998, paras 2.63–2.65, which discuss the appropriate practice in such cases; see also Fitzgerald, *Land Registry Practice* (2nd edn, Round Hall Press, 1995) pp 27–28).

20 The Commission recommended that there should be no change to the requirement of sealing for companies registered under the Companies Acts 1908 and 1963, in accordance with Table A or their Articles of Association: see LRC 56–1998, paras 2.67, 2.76 and 2.81.

21 The Commission recommended preserving the *status quo* also with respect to other corporate bodies (ie other than companies) registered in the State: see LRC 56–1998, paras 2.76 and 2.81.

22 This implements an earlier recommendation of the Commission (see LRC 44–1992, pp 3-4) and reiterated later (see LRC 56–1998, paras 2.78–2.80) to deal with difficulties relating to foreign companies operating in the State which did not have a seal. This caused particular difficulties in registering documents in the Land Registry, because its rules required sealing by a corporate body.

23 This confirms the common law rule that a deed is not effective until it is "delivered": *Evans v Grey* (1882) 9 LR Ir 539 at 544 (*per* Sullivan MR); see also *Bolton Metropolitian Borough Council v Torkington* [2004] Ch 66; Wylie and Woods, *Irish Conveyancing Law* (3rd edn, Tottel Publishing, 2005), paras 18.127–18.136.

24 Subsection (3) is an important provision to cover situations where a statute or private document refers to a "document under seal" rather than to a "deed". For example s 17(1) of the Powers of Attorney Act 1996 refers to execution by a donor of a power of attorney "where sealing is required, by his or her own seal". A deed executed in accordance with sub-s (2) will come within any such reference.

25 Subsection (4) re-enacts part of the substance of s 5 of the Real Property Act 1845 (see also s 70 and the Notes to it below). That scrapped the need to indulge in the ancient practice of "indenting" and confirms (this point was never quite so clear) that it is no longer necessary to use the heading "INDENTURE" in a deed: see Wylie and Woods, *Irish Conveyancing Law* (3rd edn, Tottel Publishing, 2005), para 18.07.

26 These last words were added to confirm the point mentioned in Note 25 above.

[110]

65.—(1) Any rule of law to the effect that the affixing of a corporate seal to an instrument effects delivery by that body corporate is abolished.[2]

(2) An instrument executed by a body corporate in accordance with *section 64(2)(b)* is capable of operating as an escrow in the same circumstances and with the same consequences as an instrument executed by an individual.[3]

Escrows by corporate bodies.[1]

Definitions

See s 3 for definition of: "instrument".

Notes

1 Section 65 implements the Law Reform Commission's recommendation that doubts as to whether a body corporate could deliver a deed "in escrow" should be removed (see LRC 56-1998, para 2.71). At common law the presumption (albeit rebuttable) was that affixing a corporate seal "imported" delivery (and, therefore, due execution: see *McArdle v Irish Iodine Co* (1864) 15 ICLR 146 at 153 (*per* Pigot CB) and this led to the suggestion that a corporation could not deliver a deed in escrow (see *Gartside v Silkstone* (1882) 21 Ch D 762 at 768 (*per* Fry J)). It is doubtful whether that view was correct, given that an escrow is based on the intention of the party executing the deed (see *Staple of England v Bank of England* (1887) 21 QB 160 at 165–6 (*per* Wills J); *Beesly v Hallwood Estates Ltd* [1961] Ch 105; Wylie and Woods, *Irish Conveyancing Law* (3rd edn, Tottel Publishing, 2005), para 18.132).

2 This removes the presumption at common law (see Note 1 above) and treats corporations like individuals so far as escrows are concerned. Subsection (1) operates only with respect to execution of instruments by a corporation from 1 December 2009, the date it came into operation.

3 This resolves the particular doubt which stemmed from the common law presumption (see Note 1 above). In so far as the doubt was probably baseless, it probably has not changed the law.

---

[111]

66.—(1)[2] Any property[3] may be conveyed by a person to that person jointly[4] with another person in the same way in which it might be conveyed by that person to another person.

(2) Subject to *subsection (3)*—

    (*a*)[5] a person may convey, but not lease,[6] property to that same person in a different capacity,[7]

    (*b*)[8] two or more persons may convey, and have always been capable of conveying, any property vested in them to

Conveyance to oneself.[1]

[LPAA 1859, s. 21]
[CA 1881, s. 50]

any one or more of themselves in the same way in which they could convey it to a third person.

(3) *Subsection (2)* does not validate a conveyance made in breach of trust or other fiduciary obligation.[9]

(4) Without prejudice to *section 83*,[10] this section does not affect any rule of law under which a covenant entered into with oneself is unenforceable.[11]

Definitions

See s 3 for definitions of: "conveyed"; "covenant"' "lease"; "property".

Notes

1   Section 66 consolidates provisions in s 21 of the Law of Property Amendment Act 1859 and s 50 of the Conveyancing Act 1881, as recommended by the Law Reform Commission: see LRC CP 34–2004, paras 8.36–37 and 8.43.

2   Subsection (1) enables a person to convey property jointly to himself or herself and another person. Prior to the statutory provisions referred to in Note 1, land could only be conveyed by A to A and B using a conveyance to uses executed by the Statute of Uses (Ireland) 1634 (repealed by Schedule 2): see Wylie, *Irish Land Law* (3rd edn, Tottel Publishing, 1997), para 3.020. Such a conveyance is no longer necessary: see s 62 (and the Notes to that section).

3   Note that, as with the replaced provisions, sub-s (1) applies to any property, not just land.

4   The conveyance must be to the grantor and another person *jointly*. The common law rule that a person cannot convey land to himself or herself *alone* remains. The exception to this is that a personal representative can execute an assent in favour of himself or herself alone: s 52(*b*)(i) and (2) of the Succession Act 1965. This may not be strictly necessary but arguably it is good practice to provide a document of title in this way: see *Mohan v Roche* [1991] 1 IR 560: Wylie and Woods, *Irish Conveyancing Law* (3rd edn, Tottel Publishing, 2005), para 16.41. Section 83 deals with enforcement of covenants in such cases (see the Notes to that section): note also sub-s (4) and Note 10 below.

5   Paragraph (*a*) extends existing law and enables, eg, a trustee to convey property to himself or herself and a beneficiary or the donee of a power of appointment to make an appointment in favour of himself or herself and another object of the power. But note sub-s (3) and Note 9 below.

6   This is because a lease is based on contract and one cannot contract with oneself, so that there would be difficulties about enforcing covenants in the lease (see sub-s (4) and Note 11 below): see *Rye v Rye* [1962] AC 496 at 513 (*per* Lord Denning). *Clydesdale Bank plc v Davidson* [1997] NPC 182. However it has been held that the owner of land could lease it to a nominee: *Ingram v IRC* [2002] 1 AC 293.

7   Paragraph (*a*) is dealing with a conveyance to oneself in a "different" capacity (see Note 5 above). Subsection (1) deals with conveyances to oneself in the same capacity.

8   Paragraph (*b*) confirms the common law position, that co-owners of property may convey it to a *lesser* number of themselves.

9   This is particularly relevant where the grantor is a trustee or donee of a power in the nature of a trust: cf s 27(2) (and Notes 8–10 to that section).

10 Section 83 renders the covenant enforceable by the *other* person (see the Notes to that section).

11 This confirms the general contractual rule: see Note 6 above.

---

[112]

67.—(1)[2] A conveyance of unregistered land with or[3] without words of limitation, or any equivalent expression, passes the fee simple or the other entire estate or interest which the grantor had power to create or convey, unless a contrary intention appears in the conveyance.

Words of limitation.[1]
[CA 1881, s. 51]

(2)[4] A conveyance of unregistered land to a corporation sole[5] by that person's corporate designation without the word "successors" passes to the corporation the fee simple or the other entire estate or interest which the grantor had power to create or convey, unless a contrary intention appears in the conveyance.

(3)[6] Where an interest in land is expressed to be given[7] to—

   (*a*)   the heir or heirs,[8] or

   (*b*)   any particular heir, or

   (*c*)   any class of heirs, or

   (*d*)   issue,

of any person in words which, under the rule known as the Rule in *Shelley's Case*, would have operated to give that person a fee simple, those words operate as words of purchase[9] and not of limitation and take effect in equity accordingly.[10]

(4) Subject to *section 68, subsections (1) to (3)* apply to conveyances executed before the commencement of this Chapter,[11] but without prejudice to any act or thing done or any interest disposed of or acquired before that commencement in consequence of the failure to use words of limitation in such a conveyance or the application of the Rule in *Shelley's Case*.[12]

Definitions

See s 3 for definitions of: "conveyance"; "land"; "unregistered land".

Notes

1   Section 67 implements the Law Reform Commission's recommendation that the position with respect to registered land transfers (see s 123 of the Registration of Title Act 1964) should be replicated for unregistered land: see LRC 44–1992, pp 6–7, reiterated in LRC CP 34–2004, para 8.43 (in relation to s 51 of the Conveyancing Act 1881). It is important to appreciate the significance of this provision. It is essentially a "default" provision which may correct an oversight by a conveyancer or resolve a doubt as to the effect of a conveyance, ie, the failure to include words of limitation will not mean, as previously, that the grantee will obtain a lesser interest (eg a life interest only) than he was expecting or less than the grantor had title to convey (see Lyall, *Land Law in Ireland* (2nd edn, Round Hall, 2000), pp 227–228; Wylie, *Irish Land Law* (3rd edn, Tottel Publishing, 1997), paras 4.024–4.030). It does not, however, mean that conveyancers should adopt the practice of leaving out such words. As is explained in relation to s 80, it is necessary to include them if the benefit of the statutory covenants for title set out in Schedule 3 is to be obtained (see Note 7 to that section). Conveyancers can continue to use the expressions previously recognised as words of limitation for a fee simple (a fee tail cannot be created since 1 December 2009: see s 13 and the Notes to it), ie, the common law formula "and his heirs" or the alternative introduced by s 51 of the 1881 Act, "in fee simple". That section is repealed (see Schedule 2), but that repeal does not affect the previous operation of the section in providing that alternative: see s 27(1)(*b*) of the Interpretation Act 2005.

2   This largely reproduces the wording of s 123(1) of the Registration of Title Act 1964, adapted to a conveyance of unregistered land.

3   The words "with or" were added at the Dáil Committee Stage. They do not appear in s 123(1) of the Registration of Title Act 1964, but were added to confirm the point made at the end of Note 1 above, ie that the old words of limitation remain valid and effective: see Mee, "Words of Limitation Revisited" (2007) 12(2) CPLJ 55.

4   This largely reproduces the wording of s 123(2) of the Registration of Title Act 1964, again adapted to unregistered land. A failure to use the formula "and his successors" would give corporation sole a life interest only. Use of the formula for individuals, "and his heirs", would give the corporation sole a fee simple, but in his or her private capacity only: see Lyall, *Land Law in Ireland* (2nd edn, Round Hall, 2000), p 163; Wylie, *Irish Land Law* (3rd edn, Tottel Publishing, 1997), para 4.028.

5   For example a Minister of the Government: see Ministers and Secretaries Act 1924, s 2.

6   Subsection (3) reverses the rule in *Shelley's Case*, so as to make a disposition coming within that rule operate as the grantor is most likely to have intended, ie, that the "heirs" or "issue" referred to in the disposition should take the land in due course: see Lyall, *Land Law in Ireland* (2nd edn, Round Hall, 2000), pp 166–173; Wylie, *Irish Land Law* (3rd edn, Tottel Publishing, 1997), paras 4.034–4.042.

7   The rule could apply to both *inter vivos* conveyances and dispositions by will.

8   These words are now to be construed as meaning the person or persons (other than a creditor) who would be beneficially entitled to a deceased person's (ancestor's)

estate if that person had died intestate (under Part VI of the Succession Act 1965): see s 15(3) of the 1965 Act.

9   That is the persons take an interest instead of the holder of the prior estate getting a fee simple by virtue of the words being treated as words of limitation delimiting that prior estate.

10 The fee simple going to the heirs is not in possession and so cannot be a legal estate under s 11 (see the Notes to that section).

11 This renders somewhat controversially (see Mee, "Words of Limitation Revisited" (2007) 12(2) CPLJ 55), the "curative" effect of sub-ss (1) and (2), and the change made by sub-s (3), retrospective, but subject to safeguards in the subsection and s 68 (see the Notes to that section). Those safeguards were viewed as satisfying both constitutional and human rights requirements.

12 This preserves the interest of any person which vested or was claimed in consequence of a deed being defective for want of words of limitation or application of the rule in *Shelley's Case*. However, such a person must, since 1 December 2009, take steps to protect it by applying to the court under s 68.

---

[113]

68.—(1)[2] An interest—

(a)   to which a person was entitled, or

(b)   acquired by a person,

before the commencement of this Chapter[3] in consequence of the failure to use words of limitation in a conveyance executed before that commencement[4] or the application of the Rule in *Shelley's Case*[5] is extinguished[6] unless the person claiming to be entitled to the interest or to have acquired it—

(i)   applies to the court,[7] within 12 years from the commencement of this Chapter,[8] for an order under this section, and

(ii) registers any order made under this section in accordance with *subsection (3)*.[9]

(2)[10] On such an application the court may[11]—

(a)   make an order declaring that the applicant is entitled to the interest or has acquired it,[12]

(b)   refuse to make such an order if it is satisfied that no substantial injustice will be done to any party,[13] or

(c)   in lieu of a declaration in favour of the applicant, order payment by another party of such compensation to the applicant as the court thinks appropriate.[14]

Extinguishment of certain interests.[1]

(3) An order under this section shall be registered in the Registry of Deeds or Land Registry, as appropriate.[15]

Definitions

See s 3 for definitions of: "conveyance"; "court"; "Land Registry"; "Registry of Deeds".

Notes

1   Section 68 (which in the original Bill was part of what is now 67, but was split into a separate section at the Dáil Report Stage) supplements s 67(4).

2   Subsection (1) requires a person protected by the saving in s 67(4) from the retrospective operation of s 67 (see Notes 11 and 12 to that section) to take positive action to preserve that protection. The point is that it may not be obvious to subsequent purchasers of the land whether such persons exist or what interests they may be claiming. Often the lack of words of limitations, will have gone unnoticed or not have been acted upon. The requirement to obtain a court order confirming a claim within 12 years and to register it will facilitate conveyancing in due course. After that period has expired a purchaser will be able to ignore the possibility of a claim (unless it has been protected by registration of a court order, which will be revealed by the usual searches) and rely upon the retrospective operation of s 67.

3   This connects sub-s (1) to the saving in s 67(4) (see Note 2 above).

4   This is linked with the "curative" effect of s 67(1) and (2) which were given retrospective effect by s 67(4) (see Note 11 to that section).

5   This is linked with s 67(3) (see Notes 6–10 to that section).

6   The interest is, therefore, lost and a purchaser need not be concerned with it (see Note 2 above).

7   The Circuit Court has concurrent jurisdiction with the High Court (see the definition in s 3 and Notes 21–23 to that section). Rules of court will provide for applications under this section.

8   This period, which equates to the limitation period for actions to recover land under the Statute of Limitations 1957 (see s 13), was considered to be more than adequate to allow persons to protect interests which would otherwise be extinguished under s 67(4). The European Court of Human Rights Grand Chamber upheld the doctrine of adverse possession as a proportionate control of the use of land, rather than a deprivation of possession, in *JA Pye (Oxford) Ltd v United Kingdom* (2007) 46 EHRR 1083 (see paras 28–29 of the Introduction earlier).

9   The court order must also be registered – note the "and" preceding subparagraph (ii). Note that it is the application to the court that must be made within 12 years, not the court order or its registration. However, a purchaser can check the register of *lis pendens* maintained under s 121 (see the Notes to that section). A failure to register this may mean that a purchaser will take free of the claim under s 125 (see the Notes to that section).

10 Subsection (2) gives guidance as to the orders which a court may make, but the matter rests ultimately in the discretion of the court (see Note 11 below).

11 This confirms the court's discretion (see Note 10 above).

12 This will secure the permanent protection of the claimant's interest and prevent retrospective operation of s 67.

13 This goes to the proportionate operation of s 67 (see Notes 2 and 8 above).

14 The possibility of compensation has long been an important factor in validity of provisions under the Constitution.

15 See Registration of Deeds (No 2) Rules 2009 (SI 457/2009); Land Registration (No 2) Rules 2009 (SI 456/2009).

---

[114]

69.—(1)[2] A reservation of a legal estate or interest in a conveyance of land operates, without execution of the conveyance or of any regrant by the grantee, to— **Reservations.[1]**

  (*a*) vest that estate or interest in the grantor or other person for whose benefit it is made, and **[CA 1881, s. 62**

  (*b*) annex it to the land, if any, for the benefit of which it is made.[3]

(2) A conveyance of land expressed to be subject to a legal estate or interest which is not in existence immediately before the date of the conveyance operates as a reservation within the meaning of *subsection (1)*, unless a contrary intention is expressed in the conveyance.[4]

(3) For the purpose of construing the effect of a conveyance of land, a reservation shall not be treated as taking effect as a regrant.[5]

(4) This section applies only to reservations made after the commencement of this Part.[6]

Definitions

See s 3 for definitions of: "conveyance"; "land"; "legal estate"; "legal interest".

Notes

1 Section 69 replaces s 62 of the Conveyancing Act 1881 and, in so doing, greatly simplifies the law relating to reservations in a deed (eg where the grantor reserves easements over the land sold for the benefit of land the grantor retains: see Wylie and Woods, *Irish Conveyancing Law* (3rd edn, Tottel Publishing, 2005), paras 18.73–18.81).

2 Subsection (1) makes a reservation in a conveyance fully effective without the need for the grantee to execute the deed. It also removes the need to use the cumbersome method of a use executed by the Statute of Uses (Ireland) 1634, which was provided for by s 50 of the 1881 Act: see Bland, *The Law of Easements and Profits à Prendre* (Round Hall, 1997), para 11.07. Under s 62(2) a conveyance executed after 1

December 2009 is "fully effective" without the need for "any" conveyance to uses (see Notes 5–7 to that section). The 1634 Statute is repealed (see Schedule 2).

3   Most reservations relate to rights like easements and other appurtenant rights intended to benefit land retained by the grantor.

4   Subsection (2) confirms a long-established distinction – that a reservation relates to a *new* right being created by the conveyance (as where a landowner divides the land, sells off part and reserves an easement over the part sold; prior to the subdivision there could be no easement because both parts where held by the same owner – there were no dominant and servient lands (tenements): see Part 8, Chapter 1 (and the Notes to it)). A "reservation" is to be distinguished from an "exception" which relates to an *existing* right or matter (something *in esse*), ie already in existence before the conveyance is made, such as minerals: see Wylie and Woods, *Irish Conveyancing Law* (3rd edn, Tottel Publishing, 2005), paras 18.73–18.75. See on the English equivalent (s 65(2) of the Law of Property Act 1925) *Wiles v Banks* (1984) 50 P & CR 80.

5   This reverses an odd rule of construction that applies to reservations at common law. A reservation was, in effect, regarded as a regrant of the right in question by the grantee of the conveyance in favour of the grantor, hence the rule (abolished by sub-s (1): see Note 2 above) that the conveyance had to be executed by the grantee (as well as the grantor). The result was, in accordance with the principle that "a grantor should not derogate from the grant" (recognised by s 40: see the Notes to that section), that the wording of a reservation (notwithstanding that it was for the benefit of the grantor *of the conveyance*) was construed against the grantee *of the conveyance* (but regarded as the grantor *of the reservation*): see *South Eastern Railway v Associated Portland Cement Co* [1910] 1 Ch 12; *Foster v Lyons* [1927] 1 Ch 219; Wylie and Woods, *Irish Conveyancing Law* (3rd edn, Tottel Publishing, 2005), para 18.78. This ran counter to the usual *contra proferentem* rule for deeds, that it is construed against the grantor: see Wylie and Woods, *Irish Conveyancing Law* (3rd edn, Tottel Publishing, 2005), para 17.22. Subsection (3) substitutes the general rule for reservations as well. The English equivalent of s 69 (s 65 of the Law of Property Act 1925) does not contain an equivalent of sub-s (3) and the courts there have continued to apply the rule of construction against grantees: *Cordell v Second Clanfield Properties Ltd* [1969] 2 Ch 9; *St Edmundsbury and Ipswich Diocesan Board of Finance v Clark (No 2)* [1975] 1 WLR 468. This has been much criticised: see Megarry and Wade, *The Law of Real Property* (7th edn, Sweet & Maxwell, 2008), para 28.007.

6   Section 69 changes the law in several respects (see Notes 1–5 above) and so applies only to reservations made after 1 December 2009.

---

[115]

Benefit of deeds.[1]
[RPA 1845, s. 5]

70.—(1) Where a deed is expressed to confer an estate or interest in land,[2] or the benefit of a covenant or right relating to land,[3] on a person, that person may enforce the deed whether or not named a party to it.[4]

(2) Nothing in this section otherwise affects the doctrine of privity of contract.[5]

Definitions

See s 3 for definitions of : "covenant"; "deed"; "land".

Notes

1　Section 70 re-enacts much of the substance of s 5 of the Real Property Act 1845 and clarifies its operation (another part of it is re-enacted in s 64(4): see Note 25 to that section). In essence it deals with the extent to which someone who is not a party to the deed can nevertheless claim a benefit under it.

2　Like s 5 of the 1845 Act the section is confined to deeds relating to land (cf the controversial English replacement, s 56 of the Law of Property Act 1925: see Megarry and Wade, *The Law of Real Property* (7th edn, Sweet & Maxwell, 2008), paras 32.006–32.008).

3　Note that it is concerned only with the "benefit" of a covenant or right.

4　At common law the benefit of a provision in a deed poll could be taken by any person whether or not named in the deed, for such a deed is addressed to the world at large. It followed that any person with whom the person executing the deed poll purported to contract or to benefit could claim the benefit of the deed: see *Chelsea & Waltham Green Building Society v Armstrong* [1951] Ch 853. The rule for a deed *inter partes* (made by more than one party) was, on the other hand, the strict one that only a person made a party to the deed could sue on it: see *Lord Southampton v Brown* (1827) 6 B & C 718. Section 5 of the 1845 Act purported to reverse this strict rule, but it has been a matter of some controversy just how far it did so. One view, arguably the better one, is that a person not named as the party to the deed can sue on it only if the deed, or, more usually, the covenant in the deed is nevertheless made "with" him or her (see *Beswick v Beswick* [1968] AC 58, p 106, *per* Lord Upjohn), ie, it "can be called in aid only by a person who, although not a party to the conveyance or other instrument in question, is yet a person to whom that conveyance or other instrument purports to grant something or with whom some agreement or covenant is thereby purported to be made" *per* Crossman J in *Re Foster* [1938] 3 All ER 357 at 365; see also *White v Bijou Mansions Ltd* [1937] Ch 610 at 625 (*per* Simonds J); *Lyus v Prowsa Developments Ltd* [1982] 1 WLR 1044 at 1049 (*per* Dillon J). The contrary views expressed by Lord Denning must be doubted: see *Smith v River Douglas Catchment Board* [1949] 2 KB 500; *Drive Yourself Hire Co (London) Ltd v Strutt* [1954] 1 QB 250; see also the Court of Appeal decision in the *Beswick v Beswick* [1968] AC 58. Thus, if in a deed made between A and B, A covenants with B that A will grant a lease to C, C cannot invoke the benefit under s 70. Under the deed A has purported to covenant with B only and B alone can enforce it. If, on the other hand, the covenant by A was expressed to be made with B *and* C, then C can enforce it under s 70, even though he or she is not otherwise named as a party to the deed. Similarly where a covenant is made by a vendor with the purchaser of the land conveyed and "the owners for the time being" of adjacent plots of land. Those owners in existence at the time of the conveyance can also enforce the covenant: see *Kelsey v Dodd* (1881) 52 LJ Ch 34; *Westhoughton UDC v Wigan Coal & Iron Co Ltd* [1919] 1 Ch 159; *White v Bijou Mansions Ltd* [1937] Ch 610, *Re Ecclesiastical Commissioners for England's Conveyance* [1936] Ch 430. It also seems clear that s 70 can only be invoked by persons in existence at the date of execution of the deed in question: *Kelsey v Dodd* (1881) 52 LJ Ch 34. However, future owners of the land intended to be benefited may be able to enforce the covenant in question as successors in title, under s 49 (see the Notes to that section); that replaces s 58 of the CA 1881: as to which see *Forster v Elvet Colliery Co Ltd* [1908] 1 KB 629, on appeal *sub nom Dyson v Forster* [1909] AC 98.

5   Subsection (2) clarifies a controversial point which arose in respect of the English equivalent (see Note 2), Section 70 does not otherwise affect the general doctrine of privity of contract (as to which see McDermott, *Contract Law* (Tottel Publishing, 2001), ch 18).

---

[116]

Features and rights con-veyed with land.[1]
[CA 1881, s. 6]

71.—(1)[2] A conveyance of land includes, and conveys with the land, all—

(*a*)   buildings, commons, ditches, drains, erections, fences, fixtures, hedges, water, watercourses and other features forming part of the land,[3]

(*b*)   advantages, easements, liberties, privileges, *profits à prendre* and rights appertaining or annexed to the land.[4]

(2)[5] A conveyance of land which has houses or other buildings on it includes, and conveys with the land, houses or other buildings all—

(*a*)   areas, cellars, cisterns, courts, courtyards, drainpipes, drains, erections, fixtures, gardens, lights, outhouses, passages, sewers, watercourses, yards and other features forming part of the land, houses or other buildings,

(*b*)   advantages, easements, liberties, privileges, *profits à prendre* and rights appertaining or annexed to the land, houses or other buildings.

(3)[6] This section—

(*a*)   does not on a conveyance of land (whether or not it has houses or other buildings on it)—

(i)   create any new interest or right or convert any quasi-interest or right existing prior to the conveyance into a full interest or right,[7] or

224

      (ii) extend the scope of, or convert into a new interest or right, any licence, privilege or other interest or right existing before the conveyance,[8]

  (*b*)[9] does not—

      (i) give to any person a better title to any land, interest or right referred to in this section than the title which the conveyance gives to the land expressed to be conveyed, or

      (ii) convey to any person any land, interest or right further or other than that which could have been conveyed to that person by the grantor,

  (*c*) takes effect subject to the terms of the conveyance.[10]

Definitions

See s 3 for definitions of: "conveyance"; "land".

Notes

1   Section 71 re-enacts much of the substance of s 6 of the Conveyancing Act 1881 but, in doing so, clarifies its operation as recommended by the Law Reform Commission: see LRC CP 34–2004, paras 7.24–7.27 and 8.43. It deals with controversial aspects connected with acquisition of easements and profits by implication (see Notes 7–8 below). In fact s 6 was never really intended to deal with *creation* of such rights but was one of a number of "word-saving" provisions in the 1881 Act designed to shorten conveyances by reading in words which the conveyancer might otherwise feel obliged to insert for completeness' sake: Wylie and Woods, *Irish Conveyancing Law* (3rd edn, Tottel Publishing, 2005), para 18.54. Note that s 71 does not re-enact sub-s (3) of s 6, which related to conveyances of "manors", a feudal concept which has disappeared from our law: Lyall, *Land Law in Ireland* (2nd edn, Round Hall, 2000), pp 46–47; Wylie and Woods, *Irish Conveyancing Law* (3rd edn, Tottel Publishing, 2005), paras 2.29–2.33 and 6.066.

2   Subsection (1) lists all the constituent physical parts (or features) of land which are deemed to be conveyed along with the land identified by a general description in the deed and which, therefore, do not have to be specifically referred to: see Wylie and Woods, *Irish Conveyancing Law* (3rd edn, Tottel Publishing, 2005), para 18.54. It also indicates that various rights, such as easements and profits, which already relate to the land (see Note 4 below) pass under the conveyance.

3   Paragraph (*a*) relates to physical features.

4   Paragraph (*b*) relates to rights. Note that this concerns only the *benefit* of such rights attaching to the land conveyed. It has nothing to do with *burdens* to which that land may be subject.

5   Subsection (2) is the equivalent provision to that in sub-s (1) for conveyances of land which includes houses or other buildings on it (see Notes 3 and 4 above).

6   Subsection (3) contains the clarifications the Law Reform Commission recommended (see Note 1 above).

7   Subparagraph (*a*)(i) resolves a controversial issue as to whether the provision can create new rights or extend the scope of existing ones. As to the former, it confirms that it cannot operate in the typical *Wheeldon v Burrows* situation, where a landowner sells off part of land and the grantee obtains as a new easement a right over the part retained. As it is sometimes put, there must have been diversity of ownership or possession *prior* to the conveyance and the rights must have already been in existence for them to pass under the section. This accords with the view expressed by the Supreme Court in *William Bennett Construction Ltd v Greene* [2004] IESC 15 and the English law lords in *Sovmots Investments Ltd v Secretary of State for the Environment* [1977] 2 All ER 385 at 391 (*per* Lord Wilberforce) and 397–398 (*per* Lord Edmund-Davies) (see also Harpum, "Easements and Centre Point: Old Problems Resolved in a Novel Setting" (1977) 41 Conv 415; Smith, "Centre Point: Faulty Towers with Shaky Foundations" [1978] Conv 449; Harpum, "*Long v Gowlett*: A Strong Fortress" [1979] Conv 113).

8   Paragraph (*a*)(ii) deals with another very controversial point, at least in England and Wales. A series of cases there have held that the equivalent provision (s 62 of the Law of Property Act 1925) converts what previously may have been a purely personal and informal arrangement with respect to the land into a full legal easement. Thus if a landlord of land A, who also owns and occupies adjacent land (land B), gives the tenant of land A mere permission (licence) to use a path through land B as a temporary short-cut and then conveys the reversion of land A to the tenant, that is a "conveyance" and converts the previous mere licence into a full legal and permanent (attaching to the freehold conveyed to the tenant) easement over land B: see *International Tea Stores Ltd v Hobbs* [1903] 2 Ch 165; *White v Williams* [1922] 1 KB 727; *Wright v Macadam* [1949] 2 QB 744; *Goldberg v Edwards* [1950] Ch 247; *Graham v Philcox* [1984] QB 747. This line of authorities has provoked criticism: see Tee, "Metamorphoses and Section 62 of the Law of Property Act 1925" [1998] Conv 115. There is some suggestion that the Irish courts might have once taken the same view (*Jeffers v Odeon (Ireland) Ltd* (1953) 87 ILTR 187 (Circuit Court) but the Supreme Court in *William Bennett Construction Ltd v Greene* [2004] IESC 15 took the view that s 6 of the 1881 Act could not "enlarge" rights passing with the conveyance. Subparagraph (*a*)(ii) confirms this view.

9   Paragraph (*b*) re-enacts the substance of s 6(5) of the 1881 Act.

10   As under s 6 of the 1881 Act (see sub-s (4) to it) s 71 is subject to express provisions to the contrary in the conveyance.

---

[117]

Supplemen-
tal instru-
ments.[1]
[CA 1881,
s.53]

72.—(1) Any instrument expressed to be supplemental[2] to a previous instrument, or directed to be read as an annex to such an instrument, is, so far as is appropriate, to be read and has effect as if the instrument so expressed or directed—

(*a*)   were made by way of endorsement on the previous instrument, or

(*b*)   contained a full recital of the previous instrument.

(2) This section does not confer on a purchaser any right to an abstract, copy or production of any such previous instrument and a purchaser may accept the same evidence that the previous instrument does not affect the title as if it had merely been mentioned in the supplemental instrument.

Definitions

See s 3 for definitions of: "instrument"; "purchaser".

Notes

1   Section 72 re-enacts the substance of s 53 of the Conveyancing Act 1881 but, as recommended by the Law Reform Commission, extends it to cover any instrument (as s 58 of the English Law of Property Act 1925 did): see LRC CP 34–2004, para 8.43. The section facilitates the use of a separate instrument to supplement an existing one, so that it can be read as one with it, instead of having to make endorsements on the existing instrument.

2   For a precedent see Precedent F.1.6 in *Laffoy's Irish Conveyancing Precedents* (Bloomsbury Professional).

[118]

73.—(1)[2] A release of part of land from—

Partial releases.[1]
[LPAA 1859, ss. 10 and 11]

(*a*)   a rentcharge does not extinguish the rentcharge, but bars only the right to recover any part of the rentcharge out of the land released,

(*b*)   a judgment charged on the land does not affect the validity of the judgment as regards any of the land not specifically released.

(2) *Subsection (1) does not—*

(*a*)   prejudice the rights of any person interested in the land unreleased and not concurring in or confirming the release,[3] or

(*b*)   prevent recovery of the whole of the rentcharge or enforcement of the whole judgment against the land unreleased, unless those interested agree otherwise.[4]

Definitions

See s 3 for definitions of: "land"; "rentcharge".

Notes

1   Section 73 re-enacts the substance of ss 10 and 11 of the Law of Property Amendment Act 1859. Those sections reversed the common law rule that a "partial" release, ie a release of part of land from a rentcharge or judgment on it, released the entire land: see *Coke upon Littleton* (19th edn, 1832) 147*b* and 147*c*; *Handcock v Handcock* (1850) 1 Ir Ch R 444. Note, however, that, so far as rentcharges are concerned, the provisions of this section must be read subject to s 42, which provides that rentcharges are enforceable as a contract debt only (see the Notes to that section), but that is subject to other statutory provisions which may provide otherwise.

2   Subsection (1) ensures that a partial release does not extinguish the rentcharge or affect the validity of the judgment as regards any part of the land not covered by the release.

3   If the owner of the land does not concur in or confirm the release, his or her liability cannot be increased by the release. Thus where part only of the land is released, the remaining part will remain charged with or subject to the judgment only to an apportioned extent: see *Booth v Smith* (1884) 14 QBD 318. If, however, the owner concurs in or confirms the release, the unreleased land will remain subject to the entire rentcharge or judgment: see *Price v John* [1905] 1 Ch 744.

4   As a result of the statutory provisions a partial release can either release the entire land from part of the rentcharge or judgment or release part of the land from the whole of the rentcharge or judgment.

---

[119]

Fraudulent dispositions.[1]
[CA 1634, ss. 1 to 5, 10, 11 and 14]
[VCA 1893]

74.—(1)[2] Subject to *subsection (2)*, any voluntary disposition of land[3] made with the intention of defrauding[4] a subsequent purchaser[5] of the land is voidable[6] by that purchaser.

(2) For the purposes of *subsection (1)*, a voluntary disposition is not to be read as intended to defraud merely because a subsequent disposition of the same land was made for valuable consideration.[7]

(3)[8] Subject to *subsection (4)*, any conveyance of property[9] made with the intention of defrauding a creditor or other person[10] is voidable by any person thereby prejudiced.[11]

(4) *Subsection (3)* does not—

   (*a*)[12] apply to any estate or interest in property conveyed for valuable consideration[13] to any person in good faith not having, at the time of the conveyance, notice of the fraudulent intention, or

   (*b*)   affect any other law relating to bankruptcy of an individual[14] or corporate insolvency.[15]

Definitions

See s 3 for definitions of: "conveyance"; "disposition"; "land"; "notice"; "purchaser"; "valuable consideration".

Notes

1 Section 74 replaces the somewhat convoluted and confusing provisions in ss 1–5, 10, 11 and 14 of the Conveyancing Act (Ireland) 1634, as amended by the Voluntary Conveyances Act 1893: see LRC CP 34–2004, paras 8.22–8.25 (which drew attention to the much simpler English s 173 of the Law of Property Act 1925).

2 Subsection (1) replaces ss 1–5 of the 1634 Act and deals with *voluntary* conveyances of land made with the intention of defrauding a subsequent purchaser of the land.

3 This covers a wide range of voluntary transactions, but only relating to land: see *Blake v Hyland* (1838) 2 Dr & Wal 297; *Fitzmaurice v Sadlier* (1846) 9 Ir Eq R 595; *Scott v Scott* (1854) 4 HLC 1065.

4 See sub-s (2) and Note 7 below.

5 The object of the provision is to protect a purchaser of land from a prior voluntary and fraudulent disposition.

6 Not "void", which s 1 of the 1634 Act stated, though the courts interpreted that as meaning that the aggrieved purchaser had to take actions to "avoid" the voluntary conveyance: see *Gardiner v Gardiner* (1861) 12 ICLR 565; *Hamilton v Molloy* (1880) 5 LR Ir 339; *Lee v Matthews* (1880) 6 LR Ir 530.

7 This re-enacts the amendment made by the 1893 Act to counter the view taken by the English courts: cf *National Bank Ltd v Behan* [1913] 1 IR 512; *Re Moore* [1918] 1 IR 169; see Wylie, *Irish Land Law* (3rd edn, Tottel Publishing, 1997), para 9.078. As regards what constitutes "valuable" consideration see s 3 (and Note 95 to that section).

8 Subsections (3) and (4) re-enact the substance of ss 10, 11 and 14 of the 1634 Act. These provisions are regularly invoked in modern times: see *McQuillan v Maguire* [1996] 1 ILRM 394; *Motor Insurance Bureau of Ireland v Stanbridge* [2008] IEHC 389.

9 Unlike sub-ss (1) and (2), sub-ss (3) and (4), as under the 1634 Act, apply to a conveyance of "any property".

10 Such intention must be established (see *Bryce v Fleming* [1930] IR 36) but the circumstances of the case may give rise to a presumption of fraud, especially where the result was that creditors or others were clearly disadvantaged: see *Re Moroney* (1887) 21 LR Ir 27 at 61–62 (*per* Palles B), approved by Costello J in *McQuillan v Maguire* [1996] 1 ILRM 394; see also *Motor Insurance Bureau of Ireland v Stanbridge* [2008] IEHC 389. It is not necessary that the grantor of the conveyance was insolvent at the time it was made; an intention to defraud potential creditors is enough: see *Murphy v Abraham* (1864) 15 Ir Ch R 371; cf *Re Kelleher* [1911] 2 IR 1. On the other hand, merely preferring one creditor to another is not necessarily fraudulent: see *Nolan v Neill* (1899) 33 ILTR 129; *Re Ryan* [1937] IR 367; *Rose v Greer* [1945] IR 503.

11 That is not just creditors: see *Cadogan v Cadogan* [1977] 3 All ER 831.

12 Paragraph (*a*) recasts provisions in s 14 of the 1634 Act. It protects a *bona fide* purchaser for value without notice of the fraud.

13 The 1634 Act used the expression "for money or other good consideration", which was interpreted as including marriage consideration but not "natural love and affection": see *Re Rorke's Estate* (1865) 15 Ir Ch R 316; *Bryce v Fleming* [1930] IR 376. The definition in s 3 makes it clear that it does not include marriage nor a nominal consideration in money.

14 For example ss 57–59 of the Bankruptcy Act 1988.

15 For example s 286 of the Companies Act 1963 (as substituted by s 135 of the Companies Act 1990).

---

[120]

CHAPTER 4[1]
Contents of deeds[2]

Notes

1 Chapter 4 deals with various aspects of the contents of deeds and replaces various provisions in the Real Property Act 1845 and Conveyancing Act 1881.

2 In addition to replacing 19th century statutory provisions Chapter 4 also includes provisions recommended by the Law Reform Commission to facilitate conveyancing: see especially ss 75 and 85 below.

---

[121]

Construction
of instru-
ments.[1]

75.—Particular words and expressions used in any instrument[2] relating to land[3] executed or made after the commencement of this Chapter,[4] unless the context otherwise requires[5]—

(*a*) are subject to the same general rules of construction as are applicable to such words and expressions used in Acts of the Oireachtas under Part 4 of the Act of 2005,[6]

(*b*) have the same particular meaning, construction or effect as assigned to such words and expressions used in Acts of the Oireachtas by Part 1 of the Schedule to that Act[7] or by *section 3* of this Act,[8] whichever is more appropriate.[9]

Definitions

See s 3 for definitions of: "instrument"; "land".

Notes

1   Section 75 implements a recommendation by the Law Reform Commission that definitions, such as those in the Interpretation Act (now 2005), which are under that Act applicable only to statutes, should be made applicable also to private documents relating to land: see LRC 30–1989, paras 21–23 (reiterated in LRC CP 34–2004, para 8.43). In fact the section extends what was recommended (see Note 8 below).

2   Note that the section applies to any instrument, not just a deed.

3   But the instrument must relate to land.

4   That is after 1 December 2009.

5   The provisions of the section give way to express provisions in the instrument. Conveyancers will still need to consider what express definitions to put in a deed or other instrument, since the statutory ones otherwise applicable by virtue of s 75 may not be appropriate to the document or transaction in question. What the section does do is to provide a "default" position, which may fill a gap in the document or resolve a doubt which might otherwise exist.

6   Paragraph (*a*) imports into private instruments the general rules of construction in Part 4 of the 2005 Act. This includes, in particular, s 18 which covers things like the singular including the plural, masculine gender importing the feminine gender and *vice versa* and "person" including a body corporate.

7   This imports the definitions of particular words listed in Part 1 of the Schedule to the 2005 Act, such as "month" (meaning a "calendar" month rather than a "lunar" month: *Vone Securities v Cooke* [1979] IR 59), "year" and "writing".

8   This extends the Law Reform Commission's recommendation by making the definitions in s 3 also applicable. In the event of a conflict or variation between s 3 and the 2005 Act (eg compare the much wider definition of "land" in s 3 with that in Part 1 of the 2005 Act's Schedule) it would be for a court to determine which was more appropriate (see Note 9 below).

9   Which would be more appropriate would be governed largely by the instrument in question and the context in which it was executed.

---

[122]

76.—(1) Subject to *subsection (2)*, a conveyance[2] of land passes all the claim, demand, estate, interest, right and title which the grantor has or has power to convey in, to or on the land conveyed or expressed or intended to be conveyed.

All estate clause.[1]
[CA1881, s. 63]

(2) This section takes effect subject to the terms of the conveyance.[3]

Definitions

See s 3 for definitions of: "conveyance"; "land".

Notes

1 Section 76 re-enacts s 63 of the Conveyancing Act 1881. That section rendered it unnecessary to include an "all estate" clause in conveyances: *Price v John* [1905] 1 Ch 744. The effect of such a clause is to pass along with the estate expressed to be conveyed all other estates or interests vested in the grantor: see *Thellusson v Liddard* [1900] 2 Ch 635; Wylie and Woods, *Irish Conveyancing Law* (3rd edn, Tottel Publishing, 2005), paras 18.82–18.83.

2 Originally the English courts construed s 63 of the 1881 Act strictly and ruled that a deed of "conveyance" could not be deemed to also make an appointment the grantor might also have power to make (other grants coming within the meaning of a "conveyance" could not be read into it *mutatis mutandis*): see *Hanbury v Bateman* [1920] 1 Ch 313 at 320 (*per* Sargant J). However, more recently it was held that an assent executed under seal by personal representatives conveyed the legal estate vested in them, even though technically they had no power to execute an assent in that case because of the way the estate had devolved: see *Re Stirrup's Contract* [1961] 1 WLR 449. There seems no reason why the wide definition in s 3 should not be fully utilised. The English courts have applied the "all estate" provision to a claim for rectification of an earlier deed of transfer (see *Berkeley Leisure Group Ltd v Williamson* [1996] EGCS 18) and to a claim by the assignee of a lease that the benefit of a break clause passed to him (see *Harbour Estates Ltd v HSBC Bank plc* [2004] 3 All ER 1057).

3 Subsection (2) makes it clear that s 76 cannot apply where there is a contrary intention expressed in the conveyance, eg, the terms of a lease would clearly negate the passing of the freehold: see *Buckler's Case* (1597) 2 Co 55.

---

[123]

Receipts in deeds.[1]
[CA 1881, ss. 54 to 56]

77.—(1)[2] A receipt for consideration in the body of a deed is sufficient discharge for the consideration to the person giving it, without any further receipt being endorsed on the deed.

(2)[3] A receipt for consideration in the body of a deed[4] is, in favour of a subsequent purchaser (not having notice[5] that the consideration so acknowledged to be received was not, in fact, given wholly or in part), conclusive evidence of the giving of the whole consideration.[6]

(3)[7] Where a solicitor produces a deed[8] which—

(a) has in its body a receipt for consideration,[9] and

(b) has been executed by the person entitled to give a receipt for the consideration,[10]

the deed is conclusive authority to the person liable to give the consideration[11] for giving it to the solicitor, without the solicitor producing any separate or other authority or direction in that behalf from the person who executed or signed the deed or receipt.[12]

(4) In *subsection (3)* "solicitor" includes any employee of a solicitor, and any member or employee of a firm in which the solicitor is a partner,[13] and any such employee or member of another firm acting as agent of the solicitor or firm.[14]

Definitions

See s 3 for definitions of: "deed"; "notice"; "purchaser".

Notes

1 Section 77 re-enacts ss 54–56 of the Conveyancing Act 1881, with some modifications recommended by the Law Reform Commission: see LRC CP 34–2004, para 8.43.

2 Subsection (1) re-enacts the substance of s 54 of the 1881 Act. Prior to that Act the receipt was usually endorsed on the back of the deed and its absence was held to put a subsequent purchaser on notice of possible existence of a vendor's lien for unpaid purchase money: see *Lloyd's Bank v Bullock* [1896] 2 Ch 192; *Bateman v Hunt* [1904] 2 KB 530; *Capell v Winter* [1907] 2 Ch 383. Subsection (1) sanctions continuance of the modern practice of putting the receipt clause in the body of the deed immediately after the statement of consideration: see Wylie and Woods, *Irish Conveyancing Law* (3rd edn, Tottel Publishing, 2005), para 18.43; *Laffoy's Irish Conveyancing Precedents* (Bloomsbury Professional), Division E; *London and Cheshire Insurance Co Ltd v Laplagrene Property Co Ltd* [1971] 1 All ER 766. Cf the statutory provision for discharge of mortgages by way of endorsed receipt under s 18 of the Housing Act 1988 and s 27(2) of the Building Societies Act 1989.

3 Subsection (2) re-enacts the substance of s 55 of the 1881 Act but renders a receipt in the body of the deed now "conclusive" rather than simply "sufficient" (as recommended by the Commission). (There was no need to make this change in sub-s (1) as that is simply providing an alternative way of showing the receipt.)

4 The reference in s 55 to "indorsed" was dropped as this is no longer the practice, except in the case of mortgage discharges where separate legislation deals with the matter (see Note 2 above).

5 Which includes "constructive" notice: see the definition in s 3 and s 86 (and the Notes to that section) and *Saunders v Leslie* (1814) 2 Ba & B 509 at 514 (*per* Lord Manners LC); see also *Spencer v Clarke* (1878) 47 LJ Ch 692. However, see Note 6 below.

6 Notwithstanding the reference to notice (see Note 5 above) by declaring that the receipt is "conclusive" in favour of a subsequent purchaser it is difficult to see on what basis a court would hold such a purchaser subject to a previous vendor's lien for unpaid purchaser money. It is likely that the purchaser would only be affected if he or she was guilty of fraud, eg, by knowingly participating in a transaction designed to defeat the vendor's claim – "fraud unravels all".

7   Subsection (3) re-enacts the substance of s 56 of the 1881 Act but again renders the receipt clause "conclusive" authority rather than "sufficient", as recommended by the Commission. Section 56 was designed to counter the view that a solicitor needed express authority to receive the purchase money to be given by a separate document: see *Viney v Chaplin* (1858) 2 De G & J 468 at 482 (*per* Turner LJ); see also *Re Shanks* (1879) 11 Ch D 525. The provision has been much relied upon in practice over the years, though often without appreciating its limitations which sub-s (4) seeks to remove: see Wylie and Woods, *Irish Conveyancing Law* (3rd edn, Tottel Publishing, 2005), para 18.46 and Notes 13–14 below.

8   That is not merely to have it in his or her custody or possession. Note that it must be a deed: see Wylie and Woods, *Irish Conveyancing Law* (3rd edn, Tottel Publishing, 2005), para 18.46.

9   Again paragraph (*a*) drops the reference to indorsed receipts: see Note 4 above.

10 That is the vendor.

11 That is the purchaser.

12 See Note 7 above.

13 This confirms what has long been assumed in practice, but doubts were expressed as to whether "solicitor" meant this in s 56 of the 1881 Act (it was not defined by that section): cf *Day v Woolwich Equitable Building Society* (1889) 40 Ch D 491.

14 Again this confirms the practice of having a closing carried out by another solicitor or firm acting as agent. This was held not to be covered by s 56 of the 1881 Act in England: see *Re Hetling and Merton's Contract* [1893] 3 Ch 269; see also the *Day* case (Note 13 above); cf *Re King* [1900] 2 Ch 425.

---

[124]

Conditions and covenants not implied.[1]
[RPA 1845, s. 4]

78.—(1) An exchange or other conveyance of land does not imply any condition in law.[2]

(2) Subject to any statutory provision,[3] use of the word "give" or "grant" in any conveyance does not imply any covenant.[4]

Definitions

See s 3 for definitions of: "conveyance"; "land".

Notes

1   Section 78 re-enacts the substance of part of s 4 of the Real Property Act 1845. The rest of that section dealt with arcane law to do with feoffments and destruction of contingent remainders, both of which are rendered irrelevant by the 2009 Act: see ss 16(*a*) and 62(4) (and the Notes to those sections).

2   This was designed to ensure that deeds did not have an unintended effect – "conditions" are rarely, if ever, included in deeds nowadays, where obligations are usually couched as covenants.

3   Note the provisions for implied covenants in ss 79–81 below (see the Notes to those sections).

4   This reversed the common law rule that such words implied a warranty as to title: see Cruise, *A Digest of the Laws of England* (4th edn by White, 1835) title 32, c 24; *Doe d Starling v Prince* (1851) 20 LJCP 223. Under ss 80–81 below special words have to be used in order to imply the covenants, eg conveying "as beneficial owner". However, the word "grant" implies certain covenants for title by promoters of statutory undertakings under s 132 of the Lands Clauses Consolidation Act 1845: see McDermott and Woulfe, *Compulsory Purchase and Compensation in Ireland: Law and Practice* (Tottel Publishing, 1992), pp 5–15.

---

[125]

79.—In *sections 80* and *81*—

    (a)   "conveyance"[2]—

        (i)   does not include the granting of a tenancy,[3]

        (ii)   means a conveyance made after the commencement of this Chapter,[4]

    (b)   any reference to a person being expressed to "convey", or to an estate or interest or land being expressed to be "conveyed" does not mean that the words "convey" or "conveyed" must be used in the conveyance for the covenant to be implied.[5]

Scope of sections 80 and 81.[1]

Definitions

Apart from the definitions provided by this section, see the definitions in s 3 of: "land"; "tenancy".

Notes

1   Section 79 provides special definitions for ss 80 and 81 which, together with Schedule 3, replace the confusing and convoluted provisions relating to covenants for title in s 7 of the Conveyancing Act 1881: see Wylie and Woods, *Irish Conveyancing Law* (3rd edn, Tottel Publishing, 2005), paras 21.05–21.33.

2   Cf the definition in s 3 (see Notes 18–20 to that section).

3   The reason for this is that ss 80 and 81 are not concerned with covenants for title implied on the *grant* of a tenancy. That subject is covered by s 41 of the Landlord and Tenant Amendment Act, Ireland 1860 (Deasy's Act): see Wylie, *Landlord and Tenant Law* (2nd edn, Tottel Publishing, 1998), paras 14.04–14.05. Note, however, that s 81 applies to *assignments* of an existing tenancy (see the Notes to that section).

4   The reason for this is that various important changes are made to the provisions previously in s 7 of the 1881 Act and these operate only in respect of conveyances made after 1 December 2009.

5 Paragraph (*b*) makes it clear that the implied covenants provided for by ss 80 and 81 still operate in a "conveyance" even though the wording of that conveyance does not use the word "convey" or "conveyed": eg, an assignment of a lease (see Note 3 above) might use the word "assign" or "assigned".

---

[126]

Covenants for title.[1]
[CA 1881, s.7]

80.—(1)[2] In a conveyance of any class referred to in *subsection (2)*[3] there are implied[4] the covenants specified in relation to that class in *Part 2* of *Schedule 3*,[5] and those covenants are deemed to be made—

    (*a*)[6] by the person or by each person who conveys, to the extent of the estate or interest or share of the estate or interest expressed to be conveyed[7] by such person ("the subject-matter of the conveyance"),

    (*b*)[8] with the person to whom the conveyance is made, or with the persons jointly and severally,[9] if more than one, to whom the conveyance is made as joint tenants, or with each of the persons, if more than one, to whom the conveyance is made as tenants in common,

and have the effect specified in *Parts 1* and *2* of *Schedule 3*.

(2) The classes of conveyance referred to in *subsection (1)*[10] are—

Class 1: A conveyance (other than a mortgage[11]) for valuable consideration of an estate or interest in land (other than a tenancy[12]) made by a person who is expressed to convey "as beneficial owner";[13]

Class 2: A conveyance (other than a mortgage) for valuable consideration of land comprised in a lease[14] made by a person who is expressed to convey "as beneficial owner";

Class 3: A conveyance comprising a mortgage of land[15] (other than land comprised in a lease[16]) made by a person who is expressed to convey "as beneficial owner";

Class 4: A conveyance comprising a mortgage of land comprised in a lease[17] made by a person who is expressed to convey "as beneficial owner";

Class 5: A conveyance made by a person who is expressed to convey "as trustee", "as mortgagee", "as personal representative" or under an order of the court.[18]

(3)[19] Where a conveyance is made by a person who is expressed to convey by direction of another person who is expressed to direct "as beneficial owner", then, whether or not that other person is also expressed to convey "as beneficial owner", the conveyance is for the purposes of this section a conveyance made by that other person expressed to convey "as beneficial owner" to the extent of the subject-matter of the conveyance made by that other person's direction.

(4)[20] Without prejudice to section 52(6) of the Act of 1965,[21] where in a conveyance a person conveying is not expressed to convey "as beneficial owner", "as trustee", "as mortgagee", "as personal representative", under an order of the court or by a direction of a person "as beneficial owner", no covenant on the part of the person conveying is implied in the conveyance.

(5)[22] The benefit of a covenant implied under this section—

    (*a*)   is annexed to and passes with the estate or interest of the implied covenantee,

    (*b*)   is enforceable by every person, including a tenant, mortgagee and any other person deriving title from or under the implied covenantee,[23] in whom that estate or interest, or any part of it, or an estate or interest derived out of it, is vested from time to time.

(6)[24] A covenant implied under this section may, by the terms of the conveyance, be—

    (*a*)   excluded but not so that a sole covenant or all (as distinct from some only) of the covenants implied in relation to a person expressed to convey as specified in *subsection (2)* are excluded,[25]

    (*b*)   modified and, if so modified, operates as if the modification was included in this section and *Schedule 3*.

(7)[26] Any covenant implied under this section by reason of a person being expressed to convey "as beneficial owner" may, by express reference to this section, be incorporated, with or without modification, in a conveyance, whether or not for valuable consideration, by a person who is expressed to convey as specified in Class 5 of *subsection (2)*.

Definitions

In addition to those provided by s 79 see s 3 for definitions of: "Act of 1965"; "covenant"; "land"; "lease"; "mortgage"; "mortgagee"; "personal representative"; "tenant"; "valuable consideration".

Notes

1   Section 80 (along with s 81) implements the Law Reform Commission's recommendation that the convoluted provisions of s 7 of the Conveyancing Act 1881 should be recast in a more straightforward way and modified to improve their efficacy: see LRC CP 34–2004, para 8.43. Those provisions relate to the statutory covenants for title which are implied in conveyances of land, provided the appropriate formula is used in the conveyance: see Wylie and Woods, *Irish Conveyancing Law* (3rd edn, Tottel Publishing, 2005), paras 21.05–21.33. Section 80 (and s 81) contains the key provisions governing the operation of the covenants, but the actual covenants themselves are set out in Schedule 3 (see the Notes to that Schedule). Section 7 of the 1881 Act was essentially a "word-saving" provision designed to relieve conveyancers of the necessity to set out in detail the various covenants for title which a purchaser would be able to invoke if, after the conveyance had been made, a defect in title came to light: see the discussion by Powell J in *Re Geraghty and Lyon's Contract* (1919) 53 ILTR 57. It must be reiterated that s 80 does not apply to the *grant* of a tenancy (see Note 3 to s 79), but s 81 does apply to an *assignment* of a existing tenancy, ie, one that was previously granted (see the Notes to that section). It is very doubtful what use the implied covenants are in a transfer of *registered* land, except, perhaps, in cases where the title is not absolute, eg it is a qualified or possessory one only: see Wylie and Woods, *Irish Conveyancing Law* (3rd edn, Tottel Publishing, 2005), para 21.06. Finally, s 80 (and s 81) implies the statutory covenants set out in Schedule 3 only if the deed contains no express ones: see sub-s (6) (and the Notes to it). In fact, in practice the statutory covenants are usually relied upon and it is rare to exclude or modify them: see *Laffoy's Irish Conveyancing Precedents* (Bloomsbury Professional), Division E.

2   Subsection (2) is the operative provision bringing the covenants set out in Schedule 3 into play.

3   Subsection (3), as did s 7 of the 1881 Act, distinguishes between different "classes" of conveyance according to the *nature* of the conveyance and the *capacity* of the person expressed to convey (see Notes 10–18 below).

4   This reiterates that s 80 is concerned with implying covenants and will give way to any express provision excluding or modifying it: see sub-s (6) and the Notes to it.

5   Part 2 of Schedule 3 sets out the terms of the actual covenants, with different ones being implied according to each class specified in sub-s (2) (see the Notes to Schedule 3).

6   Paragraph (*a*) refers to the covenantor(s) and the extent of the burden (or liability) under the covenant is set out in Part 1 of Schedule 3 (see the Notes to that Part).

7　There are two vital points to be made about this wording. First, the implied covenants attach only to the "estate or interest" which is "expressed to be conveyed" in the conveyance. It is, therefore, vital to continue to use appropriate words of limitation to indicate that estate or interest, notwithstanding the provisions of s 67 (see the Notes to that section): see *Laffoy's Irish Conveyancing Precedents* (Bloomsbury Professional), Division E. The view was taken that it was not appropriate to imply covenants in a case where no words of limitation are used and to attach them to the estate or interest which passes under that section by way of default. That section operates subject to a contrary intention and, while it is one thing to say that a vendor must stand over something which he has committed himself or herself to expressly, it would be quite another to say that he or she must stand over something to which he or she did not give an express commitment and which arises only by way of default. Secondly, sub-s (1) corrects one of the most controversial features of s 7 of the 1881 Act. It contained the additional words of "conveys and" before the word "expressed". These were added to the 1881 Bill during its passage through the Westminster Parliament and, as was later held by English case law, greatly reduced the effectiveness of the covenants. In effect, it meant that they applied only where, not only was the grantor expressed to convey a particular estate or interest, but did also actually convey it. This resulted in the covenants not applying in the very case where they were most needed: where a grantor purported to convey a particular estate or interest but did not actually do so because he or she had no title to it: see *Fay v Miller, Wilkins & Co* [1941] Ch 360; *Pilkington v Wood* [1953] Ch 770; *Re Robertson's Application* [1969] 3 All ER 257. This risk of non-applicability of the covenants for title meant that, in practice, purchasers had to rely upon contractual rights surviving the conveyance, by virtue of the "non-merger" provision in Condition 48 of the Law Society's *General Conditions of Sale (2001 Edition)*; see Wylie and Woods, *Irish Conveyancing Law* (3rd edn, Tottel Publishing, 2005), para 21.03.

8　Paragraph (*b*) refers to the covenantee(s), including joint tenants or tenants in common to whom the conveyance is made.

9　Note that any co-covenantees can now sue separately, whether joint tenants or tenants in common. Under s 7 of the 1881 Act only the latter could do this and joint covenantees had to join together in order to sue: see Wylie and Woods, *Irish Conveyancing Law* (3rd edn, Tottel Publishing, 2005), para 21.13.

10　And Schedule 3 specifies different covenants in relation to each class (see the Notes to that Schedule).

11　Mortgages are covered by Class 3.

12　This refers to a conveyance (assignment) of an existing tenancy (ie one previously granted): see Note 1 above and Note 14 below.

13　This is the formula (express phrase) which must be used in the conveyance in order to incorporate the covenants for Class 1 set out in Schedule 3: see Wylie and Woods, *Irish Conveyancing Law* (3rd edn, Tottel Publishing, 2005), paras 21.15–21.16.

14　This refers to an assignment of an existing lease. Covenants implied in the *grant* of a new lease are governed by s 41 of the Landlord and Tenant Law Amendment Act, Ireland 1860 (Deasy's Act): see *Bowes v Dublin Corporation* [1965] IR 476; *Lapedus v Glavey* (1965) 99 ILTR 1; Wylie, *Landlord and Tenant Law* (2nd edn,

Tottel Publishing, 1998), ch 14. Note the additional provisions in s 81 (see the Notes to it).

15 This refers to a conveyance by way of mortgage, which since 1 December 2009 must be executed as a charge only: see s 89(1) (and the Notes to that section).

16 A mortgage of leasehold property is covered by Class 4. Note that Class 3 covers the case where the mortgagor conveys "as beneficial owner". Class 5 deals, *inter alia*, with a conveyance by a mortgagee "as mortgagee" (see Note 18 below).

17 This covers a mortgage of a leasehold interest.

18 Class 5 covers a number of "special" cases where, because of the status of the person conveying, a much more limited covenant is implied than is the case where a person conveys "as beneficial owner": see the Notes to Schedule 3 and Wylie and Woods, *Irish Conveyancing Law* (3rd edn, Tottel Publishing, 2005), para 21.18.

19 Subsection (3) re-enacts the substance of s 7(2) of the 1881 Act and in essence provides that where a person conveys by the direction of another person the same covenants are implied in respect of the directing person as if he or she had been expressed to convey as beneficial owner. This may be appropriate in the case of a subsale, where the purchaser under a contract for sale instructs the vendor to convey directly to a subpurchaser: see (1962) 106 Sol Jo 132. On the other hand, if the purchaser joins in, the vendor may convey simply "as trustee": see *Laffoy's Irish Conveyancing Precedents* (Bloomsbury Professional), Precedent E.10.1; Wylie and Woods, *Irish Conveyancing Law* (3rd edn, Tottel Publishing, 2005), paras 21.18–21.19. Note that s 80 does not re-enact s 7(3) of the 1881 Act which provided that a wife should be deemed to convey by the direction of her husband and implied covenants on his behalf accordingly. This was viewed as based on an outmoded notion of the relationship between spouses: see Wylie and Woods, *Irish Conveyancing Law* (3rd edn, Tottel Publishing, 2005), para 21.20.

20 Subsection (4) re-enacts the substance of s 7(4) of the 1881 Act and confirms that if the "magic" formula appropriate to one of the classes of conveyance set out in sub-s (2) is not used, no covenants will be implied by ss 80 and 81: see Note 13 above.

21 This exception was provided for by s 52(6) of the Succession Act 1965, under which covenants appropriate to Class 5 are implied in an assent by a personal representative, whether or not the personal representative is expressed to convey as such: see Brady, *Succession Law in Ireland* (2nd edn, Tottel Publishing, 1995), para 10.47; *Keating on Probate* (2nd edn, Round Hall, Sweet and Maxwell, 2002), para 8.53; Wylie and Woods, *Irish Conveyancing Law* (3rd edn, Tottel Publishing, 2005), para 21.18. Section 52(6) should now be taken to refer to the covenants implied by s 80: see s 8(2)(*c*) (and Note 3 to that section).

22 Subsection (5) re-enacts, but extends (see Note 23 below), s 7(6) of the 1881 Act. In essence an implied covenant for title can be invoked by the covenantee's successors in title, as is the position now generally with freehold covenants under s 49 (see the Notes to that section). The enforceability of leasehold covenants generally is governed by ss 10 and 11 of the 1881 Act (still in force: see the Notes to Schedule 2 of the 2009 Act) and ss 12 and 13 of the Landlord and Tenant Law Amendment Act, Ireland 1860 (Deasy's Act). In order for a successor to succeed in enforcing a covenant in an earlier deed, there must be an unbroken chain of covenants in successive deeds (ie, each person conveying in those deeds must have been

expressed to convey "as beneficial owner" or in the other appropriate capacity): see *David v Sabin* [1893] 1 Ch 523; *Wyld v Silver* [1963] 1 QB 169. The onus is on the plaintiff to establish which person in the chain broke the covenant: see *Howard v Maitland* (1883) 11 QBD 695; *Stoney v Eastbourne RDC* [1927] Ch 367; Wylie and Woods, *Irish Conveyancing Law* (3rd edn, Tottel Publishing, 2005), para 21.22. Note that the liability of the covenantor (the *burden*) is dealt with by Part 1 of Schedule 3 (see the Notes to that Schedule).

23 Under s 7(6) of the 1881 Act the benefit of the implied covenants passed only to a successor who succeeded to the *same* estate or interest of the original covenantee: see *Onward Building Society v Smithson* [1893] 1 Ch 1. Subsection (5)(*b*) extends this to persons deriving title "from or under" the original covenantee or such a successor: see Wylie and Woods, *Irish Conveyancing Law* (3rd edn, Tottel Publishing, 2005), paras 21.22.

24 Subsection (6) re-enacts the substance of s 7(7) of the 1881 Act and permits exclusion or modification of the implied covenants by the terms of the particular conveyance.

25 Paragraph (*a*) qualifies the provision in s 7(7) of the 1881 Act by not allowing the entire covenant (where one only is implied, as in special cases: see Part 2, paragraph 5 to Schedule 3 and the Notes to that Schedule) or the entire set of covenants to be excluded, where the conveyance still uses the magic formula for implying covenants (see Notes 1 and 13 above): see *David v Sabin* [1893] 1 Ch 523. Total exclusion in a deed employing the magic formula is an inherent contradiction. If the intention is to exclude the covenants in their entirety the way to do this is not to use the magic formula, as sub-s (4) provides: see Note 20 above.

26 Subsection (7) is a new provision which enables the more extensive covenants implied in a conveyance for valuable consideration where a person conveys "as beneficial owner" (Class 1) to be incorporated, with or without modification, in a conveyance by a person in a special capacity (Class 5), where there would otherwise be a limited covenant only (see Part 2 of Schedule 3 and the Notes to it).

---

[127]

81.—(1)[2] In a conveyance of any class referred to in *subsection (2)*[3] there are implied, in addition to the covenants referred to in *section 80(1)*,[4] the covenants specified in relation to that class in *Part 3* of *Schedule 3*, and those covenants are deemed to be made—

Additional covenants for land comprised in a lease[1]

    (*a*) by the person, or by the persons jointly and severally, if more than one, so specified in relation to any class of conveyance,

    (*b*) with the person, or with the persons jointly and severally, if more than one, who is the other party, or are the other parties, to the conveyance, and have the effect specified in *Parts 1* and *3* of *Schedule 3.*[5]

(2) The classes of conveyance referred to in *subsection (1)* are—

Class 6:   A conveyance (other than a mortgage) for valuable consideration of[6]—

(a) the entirety of the land comprised in a lease, or

(b) part of the land comprised in a lease, subject to a part of the rent reserved by the lease which has been, or is by the conveyance, apportioned with the consent of the lessor,

for the residue of the term or interest created by the lease;

Class 7:   A conveyance (other than a mortgage) for valuable consideration of part of the land comprised in a lease, for the residue of the term or interest created by the lease, subject to a part of the rent reserved by the lease which has been, or is by the conveyance, apportioned without the consent of the lessor.[7]

(3) Where in a conveyance (other than a mortgage) part of land comprised in a lease is, without the consent of the lessor,[8] expressed to be conveyed—

(a)   subject to the entire rent, then *covenant (1)* in *paragraph (2)* of *Part 3* of *Schedule 3* has effect as if the entire rent were the apportioned rent,[9]

(b)   exonerated from the entire rent, then *covenant (2)* in *paragraph (2)* of *Part 3* of *Schedule 3* has effect as if the entire rent were the balance of the rent, and "(other than the covenant to pay the entire rent)" were omitted from the covenant.[10]

(4)[11] The benefit of a covenant implied under this section—

(a)   is annexed to and passes with the estate or interest of the implied covenantee,

(b)   is enforceable by every person, including a tenant, mortgagee and any other person deriving title from or under the implied covenantee, in whom that estate or interest, or any part of it, or an estate or interest derived out of it, is vested from time to time.

(5)[12] Any covenant implied under this section may, by the terms of the conveyance, be—

(*a*)   modified by the express provisions of the conveyance and, if so modified, operates as if the modification were included in this section and *Schedule 3*,

(*b*)   extended by providing expressly in the conveyance that—

(i)   the land conveyed, or

(ii) the part of the land which remains vested in the covenantor,

stands charged with the payment of all money which would otherwise become payable under the implied covenant.[13]

Definitions

In addition to those in s 79, see s 3 for definitions of : "consent"; "covenant"; "land"; "lease"; "lessor"; "mortgage"; "rent"; "valuable consideration".

Notes

1   Section 81 introduces new provisions to cover assignments of existing leases. It provides for additional covenants (ie in addition to those provided by s 80: see Note 14 to that section) to be implied to remove the need to include various covenants to perform the obligations in the lease and to indemnify the assignor usually included expressly in such assignments: see Wylie and Woods, *Irish Conveyancing Law* (3rd edn, Tottel Publishing, 2005), para 19.31 and *Laffoy's Irish Conveyancing Precedents* (Bloomsbury Professional), Division E.2 precedents. Where the assignment relates to part only of the land comprised in the lease, different provisions apply to apportionment or charging of rent, depending on whether the lessor has agreed an apportionment (see Notes 6–9 below).

2   Subsection (1) mirrors the provisions in s 80(1) (see Notes 2–9 to that section).

3   In effect an assignment of the whole or part of land comprised in an existing lease.

4   Given the classes referred to in sub-s (2) (ie Classes 6 and 7) this refers to the Class 1 covenants referred to in s 80(2).

5   See the Notes to Schedule 3.

6   Class 6 deals with two situations: paragraph (*a*) covers an assignment of the *entirety* of the land comprised in a lease; paragraph (*b*) covers an assignment of *part* only of the land comprised in the lease, but where the lessor has agreed to an *apportionment* of the rent between the assignor and assignee. The Class 6 additional covenants and indemnity accordingly relate to the entire rent and land or the apportioned rent and part of the land assigned.

7   Class 7 deals with the case where, on an assignment again of *part* only of the land comprised in the lease, the lessor has *not* agreed to the *apportionment* of the rent as between the assignor and assignee. Subsection (3) deals with the situation where the assignor and assignee do not apportion the rent and adapts the Class 7 covenants set

out in Schedule 3 to the situations where the assignee either undertakes to be liable for the whole rent or the assignor retains full liability (see Notes 8–10 below).

8 Subsection (3) also deals with the situation where the lessor has not agreed with whatever arrangement the assignor and assignee have agreed with respect to the rent payable under the lease of the entire land (ie both the part assigned to the assignee and the part retained by the assignor). It adapts the Class 7 covenants according to the arrangement.

9 In this scenario the assignee has agreed with the assignor to be liable for the entire rent payable under the lease of the whole land, so the covenant in Schedule 3 is adjusted accordingly.

10 In this scenario the assignor has agreed to retain liability for the whole rent, notwithstanding that part of the land held under the lease has been assigned to the assignee. Again the Class 7 covenants are adjusted.

11 Subsection (4) mirrors sub-s (5) in s 80 (see Notes 22–23 to that section).

12 Subsection (5) mirrors part of sub-s (6) in s 80 (see Note 24 to that section). It allows modification, but not exclusion of the Class 6 and Class 7 implied covenants (again exclusion was viewed as inherently inconsistent: see Note 25 to s 80).

13 Paragraph (*b*) permits the creation of an indemnity rentcharge in the scenario covered by sub-s (3) (see Notes 9–10 above). The creation of such a rentcharge is permitted under s 41(2)(*c*) (see Note 6 to that section).

---

[128]

Covenants by or with two or more persons.[1]

[CA 1881, s. 60]

82.—(1) Where under a covenant persons are—

(*a*) covenantors, the covenant binds them and any two or more of them jointly and each of them severally,[2]

(*b*) covenantees, the covenant shall be construed as being also made with each of them.[3]

(2)[4] A covenant made with persons jointly to convey, pay money or do any other act to them or for their benefit, implies an obligation to do the act to, or for the benefit of—

(*a*) the survivor or survivors of them, or

(*b*) any other person on whom the right to sue on the covenant devolves.

(3)[5] This section takes effect subject to the terms of the covenant or conveyance in which it is contained or implied or of any statutory provision implying the covenant.

(4) In this section "covenant" includes an express or implied covenant and a bond or obligation contained in a deed.[6]

Definitions

In addition to the provisions in sub-s (4), see s 3 for definitions of: "conveyance"; "covenant".

Notes

1   Section 60 re-enacts the substance of s 60 of the Conveyancing Act 1881. It is another "word-saving" provision and, in essence, provides that where a *covenant* is entered into by or with two or more persons, it is deemed to be made with them jointly *and severally* and binds their respective survivors when one or more of them dies: see *White v Tyndall* (1888) 13 App Cas 263. It also gets round the common law rule that a person could not covenant with himself or herself, because in the case A covenanting with A and B the covenant was deemed to be *a joint* one only, so that both A and B would have to sue A to enforce it: see *Napier v Williams* [1911] 1 Ch 361; *Rye v Rye* [1962] AC 496; Wylie and Woods, *Irish Conveyancing Law* (3rd edn, Tottel Publishing, 2005), paras 18.96–18.97. This is reiterated by the general provision in s 83 (see the Notes to that section). Note also the equivalent provisions relating to covenants for title in ss 80(1)(*b*) (see Note 9 to that section) and 81(1) (see Note 2 to that section). These replace s 60(2) of the 1881 Act. As regards *conveyances* to oneself see s 66 (and the Notes to it).

2   Thus each of the several covenantors can be sued separately on the covenant as if he or she were the sole covenantor.

3   Thus any one of several covenantees can sue separately to enforce the covenant.

4   Subsection (2) makes it clear that in the case of joint covenantees, on the death of any one of them the survivor or survivors or any person to whom the benefit devolves on the death of the last survivor (initially that person's personal representative) may enforce the covenant.

5   This makes it clear that the terms of the conveyance in which a covenant is contained or of the covenant itself may exclude or vary the provisions of s 82.

6   This definition reflects the terms used in s 60 of the 1881 Act and supplements the definition in s 3 (see Note 24 to that section).

[129]

83.—A covenant, whether express or implied, entered into by a person with that person jointly with another person or other persons shall be construed and is enforceable as if it had been entered into with that other person or persons alone.[2]

Covenants by person jointly with others.[1]

Definitions

See s 3 for the definition of: "covenant".

Notes

1 Section 83 is the equivalent for covenants of the provisions in s 66 for conveyances (see the Notes to that section). Both are designed to get round the common law restriction that one cannot contract with oneself, so that a covenant with or conveyance to oneself was generally unenforceable. Sections 66 and 83 create an exception where the covenant or conveyance is jointly with or to oneself *and another or others*. It is enforceable by or effective as regards that other or others.

2 Thus a covenant entered into by A and B with A is enforceable by B against A as if it had been entered into with B alone. As regards the converse position, a covenant by A with A and B, again A can enforce the covenant against B: ss s 82(1)(*a*) (see Note 2 to that section).

---

[130]

Production and safe custody of documents.[1]
[CA 1881, s. 9]

84.—(1) Where a person retains possession of documents[2] and gives to another person[3] in writing—

    (a) an acknowledgment of the right of that other to production of those documents and to delivery of copies of them ("the acknowledgment"[4]),

    (b) an undertaking for the safe custody of those documents ("the undertaking"[5]),

the acknowledgment and the undertaking have the effect specified in this section.

(2)[6] The obligations imposed by an acknowledgment are to—

    (*a*) produce the documents or any of them at all reasonable times for the purpose of inspection and of comparison with abstracts or copies of the documents, by the person entitled to request production or by any person authorised in writing by that person,

    (*b*) produce the documents or any of them in court or any other place where, or on any occasion when, production may properly be required for proving or supporting the title or claim of the person entitled to request production, or for any other purpose relating to that title or claim,

    (*c*) deliver[7] to the person entitled to request them such copies or abstracts, attested or unattested, of or from the documents or any of them.

(3) The obligation imposed by an undertaking is to keep the documents complete, safe, uncancelled and undefaced.[8]

(4)[9] The obligations shall be performed from time to time—

(*a*) in the case of the acknowledgment, at the request in writing of,

(*b*) in the case of the undertaking, in favour of,

the person to whom it is given, or any person, not being a tenant, who has or who claims any estate, interest or right through or under that person or who otherwise becomes through or under that person interested in or affected by the terms of the document to which the acknowledgment or undertaking relates.

(5)[10] The acknowledgment and undertaking bind the documents to which they relate in the possession or under the control of the person who retains them and every other person having possession or control of them from time to time but they bind each such individual possessor or person as long only as that person has possession or control.[11]

(6) Each person having possession or control of such documents is bound specifically to perform the obligations imposed by this section, unless prevented from doing so by fire or other inevitable accident,[12] but all costs and expenses of or incidental to specific performance of the acknowledgment shall be paid by the person requesting performance.[13]

(7) The acknowledgment does not confer any right to damages for loss or destruction of, or injury to, the documents to which it relates, arising from whatever cause.[14]

(8) Any person claiming to be entitled to the benefit of an undertaking may apply to the court for damages for any loss or destruction of, or injury to, the documents or any of them to which it relates.[15]

(9) Upon such application the court may direct such inquiries and make such order as to costs or other matters as it thinks fit.[16]

(10) An acknowledgment or undertaking under this section satisfies any liability to give a covenant for production and delivery of copies of or extracts from documents or for safe custody of documents.[17]

(11) The rights conferred by an acknowledgment or undertaking under this section are in addition to all such other rights relating to production, inspection or obtaining copies of documents as are not satisfied by the giving of the acknowledgment or undertaking.[18]

(12) This section—

    (*a*)   has effect where an acknowledgment or undertaking is given by a person to that same person in different capacities in the same way as where it is given by one person to another,[19]

    (*b*)   takes effect subject to the terms of the acknowledgment or undertaking.[20]

Definitions

See s 3 for the definitions of: "court"; "tenant".

Notes

1   Section 81 re-enacts, with some modification, the substance of the provisions in s 9 of the 1881 Act. It deals with the situation where part of land is being conveyed. Normally a vendor of *unregistered land* is expected to hand over to the purchaser the title documents on the closing of the sale, but, where part only is being sold, the vendor will usually expect to retain those documents because they relate also to the part retained and will have to be produced in future transactions relating to that retained part. Instead, the Law Society's *General Conditions of Sale (2001 Edition)* require the vendor to give the purchaser the "usual statutory acknowledgment of the right of production" (so as to enable the purchaser to produce them when carrying out future transactions relating to the part sold) and "undertaking for safe custody" of all documents retained by the vendor. This was a reference to s 7 of the 1881 Act and now to s 84: see Wylie and Woods, *Irish Conveyancing Law* (3rd edn, Tottel Publishing, 2005), paras 18.102–18.106. Section 84 is another "word-saving" provision which saves the detailed provisions having to be included expressly in a conveyance; instead a brief reference to the acknowledgment and undertaking will incorporate the provisions of s 84: see *Laffoy's Irish Conveyancing Precedents* (Bloomsbury Professional), Precedent E.7.2, E.10.3 and E.10.4. Cf the provisions of s 61 (see the Notes to that section).

2   In this context "possession" means physical possession (cf the definition in s 3) and the acknowledgment and undertaking should only be given by a person who retains this. A mortgagee is entitled to possession of the title documents (see s 90(2) and Note 7 to that section), but it was usual for a mortgagee to give only an acknowledgment: see *Laffoy's Irish Conveyancing Precedents* (Bloomsbury Professional), Precedent E.7.2. Indeed, it was doubted whether a mortgagee could be compelled to give either an acknowledgment or undertaking in the absence of an express provision: see *Re Pursell and Deakin's Contract* [1893] WN 152. That is changed by s 90(3), which now compels a mortgagee to give both (see the Notes to that section). It was not usual to give either in a transfer of *registered* land (and none was contained in the prescribed forms): see Wylie and Woods, *Irish Conveyancing Law* (3rd edn, Tottel Publishing, 2005), para 18.106. This has become irrelevant with the abolition of land and charge certificates under s 73 of the Registration of Deeds and Title Act 2006. See Note 29 to s 21.

3   Section 9 of the 1881 Act could not operate where a personal representative executed an assent in his or her own favour: see *Re Skeat's Settlement* (1889) 42 Ch D 522. However, sub-s (12)(*a*) corrects this limitation: see Note 19 below.

4   As to the obligations imposed by an acknowledgment see sub-s (2) and Notes 5–6 below.

5   As to the obligation imposed by an undertaking see sub-s (3) and Note 8 below.

6   Subsection (2) re-enacts the substance of s 9(4) of the 1881 Act.

7   Note that this does not permit the person requesting the copies to make his or her own copies of the documents.

8   Subsection (3) re-enacts the substance of s 9(9) of the 1881 Act. Note that under sub-s (1) this obligation arises only in respect of a person who retains possession of the documents: see Note 2 above.

9   Subsection (4) re-enacts the substance of s 9(3) of the 1881 Act and provides that the benefit of both the acknowledgment and, now, the undertaking pass to the original purchaser's successors in title (but not a tenant holding under such a person). Section 9 curiously only provided for the passing of the benefit in the case of the acknowledgment: see Wylie and Woods, *Irish Conveyancing Law* (3rd edn, Tottel Publishing, 2005), para 18.105.

10 Subsection (5) re-enacts the substance of parts of s 9(2) and 9(9) of the 1881 Act.

11 The liability lasts only so long as the person has possession or control, so that there is no need to seek an indemnity when that is passed on to someone else, eg, a mortgagee returning the title deeds to the mortgagor on redemption of the mortgage.

12 This important limitation was also contained in s 9(2) and (9) of the 1881 Act: see also sub-s (7) and Note 14 below.

13 This re-enacts the substance of s 9(5) of the 1881 Act.

14 Subsection (7) re-enacts the substance of s 9(6) of the 1881 Act. This is why it is important to accompany the acknowledgment in most cases with an undertaking for safe custody. An action for damages lies in the case of the latter: see sub-s (8) and Note 15 below.

15 Subsection (8) re-enacts the substance of part of s 9(10) of the 1881 Act. However, since destruction of title documents merely affects *proof* of title, not the validity of the title, damages will usually be restricted to the cost of furnishing equivalent proof, such as statutory declarations: see Wylie and Woods, *Irish Conveyancing Law* (3rd edn, Tottel Publishing, 2005), paras 14.81 and 18.105.

16 Subsection (9) re-enacts the substance of another part of s 9(10) of the 1881 Act.

17 Subsection (10) re-enacts the substance of s 9(8) of the 1881 Act. At common law liability to give such a covenant arose in respect of title documents subsequent to the root of title: see *Cooper v Emery* (1844) 1 Ph 388.

18 Subsection (11) re-enacts the substance of s 9(12) of the 1881 Act. This makes it clear that other rights may be conferred by the conveyance in question: see also Note 20 below.

19 Paragraph (*a*) deals with a limitation which existed under s 9 of the 1881 Act, that the statutory acknowledgment or undertaking could be given only to "another" person: see Note 3 above.

20 Paragraph (*b*) re-enacts the substance of s 9(13) of the 1881 Act. Like sub-s (11) (see Note 18 above), it confirms that the statutory acknowledgment and undertaking can be varied by the terms of the conveyance.

[131]

Notices.[1]

85.—(1) Subject to *subsection (2)*, where an instrument[2] makes provision for giving or serving a notice it may be given or served as if it were authorised or required to be given or served under this Act.[3]

(2) *Subsection (1)* takes effect subject to the terms of the instrument.[4]

Definitions

See s 3 for definition of: "instrument".

Notes

1 Section 85 implements the Law Reform Commission's recommendation that the statutory provisions for service of notices under the Act should apply also to private transactions as a "default" provision: see LRC CP 34–2004, para 8.43. A similar recommendation with respect to statutory definitions is implemented by s 75 (see the Notes to that section).

2 Note that, like s 75 (see Note 2 to that section) the "default" provision applies to any instrument as defined by s 3.

3 That is in accordance with s 4 (see the Notes to that section).

4 This confirms that sub-s (1) is a "default" provision only: see Note 1 above. It is open to the parties to a particular instrument to specify expressly how notices to be given or served under that instrument should be given or served.

[132]

CHAPTER 5[1]

General provisions[2]

Notes

1 Chapter 5 contains some general provisions relating to contracts and conveyances, some of which re-enact the substance of provisions in the Conveyancing Act 1881.

2 The Chapter also implements a recommendation by the Law Reform Commission that power should be conferred by statute to make regulations governing conveyancing practice: see s 88 (and the Notes to it).

[133]

86.—(1) A purchaser[2] is not affected prejudicially by notice of any fact, instrument, matter or thing unless—

    (*a*)   it is within the purchaser's own knowledge[3] or would have come to the purchaser's knowledge[4] if such inquiries and inspections[5] had been made as ought reasonably[6] to have been made by the purchaser, or

    (*b*)[7] in the same transaction with respect to which a question of notice to the purchaser arises,[8] it has come to the knowledge of the purchaser's counsel, as such,[9] or solicitor or other agent, as such,[10] or would have come to the knowledge of the solicitor or other agent if such inquiries and inspections had been made as ought reasonably to have been made by the solicitor or agent.[11]

(2)[12] Without prejudice to *section 57(4)*,[13] *subsection (1)* does not exempt a purchaser from any liability under, or any obligation to perform or observe, any covenant, provision or restriction contained in any instrument under which the purchaser's title is derived, immediately or mediately; and such liability or obligation may be enforced in the same manner and to the same extent as if this section had not been enacted.

(3)[14] A purchaser is not, by reason of anything in this section, affected by notice in any case where the purchaser would not have been so affected if this section had not been enacted.

Restrictions on constructive notice.[1] **[CA 1882, s. 3]**

Definitions

See s 3 for definitions of: "instrument"; "purchaser".

Notes

1   Section 86 re-enacts the substance of s 3 of the Conveyancing Act 1882. It contains the statutory provision governing the doctrine of notice, in particular the concept of "constructive" notice: see Lyall, *Land Law in Ireland* (2nd edn, Round Hall, 2000), pp 123–133 and 489–499; Wylie, *Irish Land Law* (3rd edn, Tottel Publishing, 1997), paras 3.069–3.083; Keane, *Equity and the Law of Trusts in the Republic of Ireland* (Tottel Publishing, 1998), ch 5; Delany, *Equity and the Law of Trusts in Ireland* (4th edn, Round Hall, 2007), pp 45–51. Although this doctrine has little relevance to registered land, and its relevance to unregistered land was greatly reduced by the operation of the Registry of Deeds system and is further reduced by the overreaching provisions of s 21 (see the Notes to that section), it will remain of some significance. Even under s 21 a purchaser may be affected by notice of the right of a person in "actual occupation" of the land (see Notes 32–33 to s 21): see Note 5 below. Furthermore, the courts have adapted the concept of constructive notice in order to

impose on lending institutions a duty to ensure that a spouse's consent under the Family Home Protection Act 1976 is "informed": see *Bank of Ireland v Smyth* [1996] 1 ILRM 241; *Allied Irish Banks plc v Finnegan* [1996] 1 ILRM 401; Lyall, *Land Law in Ireland* (2nd edn, Round Hall, 2000), pp 489–499; Wylie and Woods, *Irish Conveyancing Law* (3rd edn, Tottel Publishing, 2005), para 16.57. Apart from that the concept of notice is referred to in ss 74(4)(*a*) (see Notes 12–13 to that section) and s 77(2) (see Note 5 to that section).

2   Note the definition in s 3 (see Notes 75–76 to that section).

3   This is what is usually referred to as "actual" notice (to be distinguished from "constructive" notice). "Knowledge" must be more than mere rumours or "flying reports": see *O'Connor v McCarthy* [1982] IR 161 at 174, where Costello J adopted Lord Cairns' test in *Lloyd v Banks* (1868) 3 Ch App 488: "knowledge which would operate upon the mind of any rational man, or man of business, and make him act with reference to the knowledge he had so acquired." See also *Welch v Bowmaker (Ireland) Ltd* [1980] IR 251. Note that paragraph (*a*) does not begin, as does paragraph (*b*), with the words "in the same transaction". It does not matter how the purchaser gained the actual acknowledge (notice), so long, of course, as it relates to the transaction in respect of which notice has become an issue.

4   This is what is usually referred to as "constructive" notice: see *Abbott v Geraghty* (1854) Ir Ch R 15; *Re Riley* [1942] IR 416.

5   The Supreme Court ruled that the test of what ought to be done by a purchaser is an objective one: see *Northern Bank Ltd v Henry* [1981] IR 1. A purchaser must investigate facts or circumstances further if a reasonable person in his or her situation would do so: see *Re Flood's Estate* (1862) 13 Ir Ch R 312; *Waldron v Jacob* (1870) IR 5 Eq 131; cf *Aldritt v Maconchy* [1908] 1 IR 333. Constructive notice cannot be avoided by "turning a blind eye" to such factors or circumstances and refraining from pursuing them: see *Justice v Wynne* (1860) 12 Ir Ch R 289; *Re Olden* (1863) 9 Ir Jur (ns) 1; *Heneghan v Davitt* [1933] IR 375. In recent times the doctrine has been invoked regularly in respect of persons in actual occupation of the land: see *Somers v Weir* [1979] IR 94; *Ulster Bank Ltd v Shanks* [1982] NI 143; *Allied Irish Banks Ltd v McWilliams* [1982] NI 156.

6   The Supreme Court ruled that "legal reasonableness" is not to be equated with "business prudence": *Northern Bank Ltd v Henry* [1981] IR 1 at 11–12 (*per* Henchy J).

7   Paragraph (*b*) relates to "imputed" notice, ie actual *or* constructive notice of an agent (eg solicitor) which is imputed or fixed on the purchaser. In practice, in most conveyancing transactions it is imputed notice which is fixed on the purchaser and results in him or her taking the land subject to prior claim, right or interest.

8   Note this qualification which does *not* apply to paragraph (*a*) which deals with the purchaser's own notice: see Note 3 above. This changed the common law, under which notice gained in a previous transaction could be imputed in a later one: see *Nixon v Hamilton* (1838) 1 Ir Eq R 238; *Tucker v Henzill* (1854) 4 Ir Ch R 513; see also *Hargreaves v Rothwell* (1836) 1 Keen 154.

9   That is in the agent's capacity as agent for the purchaser. Note that this restriction does *not* apply in relation to a spouse's consent under the Family Home Protection 1976, so that a purchaser will be fixed with the solicitor's, or other agent's, notice

however it was acquired: see s 3(7) of the 1976 Act and *H & L v S* [1979] I ILRM 105.

10 See Note 9 above.

11 This confirms that it is not just as agent's "actual" knowledge (notice) which is imputed, but also "constructive" notice: see Note 7 above.

12 Subsection (2) re-enacts the substance of s 3(2) of the 1882 Act. It confirms that, while a *bona fide* purchaser of a legal estate or interest may take free of a prior equitable interest of which he or she has no notice, he or she is otherwise bound by the title which has been bought.

13 This saving refers to the reversal of the rule in *Patman v Harland*: see Notes 13–17 to s 57).

14 Subsection (3) re-enacts s 3(3) of the 1882 Act. It has been suggested that s 3 of the 1882 Act was largely declaratory of the previous law: see the discussion by Kenny J in *Northern Bank Ltd v Henry* [1981] IR 1.

---

[134]

87.—(1) Without prejudice to any ground of appeal against any order, an order of the court under any statutory or other jurisdiction is not invalid as against a purchaser on the ground of want of—

Court orders.[1]
[CA 1881, s.70]

  (*a*) jurisdiction,[2] or

  (*b*) any concurrence, consent, notice or service.[3]

(2) This section applies to any lease, sale or other act under the authority of the court and purporting to be in pursuance of any statutory provision, notwithstanding any exception in that provision.[4]

Definitions

See s 3 for definitions of: "consent"; "court"; "lease"; "purchaser".

Notes

1   Section 87 re-enacts the substance of s 70 of the 1881 Act. It confirms the validity of any titles acquired by a purchaser dependent on a court order, such as an order for sale: see *Neville v Driscoll* (1902) 36 ILTR 209; *Woods v Brown* [1915] 1 IR 79; Wylie and Woods, *Irish Conveyancing Law* (3rd edn, Tottel Publishing, 2005), paras 8.13 and 11.02–11.07.

2   Paragraph (*a*) covers any irregularity of procedures which might affect jurisdiction: see *Jones v Barrett* [1900] 1 Ch 370 at 374 (*per* Lindley MR); see also *Re Montagu* [1897] 2 Ch 8.

3   Re paragraph (*b*) see *Woods v Brown* [1915] 1 IR 29; see also *Re Hall-Dare's Contract* (1882) 21 Ch D 41; *Mostyn v Mostyn* [1893] 3 Ch 376; *Re Whitham* (1901) 84 LT 585; *Re Harrowby and Paine's Contract* [1902] WN 137.

4   Once the court has made an order confirming a sale to a purchaser it is conclusive so
     far as the purchaser is concerned: see *Woods v Brown* [1915] 1 IR 29 at 34 (*per*
     O'Brien LC); Wylie and Woods, *Irish Conveyancing Law* (3rd edn, Tottel
     Publishing, 2005), para 11.07. See also the Notes to s 94 below.

---

[135]

Regulations   **88.**—With a view to facilitating electronic conveyancing of land[2]
for Part 9.[1]   or providing further protection for the interests of vendors and
                         purchasers of land,[3] the following matters may be prescribed:

> (*a*)   the general conditions of sale applicable to a contract
>   for the sale or other disposition of an estate or interest in
>   land;[4]
>
> (*b*)   any other matter referred to in this Part.[5]

Definitions

See s 3 for definitions of: "disposition"; "land"; "purchaser".

Notes

1   Section 88 implements the Law Reform Commission's recommendation that a
     power to make regulations concerning contracts for sale of land and other
     conveyancing matters should be introduced: see LRC CP 34–2004, paras 8.04, 8.06
     and 8.07. The Commission's early reports on risk passing to a purchaser on entering
     into a contract and completion notices (see LRC 39–1991 and LRC 40–1991) were,
     in fact, largely implemented by the Law Society's *General Conditions of Sale (2001
     Edition)*. The Commission's *Report on Gazumping* (LRC 59–1989) recommended a
     power to cover conditions of sale by regulation and other matters such as a statutory
     form of receipt for booking deposits and regulation of advertisements for sales of
     new properties. It was also envisaged that such a power could be useful in
     facilitating the introduction of electronic conveyancing: see LRC CP 34–2004, para
     8.04. As a consequence the original draft of s 88 referred to a wide range of such
     matters (see s 91 of the Bill appended to the Report LRC 74–2005), but the Bill
     ultimately introduced to the Seanad contained the truncated version which is now
     s 88. The reason is that many of the matters referred to above are covered by other
     legislation now before the Oireachtas. Thus the Property Services (Regulation) Bill
     2009 (No 28 of 2009), which implements the *Report of the Auctioneering/Estate
     Agency Review Group* (2004), contains various new provisions regulating the sale or
     letting of land, including sales by auction (replacing the Sale of Land by Auction Act
     1867), and contains its own power to make regulations relating to matters such as
     advertisements, booking deposits, terms of building contracts (including stage
     payments) and terms of auction or tender sales (see s 60 of the Bill). The Multi-unit
     Developments Bill 2009 (No 32 of 2009) contains various provisions regulating
     developers and management companies and it too contains various powers to make

regulations concerning matters such as service charges, sinking funds and "house rules" for multi-unit developments (see ss 14, 15 and 17 of the Bill).

2   See the Commission's *Report on eConveyancing: Modelling of the Irish Conveyancing System* (LRC 79–2006) and the Law Society's eConveyancing Task Force's "eVision" – *eConveyancing: Back to Basic Principles* (March 2008).

3   It was this which drove the Commission's earlier recommendations: see Note 1 above.

4   It remains to be seen whether this subject will continue to be governed instead by the Law Society's *General Conditions of Sale*, the current (2001) Edition of which is being revised to take account of the Act.

5   That is contracts and conveyances.

---

[136]

PART 10[1]
MORTGAGES[2]

Notes

1   Part 10 is likely to prove one of the most controversial Parts of the Act. At first sight that may seem surprising since much of it comprises a re-enactment of various provisions relating to mortgages contained in the Conveyancing Acts 1881–1911. However, especially as ultimately enacted, Part 10 does much more than that. The essential points to note from the outset are these:

(1)   As recommended by the Law Reform Commission, the Act greatly simplifies the method of creating a legal mortgage and aligns it with the Land Registry system, which has long used a simple charge on land.

(2)   Although the Commission initially did not view the provisions as forming part of the consumer protection regime, such as exists under the Consumer Credit Act 1995 (see LRC CP 34–2004, paras 9.09–9.11), what became Part 10 of the Bill assumed various consumer protection aspects as it passed through the Oireachtas. This was partly driven by the collapse of the property market and the pressure both borrowers and lenders came under.

(3)   Initially the Bill adopted the approach of the Conveyancing Acts 1881–1911, of providing a range of statutory "default" provisions which lenders were free to adopt or adapt to particular mortgages. However, once the Government decided to incorporate consumer protection elements, it was decided that that freedom had to be curtailed.

(4)   It was realised during the Bill's passage through the Oireachtas, following representations from lending institutions and lawyers specialising in commercial mortgages, that incorporation of consumer protection elements would cause considerable difficulties in the commercial lending industry, particularly that operating in the IFSC and involving many overseas institutions. The essential point was that it was common practice for the

statutory provisions (particularly those involving mortgagee remedies) to be incorporated, often with some modification, in commercial mortgage or debenture documents. The 1881–1911 Acts were not confined to mortgages of "land", but applied for the most part to mortgages of any "property" (that is also true of Part 10: see Note 2 below). Such incorporation with modifications would become impossible if the Act prohibited its provisions from being altered. In the end it was decided to draw a distinction between "housing loan" mortgages, where it was deemed that the consumer protection element was most needed, and other (commercial) mortgages, where the freedom to adapt the statutory provisions would remain.

(5)   The result of all this was that the provisions of Part 10 underwent numerous changes and amendments during the Bill's passage, as the Notes to its particular sections which follow detail. As is often the case when legislation is the subject of substantial changes during its parliamentary process, it may be felt by some that the ultimate version contains particular provisions which may not appear to fit together quite as tightly or coherently as might otherwise have been the case. Much time and effort was spent in dealing with consequential changes and avoidance of unintended consequences.

2   Part 10 deals with "mortgages" and not other methods of creating security. As the definition in s 3 indicates, this includes a charge or lien on property, any property and not just land (though some of Part 10 is confined to mortgages of land, eg Chapter 1: see the Notes to that Chapter). In this respect Part 10 reflects the wider scope of many of the provisions which derive from the 1881–1911 Acts. However, particularly in view of the distinction introduced during the Bill's passage between "housing loan" mortgages and other (commercial) mortgages, lending institutions have had to revise their mortgage and other security documentation to take account of the way the 1881–1911 Acts are replaced by the 2009 Act. In particular, in the case of "other" mortgages, the likelihood is that even more "derogation" from the statutory provisions will be thought appropriate. This is being reflected in the Irish Mortgage Council's recommended new mortgage forms and new mortgage conditions. The alternative in the case of non-housing loan mortgages would be to ignore the 2009 Act and not seek to adapt its provisions for incorporation, instead to insert express provisions. Arguably this would not be a desirable alternative. Apart from the effect this would have in complicating and lengthening what already tend to be lengthy documents, it would lose some of the considerable benefits of incorporating the statutory provisions, such as the protection given to purchasers when a mortgagee exercises the power of sale (see ss 105 and 106 and the Notes to those sections). Finally, it should be noted that Part 10 is not a consolidation of statutory provisions relating to mortgages and other provisions, especially post-1922 ones, are unaffected by it, eg, the provisions for discharge by endorsed receipt in s 27 of the Building Societies Act 1989 and s 18 of the Housing Act 1988 and for satisfaction or release under s 65 of the Registration of Title Act 1964.

[137]

CHAPTER 1[1]
Creation of mortgages[2]

Notes

1　Chapter 1 implements the Law Reform Commission's recommendation that the methods of creating a legal mortgage of *unregistered* land should be simplified; in effect, the only method should be by way of a "charge", which has long been the sole method for *registered* land (see ss 62–67 of the Registration of Title Act 1964; Lyall, *Land Law in Ireland* (2nd edn, Round Hall, 2000), pp 784–785; Wylie, *Irish Land Law* (3rd edn, Tottel Publishing, 1997), paras 12.24–12.27: see LRC CP 34–2004, paras 9.03–9.06). The traditional way of creating a mortgage of unregistered land, particularly by conveyance of the borrower's freehold, or assignment of the borrower's leasehold, interest had long been a poor reflection of the true nature of a mortgage transaction. It should not be a method of making the lender the owner of the land (however temporary and subject to conditions, such as the right of redemption), but rather simply a method of creating security for a loan. Hence the oft-quoted criticisms by distinguished equity lawyers like Maitland (who described the traditional form of mortgage deed as one long "*suppressio veri* [suppression of the truth] and *suggestio falsi* [suggestion of falsehood]": *Equity* (revised edition by Brunyate, CUP, 1936), p 182) and judges (such as Lord Macnaghten who remarked: "No one ... by the light of nature ever understood an English mortgage of real estate": *Samuel v Jarrah Timber and Wood Paving Corp* [1904] AC 323 at 326).

2　Unlike Chapters 2 and 3 (but like Chapter 4) Chapter 1 is confined to mortgages of land.

---

[138]

89.—(1) A legal mortgage of land may only[2] be created by a charge by deed[3] and such a charge, unless the context requires otherwise, is referred to in this Part as a "mortgage";[4] and "mortgagor" and "mortgagee" shall be read accordingly.[5]

Legal mortgages.[1]

(2)[6] Subject to *subsection (3)*, from the commencement of this Chapter[7]—

(*a*)　any instrument which would, but for the provisions of this section, convey a legal estate or interest in land by way of mortgage,[8] or

(*b*)　any other transaction which under any instrument would operate, but for the provisions of this section, as a mortgage by conveyance of a legal estate or interest in land,[9]

does not create a legal mortgage.[10]

(3) From the commencement of this Chapter, any transaction which under any statutory provision would, but for the provisions of this section, operate as a mortgage by conveyance of a legal estate or interest in land operates as if it were a mortgage under this Part.[11]

(4) From the commencement of this Chapter, any power, whenever created, to mortgage or lend money on mortgage of a legal estate or interest in land operates as a power to mortgage the legal estate or interest by a mortgage under this Part or to lend money on the security of such a mortgage.[12]

(5) This Part applies to both unregistered and registered land.[13]

(6) Nothing in this section affects the creation of equitable mortgages of land.[14]

(7) From the commencement of this Chapter, it is not possible to create a Welsh mortgage and any purported creation of such a mortgage is void.[15]

(8) For the purposes of *subsection (7)*, a "Welsh mortgage" includes any transaction under which a grantee or chargee of land is entitled to hold possession, and take rents and profits in lieu of interest on a loan, of land without the grantor or chargor being under a personal obligation to repay the loan, but being entitled to redeem.[16]

Definitions

See s 3 for definitions of: "deed"; "instrument"; "land"; "legal estate"; "legal instrument"; "mortgage"; "registered land"; "unregistered land".

Notes

1   Section 89 prescribes the method of creating a *legal* mortgage of *land* since 1 December 2009: see Note 1 to Chapter 1 above.

2   The result is that using the traditional methods of a conveyance of the freehold, assignment of a leasehold or sub-demise are no longer effective to create a *legal* mortgage. Any attempt to use these methods since 1 December 2009 is ineffective (see sub-s (2) and Notes 5–9 below), but it may create an equitable mortgage (see Note 14 below).

3   This adapts to *unregistered* land the charges system which has long operated in respect of *registered* land (see Note 1 to Chapter 1 above).

4   The point about this is that the charge under this provision, as in the case of registered land (see s 62(6) of the Registration of Title Act 1964, now amended by the 2009 Act: see Schedule 1), operates as a mortgage. This distinguishes both a s 89 and s 62 charge from other charges which do not necessarily confer the same security rights over land: see Wylie, *Irish Land Law* (3rd edn, Tottel Publishing,

1997), paras 12.19–12.20. The original draft of the Bill and the Bill as introduced to the Seanad, adapting the terminology of the equivalent English provision, referred to it as a "charge by way of legal mortgage" (see Law of Property Act 1925, s 86), but this was later deemed to be too clumsy a title and it was dropped at the Seanad Committee Stage. Despite that, the status of a mortgage created by a charge by deed, as being equivalent of a mortgage created by the traditional (but abolished) methods is confirmed by s 90 (see Notes to that section).

5   This facilitates the continued use in Part 10 of the terms "mortgage", "mortgagor" and "mortgagee" (rather than "charge", "chargor" and "chargee"): see Note 4 above. It does *not* mean that the rest of Part 10 is confined to mortgages of *land*. As with the Conveyancing Acts 1881–1911 many of the provisions relate to mortgages of "property" (as defined in s 3: see Note 1 (4) to Part 10.

6   Subsection (2) underwent several versions. The original draft of the Bill, and the Bill as introduced to the Seanad, contained a provision to the effect that a purported use of the traditional methods (eg by way of conveyance: see Note 2 above) would not be fatal after 1 December 2009, but would instead operate as a charge under sub-s (1). The wording was slightly modified at the Seanad Committee Stage, but later the view was taken that this ran counter to the policy behind sub-s (1) of getting rid of the old methods altogether. The final version now in the Act was substituted at the Dáil Select Committee Stage.

7   The new requirement to use only a charge by deed operates only from 1 December 2009.

8   That is an instrument purporting to convey the borrower's estate or interest, which is one of the traditional methods now prohibited: see Note 5 above.

9   Note that "conveyance" under s 3 includes an "assignment" and a "lease", so that paragraph (*b*) also catches purported mortgages by assignment of the borrower's leasehold interest or by demise (or sub-demise): see Lyall, *Land Law in Ireland* (2nd edn, Round Hall, 2000), pp 781–782; Wylie, *Irish Land Law* (3rd edn, Tottel Publishing, 1997), paras 12.35–12.38.

10   This confirms that purported creation of a mortgage by using the old methods is ineffective since 1 December 2009, at least if that is all that is done. If the deed also purports simply to charge the land, the addition of a purported conveyance or demise (which is rendered ineffective by sub-s (2)) may still create a valid mortgage. A court might be prepared to ignore or strike out the ineffective provision and enforce the valid charge provision. Note the position as regards registered land discussed in Note 13 below.

11   Subsection (3) is a saving for any statutory provisions relating to creation of mortgages which may refer to the old methods or even require creation of a mortgage by such methods – use of the method prescribed by the statute in question will still be valid after 1 December 2009.

12   Subsection (4) is a saving for any power, including a pre-1 December 2009 power, to mortgage land – it is to operate as if it were a power to mortgage by the new charge system.

13   Subsection (5) confirms the alignment of unregistered land with registered land (see Note 3 above). It means that the same deed can be used to charge both registered and

unregistered land. It should also be noted that an important amendment to the Registration of Title Act 1964 is made by Schedule 1 (see the Notes to that section). This was inserted at the request of the Property Registration Authority at the Dáil Select Committee Stage. It removes from ss 62(2) and 64(2) of the 1964 Act the power of the Authority to accept as sufficient to charge registered land a form other than the prescribed form: see Fitzgerald, *Land Registry Practice* (2nd edn, Round Hall Press, 1995), ch 9. Since 1 December 2009 the PRA prescribed forms must be used. As part of its move towards increasing electronic registration these forms are short one-page forms. In order to comply with the new requirements the form will have to be incorporated, perhaps as a schedule, in larger security documents, such as a debenture which charges a wide range of assets, both personal property and land, which may comprise parcels of both registered and unregistered land. The PRA should receive electronically only the prescribed form charging the parcel(s) of registered land.

14 Subsection (6) is a saving for equitable mortgages which may continue to be created informally. An obvious method is the once common creation by deposit of title documents: see Lyall, *Land Law in Ireland* (2nd edn, Round Hall, 2000), p 783; Wylie, *Irish Land Law* (3rd edn, Tottel Publishing, 1997), paras 12.28–12.29 and 12.43–12.46. This has become less common in recent times because of the administrative burden of storing physically huge numbers of title deeds. It will become even less common since the PRA has ceased to issue land and charge certificates in respect of registered land and existing equitable mortgages previously protected by deposit of such certificates have to be protected by a registered lien from 1 January 2010: see Note 29 to s 21. Apart from that, other ways of creating an equitable mortgage continue since 1 December 2009, such as a charge over an equitable interest only or a mere contract to creat a legal mortgage (not completed yet by a charge by deed), which passes the beneficial interest under s 52 (see the Notes to that section): see Lyall, *Land Law in Ireland* (2nd edn, Round Hall, 2000), pp 782–783; Wylie, *Irish Land Law* (3rd edn, Tottel Publishing, 1997), paras 12.39–12.42. There seems no reason to suppose that the courts will not continue to exercise their equitable jurisdiction on occasion to view a failed attempt to create a legal mortgage (eg because the requisite formalities have not been complied with) as a contract to create the legal mortgage, which may be specifically enforceable: see *Eyre v McDowell* (1861) 9 HLC 619; *Re Stewart's Estate* (1893) 31 LR Ir 405; *Re Hurley's Estate* [1894] 1 IR 488. Thus it is possible that, notwithstanding the provisions of sub-s (2) (see Note 9 above), a post-1 December purported creation of a legal mortgage by using one of the old methods (instead of a charge by deed as prescribed by sub-s (1)) may be regarded by a court as a clear intention on the part of the landowner to create a mortgage, to be given effect to by construing it as a contract for a mortgage and thereby creating an equitable mortgage.

15 Subsection (7) implements the Commission's recommendation that "Welsh" mortgages should no longer be capable of creation. These had several "anomalous" features, such as enabling the lender to take possession of the land and its rents and profits in lieu of interest or, even, capital repayments. Such features were deemed inconsistent with the modern concept of a mortgage providing security only, which

the Act seeks to promote (see Note 1 to Chapter 1 above): see LRC CP 34–2004, para 9.18. Such mortgages are unheard of in modern times.

16 Subsection (8) defines a "Welsh" mortgage by reference to features commonly found in them, as illustrated by the case law: see, eg, *Balfe v Lord* (1842) 2 Dr & War 480 at 486 (*per* Sudgen LC); *Cassidy v Cassidy* (1889) 24 LR Ir 577 at 578–579 (*per* Johnson J); *Johnston v Moore* (1904) 4 NIJR 218; *Re Cronin* [1914] 1 IR 23; Lyall, *Land Law in Ireland* (2nd edn, Round Hall, 2000), pp 778–779; Wylie, *Irish Land Law* (3rd edn, Tottel Publishing, 1997), paras 12.22–12.23.

---

[139]

90.—(1) Subject to this Part,[2] where a mortgage is created after the commencement of this Chapter—

Position of mortgagor and mortgagee.[1]

(*a*) the mortgagor has the same powers and rights and the same protection at law and in equity as the mortgagor would have been entitled to,[3]

(*b*) the mortgagee has the same obligations, powers and rights as the mortgagee would have had,[4]

if the mortgagee's security had been created by a conveyance before that commencement of the legal estate or interest in the land of the mortgagor.[5]

(2) Without prejudice to the generality of *subsection (1)(b)* and subject to *subsection (3)*,[6] a first mortgagee has the same right to possession of documents of title as such mortgagee would have had if the security had been created by a conveyance before the commencement of this Chapter.[7]

(3)[8] Notwithstanding any stipulation to the contrary,[9] a mortgagee who retains possession or control of documents of title relating to the mortgaged land is, in addition to being subject to the mortgagor's rights under *section 91*,[10] responsible for their safe custody as if an undertaking for this were given under *section 84*.[11]

Definitions

See s 3 for definitions of: "conveyance"; "land"; "legal estate"; "legal interest"; "mortgage"; "mortgagee"; "mortgagor".

Notes

1 Section 90 confirms that a charge by deed, the new method of creating a mortgage of unregistered land (see s 89 and the Notes to it), like a charge of registered land, is fully effective to confer on the mortgagee the same security as the old methods of creating mortgages of unregistered land. Furthermore it confirms that the

mortgagor's protection is the same. All of this is, of course, subject to any changes to the previous law made by Part 10: see Note 2 below.

2   Chapters 2, 3 and 4 contain various changes to the previous position, as the Notes to the individual sections indicate.

3   Paragraph (*a*) preserves, in particular, the protection long given to mortgagors through equitable doctrines like "clogs on the equity of redemption", undue influence and similar principles: see Lyall, *Land Law in Ireland* (2nd edn, Round Hall, 2000), pp 812–819; Wylie, *Irish Land Law* (3rd edn, Tottel Publishing, 1997), paras 13.089–13.099.

4   This preserves, in particular, the various remedies and other security rights a mortgagee traditionally has had, as opposed to other chargees or security holders: see Note 4 to s 89 and s 104 (2)(*a*) (and Notes 1 and 4 to that section).

5   That is by using one of the old traditional methods of creating a legal mortgage prior to 1 December 2009.

6   Subsection (3) changes the mortgagee's position as regards looking after title documents: see Note 8 below.

7   This preserves the right of the first legal mortgagee to retain possession of title documents as part of the security (they would have to be produced in order for the mortgagor to engage in further transactions with respect to the land): see Lyall, *Land Law in Ireland* (2nd edn, Round Hall, 2000), pp 785–786; Wylie, *Irish Land Law* (3rd edn, Tottel Publishing, 1997), paras 13.003–13.006. Previously a mortgagee of registered land obtained a charge certificate, but these are no longer issued (nor is a land certificate): see Note 29 to s 21 and Note 14 to s 89.

8   Subsection (3) reverses the view that a mortgagee who retains title documents was not responsible for their safe custody: see *Gilligan v National Bank Ltd* [1901] 2 IR 513. The Commission took the opposite view: see LRC CP 34–2004, para 9.24.

9   A mortgagee cannot contract-out of the new duty.

10 See the Notes to s 91.

11 This is an obligation to keep the documents "complete, safe, uncancelled and undefaced": see s 84(3) (and the Notes to that section).

---

[140]

CHAPTER 2[1]

Powers and rights of mortgagor[2]

Notes

1   Chapter 2 largely re-enacts the provisions in the Conveyancing Act 1881 relating to the position of the mortgagor. It does, however, contain a new provision relating to housing loan mortgages enabling a mortgagor who may be dissatisfied with how the mortgagee is exercising its power to have the matter reviewed by the court: see s 94 and the Notes to it.

2   The position of the mortgagee is dealt with by Chapter 3.

---

[141]

91.—(1) Subject to *subsection (2)*, a mortgagor, as long as the right to redeem exists, may from time to time, at reasonable times, inspect and make copies or abstracts of or extracts from the documents of title relating to the mortgaged property in the possession or power of the mortgagee.[2]

(2)[3] Rights under *subsection (1)* are exercisable—

(*a*)   on the request of the mortgagor, and

(*b*)   on payment by the mortgagor of the mortgagee's reasonable costs and expenses in relation to the exercise.

(3) *Subsection (1)* has effect notwithstanding any stipulation to the contrary.[4]

Documents of title.[1]
[CA 1881, s. 16]

Definitions

See s 3 for definitions of: "mortgagee"; "mortgagor".

Notes

1   Section 91 re-enacts the substance of s 16 of the Conveyancing Act 1881. Prior to the 1881 Act it was held that a mortgagor could not see the deeds after the mortgage had been created, without repayment of the capital, plus interest and costs: see *Chichester v Marquis of Donegal* (1870) LR 5 Ch 497 at 505; *Bank of New South Wales v O'Connor* (1889) 14 App Cas 273 at 283.

2   See *Re Lee and the Conveyancing Act* (1902) 36 ILT 79; *Gilligan v National Bank Ltd* [1901] 2 IR 513. Note the new obligation on a mortgagee to keep the documents of title in safe custody: see s 90 (3) (and Notes 8–11 to that section).

3   In *Armstrong v Dickson* [1911] 1 IR 435 the court declined to order lodgment in court where the first mortgagee made an offer under s 16 of the 1881 Act to produce deeds and permit copies to be made after he had been served with notice of an order for sale obtained by the second mortgagee, but not acted upon.

4   This was also the position under s 16 of the 1881 Act: see s 16(2).

---

[142]

92[2].—Notwithstanding any stipulation to the contrary,[3] a mortgagor is entitled to redeem any housing loan mortgage[4] without having to pay any money due under any other mortgage with the same mortgagee,[5] whether that other mortgage is of the same[6] or other property.[7]

Restriction on consolidation of certain mortgages.[1]
[CA 1881, s. 17]

Definitions

See s 3 for definitions of: "housing loan"; "mortgage"; "mortgagor".

Notes

1   Section 92 replaces s 17 of the Conveyancing Act 1881. Under the general law prior to that Act, where a mortgagor had two or more mortgages of *different* properties with the *same* mortgagee, the mortgagee could insist that all the mortgages be redeemed together, to prevent the mortgagor redeeming one (which might be well secured) and leaving unredeemed another (which might not be sufficient security for the outstanding loan). Irish judges were critical of this right of consolidation (see *Re Thomson's Estate* [1912] 1 IR 194 (*per* Ross J) and 460 (*per* Barry LC)); an English judge once described its results as "monstrous" (*Chesworth v Hunt* (1880) 5 CPD 266 at 271 *per* Lindley J): see Lyall, *Land Law in Ireland* (2nd edn, Round Hall, 2000), pp 806–808; Wylie, *Irish Land Law* (3rd edn, Tottel Publishing, 1997), paras 13.069–13.073. The Law Reform Commission took the view that a mortgagor should not be forced into having to rescue a mortgagee who has discovered that some loans are good and some are bad. It, therefore, recommended that it be abolished rather than, as s 17 of the 1881 Act did, simply requiring a mortgagee to retain the right by an express provision in the mortgage: see LRC CP 34–2004, para 9.24.

2   The original Bill, and the Bill as introduced to the Seanad, implemented the Commission's recommendation (see Note 1 above), but it was subsequently amended at the Dáil Select Committee Stage as part of the general policy then introduced of distinguishing between "housing loan" mortgages and other mortgages: see Note 2 to Part 10 and Note 1 to Chapter 3.

3   The mortgage deed cannot contract-out of this provision.

4   Section 92 is confined to such a mortgage. The result is that the right of consolidation remains with respect to commercial mortgages and, unlike the previous position under s 17 of the 1881 Act, there is no need to reserve it expressly (see *Gore-Hickman v Alliance Assurance Co Ltd* [1936] IR 721).

5   The right of consolidation exists only where there is the same mortgagor and mortgagee, however many mortgages exist: see *Hughes v Britannia Permanent Building Society* [1906] 2 Ch 607; see also *Pledge v White* [1896] AC 187. The right of consolidation should not be confused with a "cross-security" arrangement, eg where a number of loans are each secured by separate "all sums" mortgages over several properties. If the mortgagor pays off one loan, that cannot alter the fact that the remaining loans are still secured on the several properties. There is no question of consolidation in such circumstances because *all* the properties remain mortgaged in respect of the remaining loans. Consolidation can only arise where the payment removes the mortgage from one property, with the consequence that the other properties are not adequate security for the remaining loans.

6   The view in *Re Salmon* [1903] 1 KB 147 that consolidation may apply in respect of mortgages of the *same* property is usually regarded as unsound: see Megarry and Wade, *The Law of Real Property* (7th edn, Sweet & Maxwell, 2008), para 25.066.

7   It is settled that consolidation can apply to mortgages on different properties, eg, one
land and the other personalty (see *Tassell v Smith* (1858) 2 De F & J 713) or both
perso.ialcy (see *Watts v Smith* (1851) 3 De FM & G 240). It can also apply where one
mortgage is legal and the other equitable (see *Cracknell v Janson* (1877) 11 Ch D 1)
or both equitable (see *Tweedale v Tweedale* (1857) 23 Beav 341).

---

[143]

93.—(1) A mortgagor who is entitled to redeem[2] may, subject to
compliance with the terms on which the mortgagor would be
entitled to require a discharge, require the mortgagee, instead of
discharging the mortgage, to assign the mortgage debt and
transfer the mortgage to any third person, as the mortgagor
directs, and on the mortgagor so directing, the mortgagee is
bound to assign and transfer accordingly.[3]

**Transfer in
lieu of dis-
charge.**[1]
**[CA 1881,
s. 15]**
**[CA 1882,
s. 12]**

(2)[4] The rights conferred by *subsection (1)* belong to and may be
enforced by each incumbrancer or the mortgagor
notwithstanding any intermediate incumbrance, but a requisition
of an incumbrancer prevails over a requisition of the mortgagor
and, as between incumbrancers, a requisition of a prior
incumbrancer prevails over a requisition of a subsequent
incumbrancer.

(3) This section—

(*a*)   does not apply in the case of a mortgagee being or
having been in possession,[5]

(*b*)   applies notwithstanding any stipulation to the contrary.[6]

Definitions

See s 3 for definitions of: "incumbrance"; "mortgage"; "mortgagee"; "mortgagor";
"possession".

Notes

1   Section 93 re-enacts the substance of s 15 of the Conveyancing Act 1881, as
amended by s 12 of the Conveyancing Act 1882. It entitles the mortgagor, instead of
redeeming the mortgage, to require the mortgagee to assign the debt and transfer the
mortgage to a third person: see Wylie, *Irish Land Law* (3rd edn, Tottel Publishing,
1997), para 13.106. This right is rarely invoked in practice, but the Commission saw
no reason to remove it: LRC CP 34–2004, para 9.24.

2   This includes an equitable mortgagor: see *Everitt v Automatic Weighing Machine Co*
[1892] 3 Ch 506. The section is unqualified as to the mortgagors and the suggestion
in English case law that it does not apply to a building society mortgage seems
unsound: see *Re Rumney v Smith* [1827] 2 Ch 351; *Sun Building Society v Western*

Suburban and Harrow Road Building Society [1921] 2 Ch 438. There is Irish authority to the contrary (see *Ulster Permanent Building Society v Glenton* (1888) 21 LR Ir 124) and in view of this and in view of the provision's rare use, it was felt unnecessary to include a specific provision on this point: cf LRC CP 34–2004, para 9.24.

3   It is not possible to contract-out of this provision: see Note 6 below.

4   Subsection (2) re-enacts the extension of s 15 of the 1881 Act made by s 12 of the 1882 Act: see *Re Magenta Time Co Ltd* [1915] WN 318.

5   Subsection (3) re-enacts the substance of s 15(2) of the 1881 Act. The reason for this exception is that a mortgagee in possession is under a strict liability to the mortgagor and would remain so even after such a transfer: see *Re Prytherch* (1889) 42 Ch D 590. It was considered unfair to allow the mortgagor to compel such a mortgagee to transfer the mortgage: see *Hall v Heward* (1886) 32 Ch D 430; *Gaskill v Farling* [1896] 1 QB 669.

6   As under the 1881 Act it is not possible to contract-out of sub-s (1) and (2): see s 15(3) of the 1881 Act.

---

[144]

Court order for sale.[1]   **94.**—(1) This section applies to any action brought by a mortgagor[2] for—

(*a*)   redemption, or

(*b*)   sale, or

(*c*)   the raising and payment in any manner of the mortgage debt, or

(*d*)   any combination of these in the alternative.[3]

(2) In any action to which this section applies the court may, if it thinks fit, direct a sale of the mortgaged property on such terms as it thinks fit.[4]

(3) Without prejudice to the generality of the court's discretion under *subsection (2)*, it may[5]—

(*a*)   allow any time for redemption or payment of the mortgage debt,

(*b*)   require lodgment in court of a sum to meet the expenses of a sale and to secure a performance of its terms,

(*c*)   give directions as to costs and require the giving of security for costs,

(*d*)   direct a sale without previously determining priorities of incumbrances,

(*e*)   give the conduct of the sale to a particular party,

(*f*) make a vesting order conveying the mortgaged property to a purchaser or appoint a person to make such a conveyance.

(4) Except in the case of a housing loan mortgage, this section takes effect subject to the terms of the mortgage.[6]

Definitions

See s 3 definitions of: "conveyance"; "court"; "housing loan"; "incumbrance"; "mortgage"; "mortgagor"; "purchaser".

Notes

1   Section 94 implements the Commission's recommendation that a provision in the English legislation (see s 91 of the Law of Property Act 1925) entitling a mortgagor to seek a court order requiring a mortgagee to exercise its remedies in a reasonable fashion, eg by requiring it either to sell the property, or let it pending a sale, so as to reduce the debt exposure, be enacted: see LRC CP 34–2004, para 9.16. The English provision was based on s 25 of the Conveyancing Act 1881, but that section put on a statutory basis the court's power to order a sale instead of foreclosure: see Megarry and Wade, *The Law of Real Property* (7th edn, Sweet & Maxwell, 2008), para 25.011. That primary purpose explains why that particular section did not, unlike most of the 1881 Act, apply to Ireland. By then the Irish courts had ceased to grant foreclosure orders (and the remedy is now abolished by s 96(2) of the 2009 Act: see Note 10 to that section). The English provision may be used by an equitable mortgagee to obtain an order for sale of the legal title where the mortgage has not been created by a deed (and so the statutory power of sale does not apply – see s 96(1)(*a*) of the 2009 Act and Note 4 to that section). However the Irish courts have long taken the view that there is an inherent jurisdiction to order a sale on application by an equitable mortgagee: see *Antrim County Land Building and Investment Co Ltd v Stewart* [1904] 2 IR 357; *Re O'Neill* [1967] NI 129. So the section was not needed for this. The English provision has also been invoked on occasions by a mortgagee who had exercised the statutory power to sell out of court, but then found the purchaser reluctant to complete because the mortgagor was threatening proceedings to challenge whether the exercise was valid: see *Arab Bank Plc v Mercantile Holdings Ltd* [1994] 2 All ER 64. Obtaining a court order for sale renders the purchaser's title unimpeachable (see s 87 of the 2009 Act and the Notes to it). However the right of a mortgagee to obtain a court order for sale has long been recognised in Ireland as part of the court's inherent jurisdiction and is provided for by the Rules of the Superior Courts, Orders 51 and 54: see *Bank of Ireland v Waldron* [1944] IR 303. So again the section was not needed for this purpose. Instead what the Commission had in mind was another use of the English provision, namely an action by a *mortgagor* who is faced with enforcement action by the mortgagee, as illustrated by *Palk v Mortgage Services Funding Plc* [1993] Ch 330. In that case the mortgagee was seeking possession in order to let the mortgaged property until the market rose to a point where a sale would produce sufficient to repay the mortgage debt. The mortgagors objected to this because the rental income

was likely to fall far short even of the interest which would accrue on the debt. They succeeded in persuading the court to order a sale instead, the proceeds of which would substantially reduce the debt. The court took the view that the mortgagee was gambling on a rise in property prices at the mortgagor's expense. They would remain liable for the balance of the debt on their personal covenant. Furthermore, the mortgagee would be permitted to buy the property (in effect from itself) and thereby benefit from any later increase in its market value. The English courts have made it clear that such jurisdiction will be exercised in favour of the mortgagor against the mortgagee's wishes in exceptional circumstances only, especially where a sale is unlikely to discharge the entire debt: see *Polonski v Lloyds Bank Mortgages Ltd* [1998] 1 FLR 896: *Cheltenham and Gloucester Plc v Krausz* [1997] 1 All ER 21; Megarry and Wade, *The Law of Real Property* (7th edn, Sweet & Maxwell, 2008), para 25.023. It is arguable that the Irish courts already have such jurisdiction because of the wide jurisdiction they have long claimed in respect of mortgaged property, but the Commission considered it appropriate to put it on a statutory footing. The wording of the provision in the original Bill, and as introduced to the Seanad (see s 91 of that Bill) was modified at the Dáil Report Stage to reflect the primary purpose the Commission had in mind.

2   The object of the section is to enable the mortgagor to go to court to have the action being taken or proposed by the mortgagee reviewed: see Note 1 above.

3   Paragraphs (*a*)–(*d*) give the mortgagor flexibility as to how the action is framed. Rules of Court will be made to deal with such applications.

4   This gives the court a general discretion to direct a sale and to fix the terms of the order: see the *Palk* case referred to in Note 1 above and Note 5 below. Note that under s 3 the Circuit Court has concurrent jurisdiction with the High Court.

5   Paragraphs (*a*)–(*f*) give the court guidance as to the terms upon which it might make an order under sub-s (2). These are not exhaustive as the initial clause in sub-s (3) makes clear. There was a further paragraph (*g*) in the original Bill referring to an equitable mortgagee seeking power to sell the legal title, but that was dropped at the Dáil Report Stage as unnecessary: see Note 1 above.

6   Subsection (4) was also added at the Dáil Report Stage to reflect the general distinction between housing loan mortgages and other mortgages which had been introduced to Part 10 generally: see Note 2 to Part 10 above and Note 11 to s 96 below.

---

[145]

Advances on joint account.[1]
[CA 1881, s. 61]

95.—(1) Where—

(*a*)   money advanced or owing under a mortgage,[2] or any part of it, is expressed to be advanced by or owing to two or more persons out of money, or as money, belonging to them on a joint account, or (*b*) such a mortgage is made to two or more persons jointly and not in shares,

the mortgage debt, or other money or money's worth for the time being due to those persons, shall, as between them and the mortgagor, be deemed to belong to them on a joint account.

(2) The receipt in writing of—

(*a*) the survivors or last survivor of those persons, or

(*b*) the personal representative of the last survivor,

is a complete discharge[3] for all money or money's worth for the time being due, notwithstanding any notice to the payer of a severance of such joint account.

(3) This section takes effect subject to the terms of the mortgage.[4]

(4) In this section "mortgage" includes an obligation for payment of money and a transfer of a mortgage or of such an obligation; and "mortgagor" shall be read accordingly.[5]

Definitions

See s 3 for definitions of (but note also sub-s (4): see Note 2 below): "mortgage"; "mortgagor".

Notes

1   Section 95 re-enacts the substance of s 61 of the Conveyancing Act 1881. That section rendered it unnecessary to include an express "joint account" clause in a mortgage involving more than one mortgagee, whereby the survivor could give a valid receipt and make the discharge fully effective. Note that the mere presence of a joint account clause is not notice of the existence of a trust: see *Re Harman and Uxbridge and Rickmansworth Railway Co* (1883) 24 Ch D 720; cf *Re Blaiberg and Abrahams* (1899) 2 Ch 340; *Re Chafer and Randall's Contract* [1916] 2 Ch 8.

2   Note the extended meaning of "mortgage" given by sub-s (4): this also applied under s 61 of the 1881 Act, but has been put in a separate subsection to make sub-s (1) easier to read.

3   As regards the mortgagor. As between the mortgagees the joint account can be rebutted: see *Re Jackson* (1887) 34 Ch D 732; see also *AIB Finance Ltd v Sligo County Council* [1995] ILRM 81.

4   Section 95 can be excluded or varied by the terms of the mortgage.

5   This was also the position under s 61 of the 1881 Act: see Note 1 above.

---

[146]

CHAPTER 3[1]
Obligations, powers and rights of mortgagee[2]

Notes

1   Chapter 3 deals with the various rights and remedies of a mortgagee and implements to some extent the recommendations of the Law Reform Commission: see LRC CP 34-2004, paras 9.13–9.17. However, these are the provisions which were most affected by the consumer protection element introduced during the Bill's passage through the Oireachtas: see Note 1 to Part 10 above. In particular Chapter 3 is where the distinction between a "housing loan" mortgage and other mortgages is crucial. The provisions can only be contracted out in the case of the latter: see Note 15 to s 96 below.

2   Sections 96–111 deal with various powers and rights of the mortgagee and lay down obligations of the mortgagee which the mortgagee must comply with in the exercise of those powers and obligations: see, eg, s 103 re obligations on selling and s 109 re application of money received by a receiver. This is why the heading refers to "obligations" in addition to "powers and rights". The obligations do not stand alone: see Note 2 to s 96 below.

---

[147]

Powers and rights generally.[1]

96.—(1) Subject to this Part, the powers and rights[2] of a mortgagee under *sections 97* to *111*[3]—

(a)   apply to any mortgage created by deed after the commencement of this Chapter,[4]

(b)   vest, subject to section 62 of the Act of 1964,[5] as soon as the mortgage is created,[6]

(c)   do not become exercisable unless their exercise is for the purpose of protecting the mortgaged property[7] or realising the mortgagee's security,[8]

(d)   in relation to the mortgaged property, apply to any part of it.[9]

(2) A mortgagee's right of foreclosure is abolished.[10]

(3) The provisions relating to the powers and rights conferred by this Chapter apply to any housing loan mortgage[11] notwithstanding any stipulation to the contrary[12] and notwithstanding any powers and rights expressly conferred under such a mortgage,[13] but in relation to any other mortgage, except where this Part provides to the contrary,[14] take effect subject to the terms of the mortgage.[15]

Definitions

See s 3 for definitions of: "Act of 1964"; "deed"; "housing loan"; "mortgage"; "mortgagee"; "property".

Notes

1 Section 96 is fundamental to the operation of Chapter 3 as it both defines its scope and lays down principles which underpin its operation. In doing so it implements several of the Law Reform Commission's recommendations, but, as mentioned earlier, various modifications were made during the Bill's passage.

2 Chapter 3 is concerned with various powers and rights and imposes obligations as to their exercise: see Note 2 to Chapter 3 above.

3 This refers to the entirety of Chapter 3 and so the provisions of s 96 apply to all of it. There are no separate "obligations" to which they do not apply. The reason for use of this additional word in the heading of the Chapter was explained in Note 2 to Chapter 3. Apart from that, a heading is not to be taken to be part of the Act or to be construed or judicially noticed in relation to its construction or interpretation: see s 18(*g*)(ii) of the Interpretation Act 2005.

4 Chapter 3 makes various changes to the previous law and so applies only to mortgages created *by deed* after 1 December 2009. As under the Conveyancing Act 1881, the statutory provisions apply to "any" mortgage of any property provided a deed is used. Thus they apply equally to legal and equitable mortgages and to mortgages of personal property as well as land.

5 Under s 62(2) of the Registration of Title Act 1964, no charge over registered land is created until the mortgagee is registered as owner of the charge. Note that, by virtue of an amendment to s 62(2) made by Schedule 1, as from 1 December 2009 the prescribed form must be used: see Note 13 to s 89.

6 Paragraph (*b*) implements the Commission's recommendation that, in future, a mortgagee's remedies should become available as soon as the mortgage is created. It abolishes the distinction under the previous law between some remedies (the statutory powers of sale and to appoint a receiver) "arising" and only later becoming "exercisable" and the nonsense of having to insert a short *legal* date for redemption in the deed, the sole purpose of which was to make the remedies available: see LRC CP 34–2004, para 9.13; Lyall, *Land Law in Ireland* (2nd edn, Round Hall, 2000), pp 797–798; Wylie, *Irish Land Law* (3rd edn, Tottel Publishing, 1997), paras 13.026–13.027. Paragraph (*b*) must be read with paragraph (*c*).

7 This confirms that Chapter 3 applies to mortgages of any property: see Note 4 above.

8 Paragraph (*c*) implements another of the Commission's recommendations, that, notwithstanding that a mortgagee's remedies would, in future, become available as soon as the mortgage was created (so that anyone dealing with the mortgagee would not need to check if the "legal" date for redemption had passed), they would not become *exercisable* until it was necessary for the mortgagee to protect the mortgaged property or realise its security: see LRC CP 34–2004, para 9.14. In the original draft Bill, and the Bill as introduced to the Seanad (see s 93(1)(*c*) of that Bill), there was the additional provision that 28 days' notice should be given to the

mortgagor before exercising the remedies. The view was taken later that such a blanket provision was inappropriate and it was deleted from this section and inserted, instead, in s 100 (power of sale) at the Dáil Select Committee Stage: see Note 5 to that section.

9 This provision saves having to refer to "or any part of it" every time a reference is made to the mortgaged property.

10 Subsection (2) implements the Commission's recommendation that foreclosure, which had not been granted in Ireland for well over a century, should be abolished: see LRC CP 34–2004, para 9.16. Foreclosure has an inherent unfairness in many cases because it results in the mortgagee becoming owner of the property which, in normal times, may be worth more than the outstanding debt, hence the invariable practice of the courts to order a sale instead: see *Antrim County Land, Building and Investment Co Ltd v Stewart* [1904] 2 IR 357 at 359 (*per* FitzGibbon LJ); *Bruce v Brady* [1906] 1 IR 611 (*per* Walker LC); Lyall, *Land Law in Ireland* (2nd edn, Round Hall, 2000), p 805; Wylie, *Irish Land Law* (3rd edn, Tottel Publishing, 1997), paras 13.056–13.061.

11 In the original Bill, and as introduced to the Seanad, this provision (see s 93(3) to that Bill) provided that only sub-s (1) and other provisions where so specified were "mandatory" but otherwise, as under the Conveyancing Acts 1881–1911, the provisions would take effect subject to the terms of the mortgage. However, as explained earlier, the Government decided to introduce a greater consumer protection element and the issue arose as to whether the provisions of Chapter 3 should be made mandatory for all mortgages coming within it. In the end the view was taken that, while that might be appropriate in respect of mortgages of people's homes, it would not be appropriate in respect of commercial mortgages. As was explained earlier (see Note 1 to Part 10 above), it has long been common practice to incorporate the statutory provisions in such mortgages and debentures covering a wide range of assets owned by a company. This is a very useful short-hand mechanism and has the further advantage of attracting the benefit of particular provisions, such as the protection of purchasers (see s 105 and the Notes to it). However, it is also common to vary or exclude certain aspects of the statutory provisions. The conclusion eventually come to was that this facility to modify the statutory provisions should be preserved for commercial mortgages. The way of doing this adopted in the amendments made at the Dáil Select Committee Stage was to adopt an existing statutory concept, that of a "housing loan" as used in the Consumer Credit Act 1995, as substituted by s 33 of, and Part 12 of Schedule 3 to, the Central Bank and Financial Services Authority of Ireland Act 2004. Under this a "housing loan" means—

(*a*) an agreement for the provision of credit to a person on security of a mortgage of a freehold or leasehold estate or interest in land—

    (i) for the purpose of enabling the person to have a house constructed on the land as the principal residence of that person or that person's dependants, or

> (ii) for the purpose of enabling the person to improve a house that is already used as the principal residence of that person or that person's dependants, or
>
> (iii) for the purpose of enabling the person to buy a house that is already constructed on the land for use as the principal residence of that person or that person's dependants, or
>
> (*b*) an agreement for refinancing credit provided to a person for a purpose specified in paragraph (*a*)(i), (ii) or (iii), or
>
> (*c*) an agreement for the provision of credit to a person on the security of a mortgage of a freehold or leasehold estate or interest in land on which a house is constructed where the house is to be used, or to continue to be used, as the principal residence of the person or the person's dependants, or
>
> (*d*) an agreement for the provision of credit to a person on the security of a mortgage of a freehold or leasehold estate or interest in land on which a house is, or is to be, constructed where the person to whom the credit is provided is a consumer.

Although the use of an existing concept, which lending institutions have had to grapple with for some time, is understandable, it has been pointed out that in practice some issues may arise as to the scope of this provision, as it applies to Part 10. In particular, it may extend beyond a borrower's principal private residence and cover holiday homes and residential investment properties. It may also cover collateral security linked to a housing loan, such as a life insurance policy or cash deposit.

12 This prevents contracting-out in the case of housing loan mortgages.

13 This prevents getting round contracting-out in the case of a housing loan mortgage by substituting express provisions for the statutory provisions in Chapter 3.

14 The only section where this applies is s 103 (obligations on selling under the statutory power of sale): see Note 4 to that section.

15 This preserves the general rule that the statutory provisions can be adapted and modified in the case of any mortgage other than a housing loan mortgage.

---

[148]

97.—(1) Subject to *section 98*,[2] a mortgagee shall not take possession of the mortgaged property without a court order granted under this section,[3] unless the mortgagor consents in writing[4] to such taking not more than 7 days prior to such taking.[5]

Taking possession.[1]

(2) A mortgagee may apply to the court[6] for an order for possession of the mortgaged property and on such application the court may, if it thinks fit, order that possession be granted to the applicant on such terms and conditions, if any, as it thinks fit.[7]

Definitions

See s 3 for definitions of: "court"; "mortgagee"; "mortgagor"; "possession"; "property".

Notes

1   Section 97 implements the Commission's recommendation that in future a mortgagee, instead of being able to take possession "before the ink is dry on the mortgage" (*per* Harman J in *Four-Maids Ltd v Dudley Marshall Properties Ltd* [1957] Ch 317 at 320), should be required to obtain a court order: see LRC CP 34–2004, paras 9.13–9.14 and 9.16. The need to obtain possession often arises as a preliminary to exercise of the power of sale (see s 100 and the Notes to it). It should be noted that this section, like other sections in Chapter 3, is subject to the provisions of s 96. Thus possession can be sought only for the purpose of protecting the property or realising the security (see Notes 7–8 to that section) in the case of a housing loan mortgage, but this can be excluded or varied in the case of other mortgages (see Note 11 to that section). Note also the *Code of Conduct on Mortgage Arrears* (February 2009) issued by the Financial Regulator under s 117 of the Central Bank Act 1989.

2   Section 98 allows speedier action to be taken in the case of abandoned property (see the Notes to that section).

3   The Circuit Court has concurrent jurisdiction with the High Court (see s 3), except in the case of housing loan mortgages where it has exclusive jurisdiction: see s 101(5) and the Notes to that section.

4   The original draft Bill, and the Bill as introduced to the Seanad, contained this provision that there was no need for a court order where the mortgagor consented in writing to the mortgagee taking possession and left it at that.

5   The requirement for the consent in writing to be given not more than 7 days before the taking of possession was added at the final Dáil Report Stage to prevent mortgagees putting a blanket prior consent provision in the mortgage deed. Lending institutions may take the view that this period is so short that there would be too much uncertainty as to whether consent would be forthcoming to justify putting in place the preparations for taking possession. If that is the view, an application to the court may be the only option.

6   Rules of court will be made to deal with such applications.

7   This confers a wide discretion on the court and further guidance as to the exercise of this jurisdiction is provided by s 101 (see the Notes to that section). See also *Anglo Irish Bank Corporation plc v Oisin Fanning* [2009] IEHC 141.

[149]

Abandoned property.[1]

98.—(1) Where a mortgagee has reasonable grounds for believing that—

    (*a*)   the mortgagor has abandoned the mortgaged property, and[2] (*b*) urgent steps are necessary to prevent deterioration of, or damage to, the property or entry on it by trespassers or other unauthorised persons,

the mortgagee may apply to the District Court,[3] or any court already seised of any application or proceedings relating to the mortgaged property,[4] for an order authorising the mortgagee to take possession of the property.

(2) On such an application the court may make an order authorising the mortgagee to take possession of the property on such terms and conditions as the court thinks fit,[5] notwithstanding that the mortgagor dissents or does not appear.[6]

(3) Without prejudice to the generality of *subsection (2)*,[7] an order under this section may specify[8]—

(*a*) the period during which the mortgagee may retain possession of the mortgaged property,

(*b*) works which may be carried out by the mortgagee for the purpose of—

(i) protecting the mortgaged property, or

(ii) preparing it for sale in exercise of the mortgagee's power under *section 100*,

(*c*) costs and expenses incurred by the mortgagee which may be added to the mortgage debt.

(4) The mortgagee is not liable to account strictly to the mortgagor during a period of possession under an order under this section.[9]

Definitions

See s 3 for definitions of: "mortgagee"; "mortgagor"; "possession"; "property".

Notes

1   Section 98 implements the Commission's recommendation that a more summary procedure, such as existed under s 62(7) of the Registration of Title Act 1964 (now repealed: see Schedule 2), should be available where the mortgagee needs to take "emergency" action to protect the property: see LRC CP 34–2004, paras 9.14 and 9.16. Again this provision may be excluded in the case of mortgages other than housing loan mortgages: see s 96(3) (and Notes 11–15 to that section).

2   Note that both paragraphs (*a*) and (*b*) must be satisfied in terms of the mortgagee's belief.

3   The view was taken that it would be quicker to obtain a District Court order than one from the Circuit Court under s 97. Rules of court will be made to deal with such applications.

4   If, however, the Circuit Court is already seised of an issue relating to the mortgage, eg, an application under s 97 is set for imminent hearing, it may be quicker to ask it to make an order under s 97.

5   This gives the court a wide discretion whether to make an order and as to the terms and conditions to be attached to one made. Further guidance is provided by sub-s (3) (see Notes 7–8 below).

6   This prevents the mortgagor frustrating the need for emergency action. Such action is predicated upon the mortgagee having reasonable grounds for believing that the mortgagor has abandoned the property: see sub-s (1)(*a*).

7   The guidance provided by sub-s (3) as to the terms and conditions to be attached to a possession order made under s 97 does not prevent the District Court attaching others.

8   Paragraphs (*a*)–(*c*) are indicative of the sort of terms and conditions which the District Court may set, bearing in mind the underlying purpose of an order as set out in sub-s (1)(*b*). Thus works may be necessary to prevent deterioration or damage, or to prevent entry by trespassers or other unauthorised persons.

9   The view was taken that the general rule governing mortgagees in possession should not apply in cases of emergency action "forced" on the mortgagee by the actions of the mortgagor and backed up by a court order. As to the general rule: see Lyall, *Land Law in Ireland* (2nd edn, Round Hall, 2000), pp 794–795; Wylie, *Irish Land Law* (3rd edn, Tottel Publishing, 1997), paras 13.046–13.047.

---

[150]

Mortgagee in possession.[1]   **99.**—(1) Subject to the terms of any order under *section 97* or *section 98*,[2] a mortgagee in possession (or after the mortgagee has appointed a receiver[3] and so long as the receiver acts, the receiver[4]) shall take steps within a reasonable time[5] to exercise the power to—

　　(*a*)   sell the mortgaged property under *section 100*,[6] or

　　(*b*)   if it is not appropriate to sell,[7] lease the property[8] under *section 112*[9] and use the rent and any other income received from the lessee to reduce the mortgage debt, including interest accrued or accruing.

(2) Section 34 of the Act of 1957 does not apply to a mortgagee who takes possession of land under a court order under *section 97* or *section 98*.[10]

Definitions

See s 3 for definitions of: "Act of 1957"; "land"; "lease"; "lessee"; "mortgagee"; "possession"; "property"; "rent".

Notes

1 Section 99 implements the Commission's recommendation that a mortgagee should only take possession either to protect the property or to realise the security (see s 96(1)(*c*) and Notes 7–8 to that section) and, having taken possession, should subsequently act accordingly. For this reason the section does not re-enact the provision in s 19(1)(iv) of the Conveyancing Act 1881 which permits a mortgagee to cut and sell timber and trees ripe for cutting or left standing for shelter or ornament, without apparently having to use the proceeds to reduce the mortgage debt: see Wylie, *Irish Land Law* (3rd edn, Tottel Publishing, 1997), para 13.046. The section imposes considerable restrictions on what a mortgagee, or receiver (see Note 4 below), in possession can do with the property. For this reason it is likely that commercial mortgages will expressly exclude or vary this section: (see Note 11 to s 96).

2 Section 99 may be varied by the terms of the court order for possession, which is required in the case of housing loan mortgages.

3 See s 108 and the Notes to it.

4 It is unlikely that a receiver will be appointed in the case of a housing loan mortgage. In the case of a commercial mortgage, it may be that the s 99 requirements will also be inappropriate in particular cases, eg, where the property is a commercial business which the receiver needs to put back on its feet before considering selling or leasing. If the section has not been excluded or modified by the terms of the mortgage, the court making the possession order should be asked to attach appropriate terms to the order: see Note 2 above.

5 Even where there is a derogation of the section (see Notes 2 and 4 above), this gives the mortgagee or receiver some flexibility in deciding when to sell or lease.

6 See the Notes to that section.

7 For example because of the state of the market. Note the mortgagor's right to test such an issue under s 94 (see the Notes to that section).

8 Although other items of property may be "leased", such as aircraft, ships, machinery and equipment, such an arrangement does not created the relationship of landlord and tenant, which is confined to land: see Wylie, *Landlord and Tenant Law* (2nd edn, Tottel Publishing, 1998), para 1.04. The definition of "lease" in s 3 is confined to that relationship, because it refers to granting a "tenancy" (also defined: see Notes 50 and 88–90 to s 3). The result is that "property" in paragraph (*b*) is confined to land.

9 Section 112 is also confined to leases of "land" (see the Notes to that section).

10 Subsection (2) was included to remove what was perceived to be an anomaly in the law, ie that a mortgagee in possession is also regarded as being in "adverse possession" for the purposes of the Statute of Limitations 1957 and so may become owner of the land by thereby barring the mortgagor's right of redemption. This was regarded as inconsistent with the nature of a mortgage, which should be treated as security only and not as a means of becoming owner of the land: see Note 1 to Chapter 1 above and Notes 7 and 10 to s 96. In practice this is unlikely to operate in future because the requirements of sub-s (1) will militate against a mortgagee "sitting" on the property. Note that sub-s (2) does not apply to a receiver in

possession; nor did s 34 of the 1957 Statute. Nor does it apply where possession is taken with the consent of the mortgagor.

---

[151]

Power of
sale.[1]
[CA 1881,
ss.19(1)(i), 20,
21(4), 21(6)
and (7)]
[CA 1911,
s. 5(2)]

100.—(1) Subject to *subsection (3)*[2] and *sections 101* to *107*,[3] a mortgagee or any other person for the time being entitled to receive, and give a discharge for, the mortgage debt may sell or concur with any other person in selling the mortgaged property provided[4]—

(*a*) following service of notice on the mortgagor requiring payment of the mortgage debt, default has been made in payment of that debt, or part of it, for 3 months after such service, or

(*b*) some interest under the mortgage or, in the case of a mortgage debt payable by instalments, some instalment representing interest or part interest and part capital is in arrears and unpaid for 2 months after becoming due, or

(*c*) there has been a breach by the mortgagor, or some person concurring in the mortgage, of some other provision contained in the mortgage or any statutory provision, including this Act, other than a covenant for payment of the mortgage debt or interest,

and provided in each such case 28 days' notice[5] in the prescribed form[6] has been served on the mortgagor warning of the possibility of such sale.

(2)[7] The power of sale shall not become exercisable without a court order granted under *subsection (3)*, unless the mortgagor consents in writing to such exercise not more than 7 days prior to such exercise.[8]

(3)[9] At any time after expiration of the 28 days' notice given under *subsection (1)*, a mortgagee may apply to the court[10] for an order authorising exercise of the power of sale and on such application the court may, if it thinks fit, grant such authorisation to the applicant on such terms and conditions, if any, as it thinks fit.[11]

(4) An application under *subsection (3)* may be made with an application under *section 97(2)* and, in such case, both may be heard together.[12]

(5) A mortgagee is not answerable for any involuntary loss resulting from the exercise or execution of the power of sale under this Chapter, of any trust connected with it or of any power or provision contained in the mortgage.[13]

(6) Once the power of sale becomes exercisable, the person entitled to exercise it may demand and recover from any person, other than a person having in the mortgaged property an estate or interest in priority to the mortgage, all deeds and documents relating to the property, or its title, which a purchaser under the power of sale would be entitled to demand and recover.[14]

Definitions

See s 3 for definitions of: "deed"; "mortgage"; "mortgagee"; "mortgagor"; "prescribed"; "property"; "purchaser".

Notes

1   As originally drafted this provision in the Bill (and in the Bill introduced to the Seanad: see s 103 in it) was largely a re-enactment of various provisions in ss 19–21 of the Conveyancing Act 1881, as amended by s 5 of the Conveyancing Act 1911. These provisions related to exercise of a statutory power of sale *out of court* and should not be confused with a court *order for sale*: see Wylie, *Irish Land Law* (3rd edn, Tottel Publishing, 1997), paras 13.016–13.021 and 13.040–13.041. Section 100 also relates to a sale out of court. See also *Horsham Properties Group Ltd v Clark* [2008] EWHC 2327 (Ch) and Note 7 below. However, during the Bill's passage various changes were made to introduce more of a consumer protection element (see Note 1 to Part 10 above). The section's provisions are now mandatory for housing loan mortgages but, as was commonly done with respect to the 1881 Act's provisions, the likelihood is that there will be an express contrary provision in other mortgages: see Note 1 to Chapter 3 and Note 11 to s 96.

2   Subsection (3) is one of the new consumer protection elements added at the Dáil Select Committee Stage: see Note 9 below.

3   Sections 101–107 re-enact various provisions relating to the power of sale in the 1881–1911 Acts.

4   Subsection (1), including paragraphs (*a*)–(*c*), largely re-enacts the substance of ss 19(1)(i) and 20 of the 1881 Act. Like the 1881 Act's provisions this statutory power of sale applies only where the mortgage is created by deed: see s 96(1)(*a*) (and Note 4 to that section). This includes a charge on registered land: see the amendment to s 62(6) of the Registration of Title Act 1964 in Schedule 1 (and see the Notes to that Schedule).

5   This was the notice recommended by the Commission to apply to all remedies, but it was moved to this position at the Dáil Select Committee Stage: see Note 8 to s 96.

6   Section 5 makes provision for regulations to deal with prescribed matters (see the Notes to that section).

7   Subsection (2) was also added at the Dáil Select Committee Stage to introduce further protection in relation to housing loan mortgages: see Note 8 below. In *Horsham Properties Group Ltd v Clark* [2008] EWCH 2327 (Ch) it was confirmed that the statutory power of sale was exercisable without any court order and that this long-established remedy did not infringe the European Convention on Human Rights and Fundamental Freedoms.

8   The restriction re 7 days was added at the Final Dáil Report Stage for the same reason it was added to s 97(1) (see Note 5 to that section). There may be even more difficulties in operating this in practice. Apart again from the very short timescale, it may not be clear from what date it operates, ie at what date the "exercise" of the power of sale begins. Given the cross-reference to sub-s (3), which allows an application to court for authorisation only after expiration of the 28 days' notice required by sub-s (1), it must likewise be after that date. The mortgagor's consent is an alternative to court authorisation, hence the reference to "such" exercise. Hopefully a court would adopt a pragmatic view and regard consent given not more than 7 days before a mortgagee puts the property up for sale as valid. The point is that otherwise the mortgagee might incur substantial expense in putting a sale in progress (engaging an auctioneer, arranging advertisements, etc) on the basis that the mortgagor is agreeable, only to find as the day of the auction arrives that the mortgagor refuses to give consent or has changed his or her mind. There would be considerable practical problems if the date of exercise of the power of sale was regarded as a later date, eg, entering into a contract for sale.

9   Subsection (3) was also added at the Dáil Report Stage.

10 Under s 101 the Circuit Court has *exclusive* jurisdiction to deal with applications relating to housing loan mortgages: see Note 11 to that section.

11 This gives the Circuit Court a wide discretion in dealing with applications for authorisation to exercise the power of sale.

12 That is an application for authorisation to exercise the power of sale may be made with an application for possession to facilitate the sale. An application for well-charging relief and possession as a preliminary to exercise of the statutory power of sale has long been the established procedure in the High Court: see Rules of the Superior Courts, Order 54, rule 3; Wylie, *Irish Land Law* (3rd edn, Tottel Publishing, 1997), paras 13.016–13.020. As regards the Circuit Court see now Circuit Court Rules (Actions for Possession and Well-Charging Relief) 2009 (SI 264/2009) and Practice Direction CII (Actions for Repossession), 12 November 2009.

13 Subsection (5) re-enacts a provision in s 21(6) of the 1881 Act, as amended by s 5(2) of the 1911 Act.

14 Subsection (6) re-enacts a provision in s 21(7) of the 1881 Act.

[152]

101.—(1) Upon an application for an order under, and without prejudice to the generality of, *sections 97(2)*[2] and *100(3)*,[3] where it appears to the court that the mortgagor is likely to be able within a reasonable period to pay any arrears, including interest, due under the mortgage or to remedy any other breach of obligation arising under it,[4] the court may[5]—

    (*a*)   adjourn the proceedings, or

    (*b*)   on making an order, or at any time before enforcement or implementation of such an order—

        (i)   stay the enforcement or implementation, or

        (ii)   postpone the date for delivery of possession to the mortgagee, or

        (iii)   suspend the order,

for such period or periods as it thinks reasonable and, if an order is suspended, the court may subsequently revive it.[6]

(2) Any adjournment, stay, postponement or suspension under *subsection (1)* may be made subject to such terms and conditions with regard to payment by the mortgagor of any sum secured by the mortgage or remedying of any breach of obligation as the court thinks fit.[7]

(3) The court may revoke or vary any term or condition imposed under *subsection (2)*.[8]

(4)[9] Subject to *subsection (5)*, an application under *section 97(2)* or *section 100(3)* may be made to the High Court.[10]

(5) Where an application under *section 97(2)* or *section 100(3)* concerns property which is subject to a housing loan mortgage the Circuit Court shall have exclusive jurisdiction to deal with the application and the application shall not be made to the High Court.[11]

(6) The jurisdiction of the Circuit Court to hear and determine applications under *sections 97(2)* and *100(3)* concerning property which is subject to a housing loan mortgage shall be exercised by the judge of the circuit where the property or any part of it is situated.[12]

(7) Nothing in this section affects the jurisdiction of the court under sections 7 and 8 of the Act of 1976.[13]

Applications under *sections 97* and *100.*[1]

Definitions

See s 3 for definitions of: "Act of 1976"; "court"; "housing loan"; "mortgagee"; "mortgagor"; "property".

Notes

1 Section 101 provides guidance as to how the court may deal with actions for a possession order or authorisation to exercise the statutory power of sale out of court.

2 That is an order for possession (see the Notes to s 97).

3 That is an order authorising a sale out of court (see the Notes to s 100).

4 The burden will be on the mortgagor to convince the court of this.

5 Paragraphs (*a*)–(*b*) give the court a wide discretion as to the order it makes in the particular case. Prior to 1 December 2009 it was very doubtful how far the court's jurisdiction stretched to deny a mortgagee an order for possession or to adjourn the application or suspend enforcement: see *Anglo Irish Bank Corporation plc v Oisin Fanning* [2009] IEHC 141; cf the ruling of the Master of the High Court in *GE Capital Woodchester Home Loans Ltd v Connolly* (11 February 2009), HC; Wylie, *Irish Land Law* (3rd edn, Tottel Publishing, 1997), para 13.021. Cf where a family home is involved: see Note 13 below.

6 Cf the jurisdiction under ss 7 and 8 of the Family Home Protection Act 1976.

7 Subsection (2) adds further to the discretionary jurisdiction under sub-s (1).

8 Subsection (3) also adds to the discretionary jurisdiction.

9 Subsections (4)–(6) were added at the Final Dáil Report Stage as a reaction to reports of "sub-prime" mortgagees incurring costs grossly disproportionate to the outstanding debt by applying to the High Court. It should be noted, however, that these provisions operate only in respect of mortgages created after 1 December 2009: see s 96 (1)(*a*) and Note 4 to that section.

10 The general rule under s 3 is that the Circuit Court has concurrent jurisdiction: see Notes 21–23 to that section.

11 Subsection (5) requires applications for a possession order or authorisation to sell out of court to be made to the Circuit Court, and not the High Court, in the case of housing loan mortgages created after 1 December 2009: see Circuit Court Rules (Actions for Possession and Well-charging Relief) 2009 (SI 264/2009) and Circuit Court Practice Direction CCII (Actions for Repossession), 12 November 2009. It must be doubted whether the Supreme Court view that a further advance on an existing mortgage may be viewed as a new mortgage would apply here. That view was taken in respect of the Family Home Protection Act 1976 in *Bank of Ireland v Purcell* [1989] IR 327 on the basis that the 1976 Act was primarily a "social remedial" statute and not just a "conveyancing" statute (see Walsh J at p 333): see Wylie and Woods, *Irish Conveyancing Law* (3rd edn, Tottel Publishing, 2005), paras 16.49 and 16.57. The 2009 Act is primarily a conveyancing statute, but the substantial consumer protection element for housing loan mortgages may influence the courts.

12 Subsection (6) is a standard provision.

13 This is a saving for the existing jurisdiction of the court under ss 7 and 8 of the Family Home Protection Act 1976 to adjourn proceedings by a mortgagee for possession or sale of a family home and to modify the terms of a mortgage.

---

[153]

102.—Incidental to the power of sale are the powers to—

  (*a*)   sell the mortgaged property[2]—

   (i)   subject to prior charges or not,

   (ii)   either together or in lots,

   (iii)   by public auction, tender or private contract,

   (iv)   subject to such conditions respecting title, evidence of title, or other matter as the mortgagee or other person selling thinks fit,

  (*b*)   rescind any contract for sale and resell,

  (*c*)[3]   impose or reserve or make binding by covenant or otherwise, on the sold part of the mortgaged land, or on the unsold part, any restriction or reservation with respect to building on or other user of land, or with respect to mines and minerals, for the purpose of their more beneficial working, or with respect to any other matter,

  (*d*)   sell the mortgaged land, or all or any mines and minerals apart from the surface, with or without—

   (i)   any easement, right or privilege connected with building or other purposes on the sold part of the mortgaged land or the unsold part,

   (ii)   an exception or reservation of all or any of the mines and minerals in the mortgaged land and with or without a grant, reservation or imposition of powers of working, wayleaves, rights of way, rights of water and drainage and other powers, easements, rights and privileges for or connected with mining purposes, in relation to or on the sold part of the mortgaged land or the unsold part,

   (iii)   covenants by the purchaser to expend money on the land sold.

Incidental powers.[1]
[CA 1881, s. 19(1)(i)]
[CA 1911, s. 4]

Definitions

See s 3 for definitions of: "covenant"; "land"; "mortgagee"; "property".

Notes

1   Section 102 re-enacts the substance of s 19(1)(i) of the Conveyancing Act 1881 and s 4 of the Conveyancing Act 1911. It confers considerable flexibility in carrying out a sale of mortgaged property out of court.

2   Note that this includes just part of the property: see s 96(1)(d) and Note 10 to that section.

3   Paragraphs (c) and (d) were added originally by s 4 of the 1911 Act.

---

[154]

Obligations
on selling.[1]

103.—(1) In the exercise of the power of sale conferred by this Chapter or any express power of sale,[2] the mortgagee, or any receiver[3] or other person appointed by the mortgagee, shall, notwithstanding any stipulation to the contrary in the mortgage,[4] ensure as far as is reasonably practicable that the mortgaged property is sold at the best price reasonably obtainable.[5]

(2) Within 28 days after completion of the sale, the mortgagee shall serve a notice in the prescribed form[6] on the mortgagor containing information relating to the sale.

(3) A mortgagee who, without reasonable cause, is in breach of the obligation imposed by *subsection (2)* is guilty of an offence.[7]

(4) Nothing in this section affects the operation of any rule of law relating to the duty of a mortgagee to account to a mortgagor.[8]

(5) This section does not apply to a building society within the meaning of the Act of 1989[9] or a receiver appointed under the Companies Acts.[10]

(6) In *subsection (2)* "mortgagor" includes a person last known to the mortgagee to be the mortgagor, but does not include a person to whom, without the knowledge of the mortgagee, any of the rights or liabilities of the mortgagor under the mortgage have been assigned.

Definitions

See s 3 for the definitions of: "Act of 1989"; "mortgage"; "mortgagee"; "mortgagor"; "prescribed"; "property".

Notes

1   Section 103 implements the Law Reform Commission's recommendation that the duty on building societies to get the best price reasonably obtainable when selling mortgaged property should be extended to all mortgagees: see LRC CP 34–2004,

para 9.16. This is largely declaratory of the general law as laid down by the Supreme Court in *Holohan v Friends Provident and Century Life Office* [1966] IR 1; *Re Edenfell Holdings Ltd* [1999] 1 IR 443; Lyall, *Land Law in Ireland* (2nd edn, Round Hall, 2000), pp 798–799; Wylie, *Irish Land Law* (3rd edn, Tottel Publishing, 1997), paras 13.034–13.036.

2   Section 103 applies both to the statutory power of sale conferred on mortgagees by deed by Chapter 3 and any express power of sale.

3   It has long been held that the duties in selling apply to a receiver or other agent acting for the mortgagee: *Re Edenfell Holdings Ltd* [1999] 1 IR 443; *Ruby Property Co Ltd v Kilty* [1999] IEHC 50; *Bula Ltd v Crowley* [2003] 1 IR 36; *O'Leary v Agricultural Credit Corporation plc* [2004] IEHC 123.

4   Section 103 is the one section in Chapter 3 which cannot be excluded or varied by the terms of a commercial mortgage, ie, one which is not a housing loan mortgage: see s 96(3) and Notes 11–15 to that section.

5   In essence the mortgagee, receiver or other agent must strive to obtain the fair market price for the property at the time of sale: see the discussion by Ó Dálaigh CJ in *Holohan v Friends Provident and Century Life Office* [1966] IR 1.

6   Section 5 makes provision for regulations to be made prescribing forms (see the Notes to that section). Although sub-s (2) does not say so explicitly, since it is linked with the duty in selling and is designed to give the mortgagor information by which to judge whether sub-s (1) has been complied with, it is very doubtful whether the duty to serve the notice can be excluded in the case of commercial mortgages, especially since a failure to comply is an offence.

7   As regards offences see s 6.

8   For example the duty of a mortgagee in possession to account strictly: see Lyall, *Land Law in Ireland* (2nd edn, Round Hall, 2000), pp 794–795; Wylie, *Irish Land Law* (3rd edn, Tottel Publishing, 1997), paras 13.046–13.047.

9   See s 26 of the Building Societies Act 1989.

10 See *Re Edenfell Holdings Ltd* [1999] 1 IR 443; *Ruby Property Co Ltd v Kilty* [1999] IEHC 50.

---

[155]

104.—(1) A mortgagee exercising the power of sale conferred by this Chapter, or an express power of sale,[2] has power to convey the property in accordance with *subsection (2)*—

Conveyance on sale.[1]
[CA 1881, s. 21(1)]

> (*a*)   freed from all estates, interests and rights in respect of which the mortgage has priority,
>
> (*b*)   subject to all estates, interests and rights which have priority to the mortgage.[3]

(2) Subject to *subsections (3)(b)* and *(4)*, the conveyance—

> (*a*)   vests the estate or interest which has been mortgaged in the purchaser,[4]

    (*b*)   extinguishes the mortgage, but without prejudice to any personal liability of the mortgagor not discharged out of the proceeds of sale,

    (*c*)   vests any fixtures or personal property included in the mortgage and the sale in the purchaser.

(3) This section—

    (*a*)   applies to a sale by a sub-mortgagee so as to enable the sub-mortgagee to convey the head-mortgagor's property in the same manner as the mortgagee,

    (*b*)   does not apply to a mortgage of part only of a tenancy unless any rent which is reserved and any tenant's covenants have been apportioned as regards the property mortgaged.

(4) Where the mortgaged property comprises registered land, the conveyance is subject to section 51 of the Act of 1964.[5]

Definitions

See s 3 for the definitions of: "Act of 1964"; "conveyance"; "covenant"; "mortgage"; "mortgagee"; "mortgagor"; "property"; "rent"; "tenancy".

Notes

1   Section 104 extends s 21(1) of the Conveyancing Act 1881 to deal with the new method of creating legal mortgages prescribed by s 89, whereby the estate or interest of the mortgagor is no longer conveyed to the mortgagee, which obtains a charge only: see the Notes to s 89. It implements the Law Reform Commission's recommendation that, nevertheless, the charge should confer equivalent security rights (see the general provision in s 90(1)(*b*) and Notes 4 and 5 to that section). Section 104 enables the mortgagee to sell and vest in a purchaser the mortgagor's estate or interest in the property, even though until that happens it has remained vested in the mortgagor subject to the mortgagee's charge.

2   Section 104 covers both the statutory power of sale out of court and any express power.

3   Paragraphs (*a*) and (*b*) reflect the usual rules governing priorities as between several mortgages of the same property: see Lyall, *Land Law in Ireland* (2nd edn, Round Hall, 2000), pp 825–836; Wylie, *Irish Land Law* (3rd edn, Tottel Publishing, 1997), paras 13.127–13.162.

4   This confirms that the new charge by deed has the equivalent effect of the traditional mortgage by conveyance or assignment: see Note 1 above.

5   This refers to the fundamental principle that a transfer of registered land is not effective to transfer the legal title until it is registered. Under s 3 a "conveyance" includes a transfer.

[156]

105.—(1) Where a conveyance is made in professed[2] exercise of the power of sale conferred by this Chapter, the title of the purchaser is not impeachable on the ground that—

(*a*)   no case had arisen to authorise the sale,[3] or

(*b*)   due notice had not been given,[4] or

(*c*)   the power was otherwise improperly exercised,[5]

and a purchaser is not, either before or on conveyance, required to see or inquire whether the power is properly exercised.[6]

(2) Any person who suffers loss as a consequence of an unauthorised or improper exercise of the power of sale has a remedy in damages against the person exercising the power.[7]

Protection of purchasers.[1]
[CA 1881, s. 21(2)]
[CA 1911, s. 5(1)]

Definitions

See s 3 for the definitions of: "conveyance"; "purchaser".

Notes

1   Section 105 re-enacts the substance of s 21(2) of the Conveyancing Act 1881 and s 5(1) of the Conveyancing Act 1911. It is one of the most important reasons why it has long been common to incorporate the statutory power of sale in commercial mortgages.

2   The protection for purchasers applies only where the deed executed by the mortgagee refers expressly to the statutory power of sale: *Laffoy's Irish Conveyancing Precedents* (Bloomsbury Professional), Precedent E.7.3.

3   The old distinction between the power "arising" and becoming "exercisable" is abolished by s 96(1)(*b*) (see Note 6 to that section). However, it does not become exercisable unless various conditions are met, eg there is a need to realise the security (see s 96(1)(*c*) and Note 8 to that section).

4   See s 100(1) and Notes 4–5 to that section.

5   For example, the fair market price has not been obtained: see s 103 and the Notes to that section.

6   The purchaser is not required, therefore, to make inquiries as to such matters, as might otherwise be the case under s 86 (see the Notes to that section): see *Re Irish Civil Service Building Society and O'Keeffe* (1880) 7 LR Ir 136. However, it has been held that a purchaser's protection under this provision is not absolute. The courts will not allow a statute to be used as an "instrument of fraud" and so a purchaser who has *actual knowledge* of any impropriety or irregularity in the exercise of the power of sale does *not* obtain a good title: *Lord Waring v London and Manchester Assurance Co Ltd* [1935] Ch 310 at 318 (*per* Crossman J); *Bailey v Barnes* [1894] 1 Ch 25 at 30 (*per* Stirling J). The same principle has been applied to exercise of an express power of sale: see *Jenkins v Jones* (1860) 2 Giff 99; *Selwyn v Garfit* (1888) 38 Ch D 273.

7 The remedy of the mortgagor is not against the purchaser who is protected by sub-s (1), but against the mortgagee who engaged in the unauthorised or improper exercise of the power of sale.

---

[157]

Mortgagee's
receipts.[1]
[CA 1881,
s. 22]

106.—(1) Subject to *subsection (2)*, the receipt in writing of a mortgagee is a conclusive discharge[2] for any money arising under the power of sale conferred by this Chapter, or for any money or securities comprised in the mortgage, or arising under it, and a person paying or transferring the same to the mortgagee is not required to inquire whether any money remains due under the mortgage.

(2) *Subsection (1)* does not apply where the purchaser has actual knowledge of an impropriety or irregularity in the exercise of the power of sale or knowingly participates in such an exercise.[3]

(3) Subject to *section 107(5)*, money received by a mortgagee under the mortgage or from the proceeds of securities comprised in it shall be applied as *section 107* requires as regards money arising from a sale under the power of sale conferred by this Chapter.[4]

Definitions

See s 3 for the definitions of: "mortgage"; "mortgagee".

Notes

1 Section 106 re-enacts the substance of s 22 of the Conveyancing Act 1881. It provides further protection for purchasers taking the mortgaged property from a mortgagee professing to exercise the statutory power of sale.

2 Under s 22 of the 1881 Act the mortgagee's receipt was "sufficient" only, so that a purchaser with notice of trusts affecting the mortgage money might be required to make further inquiries: see *Re Blaiberg and Abraham* (1899) 2 Ch 340; *Hockey v Western* [1898] 1 Ch 350. The Law Reform Commission recommended increasing the protection: see LRC CP 34–2004, para 9.24. Note, however, that the protection is not *absolute*: see sub-s (2) and Note 3 below.

3 This mirrors the position the courts took in relation to the provisions now in s 105: see Note 6 to that section.

4 This provides that money or proceeds of securities received under the mortgage must be applied in the same way as s 107 requires the proceeds of exercise of the power of sale to be applied. However, s 107(5) provides for a variation as regards charges, costs and expenses: see Note 6 to s 107.

[158]

107.—(1) Money received by the mortgagee which arises from the sale of mortgaged property shall be applied in the following order²—

    (*a*)   in discharge of prior incumbrances, if any, to which the sale was not made subject or payment into court of a sum to meet any such prior incumbrances,

    (*b*)   in payment of all charges, costs and expenses properly incurred by the mortgagee as incident to the sale or any attempted sale or otherwise,

    (*c*)   in discharge of the mortgage debt, interest and costs, and other money, if any, due under the mortgage.

> **Application of proceeds of sale.**[1] **[CA 1881, s. 21(3)]**

(2) Any residue of the money so received shall be held on trust[3] by the mortgagee to be paid to the person who would, but for the sale, be the mortgagee secured on the property sold next in priority after the mortgagee selling, or is otherwise authorised to give receipts for the money so received, or, if there is no such person, the mortgagor.[4]

(3) Where, in accordance with *subsection (2)*, the mortgagee gives effect to the trust of the residue by paying it to a subsequent mortgagee, the latter shall apply it in accordance with *subsections (1)(c)* and *(2)* and similar obligations attach to each subsequent mortgagee who receives any of the residue.

(4) Any mortgagee who so gives effect to the trust is discharged from any further obligation with respect to the residue.[5]

(5) For the purposes of the application of *subsection (1)(b)* to money received under *section 106(3)*, charges, costs and expenses payable include those properly incurred in recovering and receiving the money or securities, and in conversion of securities into money, instead of those incident to the sale.[6]

Definitions

See s 3 for the definitions of: "court"; "mortgage"; "mortgagee"; "mortgagor"; "property".

Notes

1   Section 107 re-enacts the substance of s 21(3) of the Conveyancing Act 1881.

2   Paragraphs (*a*)–(*c*) specify how money received by the mortgagee from a sale of the property should be applied: see *Re Thompson's Mortgage Trusts* [1920] 1 Ch 508. This must apply in the case of a housing loan mortgage, but may be replaced by a "waterfall" scheme in the case of complex commercial mortgages.

3   It has long been settled that while the mortgagee is not a trustee of the power of sale, he or she is a trustee of the proceeds of exercise of that power: see *Thorne v Heard* [1895] AC 495; *Re Counter's Charge* [1960] Ch 491; Lyall, *Land Law in Ireland* (2nd edn, Round Hall, 2000), p 800; Wylie, *Irish Land Law* (3rd edn, Tottel Publishing, 1997), para 13.036. See also s 11(8) of the Housing (Miscellaneous Provisions) Act 1992.

4   See *West London Commercial Bank v Reliance Permanent Building Society* (1884) 27 Ch D 187; *Charles v Jones* (1887) 35 Ch D 544; *Bucknell v Bucknell* [1969] 2 All ER 998.

5   Subsection (3) makes it clear that where the residue is passed on to other mortgagees, each of them must comply with the section.

6   Subsection (5) adapts the provisions of s 107 to the situation where the mortgagee receives other money under the mortgage or the proceeds from the sale of other securities. Section 106(3) provides that such money or proceeds should be applied in the same way as the proceeds of a sale of the mortgaged property, but instead of s 107(1)(*b*) requiring payment of the charges, costs and expenses of such a sale, it should be read as referring to such charges etc relating to recovering and receiving money or securities or in conversion of securities into money.

---

[159]

Appointment of receiver.[1] **[CA 1881, ss. 19(1)(iii), 24(1)—(7)]**	**108.**—(1) Where[2]—

    (*a*)   following service of notice on the mortgagor requiring payment of the mortgage debt, default has been made in payment of that debt, or part of it, for 3 months after such service, or

    (*b*)   some interest under the mortgage or, in the case of a mortgage debt payable by instalments, some instalment representing interest or part interest and part capital is in arrears and unpaid for 2 months after becoming due, or

    (*c*)   there has been a breach by the mortgagor, or some person concurring in the mortgage, of some other provision contained in the mortgage or any statutory provision, including this Act, other than a covenant for payment of the mortgage debt or interest,

the mortgagee or any other person for the time being entitled to receive, and give a discharge for, the mortgage debt, may appoint,[3] by writing, such person as the mortgagee or that other person thinks fit to be a receiver of—

    (i)   the income of the mortgaged property, or

    (ii) if the mortgaged property comprises an interest in income, or a rentcharge or other annual or other periodical sum, that property.

(2) A receiver appointed under *subsection (1)* is the agent of the mortgagor, who is solely responsible for the receiver's acts or defaults,[4] unless the mortgage provides otherwise.[5]

(3) The receiver may—

    (*a*) demand and recover all the income[6] to which the appointment relates, by action or otherwise, in the name either of the mortgagor or mortgagee, to the full extent of the estate or interest which the mortgagor could dispose of,

    (*b*) give effectual receipts accordingly for such income,

    (*c*) exercise any powers delegated by the mortgagee or other person to the receiver.[7]

(4) Any power delegated to the receiver shall be exercised in accordance with this Chapter.

(5) A person paying money to the receiver is not required to inquire whether the receiver is authorised to act.

(6) The receiver may be removed, and a new receiver may be appointed,[8] by the mortgagee or the other person in writing.

(7) The receiver may retain out of any money received, for remuneration and in satisfaction of all costs incurred as receiver,[9] a commission at the prescribed rate.[10]

(8) The receiver shall, if so directed in writing by the mortgagee, insure to the extent, if any, to which the mortgagee might have insured[11] and keep insured against loss or damage by fire, flood, storm, tempest or other perils commonly covered by a policy of comprehensive insurance, out of the money received, any property comprised in the mortgage, whether affixed to land or not, which is of an insurable nature.

Definitions

See s 3 for the definitions of: "mortgage"; "mortgagee"; "mortgagor"; "property"; "rentcharge".

Notes

1 Section 108 re-enacts the substance of ss 19(i)(iii) and 24(1)–(7) of the Conveyancing Act 1881.

2   Paragraphs (*a*)–(*c*) mirror the circumstances when the power of sale under s 100(1) can be exercised (see Note 4 to that section). However, note that the restrictions on exercise of the power of sale added at a later stage by the Oireachtas (in particular the need to give a 28-day warning notice and to obtain court authorisation to exercise of the power of sale: see Notes 5–6 and 9–12 to s 100) do not apply to appointment of a receiver. As with Chapter 3 generally the provisions of s 108 must be complied with in the case of a housing loan (where it would be rare to appoint a receiver because of the nature of the mortgaged property), but may be excluded or modified in the case of other mortgages. It is common to give receivers much greater powers in such mortgages because of the limitations of the statutory provisions: see *Re Red Sail Frozen Foods Ltd* [2006] IEHC 328.

3   No appointment can be made unless it is necessary to protect the property or to enforce the security: see s 96(1)(*c*) and Notes 7–8 to that section. A mortgagee in possession can appoint a receiver to take over possession: see *Refuge Assurance Co Ltd v Pearlberg* [1938] Ch 687.

4   Since the receiver is the agent of the *mortgagor*, the mortgagee cannot be regarded as taking possession and bears no responsibility for the receiver's actions, nor is he or she liable to account strictly to the mortgagor: see *Re Marchesa Della Rochella's Estate* (1889) 29 LR Ir 464; *Lever Finance Ltd v Needleman's Estate* [1956] Ch 375.

5   The mortgage deed can exclude or vary this immunity of the mortgagee: see *Re Hale* [1899] 2 Ch 107; *White v Metcalf* [1903] 2 Ch 567; *Re Wood's Application* [1941] Ch 112.

6   This does not include the proceeds of sale of chattels (eg a dairy herd) not forming part of the mortgaged property: see *Donohoe v Agricultural Credit Corporation* [1986] IR 165. It does, however, clearly include rent issuing out of the mortgaged property: see *Fairholme v Kennedy* (1889) 24 LR Ir 498.

7   This gives the mortgagee scope to give the receiver greater powers, such as power to sell the property: see ss 99(1) (and Note 3 to that section) and 103(1) (and Note 3 to that section). If a receiver wishes to exercise such a delegated power of sale, it will be subject to s 100 (see the Notes to that section) unless in the case of a non-housing loan mortgage there is an express provision to the contrary.

8   This includes on death of a receiver since the office is continuous: see *Re Hill (RW) Ltd and Simmons* [1920] WN 386.

9   This, like other provisions in the section, may be varied by the terms of a commercial mortgage (ie a non-housing loan mortgage): see *Red Sail frozen Foods Ltd* [2006] IEHC 328.

10 Provision is made by s 5 for such matters to be prescribed by regulation (see the Notes to that section). Section 24(6) of the 1881 Act specified 5% or such higher rate as the court allowed.

11 See s 110 and the Notes to it.

[160]

109.—(1) Subject to *section 110(4)*, the receiver shall apply all money received in the following order—

(a) in discharge of all rates, rents, taxes and other outgoings affecting the mortgaged property,

(b) in discharge of all annual sums or other payments, and the interest on all principal sums, which have priority to the mortgage under which the receiver is appointed,

(c) in payment of the receiver's commission,

(d) in payment of premiums on insurance, if any, payable under this Chapter or the mortgage,

(e) in defraying the cost of repairs as directed in writing by the mortgagee,

(f) in payment of interest accruing due[2] in respect of any principal sum due under the mortgage,

(g) in or towards discharge of the principal sum, if so directed in writing by the mortgagee.

(2) The residue (if any) of any money so received after making the payments specified in *subsection (1)* shall be paid by the receiver to the person who, but for the possession of the receiver, would have been entitled to receive that money or who is otherwise entitled to the mortgaged property.

> **Application of money received.[1]**
> **[CA 1881, s. 24(8)]**

Definitions

See s 3 for the definitions of: "mortgage"; "mortgagee"; "possession"; "property"; "rent".

Notes

1 Section 109 re-enacts the provisions in s 24(8) of the Conveyancing Act 1881. The Law Reform Commission recommended that it should be open to the mortgagee to waive or vary the order of payments laid down and the original draft Bill, and the Bill introduced to the Seanad, had a provision to this effect (see s 105(2) to that Bill). However, the view was later taken that this was not appropriate and that the view of Keane J (as he then was) in *Donohoe v Agricultural Credit Corporation* [1986] IR 165 at 170, that the order was mandatory, should be adhered to. That provision was deleted at the Seanad Committee Stage. In fact as a result of s 96(3), which was modified at the Dáil Select Committee Stage, s 109 is mandatory for housing loan mortgages but may be varied by the terms of a commercial mortgage (see Notes 11–15 to s 96).

2 It is a breach of duty if the receiver pays any arrears which are statute-barred: see *Hibernian Bank v Yourell* [1919] 1 IR 310. However, interest includes all arrears

and not just those occurring after the receiver's appointment: see *National Bank v Kennedy* [1898] 1 IR 397.

[161]

Insurance.[1]
[CA 1881,
ss. 19(1)(ii),
23]

110.—(1) A mortgagee may insure and keep insured any building, effects or other property of an insurable nature, whether affixed to the land or not, which forms part of the mortgaged property.[2]

(2) The insurance shall be for the full reinstatement cost[3] of repairing any loss or damage arising from fire, flood, storm, tempest or other perils commonly covered by a policy of comprehensive insurance.

(3) The mortgagee may give a good discharge for any money payable under any such insurance, but, subject to *subsection (4)*, so much of such money as exceeds the mortgage debt shall be dealt with by the mortgagee as if it were the proceeds of a sale of the mortgaged property.[4]

(4) The mortgagee may require any money received under such or other insurance of the mortgaged property to be applied—

(*a*)   by the mortgagor in making good loss or damage covered by the insurance,[5] or

(*b*)   in or towards the discharge of the mortgage debt.[6]

Definitions

See s 3 for the definitions of: "land"; "mortgagee"; "mortgagor"; "property".

Notes

1   Section 110 largely re-enacts the substance of ss 19(1)(ii) and 23 of the Conveyancing Act 1881. It should be noted that it omits a provision in s 19(1)(ii) to the effect that the premiums are a charge on the property with the same priority as the mortgage money and subject to the same interest charge. The view was taken that this was not necessarily appropriate to enshrine in statute, as it could involve an unexpected hidden charge for some borrowers. Since 1 December 2009 it would have to be expressly contracted for.

2   Notwithstanding the reference to property, the wording of sub-s (1), like that of s 19(1)(ii) of the 1881 Act, is concerned with mortgages of land and other property included in such a mortgage (which itself may or may not be part of the land).

3   As recommended by the Law Reform Commission, sub-s (2) modifies s 23(1) of the 1881 Act to bring it more into line with modern practice: see LRC CP 34–2004, para 9.24. Section 23(1) required cover for the amount specified in the mortgage or two-thirds the cost of restoring the property.

4   See s 107 and the Notes to that section.

5   This was the position in England also under Fires Prevention (Metropolis) Act 1774, but that did not apply to Ireland: see *Andrews v Patriotic Assurance Co* (1886) 18 LR Ir 355 at 366–369 (*per* Palles CB).

6   The Irish courts have long held that a mortgagee can insist on this: see *Re Doherty* [1925] 2 IR 246; *Myler v Mr Pussy's Nite Club* (11 December 1979), HC; cf *Halifax Building Society v Keighley* [1931] 2 KB 248.

[162]

111.—(1)[2] Where a mortgage is expressed to be created on any land for the purpose of securing future advances[3] (whether with or without present advances), the mortgagee is entitled, in priority to any subsequent mortgage, to the payment of any sum due in respect of any such future advances, except any advances which may have been made after the date of, and with express notice in writing of, the subsequent mortgage.[4]

Future advances.[1]

(2) In *subsection (1)* "future advances" includes sums from time to time due on a current account and all sums which by agreement or in the course of business between the parties are considered to be advances on the security of the mortgage.

(3) Save in regard to the making of such future advances the right to tack in any form is abolished, but without prejudice to any priority acquired by tacking before the commencement of this Chapter.[5]

(4) This section—

   (*a*)   applies to mortgages made before or after the commencement of this Chapter,[6]

   (*b*)   does not apply to registered land.[7]

Definitions

See s 3 for definitions of: "land"; "mortgage"; "mortgagee".

Notes

1   To some extent s 111 implements a recommendation by the Law Reform Commission to reform the law of tacking: see LRC CP 34–2004, para 9.18.

2   As originally drafted the Commission's Bill, and the Bill introduced to the Seanad, contained a wider provision than sub-s (1) (see s 107 of that Bill). That provision was based on provisions in s 94 of the English Law of Property Act 1925. In particular, it provided that where a prior mortgagee had committed itself to making future advances, any such advances would have priority over a subsequent mortgagee even though when made the prior mortgagee had notice of the second

mortgage. However, it was pointed out subsequently that this would put the law relating to unregistered land out of line with that relating to registered land, as governed by s 75 of the Registration of Title Act 1964. The ultimate view was taken that it would be better to align both and so a provision similar to s 75 was substituted at the Seanad Committee Stage.

3   Tacking future advances is common in mortgage transactions, because often a lender will agree to make further advances on the same security as an existing mortgage: see *Allied Irish Banks v Glynn* [1973] IR 158; *Bank of Ireland v Purcell* [1989] IR 327; Johnston, *Banking and Security Law in Ireland* (Tottel Publishing, 1998), para 10.70; Lyall, *Land Law in Ireland* (2nd edn, Round Hall, 2000), pp 832–833; Wylie, *Irish Land Law* (3rd edn, Tottel Publishing, 1997), paras 13.161–13.162.

4   Thus express notice in writing will prevent the mortgagee from tacking advances made afterwards. This reflects the Irish case law: see *Re O'Byrne's Estate* (1855) 15 LR Ir 373; *Re Macnamara's Estate* (1884) 13 LR Ir 158; *Re Keogh's Estate* [1895] 1 IR 201. Such notice must be given by the intervening mortgagee to prevent tacking securing priority for later advances. Merely registering the intervening mortgage in the Registry of Deeds is not enough, because it is well-established that such registration is not "notice" for those purposes: see *Bushell v Bushell* (1803) 1 Sch & Lef 90; *Latouche v Dunsany* (1803) 1 Sch & Lef 137. There is English authority to the effect that the mortgagor's creation of an intervening mortgage relieves the prior mortgagee from any obligation to make future advances after it has notice of the intervening mortgage: see *West v Williams* [1899] 1 Ch 132.

5   Subsection (3) implements the Commission's recommendation that other forms of tacking, in particular the method known as *tabula in naufragio* ("plank in a shipwreck") should be abolished. This has always been very controversial because it involves a later mortgagee buying out an earlier mortgage so as to squeeze out the priority of an intervening mortgagee: see Lyall, *Land Law in Ireland* (2nd edn, Round Hall, 2000), pp 830–832; Wylie, *Irish Land Law* (3rd edn, Tottel Publishing, 1997), paras 13.159–13.160. Curiously it was previously abolished by s 7 of the Vendor and Purchaser Act 1874, but restored by s 73 of the Conveyancing Act 1881. It rarely had practical effect in Ireland because of the operation of the Registry of Deeds system: see *Tennison v Sweeny* (1844) 7 Ir Eq R 511.

6   The view was taken that, apart from abolishing an obsolete form of tacking (see Note 5 above), the section is largely declaratory of existing law.

7   This is simply recognition that the same provision is in s 75 of the Registration of Title Act 1964: see Note 2 above.

---

[163]

CHAPTER 4[1]

Leases and surrenders of leases[2]

Notes

1   Chapter 4 re-enacts much of the substance of s 18 of the Conveyancing Act 1881 and s 3 of the Conveyancing Act 1911. However, it recasts the provisions and makes

a numbers of modifications as recommended by the Law Reform Commission: see LRC CP 34–2004, para 9.24.

2   As o.ig.nally drafted the Commission's Bill, and the Bill as introduced to the Seanad, contained the same provision as the 1881 and 1911 Acts did, that the provision was subject to the terms of the mortgage (see ss 108(5)(*b*) and 110(6) of that Bill). This, however, was removed at the Seanad Committee Stage as part of the introduction of a greater consumer protection element (see Note 1 to Part 10 above). Subsequently the view was taken that this change had gone too far in applying to all mortgage transactions and at the Dáil Select Committee Stage further changes were made to confine mandatory provisions to housing loan mortgages and to restore freedom to "contract out" in respect of other mortgages. This was done by insertion of what is now s 96(3) (see Notes 11–15 to that section). That subsection, however, refers only to "this Chapter", ie Chapter 3. The result is that the provisions of Chapter 4 remain mandatory and cannot be contracted out of.

---

[164]

112.—(1)[2] A mortgagor of land,[3] while in possession,[4] may, as against every other[5] incumbrancer, lease[6] the land with the consent in writing of the mortgagee,[7] which consent shall not be unreasonably withheld.[8]

Leasing powers.[1]
[CA 1881, s. 18]
[CA1911, s. 3]

(2)[9] A lease made without such consent is voidable[10] by a mortgagee who establishes that—

(*a*)   the lessee had actual knowledge[11] of the mortgage at the time of the granting of the lease, and

(*b*)   the granting had prejudiced the mortgagee.[12]

(3)[13] A mortgagee of land while in possession[14] or, after the mortgagee has appointed a receiver and so long as the receiver acts,[15] the receiver, may, as against all prior incumbrancers, if any, and the mortgagor,[16] lease the land provided[17]—

(a)   it is for the purpose of—

(i)   preserving the value of the land,[18] or

(ii)   protection of the mortgagee's security,[19] or

(iii)   raising income to pay interest due under the mortgage or otherwise reduce the debt,[20]

or

(b)   it is otherwise an appropriate use of the land pending its sale,[21] or

(c)   the mortgagor consents in writing,[22] or

(d)   the court in any action relating to the mortgaged land makes an order permitting such lease.[23]

(4) In this section "mortgagor" does not include an incumbrancer deriving title from or under the original mortgagor.[24]

(5) The power of leasing conferred by this section applies only to mortgages created after the commencement of this Part.[25]

Definitions

See s 3 for definitions of: "consent"; "incumbrance"; "land"; "lease"; "mortgage"; "mortgagee"; "mortgagor"; "possession".

Notes

1 Section 112 recasts provisions in s 18 of the Conveyancing Act 1881, but subject to some important amendments: see Notes 6, 7 and 17 below. The point should be reiterated that it is not possible to contract out of this section, but only as regards leases of land. See Note 2 to Chapter 4 above. The 1881 provisions were designed to get over various difficulties at common law about leasing mortgaged land: see Lyall, *Land Law in Ireland* (2nd edn, Round Hall, 2000), pp 822–823; Wylie, *Irish Land Law* (3rd edn, Tottel Publishing, 1997), paras 13.111–13.119. They conferred a statutory right of leasing on the mortgagor and mortgagee (whichever one of them was in possession), but for restricted periods (21 years for agricultural or occupational leases and 99 years for a building lease). Section 112 removes these restrictions but imposes others: see Notes 6–7 below. The Law Reform Commission criticised the "mixed" messages given by other legislation relating to exercise of statutory powers such as these, in particular the provisions in the Leases Acts 1849 and 1850 which suggested that non-compliance with the statutory requirements was not necessarily fatal. This was described as being an "odd way" of treating statutory requirements: see *Consultation Paper on the General Law of Landlord and Tenant* (LRC CP 28–2003), para 2.17. This view, of course, may support the fact that Chapter 4 cannot be contracted out of: see Note 2 to Chapter 4 above. The key point about a lease granted under the statutory powers is that it binds the other party or parties interested in the land: see *Munster and Leinster Bank Ltd v Hollinshead* [1930] IR 187. Section 112 does not repeat the reference in s 18 of the 1881 Act to a contract to make or accept a lease on the basis that a power to grant a lease necessarily implies a power to enter into a contract to make or accept such a grant.

2 Subsection (1) deals with the position of the mortgagor while in possession of the land.

3 Chapter 4, like the provisions in the 1881 and 1911 Acts, is confined to leases of land.

4 Where a mortgagee, or receiver appointed by the mortgagee, is in possession see sub-s (2).

5 The word "other" has slipped in here and is probably "otiose"; the mortgagor is not usually an incumbrancer in respect of the mortgaged land. The point about sub-s (1) is that the lease will bind the mortgagee and other incumbrancers.

6   As part of the Law Reform Commission's recommendations to tighten up the statutory provisions, note that the statutory power is now confined to leasing, ie use of a written instrument to create a tenancy (see the definition of "lease" in s 3). The view was taken that this was more consistent with the requirements for written consent (see Note 7 below) and the various provisions relating to execution and delivery of duplicates and copies in s 113 (see Notes 9–10 to that section). The 1881 Act extended the provisions "as far as circumstances admit" to "any letting": see s 18(17).

7   The Law Reform Commission took the view that, instead of an unrestricted power as in the 1881 Act which was usually excluded by the mortgage deed, the statutory power should be subject to obtaining the mortgagee's consent: see LRC CP 34–2004, para 9.24. Note that the consent must be in writing. It does not say "prior" consent but in view of the provisions in subs-s (2) it should be given by the time of the grant of the lease, otherwise the mortgagee may be able to avoid the lease. The point is that it may argued that it is not "made" with consent unless that consent is in existence at the time of the making.

8   This adapts the well-established concept in landlord and tenant legislation: see Part V of the Landlord and Tenant (Amendment) Act 1980 and Wylie, *Landlord and Tenant Law* (2nd edn, Tottel Publishing, 1998), chs 21–22.

9   Subsection (2) makes it clear what the position is if consent of the mortgagee as required by sub-s (1) is not obtained.

10 Note that it is *not* "void". The lease will remain valid and binding on the mortgagee until it takes steps to have it "avoided", eg by seeking a declaration of the court to this effect. To obtain this the mortgagee will have to establish the factors referred to in paragraphs (*a*) and (*b*). Cf non-compliance with the requirements of s 113: see Note 8 to that section.

11 Note that "constructive" notice is not enough: see s 86 and the Notes to that section.

12 The mortgagee will also (note the "and") have to establish the "prejudice". The most obvious one would be to show that it hinders the mortgagee in exercise of its remedies, such as selling the land with vacant possession. Another would be leasing to a tenant of poor standing, who may not be a "good covenant".

13 Subsection (3) deals with leases by the mortgagee while in possession, or a receiver appointed by the mortgagee.

14 As under the 1881 Act the mortgagee's statutory power exists only while the mortgagee is in possession of the land: see s 18(1) of that Act.

15 The power to grant leases when a receiver has been appointed was added by s 3(11) of the Conveyancing Act 1911. The point was that a mortgagee would not be in possession while the receiver was in possession. Subsection (3) enables the receiver to grant the lease but this should be done in the name of the mortgagee; in essence the receiver is exercising the mortgagee's power: *Wynne v Lord Newborough* (1790) 1 Ves 164; see *Laffoy's Irish Conveyancing Precedents* (Bloomsbury Professional), Division E.6. See also s 113(1) and Note 7 to that section. Under sub-s (3) there is no need for an express delegation of the power to the receiver.

16 That is the lease binds both prior incumbrancer and the mortgagor.

17 Subsection (3) removes the restrictions as to terms of leases in s 18 of the 1881 Act but imposes other restrictions in relation to the purposes for which leases can be granted by a mortgagee or receiver in possession (as recommended by the Commission: see Note 1 above). Note that paragraphs (*a*)–(*d*) are alternatives.

18 Getting in a tenant may be the most effective way of preserving the value of the premises pending a sale or keeping a business going and preserving goodwill.

19 Again leasing may be more appropriate than a sale in a market slump.

20 The receipt of such income is often the initial aim of a receiver: see s 108 and the Notes to that section.

21 See s 99(1)(*b*) and Notes 7–9 to that section.

22 A mortgagor is clearly bound by any lease to which he or she consents and the right to redeem will be subject to any such lease.

23 Thus under s 100(3), in authorising a sale the court might order that no sale take place immediately because of the state of the market and that the premises should be let in the meantime: see Notes 9–11 to that section.

24 This re-enacts a provision in s 3(10) of the 1911 Act.

25 This is because modifications to the previous provisions in the 1881 Act are made.

---

[165]

Exercise of leasing powers.[1]

113.—(1) A lease to be granted under *section 112* shall[2]—

    (*a*)   reserve the best rent which can reasonably be obtained,[3] taking into account any premium or other capital sum[4] paid by the lessee and other relevant circumstances,[5] and

    (*b*)   be otherwise granted on the best terms that can reasonably be obtained and accord with good commercial practice,[6]

and execution of the lease by the lessor shall be sufficient evidence of execution and delivery of the lease.[7]

(2) A purported lease which fails to comply with *subsection (1)* is void.[8]

(3) A duplicate of a lease granted in accordance with *subsection (1)* shall be executed by the lessee and delivered to the lessor.[9]

(4) In the case of a lease by the mortgagor, the mortgagor shall, within one month after making the lease, deliver to the mortgagee or, where there are more than one, the mortgagee first in priority, a copy of the lease duly executed by the lessee.[10]

(5) Failure by the mortgagor to comply with *subsection (4)* does not affect the validity of the lease.[11]

(6)[12] Where a premium or other capital sum is paid by the lessee and the lease is granted by—

(*a*)   the mortgagor, it, or, where it exceeds the mortgage debt, so much of it as is required for the purpose, shall be applied in or towards discharge of that debt, whether or not the date for redemption has arrived,

(*b*)   the mortgagee, it shall be applied in accordance with *section 107* as if it comprised the proceeds of a sale.

Definitions

See s 3 for definitions of: "lease"; "lessee"; "lessor"; "mortgage"; "mortgagee"; "mortgagor"; "rent".

Notes

1   Section 113 re-enacts other provisions in s 18 of the 1881 Act relating to the terms which a lease granted under the statutory power (whether by the mortgagor or the mortgagee or receiver) must meet. However, it introduces a change recommended by the Commission to remove the previous "mixed message" whereby a failure to comply was not necessarily fatal: see Note 1 to s 112 and Note 8 below.

2   Paragraphs (*a*) and (*b*) recast the requirements in s 18 of the 1881 Act to make them accord more with modern commercial practice.

3   The need to obtain the best rent was also a requirement under the 1881 Act: see s 18(6) and *Coutts & Co v Somerville* [1935] Ch 438.

4   Section 18(6) of the 1881 Act spoke of a best rent without any fine being taken.

5   Such as concessions which are common in the commercial market nowadays.

6   This confirms the shift towards considerations the Commission thought appropriate.

7   This re-enacts a provision in s 18(8) of the 1881 Act and is another reason why, where a receiver grants the lease under the power given by s 112, it should be executed in the name of the mortgagee: see Note 15 to that section.

8   This makes it explicit that a failure to comply with the requirements of sub-s (1) is fatal: cf s 112(2) and Note 10 to that section. This gets rid of the ambiguity surrounding s 18 of the 1881 Act, partly caused by the provisions of other legislation like the Leases Act 1849 (repealed by Schedule 2: see the Note to that Schedule): see Notes 1, 2 and 6 above and Note 1 to s 112; *Re O'Rourke's Estate* (1889) 23 LR Ir 497; *ICC Bank plc v Verling* [1995] 1 ILRM 123; *Cussens v Brosnan* [2008] IEHC 119.

9   This re-enacts a provision in s 18(8) of the 1881 Act.

10   This re-enacts a provision in s 18(11) of the 1881 Act.

11   This provision was also in s 18(11) of the 1881 Act: see *Public Trustee v Lawrence* [1912] 1 Ch 789.

12   Subsection (6) was added to take account of the more commercial slant to sub-s (1) (see Notes 2–6 above), especially the possibility that a premium or other capital sum

might be paid by the tenant. Paragraphs (*a*) and (*b*) provide what is to happen to such a sum, depending on which party exercises the power to grant a lease.

[166]

Surrenders.[1]
[CA 1911,
s. 3]

114.—(1) Subject to *subsection (2)*, a mortgagor or mortgagee in possession (or after the mortgagee has appointed a receiver and so long as the receiver acts, the receiver) may accept a surrender of a lease previously granted under *section 112*[2] or as authorised by the terms of the mortgage,[3] whether the surrender relates to the whole or part only of the land leased.

(2) *Subsection (1)* applies only where the surrender of the previous lease is for the purpose of granting a new lease under *section 112* or as authorised by the terms of the mortgage.[4]

(3) On such a surrender[5]—

(*a*)   the term of the new lease shall not be less than the unexpired term which would have existed under the surrendered lease if it not been surrendered,

(*b*)   the rent reserved by the new lease shall not be less than the rent which would have been payable under the surrendered lease if it had not been surrendered,

(*c*)   where part only of the land has been surrendered—

(i)   the rent reserved by the new lease shall not be less than is required to make the aggregate rents payable under the remaining lease and new lease not less than the rent payable under the surrendered lease if no partial surrender had been accepted, and

(ii)   any other modifications of the original lease shall comply with *section 113*.[6]

(4) A purported acceptance of a surrender which fails to comply with *subsection (3)* is void.[7]

(5) Where a surrender involves payment of a premium or consideration other than the agreement to accept surrender, the surrender is void unless, in the case of a surrender—

(*a*)   to the mortgagor, the consent of incumbrancers, or

(*b*)   to a second or subsequent mortgagee, the consent of any prior incumbrancer,

is obtained.

Definitions

See s 3 for definitions of: "land"; "lease"; "lessee"; "lessor"; "mortgagee"; "mortgagor"; "rent".

Notes

1 Section 114 largely re-enacts the provisions of s 3 of the Conveyancing Act 1911, adjusted to the provisions of ss 112 and 113: see the Notes to those sections. It authorises surrender of a lease with a view to granting a new one: see *Robbins v Whyte* [1906] 1 KB 125.

2 See the Notes to that section.

3 This would seem to cover a surrender for a purpose other than granting a lease under s 112, but the new lease would still have to comply with s 113: see sub-s (3)(*c*)(ii) and Note 5 below.

4 The surrender must be confined to these purposes: see Note 5 below.

5 Paragraphs (*a*)–(*c*) are designed to ensure that the new lease does not contain adverse terms. These terms must be complied with: see sub-s (4) and Note 7 below.

6 See the Notes to that section.

7 This was also the position under the 1911 Act: see *Barclays Bank Ltd v Stasck* [1957] Ch 28.

8 This re-enacts a provision in s 3(4) of the 1911 Act.

PART 11[1]

JUDGMENT MORTGAGES[2]

Notes

1 Part 11 implements the Law Reform Commission's recommendation that the much criticised, and often confusing, provisions of the Judgment Mortgage (Ireland) Acts 1850 and 1858 should be replaced: see *Consultation Paper on Judgment Mortgages* (LRC CP 30–2004) affirmed by LRC CP 34–2004, ch 10. Apart from doubts concerning interpretation of the 1850 and 1858 Acts, there have long been difficulties over their operation and effect: see Lyall, *Land Law in Ireland* (2nd edn, Round Hall, 2000), pp 776–778; Wylie, *Irish Land Law* (3rd edn, Tottel Publishing, 1997), paras 13.163–13.182; Maddox, "The Law and Practice of Judgment Mortgages" (2006) Bar Review 189. The 1850 and 1858 Acts are repealed (see Schedule 2 and the Notes to it).

2 As originally drafted the Commission's Bill had a provision dealing with registration of a *lis pendens* (see s 113 of the Bill introduced to the Seanad), but during the Bill's passage the Government decided to insert a new Part into the Bill (see Part 12) to deal with a number of matters relating to that subject: see the Notes to Part 12. The original Bill also had a provision dealing with registration against company debtors (see s 121 of the Bill introduced to the Seanad) designed to implement changes to the Companies Act 1963, as recommended by the

Commission (see LRC CP 30–2004, paras 2.69–2.73), but it was later decided that this was not the appropriate place to amend companies legislation. That provision was deleted at the Seanad Committee Stage.

[167]

Interpretation of *Part 11*.[1]

[JMA 1858, ss. 3 and 4]

115.—In this Part, unless the context otherwise requires—

"creditor" includes—

(*a*) an authorised agent and any person authorised by the court to register a judgment mortgage on behalf of a judgment creditor,[2]

(*b*) one or some only of several creditors who have obtained the same judgment;[3]

"judgment" includes any decree or order of any court of record.[4]

Notes

1 Section 115 provides key definitions for the rest of the Part and re-enacts provisions in ss 3 and 4 of the Judgment Mortgages (Ireland) Act 1858.

2 This retains the existing law previously in the 1858 Act that a judgment mortgage can be registered by an agent or other person authorised by the court, eg holder of a power of attorney: see *McLoughlin v Strand Housing Ltd* (1952) 86 ILTR 167; see also *Lawless v Doake* (1883) 12 LR Ir 68.

3 This retains the rule that where several plaintiffs have obtained a judgment, one or more of them can register a judgment mortgage against the debtor's land: see *Re Kane* [1901] 1 IR 520; see also *Re Ryan* (1853) 3 Ir Ch R 37; *Re Gray's Estate* (1867) IR 1 Eq 265.

4 This retains the existing law, and includes the Circuit Court (see Circuit Court (Registration of Judgments) Act 1937) and District Court (see Courts Act 1981, ss 24 and 25). In fact no method of enforcing a District Court decree has been provided and a well-charging order should be sought in the Circuit Court: see Doyle, "A Fresh Look at the Judgment Mortgage (Ir) Act" (1989) 7 ILT 304.

[168]

Registration of judgment mortgages.[1]

[JMA 1850, s. 6]

116.—(1) A creditor who has obtained a judgment against a person may apply to the Property Registration Authority to register a judgment mortgage[2] against that person's estate or interest in land.[3]

(2) A judgment mortgage shall be registered in the Registry of Deeds or Land Registry, as appropriate.[4]

(3) For the avoidance of doubt[5] it is and always has been the case that—

   (*a*)   there is no requirement to re-register a judgment mortgage in order to maintain its validity or enforceability against the land or a purchaser of the land,[6]

   (*b*)   a judgment mortgage may be registered—

   (i)   notwithstanding that the judgment debtor has obtained an order of the court granting a stay of execution, unless the court orders otherwise,[7]

   (ii)   against the interest of a beneficiary under a trust for sale of land.[8]

Definitions

Apart from those in s 115, see s 3 for the definitions of: "land"; "Land Registry"; "Registry of Deeds"; "purchaser".

Notes

1   Section 116 implements the Law Reform Commission's recommendation that the complicated and confusing provisions relating to the formalities of registration of a judgment mortgage, particularly the requirements of the affidavit as set out in s 6 of the 1850 Act, should be replaced with a much simpler system: see LRC CP 30–2004, ch 4. The requirements of s 6 gave rise to much litigation, resulting in considerable judicial debate as to how far they had to be followed strictly: see a recent example in *Dovebid Netherlands BV v Phelan* [2007] IEHC 131; see also *Dardis and Dunns Seed Ltd v Hickey* (11 July 1974), HC; *Allied Irish Banks plc v Griffin* [1992] 2 IR 70; *Irish Bank of Commerce Ltd v O'Hara* (7 April 1992), SC; Doyle, "Merits Versus Technicalities: The Judgment Mortgage (Ireland) Acts" (1993) ILT 52; "Judgment Mortgages – A False Dawn" (1993) LS Gazette 297; de Londras, "The Technical Defence to a Judgment Mortgage: Time to say Goodbye?" (2008) 13(1) CPLJ 5. Section 116 also clarifies a number of points as recommended by the Commission: see Notes 5–8 below.

2   The Commission took the view that the complicated provisions of s 6 of the 1850 Act should be replaced by more simple requirements to be set out by statutory instrument especially as regards unregistered land: cf the Registration of Deeds Rules 2008 (SI 52/2008). See LRC CP 30–2004, paras 2.13–2.40 and 4.06–4.16.

3   This covers, as did s 6 of the 1850 Act, a wide range of both legal and equitable interests in land (see also Note 8 below): see *Murray v Diamond* [1982] ILRM 113; *Containercare (Ir) Ltd v Wycherley* [1982] IR 143. It has been held to apply to a jointure annuity (see *Re Blake* (1899) 33 ILTR 182); a share of one of a deceased's next-of-kin in leasehold property (see *Tevlin v Gilsenan* [1902] 1 IR 514; cf *Tench v Glennon* (1900) 34 ILTR 157 and *Re Carolan and Scott's Contract* [1899] 1 IR 1); a specific devise left by will (see *Kavanagh v Best* [1971] NI 89); the interest of the sole proving executor of a will (see *Munster & Leinster Bank Ltd v Fanning* [1932]

IR 671); a tenancy at will (see *Devlin v Kelly* (1886) 20 ILTR 76); land subject to a court order for sale (see *Re Scanlan's Trustees' Estate* [1897] 1 IR 462; *Re Swanton's Estate* [1898] 1 IR 157). It has even been held to apply to a judgment mortgage held by the debtor against another debtor's land, thereby creating a sub-judgment mortgage: see *Rossborough v McNeill* (1889) 23 LR Ir 409. It cannot, however, be registered against a sum of money or a legacy (even though charged on land: see *Woodhouse v Annesly* (1899) 33 ILTR 153; *Re Blake's Estate* [1895] 1 IR 468). The interest in question must be vested in the debtor at the time the judgment is entered, so that a judgment mortgage cannot capture any future or contingent interest: see *Re Rae's Estate* (1877) 1 LR Ir 174. It can, however, be registered against the vendor's retained legal interest under a contract for the sale of land and against the purchaser's beneficial interest: see *Coffey v Brunel Construction Co Ltd* [1983] IR 36; *Tempany v Hynes* [1976] IR 101; see also s 52 and the Notes to it.

4 See Registration of Deeds (No 2) Rules 2009 (SI 457/2009); Land Registration (No 2) Rules 2009 (SI 456/2009).

5 The Commission recommended clarification of these matters: see Notes 6–8 below.

6 It was common to misinterpret s 4 of the 1850 Act as requiring this, but its provisions applied to judgments only, *not* judgment *mortgages*: see *Holohan v Aughey* (28 July 2004), HC; LRC CP 30–2004, paras 2.05, 2.50 and 4.26.

7 The Commission recommended that this should be confirmed: see LRC CP 30–2004, para 4.21.

8 The Commission recommended that the doubt raised by English case law (see *Irani Finance Ltd v Singh* [1971] Ch 59) as to whether an equitable interest in land held under a trust *for sale* (which under the doctrine of conversion would be regarded as an interest in the proceeds of the sale) was an interest against which a judgment mortgage could be registered prior to the actual conversion taking place, should be resolved: see LRC CP 30–2004, paras 2.74–2.75.

---

[169]

Effect of registration.[1]
[JMA 1850, ss. 7 and 8]
[JMA 1850, s. 8]

117.—(1) Registration of a judgment mortgage under *section 116* operates to charge[2] the judgment debtor's estate or interest in the land with the judgment debt and entitles the judgment mortgagee to apply to the court for an order under this section[3] or *section 31*.[4]

(2) On such an application the court may make[5]—

(*a*) an order for the taking of an account of other incumbrances affecting the land, if any, and the making of inquiries as to the respective priorities of any such incumbrances,[6]

(*b*) an order for the sale of the land, and where appropriate, the distribution of the proceeds of sale,[7] (*c*)   such other order for enforcement of the judgment mortgage as the court thinks appropriate.[8]

(3) The judgment mortgage is subject to any right or incumbrance affecting the judgment debtor's land, whether registered or not, at the time of its registration.[9]

(4)[10] For the purposes of this section, a right or incumbrance does not include a claim made in an action to a judgment debtor's estate or interest in land (including such an estate or interest which a person receives, whether in whole or in part, by an order made in the action) whether by way of claim or counterclaim in the action, unless the claim seeks an order—

(*a*)   under the Act of 1976, the Act of 1995 or the Act of 1996,[11] or

(*b*)   specifically against that estate or interest in land.

(5)[12] *Section 74* applies to a voluntary conveyance of land made by the judgment debtor before the creditor registers a judgment mortgage against that land under *section 116* as if the creditor were a purchaser for the purposes of *section 74*.[13]

Definitions

Apart from those in s 115, see s 3 for definitions of: "Act of 1976"; "Act of 1995"; "Act of 1996"; "court"; "incumbrance"; "land"; "purchaser".

Notes

1   Section 117 largely re-enacts provisions in ss 7 and 8 of the 1850 Act, but adapts them to other provisions in the 2009 Act.

2   Notwithstanding the provisions of s 7 of the 1850 Act, which suggested that registration of a judgment mortgage automatically created a full mortgage over the debtor's land, in reality this was not really the position, given that the creditor could not be sure what interest the debtor had. Thus the courts have frequently emphasised that a judgment mortgage is essentially a "process of execution": see *Containercare (Ir) Ltd v Wycherley* [1982] IR 143; *Murray v Diamond* [1982] ILRM 113. The judgment creditor's remedies really only crystallise when a court order for enforcement is obtained: see sub-s (2) and the Notes to it. Thus it has been held that the mere registration of the judgment mortgage is not a "conveyance" within the Family Home Protection Act 1976: see the *Containercare* and *Murray* cases above. Nor is registration an "alienation" by the debtor: see *Fowler v Fowler* (1865) 16 Ir Ch R 507; *Re Moore's Estate* (1885) 17 LR Ir 549. It is, however, an alienation "by operation of law": see *Reidy v Pierce* (1861) 11 ICLR 361. It seems that the judgment mortgagee can insist on rent being paid to him or her instead of to the debtor's landlord: see *Collins v Thompson* (1863) 13 ICLR App i. A judgment mortgagee can also claim possession against a tenant debtor and maintain an ejectment action (see *Gowrie Park Utility Society Ltd v Fitzgerald* [1963] IR 436)

and claim restitution under s 71 of the Landlord and Tenant Law Amendment Act, Ireland, 1860 (Deasy's Act) (see *Caulfield v Walshe* (1868) IR 2 CL 492). Subsection (1) uses the expression "charge" here to emphasise the point that mere registration does not initially create a full mortgage conferring all the remedies a mortgagee has under Part 10; note also that the definition of "mortgage" in s 3 does not include a judgment mortgage: see Note 65 to that section. The original draft Bill (and the Bill introduced to the Seanad: see ss 3 and 122) did refer to a mortgage in line with s 8 of the 1850 Act. Those references were dropped at the Seanad Committee Stage.

3 Provision will be made for such applications by rules of court. The procedure hitherto has been to seek a "well-charging" order, declaring that land identified as being owned by the debtor is well charged, and an order for sale if the debt is not paid within a specified time: see *Credit Finance Ltd v Grace* (9 June 1972), SC; *Dardis and Dunns Seeds Ltd v Hickey* (11 July 1974), HC; *Irwin v Deasy* [2004] IEHC 104, [2006] IEHC 25.

4 Section 31 deals with the situation where the debtor is one of co-owners and, along with s 30(3), makes substantial changes to enforcement of judgment mortgages against such an owner: see Notes 13–17 to s 30 and Notes 4, 9 and 19 to s 31.

5 Cf the provisions of s 31(2): see Notes 9–10 to that section.

6 As regards priorities see sub-ss (3)–(5) below and the Notes to them.

7 This is the usual order accompanying a "well-charging" order: see *Bank of Ireland v Waldron* [1944] IR 303; *Bank of Ireland v Smith* [1966] IR 646; *Re O'Neill* [1967] NI 129.

8 It has long been settled that the court may appoint a receiver: see *Herbert v Greene* (1854) 3 Ir Ch R 270; *Tressillian v Caniffe* (1855) 4 IR Ch R 399; *Holland v Cork and Kinsale Rly Co* (1868) IR 4 Eq 417; *Re Martin's Estate* (1884) 13 LR Ir 43.

9 This confirms the position of a judgment mortgagee is *not* a "purchaser" but is a *mere volunteer*. Thus the judgment mortgage is subject to prior rights or incumbrances affecting the judgment debtor's interest in the land, whether or not they have been registered and whether or not the judgment mortgagee has notice of them: see *McAuley v Clarendon* (1858) 8 Ir Ch R 121; *Eyre v McDowell* (1861) 9 HLC 620; *Quinn v McCool* [1929] IR 620; *ACC Bank plc v Markham* [2005] IEHC 437. As regards registered land, this was governed by s 71(4) of the Registration of Title Act 1964: see also *Re Murphy and McCormack's Contract* [1930] IR 322; *Re Strong* [1940] IR 382; cf *Tempany v Hynes* [1976] IR 101; Wylie, *Irish Land Law* (3rd edn, Tottel Publishing, 1997), para 13.182; Wylie and Woods, *Irish Conveyancing Law* (3rd edn, Tottel Publishing, 2005), para 12.06. See now s 71(2)(c), substituted by s 130 of the 2009 Act: see the Note to that section.

10 Subsection (4) clarifies the law as suggested by Geoghegan J in *AS v GS and AIB* [1994] 1 IR 407 and adopted by the Law Reform Commission: see LRC CP 34–2004, paras 10.03–10.04. In essence this was that the prior "equities" or "rights" subject to which a judgment mortgagee (as a volunteer) should take should not include a claim lodged in court unless it specifically seeks an order against the debtor's land or involves a family home.

11 The Family Home Protection Act 1976, Family Law Act 1995 and Family Law (Divorce) Act 1996 give the courts a wide jurisdiction to make orders in respect of land.

12 Subsection (5) re-enacts the provision in s 8 of the 1850 Act but adapts it to the other provisions of the 2009 Act. It concerns any voluntary conveyance of the land made by the judgment debtor *after* the judgment has been obtained by the creditor but *before* the judgment mortgage is registered: see *Re St George's Estate* (1879) 3 LR Ir 277.

13 By applying s 74 (see the Notes to that section) the creditor (judgment mortgagee) may be able to "avoid" the conveyance by establishing that it was made with the intention of defrauding him or her: see Notes 2–7 to s 74; see also *McAuley v Clarendon* (1858) 8 Ir Ch R 568; *McQuillan v Maguire* [1996] 1 ILRM 394.

---

[170]

118.—Registration in the Registry of Deeds[2] of a certificate of satisfaction of a judgment[3] in respect of which a judgment mortgage has been registered extinguishes the judgment mortgage.[4]

Extinguish-ment of judg-ment mortgages.[1]
[JMA 1850, s. 9]

Definitions

Apart from those in s 115 see s 3 for definition of: "Registry of Deeds".

Notes

1 Section 118 re-enacts the provision in s 9 of the 1850 Act, as amended by s 5 of the 1858 Act, relating to "satisfaction" (discharge) of a judgment mortgage.

2 Section 118 applies to unregistered land only. Registered land is covered by s 65 of the Registration of Title Act 1964.

3 The certificate is issued by the court confirming that the judgment originally obtained has been paid off.

4 Registration of the certificate extinguishes the judgment mortgage: curiously the 1850 Act did not specify this but it was added by s 5 of the 1858 Act.

---

[171]

119.—Section 32 of the Act of 1957[2] is amended by the addition of the following subsection:

Amendment of section 32 of the Act of 1957.[1]

"(3) In the case of a judgment mortgage, the right of action accrues from the date the judgment becomes enforceable and not the date on which it is registered as a mortgage."[3]

Definitions

See s 3 for definition of: "Act of 1957".

Notes

1 Section 119 implements the Commission's recommendation that the date from which an action seeking a court sale to enforce a judgment mortgage accrues should be clarified: see LRC CP 30–2004, paras 2.51–2.52.

2 Section 32 of the Statute of Limitations 1957 specifies a limitation period of 12 years (30 years in the case of a State authority): see Brady and Kerr, *The Limitation of Actions* (2nd edn, Law Society of Ireland, 1994), pp 130–131.

3 That is the date the judgment is marked in favour of the creditor, not when it is later registered as a judgment mortgage.

[172]

PART 12[1]
LIS PENDENS[2]

Notes

1 Part 12 is a new Part, added to the Bill after it had been introduced, designed to update and streamline a number of provisions relating to registration of a *lis pendens* to be found in pre-1922 statutes. It was added at the Dáil Select Committee Stage.

2 The Judgments (Ireland) Act 1844 provided a system of registration of actions against a landowner, so as to warn purchasers who might take the land subject to whatever rights or liabilities might be declared subsequently in the action: see the discussion by Kenny J in *Giles v Brady* [1974] IR 462; see also *Dorene Ltd v Suedes Ltd* [1981] IR 312; *Coffey v Brunel Construction Co* [1983] IR 36; *Re Kelly's Carpetdrome* [1984] ILRM 418; *AS v GS and AIB* [1994] 1 IR 407; see also Wylie, *Irish Land Law* (3rd edn, Tottel Publishing, 1997), para 13.165.

[173]

Interpreta-
tion of *Part*
12.[1]
	120.—In this Part—
	    "manner" includes form;
	    "prescribed" means prescribed by rules of court;[2]
	    "register" means the register of *lis pendens* maintained under *section 121.*

Notes

1 Section 120 gives definitions specific to Part 12.

2 Cf the definition in s 3: see Note 72 to that section.

---

[174]

121.—(1) A register of *lis pendens* affecting land[2] shall be maintained in the prescribed manner in the Central Office of the High Court.

Register of *lis pendens*.[1] [JA 1844, s. 10]

(2) The following may be registered as a *lis pendens*:

    (*a*)   any action in the Circuit Court or the High Court in which a claim is made to an estate or interest in land (including such an estate or interest which a person receives, whether in whole or in part, by an order made in the action) whether by way of claim or counterclaim in the action;[3] and

    (*b*)   any proceedings to have a conveyance of an estate or interest in land declared void.[4]

(3) Such particulars as may be prescribed shall be entered in the register.[5]

(4) A *lis pendens* registered under section 10 of the Judgments (Ireland) Act 1844 which has not been vacated before the repeal of that section continues to have effect as if that section has not been repealed and such registration shall be deemed to form part of the register to be maintained under *subsection (1)*.[6]

Definitions

Apart from those in s 120 see s 3 for definitions of: "conveyance"; "land".

Notes

1   Section 121 re-enacts the substance of s 10 of the 1844 Act, which is repealed (see Schedule 2 and the Notes to that section).

2   The section is concerned only with actions affecting land, hence s 125: see the Notes to that section. To be a valid registration the person registering the *lis pendens* must already have an estate or interest in land or expect to acquire one on the successful outcome of the action: see *McCourt v Tiernan* [2005] IEHC 268; *ACC Bank Ltd v Markham* [2005] IEHC 437; *Dan Morrissey (Irl) Ltd v Morrissey* [2008] IEHC 50.

3   The landowner will be entitled to have the *lis pendens* vacated on showing that the action does not involve such a claim to an estate or interest in the land or, if the action is successful, would not result in obtaining such an estate or interest: see *Cunnane v Shannon Foynes Port Co* [2002] IESC 55.

4   For example, for rescission or setting aside a deed on the ground of fraud, duress, undue influence or other inequitable or unconscionable conduct: see Wylie and

Woods, *Irish Conveyancing Law* (3rd edn, Tottel Publishing, 2005), paras 21.34–21.35.

5   It has been held that there is no requirement to register a *lis pendens* as a burden on the folio relating to registered land and that a failure to do so does not render registration under s 121 ineffective: that registration is sufficient to fix a purchaser with notice: see *Dan Morrissey (Irl) Ltd v Morrissey* [2008] IEHC 50. The view was taken that opting to register it as a burden affecting registered land under s 69(1)(*i*) of the Registration of Title Act 1964 does not seem to secure additional protection. On the other hand, it is not clear how this view can be reconciled with s 52(1) of the 1964 Act, according to which a transfer of registered land is subject only to burdens registered as affecting the land or burdens which affect it without registration (which does not include a *lis pendens*) and is "free of all other rights": see *Lonergan v Hoban* [1896] 1 IR 401; McAllister, *Registration of Title in Ireland* (1973), pp 214–215; Fitzgerald, *Land Registry Practice* (2nd edn, Round Hall Press, 1995), para 12.13. The appropriate search for a purchaser's solicitor to make in respect of a *lis pendens* is a search in the register maintained by the Central Office of the High Court under s 121: see Wylie and Woods, *Irish Conveyancing Law* (3rd edn, Tottel Publishing, 2005), para 15.45.

6   This preserves the protection of a *lis pendens* already registered under s 10 of the 1844 Act and not vacated before 1 December 2009, when that section was repealed (see Schedule 2).

---

[175]

Cancellation of entry in register.[1]
[JRA 1871, s. 21]

122.—An entry of a *lis pendens* in the register shall be cancelled—

(*a*) with the consent, given in the prescribed manner, of the person on whose application it was registered, or

(*b*) upon the lodgement in the Central Office of the High Court of a notice, given in the prescribed manner, of an order under *section 123* vacating the *lis pendens*.[2]

Notes

1   Section 122 replaces s 21 of the Judgments Registry (Ireland) Act 1871.

2   Paragraph (*b*) confirms that the courts have always had jurisdiction to vacate a *lis pendens* in appropriate circumstances without waiting until the suit has been determined. The view of Kenny J to the contrary expressed in *Giles v Brady* [1974] IR 462 was rejected by the Supreme Court in *Flynn v Buckley* [1980] IR 423. See also *Culhane v Hewson* [1979] IR 8; *Dunville Investments Ltd v Kelly* (27 April 1979), HC; *Dan Morrissey (Irl) Ltd v Morrissey* [2008] IEHC 50.

[176]

123.—Subject to *section 124*, a court may make an order to vacate a *lis pendens* on application by—

(*a*)   the person on whose application it was registered, or

(*b*)   any person affected by it,[2] on notice to the person on whose application it was registered—

  (i)   where the action to which it relates has been discontinued or determined, or

  (ii)   where the court is satisfied that there has been an unreasonable delay in prosecuting the action or the action is not being prosecuted bona fide.[3]

Court order to vacate *lis pendens*.[1]
[LPA 1867, s. 2]

Notes

1   Section 123 updates s 2 of the Lis Pendens Act 1867. Kenny J had based his view of the limited jurisdiction to vacate a *lis pendens* on the basis that the 1867 Act did not apply to Ireland but other judges took a different view: see Note 2 to s 122.

2   In *Cunnane v Shannon Foynes Port Co* [2002] IESC 55, it was held that a person affected by a *lis pendens* can apply to have it vacated where the person who registered it had not claimed any interest in the land in question nor was any interest likely to result from the action.

3   See *Dan Morrissey (Irl) Ltd v Morrissey* [2008] IEHC 50.

[177]

124.—A court shall not under *section 123* vacate a *lis pendens*, registered under section 10 of the Judgments (Ireland) Act 1844 before the repeal of that section, on a ground other than one on which the *lis pendens* could have been vacated immediately before that repeal.[2]

Transitional.[1]

Notes

1   Section 124 preserves the pre-1 December 2009 position in relation to vacation of a *lis pendens* registered before that date.

2   This provision is necessary in so far as s 123 might be perceived as extending or clarifying previous doubts as to the scope of the courts' jurisdiction to vacate a *lis pendens*: see the Notes to s 123.

[178]

<table>
<tr>
<td>Protection of purchasers.[1]
[JMA 1850, s. 5]</td>
<td>125.—A lis pendens does not bind a purchaser of unregistered land[2] without actual knowledge[3] of it unless it has been registered in the Central Office of the High Court within 5 years[4] before the making of the conveyance to the purchaser.[5]</td>
</tr>
</table>

Definitions

Apart from those in s 120, see s 3 for definitions of: "conveyance"; "land"; "purchaser"; "unregistered land".

Notes

1   Section 125 re-enacts the substance of s 5 of the Judgment Mortgage (Ireland) Act 1850, which reinforced the primary purpose of s 10 of the Judgments (Ireland) Act 1844 of putting in place a registration system to warn purchasers of the existence of a prior claim being made against the land: see Note 2 to Part 12 and the Notes to s 121.

2   Section 5 of the 1850 Act, hardly surprising given its date, applied to unregistered land only. As regards registered land, the traditional view is that a *lis pendens* does not affect a purchaser unless registered as a burden under s 69(1)(*i*) or the Registration of Title Act 1964: see Note 5 to s 121.

3   Constructive notice is not enough to bind a purchaser: see s 86 and the Notes to it.

4   This means that in order to protect rights to which the *lis pendens* relates it must be re-registered every 5 years in the case of unregistered land. In the case of registered land, once a *lis pendens* is registered as a burden on the folio (see Note 2 above) that is a permanent warning to any purchaser unless and until it is vacated: see McAllister, *Registration of Title in Ireland* (1973), p 215.

5   A volunteer such as a judgment mortgagee does not get priority over a prior claim made in respect of the land, such as an application for a property adjustment order in family proceedings, even though the claimant has not registered a *lis pendens*: *ACC Bank plc v Markham* [2005] IEHC 437.

[179]

<table>
<tr>
<td>Amendment of Second Schedule to Courts and Court Officers Act 1995.[1]</td>
<td>126.—The Courts and Court Officers Act 1995 is amended, in the Second Schedule, in paragraph 1, by substituting the following for subparagraph (xxiv):

"(xxiv) An order under section 123 of the Land and Conveyancing Law Reform Act 2009.".</td>
</tr>
</table>

Notes

1   This is a consequential amendment necessary in view of the jurisdiction conferred by s 123.

[180]

PART 13[1]
AMENDMENTS TO REGISTRATION OF TITLE ACT 1964[2]

Notes

1   Part 13 contains various, substantial amendments to the Registration of Title Act 1964, which are consequential on the provisions of the 2009 Act.

2   Other, minor amendments to the 1964 Act are contained in Schedule 1: see the Notes to that Schedule. Note also various repeals set out in Schedule 2, Part 5: see the Notes to that Schedule.

[181]

127.—Section 3 (interpretation) of the Act of 1964 is amended in subsection (1)—   **Amendment of section 3.**[1]

   (*a*)   by the insertion of the following definitions:

   "'instrument' has the meaning given to it by *section 3* of the *Land and Conveyancing Law Reform Act 2009*;[2]

   'owner' includes full owner;",[3]

   (*b*)   by the substitution of " 'freehold land' means land the ownership of which is an estate in fee simple in possession;" for the definition of "freehold land",[4]

   (*c*)   by the substitution of " 'judgment mortgage' means a mortgage registered by a judgment creditor pursuant to *section 116* of the *Land and Conveyancing Law Reform Act 2009*;" for the definition of "judgment mortgage".[5]

   (*d*)   by the substitution of " 'land' has the meaning given to it by *section 3* of the *Land and Conveyancing Law Reform Act 2009*;" for the definition of "land",[6]

   (*e*)   by the substitution of "estate" for "interest" where it first occurs in the definition of "leasehold interest",[7] and

   (*f*)   by the deletion of the definitions of "Bankruptcy Acts", "Registry of Deeds",[8] "Settled Land Acts", "settlement", "settled land", "tenant for life" and "trustees of the settlement".[9]

315

Notes

1   Section 127 adjusts the "interpretation" section in the 1964 Act (s 3) to the definitions in s 3 of the 2009 Act.

2   See Notes 37–39 to s 3 of the 2009 Act.

3   This is linked with paragraph (*b*): see Note 4 below. This is to adjust the 1964 Act to the new meaning of ownership given by Part 2 of the 2009 Act. Amendments to the 1964 Act in Schedule 1 to the 2009 Act delete the references in the 1964 Act to "full or limited". Under Part 4 of the 2009 Act a limited owner like a tenant for life no longer has a legal estate capable of registration; instead the legal ownership (the fee simple in possession) is vested in trustees and they are registered as the owners of the land: see the Notes to Part 4.

4   This too is linked to the provisions relating to ownership in Part 2 of the 2009 Act: see Note 3 above. See especially s 11 and the Notes to it.

5   This is consequential upon the substitution of the Judgment Mortgage (Ireland) Acts 1850 and 1858 by Part 11 of the 2009 Act: see the Notes to that Part.

6   This adopts the new, wide-ranging definition in s 3 of the 2009 Act: see Notes 41–56 to that section.

7   This adjusts the 1964 Act to the provisions of s 11(3) of the 2009 Act: see Notes 16–29 to that section.

8   This is now defined by s 33 of the Registration of Deeds and Title Act 2006.

9   These became redundant because of the replacement of the Settled Land Acts 1882–1890 by the provisions of Part 4 of the 2009 Act: see the Notes to that Part.

[182]

Substitution of section 25[1]   **128.**—The following section is substituted for section 25 (effect of failure to register where registration compulsory) of the Act of 1964:

> "25.—A person shall not acquire an estate or interest in land in any case in which registration of ownership of the land is or becomes compulsory under section 23 or 24 unless the person is registered as owner of the estate or interest within 6 months after the purported acquisition or at such later time as the Authority (or, in case of refusal, the court) may sanction in any particular case, but on any such registration the person's title shall relate back to the date of the purported acquisition, and any dealings with the land before the registration shall have effect accordingly.".

Note

1   Section 25 of the 1964 Act deals with the consequences of failure to comply with the compulsory registration requirements of ss 23 and 24. Section 25 was substituted by s 54 of the Registration of Deeds and Title Act 2006, but, by mistake, it referred only to s 24. This new substitution corrects that oversight.

[183]

129.—Section 69 (burdens which may be registered as affecting registered land) of the Act of 1964 is amended by the insertion in subsection (1) of the following paragraph after paragraph (*k*):

Amendment of section 69.[1]

> "(*kk*) a freehold covenant within the meaning of *section 48* of the *Land and Conveyancing Law Reform Act 2009*;".

Note

1   Section 129 is consequential on the new provisions relating to freehold covenants in s 49, which enhance their status: see the Notes to s 49. They now become burdens which may be registered as affecting registered land, like easements and profits created by express grant.

[184]

130.—The following section is substituted for section 71 (registration of judgment mortgages) of the Act of 1964:

Amendment of section 71.[1]

> "**71.**—(1) Application for registration of a judgment mortgage under *section 116* of the *Land and Conveyancing Law Reform Act 2009* shall, in the case of registered land, be in such form and in such manner as may be prescribed.
>
> (2) Registration under *subsection (1)* shall operate to charge the estate or interest of the judgment debtor subject to—
>
> (*a*) the burdens, if any, registered as affecting that estate or interest,
>
> (*b*) the burdens to which, though not so registered, that estate or interest is subject by virtue of section 72,

(*c*) all unregistered rights subject to which the judgment debtor held that estate or interest at the time of registration,

and with the effect stated in *section 117* of the said *2009 Act*.".

Note

1 This adjusts s 71 of the 1964 Act to the fact that the provisions of Part 11 replace the provisions of the Judgment Mortgage (Ireland) Acts 1850 and 1858: see the Notes to that Part.

---

[185]

PART 14[1]
MISCELLANEOUS[2]

Notes

1 The only provision of this Part which was in the original Bill (and as introduced to the Seanad) was s 133. That was amended during its passage.

2 At the final Dáil Report Stage the Minister for Justice, Equality and Law Reform introduced a provision to ban upwards-only rent reviews (see s 132). Previously the Master of the High Court had called into question the appropriateness of such clauses in the current state of the property market (in a decision on an application for appointment of an arbitrator, *Kidney v Charlton* (22 January 2009), HC). There was a campaign to ban such clauses by retail tenants who claimed that such clauses forced them to continue paying rent well above the going market rate. A dispute over the refusal by the landlord to reduce the rent of a small shop on Grafton Street, Dublin brought the controversy to a head. The Minister was responding to this. However, the introduction of s 132 proved to be equally controversial: see, eg, the articles in the *Irish Times*, 1 July 2009, Commercial Property Section (p 21). What increased this controversy was the continuing crisis in the economy generally and debts accruing to Irish banks largely caused by exposure to the property market. The development of the National Asset Management Agency (NAMA) concept meant that the Irish taxpayer had a direct interest in the value of properties used as security for loans made by the banks. It is not surprising, therefore, that s 132, unlike the rest of the Act, was not commenced on 1 December 2009 but on that date the Minister announced that s 132 will come into operation on 28 February 2010.

---

[186]

131.—In this Part, "business"[2] and "lease"[3] have the same meanings as they have in the Landlord and Tenant (Amendment) Act 1980.

Interpretation (Part 14).[1]

Notes

1   Section 131 provides special definitions for the purposes of Part 14. Note that these also govern s 133.
2   This is defined in s 3(1) of the Landlord and Tenant (Amendment) Act 1980. Note that is a very wide-ranging definition and includes activities of a non-profit-making nature, including the operation of government departments, local authorities and various bodies carrying on educational, social, sporting, cultural and charitable services: see Wylie, *Landlord and Tenant Law* (2nd edn, Tottel Publishing, 1998), para 30.15.
3   This is also defined in s 3(1) of the 1980 Act. Cf the definition in s 3 of the 2009 Act: see Note 59 to that section.

[187]

132.—(1) This section applies to a lease of land to be used wholly or partly[2] for the purpose of carrying on a business.[3]

Review of rent in certain cases.[1]

(2) *Subsection (1)* shall not apply where—

   (*a*)   the lease concerned, or

   (*b*)   an agreement for such a lease,

is entered into prior to the commencement of this section.[4]

(3) A provision in a lease to which this section applies[5] which provides for the review of the rent payable under the lease[6] shall be construed[7] as providing that the rent payable following such review may be fixed at an amount which is less than, greater than or the same as the amount of rent payable immediately prior to the date on which the rent falls to be reviewed.[8]

(4) *Subsection (3)* shall apply—

   (*a*)   notwithstanding any provision to the contrary contained in the lease or in any agreement for the lease,[9] and

   (*b*)   only as respects that part of the land demised by the lease in which business is permitted to be carried on under the terms of the lease.[10]

Definitions

Apart from those in s 131, see s 3 for definitions of: "land"; "rent".

Notes

1   As explained earlier (see Note 2 to Part 14 above), this provision was a "last-minute" addition to the Bill introduced by the Minister for Justice, Equality and Law Reform at the Dáil Report Stage. It is designed to ban "upwards-only" rent review clauses in "business" leases: on such clauses see Wylie, *Landlord and Tenant Law* (2nd edn, Tottel Publishing, 1998), para 11.25.

2   The provision applies, therefore, to a lease of mixed premises, such as a shop with living accommodation upstairs.

3   Note the very wide meaning of business: see Note 2 to s 131.

4   The section, when it comes into force on 28 February 2010 (see Note 2 to Part 14 above), will operate prospectively only. It will not apply to existing leases or to reviews to be carried out under such leases after the commencement date. It is not clear what the position would be with respect to an extension after the commencement date of a pre-commencement lease or a renewal of such a lease. Under s 27 of the Landlord and Tenant (Amendment) Act 1980, where a tenancy is "continued or renewed" or a new tenancy is created under that Act, the tenancy is (or deemed to be) "for all purposes" a "continuation of the tenancy previously existing" and is deemed "for all purposes" a "graft" on the previous tenancy. Furthermore the tenant is subject to "any rights or equities arising from its being such a graft". The view may be taken, therefore, that any post-commencement extension of or new tenancy granted in respect of a pre-commencement lease will not be caught by s 132.

5   That is a lease for business purposes.

6   This wording suggests that there must be a mechanism for review which has to be operated, whether by negotiation between the parties or use of an arbitrator or expert to resolve a dispute. It may not apply where the "review" of the rent is "preordained", eg where the lease simply provides that the rent will increase at specified intervals by a fixed rate or percentage or according to a nominated index which involves a purely mathematical calculation with no room for negotiation or variation.

7   This reinforces the point made in Note 6. The section operates by putting a statutory construction on a rent review provision in a business lease. The wording of the rest of sub-s (3) suggests that the provision must be one which contemplates the passing rent being "reviewed" and, then, construes it as meaning that the result of the review can be that the rent may go down as well as up (or stay the same). This seems to assume that the rent review provision provides both a mechanism for assessing the reviewed rent and states the basis upon which that assessment may be made (eg the usual open market rent taking into account various assumptions and disregards: see Wylie, *Landlord and Tenant Law* (2nd edn, Tottel Publishing, 1998), paras 11.17–11.43). However, if the provision in the lease does not do this and simply preordains increases at fixed rates or percentages or according to an index, so that there is no reference to the market rent at the time of the "review", it is difficult to see on what basis the rent could be fixed at a lower amount than the passing rent. Subsection (3) makes no such reference and provides no other basis for calculating a lower rent.

8   Subsection (3) would seem to operate only where a review is actually carried out. Often the review provision will provide that the landlord only can initiate a review.

It may be that s 132 will not protect a tenant if the landlord, bearing in mind the state of the market at the time for review, simply decides not to initiate a review (leases invariably provide that the passing rent continues to be payable until a review is completed: see Wylie, *Landlord and Tenant Law* (2nd edn, Tottel Publishing, 1998), paras 11.45–11.46). There is authority in England (there is no Irish authority) that, while a tenant (who has no right to initiate a review) may call upon the landlord to initiate the review, the consequence of the landlord failing to respond is simply loss of the right to a review: see *London & Manchester Assurance Co Ltd v GA Dunn & Co* [1983] 1 EGLR 111; *Amhurst v James Walker Goldsmith & Silversmith Ltd* [1983] Ch 305. The rent review provision confers a "right", which the holder is free to choose not to exercise, not an "obligation" which must be exercised.

9 It will not be possible, therefore, to contract out of s 132.

10 This confines the "overriding" provision in sub-s (3) to the business part of mixed premises held under the same lease. If there is a single rent relating to the entire mixed premises (eg a shop with living accommodation upstairs) and the upwards-only rent review provision relates to that single rent, it is not clear why the tenant only gets protection in respect of the shop. The living accommodation may be a vital part of the operation. Apart from that it is not clear how the section will apply in such a case. There is no provision for apportionment of rent as between the business and other parts and the lease will make no provision where there is a single rent.

---

[188]

133.—The power of the sheriff, or of other persons entitled to exercise the sheriff's powers,[2] to seize a tenancy[3] under a writ of *fieri facias*[4] or other process of execution[5] is abolished except in relation to a tenancy of land that is used wholly or partly for the purpose of carrying on a business.[6]

Abolition of power to seize a tenancy.[1]

Definitions

Apart from those in s 131, see s 3 for definitions of: "land"; "tenancy".

Notes

1 Section 133 implements partially the Law Reform Commission's recommendation that the power of the sheriff to seize leasehold land should be abolished: see LRC CP 34–2004, paras 10.05–10.06. The Commission had previously reviewed this method of enforcing debts and had concluded that it was rarely used and, when used, was not very effective: see *Report on Debt Collection: (1) The Law Relating to Sheriffs* (LRC 27–1988). The view was taken that it was better to rely on other methods, such as a judgment mortgage (see Part 11 and the Notes to that Part). The continuance of this method of enforcing debts meant that purchasers of leasehold land had to make searches in the Sheriff's Office: see Wylie and Woods, *Irish Conveyancing Law* (3rd edn, Tottel Publishing, 2005), para 15.46. The Commission recommended abolishing it and its draft Bill (and the Bill introduced to the Seanad) did so (see

s 119 of that Bill). However, it later emerged that the threat to use the power was often an effective method of enforcing debts owed to the Revenue Commissioners in respect of commercial leasehold premises: see Macauley and McCann, "Methods of Enforcement of Revenue Debts" (1991) Ir Tax Rev 448. Furthermore, where exercised in such cases, it was used not necessarily with a view to selling the lease but rather to occupy and use the premises to sell the tenant's stock, instead of having to remove it elsewhere for a "salvage" sale. So the Government decided to confine the abolition to non-business leasehold premises. This change was made at the Dáil Select Committee Stage.

2   Outside Dublin and Cork the powers of a sheriff reside in the County Registrars: see LRC 27–1988, paras 18–24.

3   The Commission concluded that the power of seizure was probably confined to leasehold property: see LRC 27–1988, paras 54–57.

4   A "*fi fa*" order is made by the High Court and requires the sheriff to execute a judgment order and make a return to the Court as to the manner in which it has been executed: Rules of the Superior Courts, Ord 42, r 17 and Ord 43, r 1 (and see the forms in Appendix F, Part II, Nos 1–3).

5   In the case of the Circuit Court the equivalent of a *fi fa* order is an execution order: see Circuit Court Rules 2001 (SI 510/2001), Ord 36, r 1 (and see Form 20 in the Schedule of Forms).

6   The abolition and consequential removal of the need to make Sheriff's Office searches (see Note 1 above) is confined to exclusively non-business leasehold premises. The sheriff's power of seizure remains in respect of business and mixed premises.

[189]

SCHEDULE 1[1]

AMENDMENTS[2]

Notes

1   Schedule 1 lists the various consequential amendments to other statutes specified by s 8(1). It should be noted that other general amendments to statutes which referred to the principal pre-1922 statutes replaced by the 2009 Act, the Settled Land Acts 1882–1890 and the Conveyancing Acts 1881–1911, are made by s 8(2): see Notes 2–3 to that section. Apart from that Part 13 contains various amendments to the Registration of Title Act 1964 (see the Notes to that Part) and other sections contain amendments to specific statutes: see, eg, ss 99(2) (and Note 10 to that section), 119 (and the Notes to that section) and 126 (and Note 1 to that section).

2   The various consequential amendments to the other statutes listed below fall into four categories:

   (i)   Substituting in such statutes references to the relevant provisions in the 2009 Act for those referring to statutes repealed by the Act, such as the Judgment Mortgage (Ireland) Acts 1850 and 1858 (see Part 11 and the Notes to it), Partition Acts 1868 and 1876 (see Part 7 and the Notes to it) and Vendor and Purchaser Act 1874 (see Part 9 and the Notes to it).

   (ii)   Deleting references in other statutes to concepts replaced by the 2009 Act, such as—

      (a)   settlements of land, powers of a tenant for life and a minor holding a legal estate, all of which are replaced by the trusts of land provisions of Part 4 (ses the Notes to that Part);

      (b)   mortgages by conveyance or demise and foreclosure, which are replaced by the provisions of Part 10 (see the Notes to that Part).

   (iii)   Making minor amendments to the Registration of Title Act 1964 (in addition to those made by Part 13: see the Notes to that Part), largely to reflect the changes referred to in category (ii)(a) above. [The one exception to this is the substantial change to the wording of ss 62(2) and 64(2) of the 1964 Act: see Note 13 to s 89.]

   (iv)   Adding references to new concepts created by the 2009 Act, such as a works order under Part 8, Chapter 3 (see the Notes to that Chapter).

---

[190]

Section 8(1).

Enactment (1)	Provision (2)	Nature of amendment (3)
Trustee Act 1893	Section 15	The substitution of *"sections 57 and 58 of the Land and Conveyancing Law Reform Act 2009"* for "section two of the Vendor and Purchaser Act, 1874".
Housing (Gaeltacht) Act 1929	Section 9	In subsection (2)— (a) the substitution of "legal mortgage under *Part 10* of the *Land and Conveyancing Law Reform Act 2009*" for "mortgage made by deed within the meaning of the Conveyancing Acts, 1881 to 1911", (b) the substitution of "that Act" for "those Acts" in both places where it occurs.
Minerals Development Act 1940	Section 52	In subsections (1) and (2), the deletion of the words "as tenant for life or person having the powers of a tenant for life under a settlement or".
Harbours Act 1946	Section 169	In subsection (5), the deletion of— (a) "or by reason of his being an infant", (b)"for his life, or".
Statute of Limitations 1957	Section 2	In subsection (1), the substitution of " 'judgment mortgage' means a mortgage registered by a judgment creditor under *section 116* of the *Land and Conveyancing Law Reform Act 2009;*" for the definition of "judgment mortgage".
	Section 25	In subsection (4), the deletion of "any settled land, within the meaning of the Settled Land Acts, 1882 to 1890, or".

Enactment (1)	*Provision* (2)	*Nature of amendment* (3)
Charities Act 1961	Section 34	In subsection (4), the deletion of ", or the redemption and reconveyance of land which is subject to the mortgage or charge".
	Section 37	In subsection (1)—
		(a) in paragraph (*h*), the substitution of "land," for "land.",
		(b) the insertion of the following paragraph after paragraph (*h*):
		"(*i*) the making of an application for a works order under *section 45* of the *Land and Conveyancing Law Reform Act 2009*.".
Courts (Supplemental Provisions) Act 1961	Third Schedule	In column (2) at reference number 19, the insertion of the following after paragraph (c):
		"(d) applications under *sections 94, 97* (except where the property concerned is subject to a housing loan mortgage), *100* (except where the property concerned is subject to a housing loan mortgage) and *117* of the *Land and Conveyancing Law Reform Act 2009*".
		In column (2) at reference number 22, the insertion of "and under *section 55* of the *Land and Conveyancing Law Reform Act 2009*" after "Proceedings for specific performance of contracts".
		In column (2) at reference number 23, the substitution of "Proceedings under *sections 31, 35, 50, 68,* and *84* of the *Land and Conveyancing Law Reform Act 2009*" for "Proceedings for the partition or sale of land".
		In column (2) at reference number 26, the insertion of "*Parts 4* and *5* of the *Land and Conveyancing Law Reform Act 2009* and" after "Proceedings under".

Enactment (1)	Provision (2)	Nature of amendment (3)
Companies Act 1963	Section 231	In subsection (2)(*a*), the deletion of— (a)"fee farm grant, sub fee farm grant,", (b)"any rent reserved on any such grant or".
Registration of Title Act 1964	Section 24	In subsection (1), the substitution of "on and after" for "on or after".
	Section 37	In subsection (3), the deletion of "In either case,".
	Section 38	In subsection (1), the deletion of "full or limited".
	Section 39	The deletion of "full or limited".
	Section 44	In subsection (3), the deletion of "In either case,".
	Section 45	The deletion of "full or limited".
	Section 46	The deletion of "full or limited".
	Section 47	The deletion of "full or limited".
	Section 51	In subsection (1), the substitution of "A" for "Subject, in the case of a limited owner, to the Settled Land Acts, a". In subsection (2), the deletion of "or in such other form as may appear to the Authority to be sufficient to convey the land,".
	Section 60	In subsection (2), the deletion of— (*a*) "if he is full owner," in each place where it occurs, (*b*) "and if he is not full owner, of such persons as may be prescribed", and (*c*) ", and, if he is not full owner, to such persons as may be prescribed".

Enactment (1)	Provision (2)	Nature of amendment (3)
	Section 61	In subsection (3)(a), the deletion of— (*a*) "full or limited", (*b*) ", as the case may be". In subsection (4), the deletion of "full owner or limited".
	Section 62	In subsection (2), the deletion of "(or an instrument in such other form as may appear to the Authority to be sufficient to charge the land, provided that such instrument shall expressly charge or reserve out of the land the payment of the money secured)". In subsection (6), the substitution of— (*a*) "legal mortgage under *Part 10* of the *Land and Conveyancing Law Reform Act 2009*" for "mortgage by deed within the meaning of the Conveyancing Acts", (*b*) "under such a mortgage" for "under a mortgage by deed".
	Section 64	In subsection (2), the deletion of "or in such other form as may appear to the Authority to be sufficient to transfer the charge,".
	Section 100	In subsection (1), the substitution of "any" for "the person who ought to be registered under this Act, or as to any other". In subsection (2), the deletion of "(including a limited owner exercising powers under the Settled Land Acts or this Act)".
	Section 103	In subsection (4), the deletion of "or, in the case of settled land, as assignees of the registered owner".
	Section 123	In subsection (6), the substitution of "instruments" for "those".

Enactment (1)	Provision (2)	Nature of amendment (3)
Succession Act 1965	Section 60	In subsection (1)— (*a*) in paragraph (*c*), the substitution of "a sub-lease of the land" for "a sub fee farm grant of the land, or a sub-lease thereof", (*b*) in paragraph (*c*), the deletion of "sub fee farm grant or", (*c*) the deletion of "grant or", (*d*) the deletion of "any rent reserved on such grant or".
Housing Act 1966	Section 71	In subsection (4)— (*a*) the substitution of "legal mortgage under *Part 10* of the *Land and Conveyancing Law Reform Act 2009*" for "mortgage made by deed within the meaning of the Conveyancing Acts, 1881 to 1911", (*b*) the substitution of "that Act" for "those Acts" in both places where it occurs.
Charities Act 1973	Section 4	In subsection (3), the deletion of "or the redemption and reconveyance of land which is subject to the mortgage or charge".
Bankruptcy Act 1988	Section 50	In subsection (1), the deletion of "or a leasehold interest in land".
	Section 51	The substitution of the following for subsection (1): "(1) A judgment creditor who registers a judgment mortgage under *section 116* of the *Land and Conveyancing Law Reform Act 2009* shall not, by reason of such registration, be entitled to any priority or preference over simple contract creditors in the event of the person against whom such judgment mortgage is registered being adjudicated bankrupt, unless the judgment mortgage is registered at least three months before the date of the adjudication.".

Enactment (1)	Provision (2)	Nature of amendment (3)
	Section 61	In subsection (3)(*a*)— (*a*) the deletion of "fee farm grant, sub fee farm grant,", (*b*) the deletion of "any rent reserved on any such grant or".
	Section 87	In subsection (4), the substitution of "a judgment mortgage under *section 116* of the *Land and Conveyancing Law Reform Act 2009*" for "an affidavit of a judgment mortgage under the Judgment Mortgage (Ireland) Act 1850". In subsection (5), the substitution of "judgment mortgage" for "affidavit".
Trustee Savings Bank Act 1989	Section 23	The substitution of the following for subsection (5): "(5) Where a Trustee Savings Bank is a creditor under a judgment within the meaning of *section 115* of the *Land and Conveyancing Law Reform Act 2006*, a judgment mortgage may be registered under section 116 of that Act by the secretary or other officer or the law agent of the bank duly authorised in that behalf by the bank.".
Housing (Miscellaneous Provisions) Act 1992	Section 5	In subsection (6)— (*a*) the substitution of "legal mortgage under *Part 10* of the *Land and Conveyancing Law Reform Act 2006*" for "mortgage by deed within the meaning of the Conveyancing Acts, 1881 to 1911", (*b*) the substitution of "that Act" for "those Acts" in both places where it occurs.

Enactment (1)	Provision (2)	Nature of amendment (3)
Family Law Act 1995	Section 10	In subsection (1)(*e*), the substitution of "under *section 31* of the *Land and Conveyancing Law Reform Act 2009*" for "for the partition of property or under the Partition Act, 1868, and the Partition Act, 1876".
Powers of Attorney Act 1996	Section 16	In subsection (2), the deletion of "or as a tenant for life within the meaning of the Settled Land Act, 1882, or as a trustee or other person exercising the power of a tenant for life under section 60 of that Act".
Family Law (Divorce) Act 1996	Section 15	In subsection (1)(*e*), the substitution of "under *section 31* of the *Land and Conveyancing Law Reform Act 2009*" for "for the partition of property or under the Partition Act, 1868, and the Partition Act, 1876".
Taxes Consolidation Act 1997	Section 574	In subsection (3), the deletion of "(and in particular where settled land within the meaning of the Settled Land Act, 1882, is vested in the tenant for life and investments representing capital money are vested in the trustees of the settlement)".
	Section 964	In subsection (1), the substitution of the following for paragraph (c): "(c) Any judgment mortgage to be registered by a Collector-General under *section 116* of the *Land and Conveyancing Law Reform Act 2009* may be registered by a successor."
Stamp Duties Consolidation Act 1999	Section 1	In subsection (1), in the definition of "conveyance on sale", the deletion of "(including a decree or order for, or having the effect of, an order for foreclosure)".

Enactment (1)	Provision (2)	Nature of amendment (3)
Planning and Development Act 2000	Section 99	In subsection (3A)(*c*), the substitution of "legal mortgage under *Part 10* of the *Land and Conveyancing Law Reform Act 2009*" for "mortgage made by deed within the meaning of the Conveyancing Acts 1881 to 1911".
Housing (Miscellaneous Provisions) Act 2002	Section 9	In subsection (3A)(*c*), the substitution of "legal mortgage under *Part 10* of the *Land and Conveyancing Law Reform Act 2009*" for "mortgage made by deed within the meaning of the Conveyancing Acts 1881 to 1911".
Capital Acquisitions Tax Consolidation Act 2003	Section 2	In subsection (1), in the definition of "general power of appointment", the deletion of "or exercisable by a tenant for life under the Settled Land Act 1882,".
Registration of Deeds and Title Act 2006	Section 11	In subsection (6), the insertion of "and are eligible for reappointment" after "appointment".
	Section 12	In subsection (3), the deletion of "for one further term".
	Section 32	In subsection (1), the substitution of— (*a*) "(*g*) an application to register a judgment mortgage under *section 116* of the *Land and Conveyancing Law Reform Act 2009*;" for paragraph (*g*) of the definition of "deed", (*b*) " 'land' has the meaning given to it by *section 3* of the *Land and Conveyancing Law Reform Act 2009*;" for the definition of "land".
	Section 55	The insertion of "of the Act of 1964" after "registration)".

[191]

SCHEDULE 2[1]
REPEALS[2]

Notes

1 Schedule 2 contains a long list of statutes, particularly pre-1922 statutes, which are repealed in whole or in part. This implements one of the primary objectives of the Act, as explained in the Introduction, see paras 14–15.

2 The repeals fall into a number of categories (for further detail see the Law Commission's LRC CP 34–2004):

(i) Ancient statutes whose provisions had become obsolete or are replaced by more modern provisions in the 2009 Act. Examples are: *De Donis Conditionalibus* 1285; *Quia Emptores* 1290; Statute of Uses 1634; Conveyancing Act 1634; Tenures Abolition Act 1662; Statute of Frauds 1695 (parts of s 2 only): see LRC CP 34–2004, paras 2.08 and 2.30.

(ii) Numerous early statutes conferring powers of dealing with settled land and the Settled Land Acts 1882–1890, whose provisions are replaced by Part 4 of the 2009 Act: see LRC CP 34–2004, paras 4.04, 4.08, 4.10 and 4.27.

(iii) The Conveyancing Acts 1881–1911 (except provisions dealing with leases) and other 19th century statutes dealing with conveyancing matters whose provisions are covered by Parts 9 and 10 of the Act, such as: Real Property Act 1845; Law of Property Amendment Acts 1859 and 1860; Vendor and Purchaser Act 1874.

(iv) Other 19th century statutes dealing with various aspects of land law now covered by the 2009 Act, such as: Illusory Appointments Act 1830 and Powers of Appointment Act 1874; Prescription Acts 1832 and 1858; Fines and Recoveries Acts 1833 and 1834; Satisfied Terms Act 1845; Leases Act 1849; Renewable Leasehold Conversion Acts 1849 and 1868; Judgment Mortgage Acts 1850 and 1858; Fee-Farm Rents Act 1851; Chief Rents (Redemption) Act 1864; Lis Pendens Act 1867; Sales of Reversions Act 1867; Partition Acts 1868 and 1876; Contingent Remainders Act 1877; Accumulations Act 1892; Voluntary Conveyances Act 1893: see LRC CP 34–2004, paras 2.37, 3.05, 5.05, 6.12 and 7.19.

(v) Numerous statutes dealing with former Crown land which had become obsolete especially since State land became subject to the State Property Act 1954: see LRC CP 34–2004, para 2.08.

(vi) Numerous statutes dealing with copyhold tenure which ceased to be relevant to Ireland by the latter half of the 19th century: see LRC CP 34–2004, para 2.08.

(vii) Numerous statutes relating to land drainage and other improvements to land which became obsolete with the enactment of more modern legislation such as the Arterial Drainage Acts 1945 and 1955: see LRC CP 34–2004, paras 13.12–13.13.

(viii) Various statutes dealing with tithes and tithe rentcharges long since no longer collected: see LRC CP 34–2004, para 7.06.

In addition Part 5 of Schedule 2 contains various repeals of provisions in post-1922 Acts of the Oireachtas rendered redundant by the 2009 Act, eg, because they refer to concepts abolished or replaced by the Act like settled land and related matters such as powers of a tenant for life.

Section 8(3)

PART 1
PRE-UNION IRISH STATUTES

Session and Chapter (1)	Short Title (2)	Extent of Repeal (3)
10 Chas. 1 sess. 2 c. 1	Statute of Uses 1634	The whole Act so far as unrepealed
10 Chas. 1 sess. 2 c. 3	Conveyancing Act 1634	The whole Act so far as unrepealed
10 Chas. 1 sess. 3 c. 15	Maintenance and Embracery Act 1634	Sections 2, 4 and 6
10 & 11 Chas. 1 c. 3	Ecclesiastical Lands Act 1634	The whole Act so far as unrepealed
15 Chas. 1 c. 3	Forfeiture Act 1639	The whole Act
14 & 15 Chas. 2 sess. 4 c. 19	Tenures Abolition Act 1662	The whole Act so far as unrepealed
7 Will. 3 c. 8	Life Estates Act 1695	The whole Act
7 Will. 3 c. 12	Statute of Frauds 1695	In section 2, the words "or upon any contract or sale of lands, tenements, or hereditaments, or any interest in or concerning them,".
9 Will. 3 c. 11	Clandestine Mortgages Act 1697	The whole Act
2 Anne c. 8	Plus Lands Act 1703	The whole Act
6 Anne c. 10	Administration of Justice Act 1707	Section 23
8 Geo. 1 c. 5	Boundaries Act 1721	The whole Act so far as unrepealed
10 Geo. 1 c. 5	Mining Leases Act 1723	The whole Act so far as unrepealed
9 Geo. 2 c. 7	Timber Act 1735	The whole Act

Session and Chapter (1)	Short Title (2)	Extent of Repeal (3)
15 Geo. 2 c. 10	Mining Leases Act 1741	The whole Act
23 Geo. 2 c. 9	Mining Leases Act 1749	The whole Act
1 Geo. 3 c. 8	Hospitals Act 1761	The whole Act
5 Geo. 3 c. 17	Timber Act 1765	The whole Act so far as unrepealed
5 Geo. 3 c. 20	County Hospitals Act 1765	The whole Act so far as unrepealed
7 Geo. 3 c. 8	County Hospitals (Amendment) Act 1767	The whole Act so far as unrepealed
7 Geo. 3 c. 20	Timber Act 1767	The whole Act so far as unrepealed
15 & 16 Geo. 3 c. 26	Timber Act 1775	The whole Act so far as unrepealed
17 & 18 Geo. 3 c. 15	County Hospitals Act 1777	The whole Act
17 & 18 Geo. 3 c. 35	Timber Act 1777	The whole Act
17 & 18 Geo. 3 c. 49	Leases for Lives Act 1777	The whole Act so far as unrepealed
19 & 20 Geo. 3 c. 30	Tenantry Act 1779	The whole Act so far as unrepealed
21 & 22 Geo. 3 c. 27	Leases by Schools Act 1781	The whole Act
23 & 24 Geo. 3 c. 39	Timber Act 1783	The whole Act so far as unrepealed
25 Geo. 3 c. 55	Leases by Schools Act 1785	The whole Act
25 Geo. 3 c. 62	Leases for Corn Mills Act 1785	The whole Act so far as unrepealed
29 Geo. 3 c. 30	Commons Act 1789	The whole Act so far as unrepealed
31 Geo. 3 c. 38	Commons Act 1791	The whole Act
35 Geo. 3 c. 23	Ecclesiastical Lands Act 1795	The whole Act
40 Geo. 3 c. 90	Leases for Cotton Manufacture Act 1800	The whole Act

[192]

PART 2
STATUTES OF ENGLAND

Session and Chapter (1)	Short Title (2)	Extent of Repeal (3)
13 Edw. 1 Stat. Westm. 1285 sec. c. 1	Statute De Donis Conditionalibus 1285	The whole Act so far as unrepealed
18 Edw. 1 Stat. d'ni R. de t'ris, & c.	Statute Quia Emptores 1290	The whole Act

[193]

PART 3
STATUTE OF GREAT BRITAIN 1707 TO 1800

Session and Chapter (1)	Short Title (2)	Extent of Repeal (3)
39 & 40 Geo. 3 c. 88	Crown Private Estate Act 1800	The whole Act so far as unrepealed

[194]

PART 4
STATUTES OF THE UNITED KINGDOM OF GREAT BRITAIN AND IRELAND 1801 TO 1922

Session and Chapter (1)	Short Title (2)	Extent of Repeal (3)
46 Geo. 3 c. 71	Mines (Ireland) Act 1806	The whole Act
50 Geo. 3 c. 33	School Sites (Ireland) Act 1810	The whole Act so far as unrepealed
59 Geo. 3 c. 94	Crown Land Act 1819	The whole Act
3 Geo. 4 c. 63	Crown Lands (Ireland) Act 1822	The whole Act so far as unrepealed
4 Geo. 4 c. 18	Crown Lands Act 1823	The whole Act
6 Geo. 4 c. 17	Crown Lands Act 1825	The whole Act
11 Geo. 4 & 1 Will. 4 c. 46	Illusory Appointments Act 1830	The whole Act so far as unrepealed
2 & 3 Will. 4 c. 71	Prescription Act 1832	The whole Act so far as unrepealed

Session and Chapter (1)	Short Title (2)	Extent of Repeal (3)
3 & 4 Will. 4 c. 74	Fines and Recoveries Act 1833	The whole Act so far as unrepealed
3 & 4 Will. 4 c. 106	Inheritance Act 1833	The whole Act so far as unrepealed
4 & 5 Will. 4 c. 92	Fines and Recoveries (Ireland) Act 1834	The whole Act so far as unrepealed
5 & 6 Will. 4 c. 74	Tithes Act 1835	The whole Act so far as unrepealed
5 & 6 Will. 4 c. 75	Tithing of Turnips Act 1835	The whole Act so far as unrepealed
6 & 7 Will. 4 c. 70	Sites for Schoolrooms Act 1836	The whole Act so far as unrepealed
1 & 2 Vic. c. 62	Renewal of Leases (Ireland) Act 1838	The whole Act so far as unrepealed
1 & 2 Vic. c. 109	Tithe Rentcharge (Ireland) Act 1838	The whole Act so far as unrepealed
2 & 3 Vic. c. 3	Tithe Arrears (Ireland) Act 1839	The whole Act so far as unrepealed
5 Vic. c. 1	Crown Lands Act 1841	The whole Act
5 & 6 Vic. c. 89	Drainage (Ireland) Act 1842	The whole Act
6 & 7 Vic. c. 23	Copyhold Act 1843	The whole Act
7 & 8 Vic. c. 55	Copyhold Act 1844	The whole Act
7 & 8 Vic. c. 90	Judgments (Ireland) Act 1844	Section 10
8 & 9 Vic. c. 56	Land Drainage Act 1845	The whole Act so far as unrepealed
8 & 9 Vic. c. 69	Drainage (Ireland) Act 1845	The whole Act
8 & 9 Vic. c. 99	Crown Lands Act 1845	The whole Act
8 & 9 Vic. c. 106	Real Property Act 1845	Sections 2 to 6 and 8
8 & 9 Vic. c. 112	Satisfied Terms Act 1845	The whole Act so far as unrepealed
9 & 10 Vic. c. 4	Drainage (Ireland) Act 1846	The whole Act so far as unrepealed
10 & 11 Vic. c. 32	Landed Property Improvement (Ireland) Act 1847	The whole Act so far as unrepealed
10 & 11 Vic. c. 46	Settled Land (Ireland) Act 1847	The whole Act so far as unrepealed
10 & 11 Vic. c. 79	Drainage (Ireland) Act 1847	The whole Act

Session and Chapter (1)	Short Title (2)	Extent of Repeal (3)
11 & 12 Vic. c. 13	Mining Leases (Ireland) Act 1848	The whole Act so far as unrepealed
11 & 12 Vic. c. 80	Tithe Rentcharge (Ireland) Act 1848	The whole Act so far as unrepealed
11 & 12 Vic. c. 102	Crown Lands Act 1848	The whole Act so far as unrepealed
12 & 13 Vic. c. 26	Leases Act 1849	The whole Act so far as unrepealed
12 & 13 Vic. c. 59	Landed Property Improvement (Ireland) Act 1849	The whole Act so far as unrepealed
12 & 13 Vic. c. 105	Renewable Leasehold Conversion Act 1849	The whole Act so far as unrepealed
13 & 14 Vic. c. 29	Judgment Mortgage (Ireland) Act 1850	The whole Act so far as unrepealed
13 & 14 Vic. c. 31	Public Money Drainage Act 1850	The whole Act so far as unrepealed
14 & 15 Vic. c. 7	Leases for Mills (Ireland) Act 1851	The whole Act so far as unrepealed
14 & 15 Vic. c. 20	Fee-Farm Rents (Ireland) Act 1851	The whole Act so far as unrepealed
14 & 15 Vic. c. 42	Crown Lands Act 1851	The whole Act so far as unrepealed
15 & 16 Vic. c. 34	Landed Property Improvement (Ireland) Act 1852	The whole Act so far as unrepealed
15 & 16 Vic. c. 51	Copyhold Act 1852	The whole Act
15 & 16 Vic. c. 62	Crown Lands Act 1852	The whole Act
16 & 17 Vic. c. 56	Crown Lands Act 1853	The whole Act
16 & 17 Vic. c. 130	Drainage and Improvement of Lands (Ireland) Act 1853	The whole Act
17 & 18 Vic. c. 68	Crown Land Revenues Act 1854	The whole Act
18 & 19 Vic. c. 39	Leasing Powers for Religious Worship in Ireland Act 1855	The whole Act so far as unrepealed
18 & 19 Vic. c. 110	Drainage and Improvement of Lands (Ireland) Act 1855	The whole Act
19 & 20 Vic. c. 9	Public Money Drainage Act 1856	The whole Act so far as unrepealed
19 & 20 Vic. c. 62	Drainage (Ireland) Act 1856	The whole Act so far as unrepealed

Session and Chapter (1)	Short Title (2)	Extent of Repeal (3)
21 & 22 Vic. c. 42	Prescription (Ireland) Act 1858	The whole Act so far as unrepealed
21 & 22 Vic. c. 72	Landed Estates Court (Ireland) Act 1858	The whole Act so far as unrepealed
21 & 22 Vic. c. 94	Copyhold Act 1858	The whole Act
21 & 22 Vic. c. 105	Judgment Mortgage (Ireland) Act 1858	The whole Act so far as unrepealed
22 & 23 Vic. c. 35	Law of Property Amendment Act 1859	Sections 10 to 13, 21, 23 and 24
23 & 24 Vic. c. 38	Law of Property Amendment Act 1860	Sections 7, 8 and 10
23 & 24 Vic. c. 153	Landed Property (Ireland) Improvement Act 1860	The whole Act so far as unrepealed
24 & 25 Vic. c. 123	Landed Estates Court (Ireland) Act 1861	The whole Act so far as unrepealed
25 & 26 Vic. c. 29	Landed Property Improvement (Ireland) Act 1862	The whole Act so far as unrepealed
25 & 26 Vic. c. 37	Crown Private Estates Act 1862	The whole Act so far as unrepealed
26 & 27 Vic. c. 26	Land Drainage Act (Ireland) 1863	The whole Act
26 & 27 Vic. c. 88	Drainage and Improvement of Lands Act (Ireland) 1863	The whole Act
27 & 28 Vic. c. 38	Chief Rents Redemption (Ireland) Act 1864	The whole Act so far as unrepealed
27 & 28 Vic. c. 72	Drainage and Improvement of Lands (Ireland) Act 1864	The whole Act
27 & 28 Vic. c. 107	Drainage and Improvement of Lands Supplemental Act, Ireland 1864	The whole Act
27 & 28 Vic. c. 114	Improvement of Land Act 1864	The whole Act so far as unrepealed
28 & 29 Vic. c. 52	Drainage and Improvement of Lands Amendment Act (Ireland) 1865	The whole Act
28 & 29 Vic. c. 53	Drainage and Improvement of Lands Supplemental Act (No. 2 Ireland) 1865	The whole Act
28 & 29 Vic. c. 78	Mortgage Debenture Act 1865	The whole Act

Session and Chapter (1)	Short Title (2)	Extent of Repeal (3)
28 & 29 Vic. c. 101	Land Debentures (Ireland) Act 1865	The whole Act
29 & 30 Vic. c. 26	Landed Property Improvement (Ireland) Act 1866	The whole Act so far as unrepealed
29 & 30 Vic. c. 40	Drainage and Improvement of Land (Ireland) Act 1866	The whole Act so far as unrepealed
29 & 30 Vic. c. 49	Drainage Maintenance Act 1866	The whole Act
29 & 30 Vic. c. 61	Drainage and Improvement of Lands Supplemental Act (Ireland) 1866	The whole Act
29 & 30 Vic. c. 62	Crown Lands Act 1866	The whole Act so far as unrepealed
29 & 30 Vic. c. 99	Landed Estates Court Act 1866	The whole Act so far as unrepealed
30 & 31 Vic. c. 43	Drainage and Improvement of Lands Supplemental Act (Ireland) 1867	The whole Act
30 & 31 Vic. c. 47	Lis Pendens Act 1867	The whole Act so far as unrepealed
30 & 31 Vic. c. 139	Drainage and Improvement of Lands Supplemental Act (Ireland) (No. 2) 1867	The whole Act
31 & 32 Vic. c. 3	Drainage and Improvement of Lands Supplemental Act (Ireland) (No. 3) 1867	The whole Act
31 & 32 Vic. c. 4	Sales of Reversions Act 1867	The whole Act so far as unrepealed
31 & 32 Vic. c. 40	Partition Act 1868	The whole Act so far as unrepealed
31 & 32 Vic. c. 62	Renewable Leaseholds Conversion (Ireland) Act 1868	The whole Act so far as unrepealed
32 & 33 Vic. c. 72	Drainage and Improvement of Lands Amendment Act, Ireland 1869	The whole Act
34 & 35 Vic. c. 72	Judgments Registry (Ireland) Act 1871	Section 21
35 & 36 Vic. c. 31	Drainage and Improvement of Lands Amendment Act (Ireland) 1872	The whole Act

Session and Chapter (1)	Short Title (2)	Extent of Repeal (3)
36 & 37 Vic. c. 36	Crown Lands Act 1873	The whole Act
36 & 37 Vic. c. 61	Crown Private Estates Act 1873	The whole Act so far as unrepealed
37 & 38 Vic. c. 32	Drainage and Improvement of Lands Amendment Act (Ireland) 1874	The whole Act
37 & 38 Vic. c. 37	Powers of Appointment Act 1874	The whole Act so far as unrepealed
37 & 38 Vic. c. 78	Vendor and Purchaser Act 1874	The whole Act so far as unrepealed
38 & 39 Vic. c. 11	Leasing Powers Amendment Act for Religious Purposes in Ireland 1875	The whole Act
39 & 40 Vic. c. 17	Partition Act 1876	The whole Act so far as unrepealed
40 & 41 Vic. c. 18	Settled Estates Act 1877	The whole Act so far as unrepealed
40 & 41 Vic. c. 31	Limited Owners Reservoirs and Water Supply Further Facilities Act 1877	The whole Act so far as unrepealed
40 & 41 Vic. c. 33	Contingent Remainders Act 1877	The whole Act
41 & 42 Vic. c. 59	Drainage and Improvement of Lands (Ireland) Act 1878	The whole Act
44 & 45 Vic. c. 41	Conveyancing Act 1881	Sections 2 to 9, 15 to 24, 26 to 29, 41, 44, 49 to 64, 66, 67, 69, 70, 72 and 73 and the third and fourth Schedules
44 & 45 Vic. c. 65	Leases for Schools (Ireland) Act 1881	The whole Act so far as unrepealed
45 & 46 Vic. c. 38	Settled Land Act 1882	The whole Act so far as unrepealed
45 & 46 Vic. c. 39	Conveyancing Act 1882	Sections 3, 4, 6, 10 and 12
47 & 48 Vic. c. 18	Settled Land Act 1884	The whole Act so far as unrepealed
48 & 49 Vic. c. 79	Crown Lands Act 1885	The whole Act so far as unrepealed

Session and Chapter (1)	Short Title (2)	Extent of Repeal (3)
50 & 51 Vic. c. 30	Settled Land Acts (Amendment) Act 1887	The whole Act so far as unrepealed
50 & 51 Vic. c. 73	Copyhold Act 1887	The whole Act so far as unrepealed
51 & 52 Vic. c. 37	Timber (Ireland) Act 1888	The whole Act
52 & 53 Vic. c. 36	Settled Land Act 1889	The whole Act
53 & 54 Vic. c. 69	Settled Land Act 1890	The whole Act so far as unrepealed
55 & 56 Vic. c. 58	Accumulations Act 1892	The whole Act
55 & 56 Vic. c. 65	Drainage and Improvement of Land (Ireland) Act 1892	The whole Act
56 & 57 Vic. c. 21	Voluntary Conveyances Act 1893	The whole Act
57 & 58 Vic. c. 43	Crown Lands Act 1894	The whole Act
58 & 59 Vic. c. 25	Mortgagees Legal Costs Act 1895	The whole Act
62 & 63 Vic. c. 20	Bodies Corporate (Joint Tenancy) Act 1899	The whole Act
62 & 63 Vic. c. 46	Improvement of Land Act 1899	The whole Act so far as unrepealed
6 Edw. 7 c. 28	Crown Lands Act 1906	The whole Act so far as unrepealed
1 & 2 Geo. 5 c. 37	Conveyancing Act 1911	Sections 1, 3 to 6, 9 to 11, 13 and 15
3 & 4 Geo. 5 c. 8	Crown Lands Act 1913	The whole Act

[195]

PART 5
ACTS OF THE OIREACHTAS

Number and Year (1)	Enactment (2)	Extent of Repeal (3)
No. 22 of 1933	Perpetual Funds (Registration) Act 1933	The whole Act
No. 3 of 1937	Circuit Court (Registration of Judgments) Act 1937	Section 4
No. 5 of 1957	Married Women's Status Act 1957	Sections 2(4) and 2(5)
No. 16 of 1964	Registration of Title Act 1964	Sections 3(2), 27, 37(2), 44(2), 52(3), 55(3), 61(1), 61(3)(*b*), 62(3), 62(7), 62(8), 98(4)(*a*), 99 and 101
No. 27 of 1965	Succession Act 1965	Sections 50(3), 58(2), 95 and 97
No. 3 of 1967	Landlord and Tenant (Ground Rents) Act 1967	Section 24(2)
No. 10 of 1980	Landlord and Tenant (Amendment) Act 1980	Sections 79 and 80(2)
No. 11 of 1981	Courts Acts 1981	Section 24
No. 6 of 1982	Housing (Private Rented Dwellings) Act 1982	Section 22
No. 27 of 1988	Bankruptcy Act 1988	Section 64
No. 18 of 1992	Housing (Miscellaneous Provisions) Act 1992	Section 2(2)
No. 12 of 1996	Powers of Attorney Act 1996	Section 6(3)
No. 31 of 1999	Stamp Duties Consolidation Act 1999	Section 39

SCHEDULE 3[1]
COVENANTS IMPLIED IN CONVEYANCES[2]

Notes

1   Schedule 3 is linked with the provisions in ss 80 and 81 relating to covenants for title implied in conveyances of land: see the Notes those sections.

2   Part 1 of the Schedule deals with the burden of the implied covenants, ie identifying who is bound by them. Parts 2 and 3 set out the details of the actual covenants implied in different conveyances which are referred to in ss 80 and 81.

[197]

Section 80 and 81

PART 1
EXTENT OF THE BURDEN OF COVENANTS[1]

1. In this Schedule, unless either the context otherwise requires or the contrary is expressed,[2] the covenantor's liability in respect of any covenant extends to the acts or omissions only of persons within any of the following classes:[3]

   (1)   the covenantor and any person conveying by the covenantor's direction;

   (2)   any person through whom the covenantor derives title;[4]

   (3)   any person (including a mortgagee) who either holds or has held a derivative title from the covenantor for less than the estate or interest vested in the covenantor or who holds or has held such a derivative title from any predecessor in title of the covenantor;

   (4)   any person who holds or has held in trust for the covenantor.

2. It is not a breach of a covenant contained in this Schedule where the conveyance by the covenantor was made expressly subject to the act, matter or thing which, but for this paragraph, would or might have caused such a breach. [5]

3. The covenantor has no liability for any defect in the title of which it is proved that the covenantee had actual knowledge[6] before the making of the contract to convey or the making of the conveyance (whichever is the earlier).[7]

Definitions

See s 3 for definitions of: "conveyance"; "covenant"; "mortgagee".

Notes

1 The extent of the benefit of the implied covenants is dealt with by ss 80(5) (see Notes 22–23 to that section) and 81 (4) (see Note 11 to that section).

2 The statutory provisions may be varied by the terms of the conveyance: see ss 80(6) (and Notes 24–25 to that section) and 81(5) (and Notes 12–13 to that section).

3 What follows largely re-enacts the provisions of s 7 of the Conveyancing Act 1881: see Wylie and Woods, *Irish Conveyancing Law* (3rd edn, Tottel Publishing, 2005), paras 21.23–21.25.

4 This gets rid of a curious distinction under s 7 of the 1881 Act between a vendor who took under a voluntary conveyance (and, therefore, would not have investigated the title) and one who took for value (and would have been expected to investigate it). The covenantor is now liable in both instances. The provisions of Schedule 3, like ss 80 and 81, follow the precedent in the Northern Ireland *Final Report of the Land Law Working Group* (HMSO 1990): see Volume 1, paras 2.5.45–2.5.50 and Volume 2, pp 638–643 and 991–996: see also LRC CP 34–2004, para 8.43, fn 132.

5 A purchaser cannot invoke the implied covenants in respect of any incumbrance or matter to which the conveyance was made expressly subject: see *Geraghty and Lyon's Contract* (1989) 53 ILTR 57.

6 Constructive notice is not enough: see s 86 and the Notes to that section.

7 A purchaser cannot invoke the implied covenants in respect of a covenant he or she actually knew about at the time of the conveyance. This reverses the position under s 7 of the 1881 Act: see Wylie and Woods, *Irish Conveyancing Law* (3rd edn, Tottel Publishing, 2005), para 21.27.

[198]

PART 2
IMPLIED COVENANTS[1]

Paragraph 1
Class 1 Conveyances

Covenants implied in a conveyance (other than a mortgage[2]) for valuable consideration of an estate or interest in land (other than a tenancy) made by a person who is expressed to convey "as beneficial owner".[3]

(1) That the covenantor has the right to convey the subject-matter of the conveyance, save that the covenantor's liability is only in respect of any acts or omissions of the covenantor or persons within class (ii)[4] of *paragraph 1 of Part 1*.[5]

(2) That the person to whom the conveyance is made will quietly enjoy the subject-matter of the conveyance without disturbance from any person within any class in *paragraph 1 of Part 1*.[6]

(3) That the subject-matter of the conveyance is free from all claims, demands, estates, incumbrances and interests.[7]

(4) That the covenantor will, at the covenantor's own cost, take such action as may be necessary for the better assuring of the subject-matter of the conveyance as may from time to time be reasonably required by the person to whom the conveyance is made and the persons deriving title under that person.[8]

Paragraph 2
Class 2 Conveyances

Covenants implied in a conveyance (other than a mortgage) for valuable consideration of land comprised in a lease made by a person who is expressed to convey "as beneficial owner".[9]

(1) to (4) Covenants (1) to (4) in *paragraph 1*.

(5) That the lease which created the subject-matter of the conveyance is at the time of the conveyance valid and effectual.

(6) That the rent reserved by the lease has up to the time of the conveyance been paid and the covenants expressly or impliedly contained in the lease have been performed and observed by the lessee.

The covenantor's liability in respect of covenants (5) and (6) is restricted to—

(*a*) any acts or omissions of the covenantor or persons within class (ii)[10] of *paragraph 1* in *Part 1*, and

(*b*) as regards the covenants mentioned in covenant (6), breaches caused by such acts and omissions the consequences of which could not be discovered on reasonable inspection of the land conveyed.

Paragraph 3
Class 3 Conveyances

Covenants implied in a conveyance comprising a mortgage of land (other than land comprised in a lease) made by a person who is expressed to convey "as beneficial owner".

(1) to (4) Covenants (1) to (4) in paragraph 1.

Those covenants are subject to the following variations, that is to say—

(*a*) liability in respect of any breach of the covenants extends to the acts or omissions of any person whether or not that person is within the classes of person set out in *paragraph 1* of *Part 1*;[11]

(*b*) covenant (2) (for quiet enjoyment) is not implied against any mortgagor until the mortgagee has lawfully entered into possession of the land conveyed.[12]

345

Paragraph 4

Class 4 Conveyances

Covenants implied in a conveyance comprising a mortgage of land comprised in a lease made by a person who is expressed to convey "as beneficial owner". [13]

(1) to (4) Covenants (1) to (4) in paragraph 1, subject to the variations mentioned in paragraph (3).

(5) That the grant or lease which created the estate out of which the subject-matter of the conveyance is created is at the time of the conveyance valid and effectual and that the rent reserved by the grant or lease has up to that time been paid and that the covenants expressed or implied in the grant or lease have been performed and observed.

(6) That the covenantor will from time to time, so long as any money remains owing on the security of the land conveyed, pay the rent reserved by the grant or lease and perform and observe the covenants in it and will indemnify the person to whom the conveyance is made in respect of any consequences of the breach of this covenant.

Paragraph 5

Class 5 Conveyances

Covenant implied in a conveyance made by a person who is expressed to convey "as trustee", "as mortgagee", "as personal representative" or under an order of the court.[14]

That the covenantor has not, by virtue of any act or omission of the covenantor, caused the title to the estate or interest conveyed to be liable to be impeached through the existence of any incumbrance or rendered the covenantor unable to convey that estate or interest in the manner in which it is expressed to be conveyed.

Definitions

See s 3 for definitions of: "conveyance"; "covenant"; "incumbrance"; "lease"; "mortgage"; "mortgagor"; "personal representative"; "possession"; "rent".

Notes

1   Part 2 sets out the different classes of covenants implied by s 80, depending on the type of conveyance and the capacity in which the conveying party is expressed to convey: see the Notes to that section.

2   Mortgages are covered by Classes 3 and 4.

3   This is the "magic" phrase which must be used in the conveyance to imply the covenants which follow: see Note 13 to s 80.

4   This should be "(2)".

5   This is the "full power to convey" covenant: see Wylie and Woods, *Irish Conveyancing Law* (3rd edn, Tottel Publishing, 2005), paras 21.27–21.29. Thus the covenantor is liable if he or she, or some person through whom the title was derived,

prior to the conveyance had created a defect in title, eg, by conveying part of the land to someone else: see *David v Sabin* [1893] 1 Ch 523; *May v Platt* [1900] 1 Ch 616; *Turner v Moon* [1901] 2 Ch 825; see also *Eastwood v Ashton* [1915] AC 900.

6   This is the covenant for "quiet enjoyment": see Wylie and Woods, *Irish Conveyancing Law* (3rd edn, Tottel Publishing, 2005), para 21.30. To breach this, disturbance must be physical interference such as dispossession, not, eg, the disturbance by noise: see *Howard v Maitland* (1883) 11 QBD 695; *Jenkins v Jones* (1888) 40 Ch D 71.

7   This is the covenant for "freedom from incumbrances": see Wylie and Woods, *Irish Conveyancing Law* (3rd edn, Tottel Publishing, 2005), paras 21.31–21.32. To breach this the existence of the incumbrance must lead to disturbance of possession or interruption of enjoyment: see *Cadden v McCaffrey* (20 May 1996) SC.

8   This is the covenant for "further assurance": see Wylie and Woods, *Irish Conveyancing Law* (3rd edn, Tottel Publishing, 2005), para 21.33; see also *Maguire v Armstrong* (1814) 2 Ba & B 538; *Bankes v Small* (1887) 36 Ch D 716; *Re Jones* [1893] 2 Ch 461.

9   Class 2 contains *additional* covenants (ie in addition to the Class 1 covenants) where the conveyance is of a leasehold property: see Note 14 to s 80. These provisions remove the need for express indemnities in an assignment of a lease: see *Laffoy's Irish Conveyancing Precedents* (Bloomsbury Professional), Division E.2.

10 Again should be "(2)".

11 As under s 7 of the 1881 Act the covenants by a mortgagee conveying as *beneficial owner* are unqualified: see Wylie and Woods, *Irish Conveyancing Law* (3rd edn, Tottel Publishing, 2005), para 21.16. Cf on a conveyance as *mortgagee*: see Note 14 below.

12 This reflects the fact that a mortgagee is not usually in possession: see Pritchard, "Mortgagees and Covenants for Title" (1964) 28 Conv 205.

13 The additional covenants here also remove the need for express indemnities: see Note 9 above.

14 This limited covenant implied where a person does not convey as beneficial owner, but in some other capacity also operated under s 7 of the 1881 Act: see Wylie and Woods, *Irish Conveyancing Law* (3rd edn, Tottel Publishing, 2005), para 21.18.

---

[199]

PART 3
ADDITIONAL IMPLIED COVENANTS FOR LAND COMPRISED IN A LEASE[1]

Paragraph 1
Class 6 Conveyances[2]

Additional covenants implied in a conveyance (other than a mortgage) for valuable consideration of—

   (a) the entirety of land comprised in a lease, or

(b) part of the land comprised in a lease, subject to a part of the rent reserved by the lease which has been, or is by the conveyance, apportioned with the consent of the lessor,

for the residue of the term or interest created by the lease.

(1) That the assignee, or the person deriving title under the assignee, will at all times, from the date of the conveyance or other date stated in it, duly pay all rent becoming due under the lease creating the estate for which the land is conveyed, or, as the case may be, such part of such rent as has been apportioned to the land conveyed, and observe and perform all the covenants, contained in it and on the part of the lessee to be observed and performed, so far as they relate to the land conveyed.

(2) That the assignee will at all times, from that date, indemnify the assignor and the assignor's estate and their estates from and against all claims, costs and proceedings on account of any omission to pay the rent, or the part of the rent so apportioned, or any breach of any of the covenants, so far as they relate to the land conveyed.

Paragraph 2

Class 7 Conveyances

Additional covenants implied in a conveyance (other than a mortgage) for valuable consideration of part of the land comprised in a lease, for the residue of the term or interest created by the lease, subject to a part of the rent reserved by the lease which has been, or is by the conveyance, apportioned without the consent of the lessor.

(1) *In every case* That the assignee will at all times, from the date of the conveyance, or other date stated in it, pay the apportioned rent and observe and perform all the covenants (other than the covenant to pay the entire rent) contained in the lease creating the estate for which the land is conveyed, and on the part of the lessee to be observed and performed, so far as the same relate to the land conveyed; and also will at all times from that date indemnify the assignor and the assignor's estate, from and against all claims, costs and proceedings on account of any omission to pay the apportioned rent or any breach of any of such covenants.

(2) *Where the conveying party is expressed to convey "as beneficial owner"* That the assignor, or the persons deriving title under the assignor, will at all times, from the date of the conveyance, or other date stated in it, pay the balance of the rent (after deducting the said apportioned rent and any other rents similarly apportioned in respect of land not retained) and observe and perform all the covenants (other than the covenant to pay the entire rent) contained in the lease and on the part of the lessee to be observed and performed so far as they relate to the land demised (other than the land comprised in the conveyance) and remaining vested in the

assignor; and also will at all times, from that date, indemnify the assignee, and the assignee's estate, from and against all claims, costs and proceedings on account of any omission to pay the balance of the rent or any breach of any of such covenants.

Definitions

See s 3 for definitions of: "consent"; "conveyance"; "covenant"; "land"; "lease"; "lessor"; "mortgage"; "rent".

Notes

1 Part 3 contains the additional implied covenants provided for by s 81 in a conveyance of land comprised in a lease: see the Notes to that section.

2 Class 6 covenants apply where either the entire land is conveyed or part is, but subject to an apportionment of rent consented to by the lessor.

3 Class 7 covenants apply where part only is conveyed without consent to an apportionment: see Notes 8–10 to s 81.

Index

All references are to *paragraph* numbers.